D1558742

The Marketplace of Christianity

The Marketplace of Christianity

Robert B. Ekelund Jr., Robert F. Hébert, and Robert D. Tollison

The MIT Press
Cambridge, Massachusetts
London, England

MIT Press books may be purchased at special quantity discounts for business or sales promotional use. For information, please email special_sales@mitpress.mit .edu or write to Special Sales Department, The MIT Press, 55 Hayward Street, Cambridge, MA 02142.

This book was set in Sabon on 3B2 by Asco Typesetters, Hong Kong, and was printed and bound in the United States of America.

Library of Congress Cataloging-in-Publication Data

Ekelund, Robert B. (Robert Burton), 1940–
The marketplace of Christianity / Robert B. Ekelund Jr., Robert F. Hébert, and Robert D. Tollison.
    p. cm.
Includes bibliographical references (p. 273) and index.
ISBN-13: 978-0-262-05082-1 (alk. paper)
ISBN-10: 0-262-05082-X (alk. paper)
1. Christianity—Economic aspects—History. 2. Church history—Modern period, 1500– 3. Christian sociology—History. I. Hébert, Robert F. II. Tollison, Robert D. III. Title.

BR115.E3E55 2006
270—dc22   2006046196

10 9 8 7 6 5 4 3 2 1

Contents

Preface

Economic markets tell us about the production and distribution of material goods. But humankind's spiritual needs, as manifested through the ages by the practices of magic and religion, are as pressing and durable as its material needs. The existential dilemma posed by life on planet earth was as real for the ancient hunter as it is for the modern computer programmer. For eons, religion in its myriad forms has been a binding force of human populations and a contributing factor to human survival. Can economics, the science of markets, help us understand this realm of human behavior? We believe that it can, especially when it enlists other social and biological sciences to explain religious markets in all eras of human history and, in particular, in the half-millennium from the Protestant Reformation to modern Christianity.

Our study of Christianity shows that the economics of religion has little to do with counting the money in the collection basket and much to do with understanding the background of today's religious/political divisions. Because religion is a set of organized beliefs, and a church is an organized body of worshippers, it is natural to use economics—a science that explains the behavior of individuals in organizations—to understand the development of organized religion. *The Marketplace of Christianity* applies the tools of contemporary economics to explain the existence of religion, changes in its organizational form, and the impact of contemporary religion-influenced controversies, including such hot-button issues as biologic evolution and gay marriage.

The conceptual foundation for this book began in 1981 in Ekelund and Tollison's *Mercantilism as a Rent-Seeking Society*, which established the basic research paradigm for exploring institutional, economic/political change in an emergent commercial society. That paradigm was deployed in 1996 in a book entitled *Sacred Trust* to explore the nature and operation of the medieval church. *The Marketplace of Christianity* is yet a further progression in the mode of applying economics to major historical interludes of abiding interest to social scientists. In this most recent effort, we go beyond mere historical exegesis by attempting to evaluate contemporary religious policies and practices that may help predict the future course of Christianity, including possible schisms. Christianity today is awash in controversies over matters of faith and morality: abortion, stem cell research, gay rights, women's rights, and women and gays in the clergy. We treat these factors as "shifters" in the demand for particular forms of Christian religion that will have profound effects on the whole nature of Christianity.

In Christendom, the market for religion was dominated for over a thousand years by a single institution, the Roman Catholic Church. Eventually the monopoly was challenged successfully and the market was opened to competition. The Protestant Reformation was a successful penetration of a religious market dominated by a monopoly firm. The Ninety-five Theses nailed to the Wittenberg church door in 1517 by Martin Luther was the flash point in what became a pitched battle of rivalrous market entry. In economic terms, the dominant-firm reaction to this assault on its market leadership was predictable. The Counter-Reformation accelerated the competitive process, which came to be characterized by "product differentiation" in the form of doctrinal and organizational innovations. History can be refracted through many prisms. By refracting it through the prism of economics, we can see how Christianity evolved to satisfy the changing demands of consumers/worshippers.

Critics of the economics of religion regard the attempt to explain religious behavior on economic grounds to be illegitimate or, worse, perverse. While we obviously do not share this view, we nevertheless recognize many pitfalls in the way of unbiased analysis. We seek to explain, not to judge. Our analysis takes preferences for religion as given, and analyzes their observable effects on society and the individual. In order to be intelligible to non-economists, we preface our detailed analysis of changes in religious forms with clear and nontechnical background information on economics and the economics of religion. And rather than maintain that an economic perspective is the only or preferred approach, we incorporate the research of many other disciplines to buttress our arguments.

Completion of a major project such as this brings not only a sense of accomplishment and relief but also an opportunity to acknowledge the assistance and support of many others. In particular we would like to thank friends, colleagues, and former students: James M. Buchanan, Audrey Davidson Kline, Gary M. Anderson, Sonja Langley, Lane Boyte, John Jackson, Richard Ault, Brighita Bercea, Randy Beard, Dave Kaserman, William Shughart, Bobby McCormick, Jody Lipford, Mark Thornton, Michael Maloney, and Kristine Terkun. Editors and anonymous referees of the *Journal of Political Economy*, *Kyklos*, *Economic Inquiry*, *History of Political Economy*, and Oxford University Press helped us weigh and refine various arguments that made their way into this book. Part of the research for this book was conducted while Ekelund was Vernon F. Taylor Visiting Distinguished Professor at Trinity University in San Antonio in the spring of 2003. He gratefully acknowledges that support as well as insights derived from stimulating discussions of religion with John and Mary Jane Roper. Parts of this book were the subject of seminars given at Clemson University and the University of Georgia by Tollison, who wishes to thank seminar participants at these universities as well as the participants in the Program on Religion, Political Economy, and Society at the Weatherhead Center for International Affairs at Harvard University. We would also like to thank the following journals for allowing us to excerpt materials from our published papers: *Kyklos* (Richard Ault, Ekelund, and Tollison, "The Pope and the Price of Beef: A Public Choice Perspective," 1987; Brighita Bercea, Ekelund, and Tollison, "Cathedrals as Entry-Deterring Devices," 2005); *Journal of Political Economy* (Ekelund, Hébert, and Tollison, "An Economic Analysis of the Protestant Reformation," 2002); and *Economic Inquiry* (Ekelund, Hébert, and Tollison, "Economics of the Counter-Reformation: Incumbent-Firm Reaction to Market Entry," 2004). Our project owes an enormous debt of gratitude to the MIT Press and in particular to senior editor John S. Covell, editor Kathleen Caruso, freelance editor

Amanda Nash, and editorial assistant Hiu Yan Ho. Naturally we are responsible for the final quality of this book—a project that has held our fascinated interest for two decades.

Robert B. Ekelund Jr.
Robert F. Hébert
Robert D. Tollison

1

Religion, Church, and Economics

In all history, we do not find a single religion without a church.
—Emile Durkheim, *The Elementary Forms of the Religious Life*

A glorious Church is like a magnificent feast; there is all the variety that may be, but every one chooses out a dish or two that he likes, and lets the rest alone: how glorious soever the Church is, every one chooses out of it his own religion, by which he governs himself, and lets the rest alone.
—John Selden, *Table Talk*

The concepts of religion and church are so intertwined as to be inseparable in most people's minds. By one set of definitions, *religion* is an organized system of beliefs, and *church* is an organized body of worshippers. At first blush, economics seems far removed from these constructs. In the complicated nexus of relations between the sacred and the profane, most people would place church and religion among the former and economics among the latter. But if we are rational about such things, we must recognize that organized bodies imply organization and administration. Therefore, in order to understand the workings of organized bodies, it makes sense to turn to a science like economics that seeks to explain the behavior of organizations. Economics and religion, therefore, are not such strange bedfellows after all.

The premise of this book is that the history and contemporary state of organized religions can be better understood if one uses economic principles to analyze their evolution and development. In order to do this, we must adopt a new mindset. We must be willing to employ the language and analytical methods of business and economics. This might be considered heresy to some, but there is cumulative evidence that old thought patterns are giving way to new ones, even among those ideologies most tightly wound to tradition. No church is more dominant in the history of Western Christianity than the Catholic Church. Yet the editor in chief of the *Catholic Herald*, Damian Thompson, recently wrote, using the language of business, "One of the discoveries in the sociology of religion in the last twenty-five years has been the extent to which, mutatis mutandis, patterns of religious allegiance in a pluralist society resemble those of consumption in the marketplace. People are attracted to strong brands that protect their identity; they enjoy products that suspend the boring reality of everyday life; and they demand near-infallible standards of professionalism."[1] Moreover, Thompson implicitly endorses a view we[2] advanced nearly a decade ago: "The Pope is a CEO, not a chairman, and as such has two priorities. The first is to make sure that staff and services bearing the label "Catholic" are what they say they are...[His] other priority is to improve the quality of the Church's greatest service, the liturgy of the Eucharist."[3] Although Thompson makes specific reference to the Catholic Church, the notion that organization is an essential feature of *all* churches is self-evident. He has, in other words, embraced the mindset that we employ in this book.

Religion and church are universal concepts. There are, by loose count, nearly two dozen major world religions. It is possible, indeed probable, that an economic approach to the study of religion may be fruitfully applied to any and all of them. But all scientific studies are bounded by theoretical or practical limits. Ours is no different. Here we confine our study to Christianity for three reasons: It is the largest of the world's organized religions;[4] it is the fastest-growing religion in developing countries around the world; and it has played a major role in the history and development of Western civilization. This book is not a work of history, but we wish to use history as support for our theory and its application. We will concentrate on the central transformation that occurred in Christendom in the sixteenth century—the Protestant Reformation—and its aftermath, including the initial and ongoing reaction against Protestantism by the Catholic Church. In economic terms, Protestantism may be represented as a successful penetration of a religious market dominated by a monopoly firm (the Catholic Church). Hence, the competitive process is at the heart of our inquiry. In the persistent rivalry that followed the Reformation, all manner of product differentiation was introduced; this process continues to this very day. We hope to show that as the story of Christianity unfolds it becomes increasingly evident that economics provides a useful framework for interpreting its evolution.

Is There an Economics of Religion?

No urge, primal or modern, is more fundamental than the desire to explain existence. Human curiosity concerning mankind's ultimate origins and destinations has motivated multiple belief systems and organized religions, all seeking, more or less, to provide meaning to life on earth. Although we cannot know for sure, it is quite possible that religion is as old as mankind. Can the same be said of economics? Whereas economic *behavior* is probably as old as *Homo erectus*, by a common consensus the formal study of economics is only about as old as the United States of America. The origins of formal economic theory go back to Adam Smith (1723–1790), a Scottish political economist and moral philosopher, who published his *An Inquiry into the Nature and Causes of the Wealth of Nations* in 1776. It might come as a surprise, even to some contemporary economists, that Smith wrote at length about the economics of religion.[5] But after Smith, the subject was largely ignored by the chief architects of economic theory.

Two centuries later, economists Corry Azzi and Ronald G. Ehrenberg (1975) reawakened their peers' interest in the subject by examining church attendance within the context of modern economics.[6] Their work is a watershed in what has since become a burgeoning field—the economics of religion. The distinguishing feature of this field is the belief that religion and religious behavior are rational constructs. In religious activity, as in commercial activity, people respond to costs and benefits in a predictable way, and therefore their actions are amenable to economic analysis (as well as sociological, historical, psychological, and anthropological analysis). This view is becoming increasingly commonplace, as manifest by an ever-expanding volume of literature from economics and the other social sciences.[7] We see this book as a continuation of this young tradition. We take our inspiration from Adam Smith. But our attachment to Smith is more fundamental than the shared assumption of rationality—which, after all, is the foundation of *all* modern economic investigation. By refusing to make pejorative judgments about religion, Smith distanced himself from his great friend and mentor, Scottish philosopher David Hume (1711–1776), who considered organized religion to be an elixir for the ill-informed and superstitious. Like Smith, we seek to avoid value judgments about religion. Consequently, we take preferences for religion as given and attempt to analyze their effects. We do not argue about why preferences for religion exist, or about whether or not people should believe in supernatural phenomena. For very good reasons, some of which we analyze in chapter 3, individuals have, since the beginning of recorded time, believed in the presence of an eternal spirit or deity, an afterlife, ultimate rewards and punishments, magic, and the existence of phenomena outside the corporeal or empirical. The economist, as any other scientific observer, does not attempt to explain whether such preferences are good or bad. Rather, given that they exist for reasons that are deemed rational, the economist asks what their actual effects might be on society, or on individual or collective welfare.

Limitations of the Economic Approach

The extension of Adam Smith's analysis of the economics of religion is even more appropriate today for two reasons: Religion remains at the center of culture and civilization, and economic theory has progressed substantially in the past two and a half centuries. Contemporary economics can bring many analytical tools and concepts to bear that were not available to Smith and his contemporaries. Our study relies not only on the standard techniques of demand and supply analysis, but also on contemporary concepts of industrial organization, bureaucratic behavior, full-price analysis, time allocation, economic interest groups, economic opportunism, spatial competition, and product differentiation.[8]

Despite the many advances of modern economics, limitations do remain on what it can contribute to the understanding of human behavior. A different and troubling limitation is some people's belief that economic analysis has no place in certain realms, including the family and religion. At base, the key controversy concerns the assumption of rationality. As we've noted, rationality is the foundation of economic analysis. There is, however, a certain resistance, inside and outside the academic world, to extending this assumption to religious behavior. Admittedly there are aspects of religion and religious behavior that are wildly incompatible with typical assumptions of rationality. But these aspects can be confined to the *psychology* of belief systems, which lies beyond the realm of our investigation. It is clearly not irrational to assume, as we do, that human beliefs (however they are formed) are *given*, and to proceed accordingly. It may well be that the lynchpin of a full-blown theory of religion requires both a richer model of psychology *and* economic market analysis. While we are not equipped to advance the former, we shall try to demonstrate the effectiveness of the latter.

In proceeding this way, we merely continue on the path of contemporary microeconomics, which has embellished the theories of competition and monopoly. In earlier centuries it was common to define economics in terms of action focused on achieving wealth. The modern view is that economics is only peripherally concerned with wealth maximization. Its central concern is with utility, or satisfaction. Therefore, all markets may be studied in terms of their utility-creating effects: whether it be the market for bread or automobiles, or the market for marriage, dating, or religion. Any market—not merely traditional ones—in which both suppliers and demanders engage in rational behavior may be analyzed using the principles of economics. With appropriate imagination, we can readily apply common tools of economic analysis, such as demand and supply curves, in nontraditional markets as well. For example, the demand for religious services may be specified such that the quantity demanded is, other things equal, inversely related to the full price paid by the individual believer. *Full price* is the total cost to an individual in terms of money outlay and resources foregone. In addition to explicit (money) costs it includes implicit costs, such as time spent in delivery, search, or waiting. When the determinants of the demand for religion change, the equilibrium full price of religion (including time spent on ritual and observance of religious precepts) likewise changes. *Equilibrium price* is the price that results from the free interaction of both supply and demand. The law of demand indicates that, other things equal, quantity purchased decreases as full price increases. The law of supply indicates that, other things equal, quantity offered for sale increases as full price increases. Alternatively stated, quantity demanded is inversely related to full price; whereas quantity supplied is positively related to full price. Equilibrium quantity is traded when the desires of both demanders and suppliers are simultaneously satisfied. What is of particular interest to economists who study market behavior is how market activities are coordinated: how and on what basis participants (demanders and suppliers) make decisions, and what are the outcomes of market activity. Like other markets, religious markets may produce outcomes that are beneficial or detrimental to participants. We anticipate these results but pass no moral judgments about them.

A basic question for many people is whether the law of demand applies to religious activity. To assume that it does not is to argue that relative price changes (due, for example, to aging, or to alterations of time costs connected with ritual or belonging) do not affect behavior in religious markets. It may be that some people (e.g., Joan of Arc or Mother Teresa) do not fit the standard model of economic behavior. (On the other hand, maybe their demand curves were vertical, i.e., their demand remained unchanged regardless of price). Our observations, however, and those of many other researchers convince us that this is not the case for most demanders of religion. Studies have consistently shown that religious participation rises with age and that higher time costs change the kind of religion demanded. The fact that there may be a few exceptions does not refute the general applicability of economics to religious markets.

Objections to the use of economics to help explain church behavior have come mostly from non-economists, and are not especially persuasive. For example, William Campbell, a Roman Catholic apologist, argues that the medieval church could not be selling a commodity. In a critique of our previous work,[9] Campbell asks: "What do we put on the quantity axis that makes any sense?"[10] The answer of course is that just as insurance companies sell protection against loss, the medieval church sold a product that is a composite good that includes both temporal and supernatural elements. A demand curve may be generated that reflects the relationship between the full price of this product and corresponding quantities demanded. In any specified market a change in demand (or supply) will have predictable effects. That other motives may be involved is incontestable. It is undoubtedly true that many in the Roman Catholic Church were "shocked and distressed" at Church abuses in the Middle Ages, but it is clear that the Church, largely in an attempt to maximize wealth, was unable to prevent Protestant entry by internal reforms, as we demonstrate in chapter 5. If accepted, Campbell's metaphysical arguments concerning religion would preclude further inquiry, for he declares: "The question of whether God is also to be included among the purposive rational agents is the crux question in the interpretation of history that mere empirical evidence will probably never solve."[11] Such arguments do not carry us very far in understanding the evolution and functioning of institutions such as the Christian church.[12]

Sound research on the economics of religion does not casually apply the sweeping idea that all human activities can be reduced to market analysis. Religion is a complex good that satisfies a complicated set of individual wants. Faith, philosophy, and other intangibles play critical roles in religious markets. Like science in general, economics must abstract and simplify in order to make intellectual headway. Economics is only one avenue for explaining phenomena that may have observational equivalents. The scientific method demands, among other things, that theories be portrayed in terms that are verifiable or refutable, usually on the strength of empirical evidence. And therein lies a major problem for the economics of religion that has so far hampered progress.

For the most part, existing economic studies of religion share a common weakness: They do not accurately define the subject being studied. As a consequence, religion may, and often does, take on different meanings, some of which are amenable to empirical (or anecdotal) study, and some that are not. This ambiguity may merely reflect familiar usage in the nonscientific community, as standard dictionary definitions of religion are far from uniform. Religion is usually treated as a system of beliefs, but sometimes the system is tied to an institutional structure and sometimes it is not. One leading authority defines religion, alternatively, as "belief in and reverence for a supernatural power or powers regarded as creator and governor of the universe"; and simultaneously as a "personal or institutionalized system grounded in such belief and worship."[13] This ambiguity introduces a problem in how to count believers or members of a religion for those attempting empirical research. This problem arises because believers may or may not be members of a religion or, if they are, they may or may not attend services. Can a general (Christian) market or a particular (Methodist) market be defined by the (increasingly) standard measure of church attendance, or must it be delimited by specific (Christian vs. Methodist) beliefs? If we think of religion as a belief system, what does or can a survey of belief in God, heaven and hell, or the Ten Commandments tell us about the market for religion? These are issues that challenge investigators and trouble skeptics. They present problems that so far have proven insoluble.

As an example of the difficulties involved, consider the following: Some Christians reject institutionalized religion because they do not find a church that matches their beliefs, or satisfies their wants. These Christians may become *both* suppliers and demanders of religion—Christian or otherwise. Individuals may want to embrace religion (demand) but only on their own terms, which means changing an existing belief system to conform to individual wants (supply). Clearly, changing one's belief system involves certain costs, such as time spent learning new rituals, carrying out new responsibilities, or meeting new brethren. Costs may also be raised by the imposition of different behavioral constraints imposed by a revised belief system. Given the wide latitude concerning biblical interpretation that is characteristic of Protestantism, there is no fundamental reason why Christianity cannot be tailored to individual tastes, within limits. This point was made in an important empirical study by Robert Barro and Rachel McCleary, who first demonstrated that income and education tend to raise church attendance.[14] However, they showed that the primary factor relating economic growth to religion is the ratio of believing in certain doctrines to attendance. In other words, belief rises relative to attendance, which seems affirmed by the following survey statistics: Approximately 96 percent of Americans believe in God or a universal spirit, while only 60 percent find religion to be "very important" in their lives, and only 40 percent attend services on a regular basis.[15] Clearly, mere head counts of attendance or membership must undercount religion if it is defined as a personal belief system. Other survey data corroborate this view. In ongoing surveys conducted by the National Opinion Research Center at the University of Chicago, respondents overwhelmingly report that "faith in God" is important to some degree, that they feel "deep inner peace or harmony," and that they are "spiritually touched by the beauty of creation."[16] Yet this seems to contradict the survey data on attendance.

Rather than resolve these contradictions (which may be insoluble) we propose a different approach that asks how general forms of religion, such as Christianity, are developed and morph into other, more specific forms, either Christian or otherwise. Although our approach does not solve the empirical challenge presented by survey data, it does underscore the ramifications of the competitive process, which presumably works in religious markets just as it does in all other markets. We appreciate the fact that attendance and membership statistics provide a starting point for many researchers—one must, of course, start somewhere—but at the same time, the acknowledged deficiency of the survey approach cries out for alternatives. We regard our approach as complementary to, rather than a substitute for, the survey approach.

Advantages of the Economic Approach

The events in the United States of September 11, 2001, and their aftermath, have stirred, more than ever, awareness among social scientists of the importance of studying religion. This book seeks to contribute to our understanding of religion by demonstrating the usefulness of economic analysis for the study of Christianity, both past and present. The level of historical and theological analysis presented here is not as deep as some scholars would prefer, but such depth is neither the intent nor the justification of our effort. Our investigation convinces us that an economic approach to religion may be justified in its own right or, at the very least, as a useful accoutrement to approaches employed in other fields. Our approach particularly reaffirms the fact that economic investigations like ours must include findings from other social sciences. With regard to religion in general and Christianity in specific, the advantages that we claim on behalf of the economics of religion help us to understand many nettlesome issues that occupied Christianity in the past or that will challenge it in the future. For example, the quasi-monopoly held by the Catholic Church until the sixteenth century had a decided and predictable impact on the formation of religious markets. Economic analysis can help us understand how religious markets evolved to satisfy changing (consumer) demands, and what social, political, and economic consequences followed from the entry of new firms (churches) into religious markets. Economic analysis can also shed light on the exasperating tendency of violence to be perpetrated in the name of religion, even though most organized religions embrace the concept of peace as a moral imperative. Economic analysis can help us understand how and why new doctrinal innovations occur over time and the motivation behind religious entrepreneurship. It can help us understand (and even predict) the origins and consequences of schisms within Christian religions. It can even help us develop an informed judgment about the probable fate of ecumenical movements in contemporary Christianity. There is undoubtedly much more that economic analysis can contribute to our understanding of, and appreciation for, religion, but we make no effort to be exhaustive in this regard. Inasmuch as the field is still considered to be at the cutting edge, it is likely that more than a few of its advantages cannot easily be foreseen.

Plan of the Book

Our analysis of the evolution of Christianity in the post-Reformation period is presented in succeeding chapters. In chapter 2 we provide a limited survey of the major approaches to the economics of religion, starting with Adam Smith and moving toward the present. Using past research as a backdrop, we attempt to place our theory within the context of existing research, including studies generated by other allied social sciences. In chapter 3 we analyze religion as rational economic behavior from both historical and contemporary perspectives. This chapter attempts to develop a theory of the demand and supply for the existence and form of religion and to identify the determinants of demand and supply. Chapter 4 presents historical examples of how economic determinants affect forms of religion in religious markets. This chapter is a prelude to our theory and discussion of the Protestant Reformation in chapter 5, in which we provide historical evidence for the usefulness of economics in analyzing the critical point of entry by Protestants into the market for Christian religion. Chapter 6 explores and evaluates the Roman Catholic response to market entry, which is commonly known as the Counter-Reformation. Chapter 7 supplies economic context for the early doctrinal and organizational responses to the new market entrants (i.e., by Martin Luther, leader of the great religious revolt of the sixteenth century, and others), and traces the ensuing developments that led almost immediately to open competition in the market for religion. This chapter emphasizes the doctrinal and organizational developments of Protestant Christianity that bestowed utility-enhancing benefits on members of various denominations. In chapter 8 we examine, evaluate, and supplement the sociologist Max Weber's famous conjecture that the advent of Protestantism encouraged the development of capitalism. Finally, in chapter 9 we explore the contemporary impact of Christianity's historical evolution on today's hot-button religious issues, such as the so-called North-South (liberal-conservative) issue, sectarianism, and other highly charged controversies (e.g., women/gay clergy, gay marriage, celibacy, and competition from other religious traditions). We conclude this study with some speculations on the usefulness of an analytical method that exploits modern microeconomics to understand Christianity. Although we do not argue that modern economics is capable of explaining all facets of religion and religious institutions, we nevertheless affirm, with the backing of an ever-growing body of scientific literature, that economic analysis can improve our understanding of important aspects of religion and religious practice.

2

The Economics of Religion

Nor is it only with regard to such frivolous objects that our conduct is influenced by this principle [of utility]; it is often the secret motive of the most serious and important pursuits of both public and private life.
—Adam Smith, *The Theory of Moral Sentiments*

The genius of Adam Smith is that he saw clearly how competition promoted consumer sovereignty. This is most evident in the realm of commerce; but it is no less efficacious in the realm of religion. Smith wrote long after the Protestant Reformation occurred. Thus he faced the prospect of competing religions throughout Europe and Great Britain. A major controversy of his time concerned established religions (i.e., state-sponsored or enforced) versus non-established religions. By virtue of state sponsorship, established religions enjoyed a kind of monopoly status, whereas non-established religions competed for members, in some cases, against state-imposed sanctions. As the apostle of self-interest, Smith recognized that incentives affect individual behavior and that in religious matters individuals respond to incentives on both sides of the market, that is, from the demand side and the supply side. It may be said that he took a broad, industrial organization approach to religion, in which market *structure* has an important impact on individual and collective outcomes.

The Progenitor

The important consequences of Smith's industrial organization analysis of religion can be put into bold relief by fitting his inquiry into a more contemporary framework. For this purpose, we borrow one of the tools of contemporary microeconomics, the Coasian firm. This construct takes its name from Nobel Laureate Ronald Coase, who formally identified a kind of non-market or team production that takes place within what we call a business firm.[1] In his view, firms arise because they represent the least costly form of economic coordination; their size is determined by which scale is most efficient (least costly) for production. In many cases, for example, it has been found to be efficient to organize production in a manner in which resource allocation is directed and coordinated by managers. Such organizations (firms) have costs and benefits, the costs being represented by the necessity of monitoring economic activity to prevent shirking and so on; the benefits represented by gains in economic efficiency.

Self-Interest and Competition Outside the Firm

Religion does not play a central role in Smith's seminal work, *An Inquiry into the Nature and Causes of the Wealth of Nations*, but it becomes significant in Book V, when he embarks on a discussion of the source and use of government revenues. The critical issue for Smith throughout *The Wealth of Nations* was to show how private interest vented through free and open markets winds up promoting the public interest. In education this link was severed, Smith argued, by the practice of paying teachers from endowments: "The endowments of schools and colleges have necessarily diminished more or less the necessity of application in the teachers. Their subsistence, so far as it arises from their salaries, is evidently derived from a fund altogether independent of their success and reputation in their particular professions."[2] Smith believed that a system of remuneration based on fees paid by students would produce greater economic efficiency and public welfare. He endorsed the same idea as it pertains to the performance of clergy, noting that despite other glaring shortcomings, "In the [post-Reformation] church of Rome, the industry and zeal of the inferior clergy is kept more alive by the powerful motive of self-interest, than perhaps in any established protestant church."[3] In this regard, Smith clearly regarded competition as an energizer of enterprise, whether secular or religious: "The parochial clergy are like those teachers whose reward depends partly upon their salary, and partly upon the fees or honoraries which they get from their pupils, and these must always depend more or less upon their industry and reputation. The mendicant orders are like those teachers whose subsistence depends altogether upon their industry. They are obliged, therefore, to use every art which can animate the devotion of the common people."[4]

What makes Smith's discussion of the competitive principle in religious activity significant is the fact that he recognized and explored the nature of competition on several different levels in religious organizations. In addition to being advantageous to civil order, organized belief can threaten it as well. Religion produces certain public spillovers as well as private benefits. What Smith perceived as a threat is the tendency of religion to monopolize certain aspects of culture, in part because civil governments invariably seek to mold religious institutions to their advantage. Smith maintained that it is in the interest of civil governments to keep the clergy indolent, just as it is in the interest of church administrators to subdue rivals. Government opportunism exerts a strong tendency in favor of established churches—by endorsing a single religion, the state buys domestic tranquility, whereas by aligning itself with civil government, the church buys relief from institutional competitors. The tendency, in other words, is for established churches to become monopolies: "The interested and active zeal of religious teachers can be dangerous and troublesome only where there is, either but one sect tolerated in the society, or where the whole of a large society is divided into two or three great sects; the teachers of each acting by concert, and under a regular discipline and subordination."[5] If left free from government affiliation, many small religious sects will neither "disturb the public tranquility," nor be "productive of any very hurtful effects, but, on the contrary, of several good ones."[6]

This official alignment of church and state is capable of engendering conflict between the two.

The clergy of every established church constitute a great incorporation. They can act in concert, and pursue their interest upon one plan and with one spirit, as much as if they were under the direction of one man; and they are frequently too under such direction. Their interest as an incorporated body is never the same with that of the sovereign, and is sometimes directly opposed to it. Their great interest is to maintain their authority with the people; and this authority depends upon the supposed certainty and importance of the whole doctrine which they inculcate, and upon the supposed necessity of adopting every part of it with the most implicit faith, in order to avoid eternal misery.[7]

The question for society is how to resolve the conflict of interest that arises from what in most cases springs from the voluntary incorporation of political and religious interests.

For Smith to resolve this issue, he had to establish the goal of religion. Just as he believed that state religions created public mischief, so he believed that the separation of church and state promoted a well-ordered polity. The separation of church and state permitted competition among religions, which Smith thought was justified because beliefs regarding religious precepts (e.g., moral behavior, conditions for salvation) differed among individuals. He was keenly aware that religion is not a homogeneous good and that, in some kind of moving equilibrium, different forms of religion evolved and had to be supplied. Competition produces consumer sovereignty, which helps to establish a well-ordered society.

Consumers are sovereign by virtue of free choice among alternatives offered to them by rival vendors. Optimality in terms of meeting consumer demands is achieved by open competition in output markets— that is, between religious firms. This is essentially the position taken by Nathan Rosenberg[8] and by Gary M. Anderson[9] who have analyzed this issue. As we will see momentarily, however, Smith also analyzed consequences of consumer sovereignty produced *within* the Coasian firm.

We must remember that Smith was a historian as well as a philosopher and economist. So it is no surprise that after establishing the superiority of competitive religious markets to established religions, he introduced a bit of conjectural history.

But *if politicks had never called in the aid of religion*, had the conquering party never adopted the tenets of one sect more than those of another, when it had gained the victory, it would probably have dealt equally and impartially with all the different sects, and have allowed every man to chuse his own priest and his own religion as he thought proper. There would, in this case, no doubt, have been a great multitude of religious sects. Almost every different congregation might probably have made a little sect by itself, or have entertained some peculiar tenets of its own. Each teacher would no doubt have felt himself under the necessity of making the utmost exertion, and of using every art both to preserve and to increase the number of his disciples. But as every other teacher would have felt himself under the same necessity, the success of no one teacher, or sect of teachers, could have been very great.[10] (emphasis added)

In other words, if history could be rewritten, the desired path would be clear. But given the evolution of government and the pattern of incentives in existence between civil government and religious institutions, the deregulation of established churches into free religious markets was not likely, in Smith's view. Therefore he turned his attention to an assessment of the relative merits of various established religions and, in doing so, made a clear contribution to the theory of organizational economics—that is, to efficiencies possible *within* the religious firm.

Self-Interest and Competition within the Religious Firm
Competitive religions, Smith believed, posed no threat to civil government or individual liberties. If competition reigned in religious markets, each sect would have to respect all others and these concessions might even lead to Smith's ultimate libertarian ideal—a "pure and rational religion, free from every mixture of absurdity, imposture, or fanaticism, such as wise men have in all ages of the world wished to see established."[11] Such a world would, among other things, encourage the development of science and rationality, thereby enhancing economic growth.

By contrast, the alliance of religion and state tends to corrupt both parties. Civil government, like its partner, established religion, is influenced, to one degree or another, Smith avowed, by "popular superstition and enthusiasm." Established religions typically become bureaucratic, thereby losing touch with the common people, and creating disharmony among them. Thus we arrive at Smith's two fundamental objections to established religions: On the one hand they tend to infect civil government with instability (i.e., fanatical behavior), and on the other, they undermine consumer sovereignty. On both counts, economic development is threatened.

Since established religion was commonplace in many European states, the issue for Smith became how, under the constraints of state-established religion, preachers could be relieved of indolence and greed while consumer choice and sovereignty were maintained. Smith found the answer to this question within the organizational principles of the religious firm. This is verified by his qualified praise of the Presbyterian clergy, which, despite its standing as a state religion, established an internal organization that emphasized freedom, equality, and individual rights—the same qualities that promoted consumer sovereignty. Smith noted that some Protestant churches bestowed on their members the rights to elect their pastors, but that this alone was not sufficient to mitigate the effect of establishment, because

as long as the people of each parish preserved the right of electing their own pastors, they acted almost always under the influence of the clergy, and generally of the most factious and fanatical of the order. The clergy, in order to preserve their influence in those popular elections, became, or affected to become, many of them, fanatics themselves, encouraged fanaticism among the people, and gave preference almost always to the fanatical candidate. So small a matter as the appointment of a parish priest occasioned almost always a violent contest, not only in one parish, but in all the neighbouring parishes, who seldom failed to take part in the quarrel.[12]

However, when the rights of patronage were abolished "by the act which established presbytery in the beginning of the reign of William III, [t]hat act at least put it in the power of certain classes of people in each parish to purchase, for a very small price, the right of electing their own pastor"[13]; this reform allowed parishioners to become stakeholders in good ecclesiastical government. Although the rights of patronage were later restored under Queen Anne, Smith argued that Scotland nevertheless maintained some vestiges of concurrence by the people.

Smith made it clear that the disadvantages of established religion sprang from the twin inequalities of authority within the organization and benefices to the clergy. Hence a religion—even an established one —that provided both equality of authority and equality of benefice mitigated these disadvantages. And the way to nurture equality of authority and benefices was to introduce elements of competition into the organization of an established church. It is therefore the quasi-competitive nature of certain established religions that Smith endorsed.[14] The fact that established religions could be ranked and evaluated according to how close they came to free religious markets is inherent in Smith's qualified praise of Presbyterianism. As established religions go, Presbyterianism was not perfect, but it was, from an economic perspective, better than most alternatives.

The equality which the Presbyterian form of church government establishes among the clergy, consists, first in the equality of authority or ecclesiastical jurisdiction; and secondly, in the equality of benefice. In all Presbyterian churches the equality of authority is perfect: that of benefice is not so. The difference, however, between one benefice and another, is seldom so considerable as commonly to tempt the possessor even of the small one to pay court to his patron, by the vile arts of flattery and ostentation, in order to get a better. In all the Presbyterian churches, where the rights of patronage are thoroughly established, it is by nobler and better arts that the established clergy in general endeavour to gain the favour of their superiors; by their learning, by the irreproachable regularity of their life, and by the faithful and diligent discharge of their duty.[15]

By the same token, equality of church benefices makes for a more efficient and responsive religion, and therefore commends the Presbyterian form of internal organization over other established churches.

Where the church benefices are all nearly equal, none of them can be very great, and this mediocrity of benefice, though it may no doubt be carried too far, has, however, some very agreeable effects. Nothing but the most exemplary morals can give dignity to a man of small fortune. . . . In his own conduct, therefore, he is obliged to follow that system of morals which the common people respect the most. He gains their esteem and affection by that plan of life which his own interest and situation would lead him to follow. . . . The Presbyterian clergy, accordingly, have more influence over the minds of the common people than perhaps the clergy of any other established church. It is accordingly in Presbyterian countries only that we ever find the common people converted, without persecution, completely, and almost to a man, to the established church.[16]

Finally, Smith underscored the fact that the revenue of every established church competes with the general revenue of the state and, on that account, should not be so large as to diminish national defense. He therefore lauded the national churches of Scotland and Switzerland for their frugality and efficient administration, noting that "[the] most opulent church in Christendom does not maintain better the uniformity of faith, the fervour of devotion, the spirit of order, regularity, and austere morals in the great body of the people, than this very poorly endowed church of Scotland."[17] He added that Switzerland does an even better job with yet less funding.

For Smith, Presbyterianism provided a form of church organization that allowed a certain measure of participatory, representative democracy at the local level, which set it apart from Episcopal and Roman Catholic traditions.[18] Moreover, it allowed for some heterogeneity in the style and form of worship, according to the demands of individual church members. This internal organization within the Coasian firm was a second-best solution to open output competition, which Smith regarded as most efficient.

Protestantism in general was a religion of emancipation—in part from the medieval church but also in part from medieval government. Yet in many instances, Martin Luther included, the leaders of the new religion allowed themselves to become mere chaplains to national rulers. Some of the new religions, such as Anglicanism and Calvinism, were dictatorial, as was the Roman Catholicism that they displaced. So it is significant that the only form of established religion Smith qualifiedly condoned was Presbyterianism—as practiced in Scotland, Holland, and Switzerland. In each of these countries, religious competition was keen. In Scotland, Presbyterianism faced off against Anglicanism; in Holland and Switzerland, it confronted Roman Catholicism. The dominant religious firm in each of these countries was authoritarian and non-democratic; the new entrant stressed individualism, equality, and representative democracy.

The democratic elements of Presbyterianism are evident in its constitution, which emphasizes popular election of ministers and officers, wide dissemination of authority, and local property rights. Authority in the Presbyterian Church flows from the bottom up rather than from the top down (as it does in Anglicanism and Catholicism). Presbyterianism owes its existence largely to the efforts of John Knox and his followers. The new religion that Knox founded gained a receptive audience in Scotland, Holland, and Switzerland because it offered a more convenient or persuasive alternative to the dominant religion it displaced. Since medieval times, the social hierarchy in western Europe was based on the duties and responsibilities of the three estates: those who pray, those who fight, and those who work. The Scottish third estate was in bad shape in the sixteenth century, not so much due to wars as to the defects of social organization and Scottish government. Scottish tenants had three main grievances: The first was against the church, which placed a heavy tax burden (e.g., tithe and other ecclesiastical duties) on production: the second was against the burghs, which held a monopoly of markets and crafts[19]; the third was against a notoriously insecure system of land tenure. In response to this situation, Knox led a reform movement that was ostensibly religious, but encompassed social, economic, and political reform as well. In fact, Knox's religious reforms could be seen as a vehicle for reforming the polity and the economy.[20]

Knox used a successful entry strategy that organized the poor into a new religion. He did so, as did his counterparts in Holland and Switzerland, by lowering the cost of religion to the rural poor. It was a religion that served the preferences of its newfound constituency and thus was able to compete successfully with the incumbent monopoly. Its success and Smith's qualified admiration was due to the fact that leaders selected hardy and consumer-friendly organizational formats in the face of direct competition.

The Provocateur

Adam Smith's analysis of religion from an economic standpoint surprisingly did not encourage further work on the same subject by classical economists and their direct descendants, despite the fact that some of the early economists, such as Thomas Robert Malthus and Phillip Henry Wicksteed, were religious prelates (at a time when taking holy orders was one of the surest ways to get a university scholarship). Some writers, such as Karl Marx and Thorstein Veblen, argued that religion was an impediment to economic development, calling it an "imbecile institution." For Marx, religion hindered the emergence of a proletarian class; for Veblen, it retarded the emergence of technocracy. The great neoclassical economist, Alfred Marshall, while seeking to preserve a clear delineation between the economic and the religious in human affairs, nevertheless hinted at a connection between Protestantism and economic development.[21] But the one author whose name is linked above all others with religion and economics in the social sciences is Max Weber.[22]

Weber, a sociologist, is such a towering figure in this field, and his ideas are so enduring, that we reserve a full chapter later on for a detailed analysis of his famous thesis. Here we merely wish to place his ideas in the broad timeline that established the economics of religion, and to expose some myths surrounding his ideas. Weber's famous hypothesis, that the advent of Protestantism encouraged the development of capitalism, as laid out in *The Protestant Ethic and the Spirit of Capitalism*, has come to mean several things, some by misinterpretation rather than by careful exegesis. Generally it is interpreted to mean either that Protestantism encouraged a "pursuit of gain" that encouraged capitalism, or that Protestantism *caused* capitalism, neither of which is entirely correct. Weber went to great lengths to argue that the pursuit of gain was a feature of all ages, including the Middle Ages, during which he charged society with the "lowest forms of avarice."[23] Furthermore, a fair interpretation of Weber belies the argument that the Protestant ethic *caused* capitalism. At the end of his famous essay Weber admits the possibility that causality may run the other way, that is, that economic conditions may influence Protestant asceticism.[24] While Weber has remained open to criticism on a number of issues,[25] he did not argue, as some have supposed, for some single causal explanation for the emergence of capitalism. Indeed, he emphasized the importance of other factors leading to its development, such as free labor, the invention of double-entry bookkeeping, and the separation of business from household accounts. Nevertheless, his brilliant study of institutional change and the role of culture in fomenting such change captured the fancy of social scientists for centuries to come.[26]

We are concerned here with the fact that Weber's central argument employs a preference-based explanation of Protestantism's impact. Declaring his interest in "the influence of those psychological sanctions which, originating in religious belief and the practice of religion, gave a direction to practical conduct and held the individual to it," Weber propounded the idea of a "calling," a focus of human activity ordained by God.[27] According to Weber:

The earning of money within the modern economic order is, so long as it is done legally, the result and the expression of virtue and proficiency in a calling.... [The idea] of one's duty in a calling, is what is most characteristic of the social ethic of capitalistic culture, and is in a sense the fundamental basis of it. It is an obligation which the individual is supposed to feel and does feel towards the content of his professional activity, no matter in what it consists, in particular no matter whether it appears on the surface as a utilization of his personal powers, or only of his material possessions (as capital).[28]

Acceptance of life and toil in *this* world is the task that God sets out for man. This worldly goal was not part of Catholic psychology.

The God of Calvinism demanded of his believers not single good works, but a life of good works combined into a unified system. There was no place for the very human Catholic cycle of sin, repentance, atonement, release, followed by renewed sin. Nor was there any balance of merit for a life as a whole which could be adjusted by temporal punishments or the Churches' means of grace.[29]

"Ascetic ideals" were not achieved by withdrawal from the world but by pursuit of worldly goals in everyday activities. This Protestant psychology was buttressed by Calvin's doctrine of predestination. There was much uncertainty about who the elect would be. Calvin seemed to entertain no doubts about himself, but the doctrine (initially) caused consternation among his followers. Eventually the doctrine evolved into a belief that success at one's calling was a manifestation of God's favor and a sign of eventual salvation. In discussing the religious foundations of worldly asceticism, Weber concluded that "the complete elimination of salvation through the Church and the sacraments (which was in Lutheranism by no means developed to its final conclusions) was what formed the absolutely decisive difference from Catholicism."[30] The Calvinists wanted to be saved by faith alone, and Calvin offered a creed that promised just that.

Weber's link between religion and economic growth—too intricate to probe in great detail at this juncture—has, until recently, probably remained the single most popular investigation in the field of the economics of religion. The central supposition of Weber's analysis—that Protestantism changed preferences from the otherworldly concerns of Catholicism to the economic activities of this world—introduces a clearly defined change on the demand side of religious (and economic) behavior. The basic tenet of Roman Catholicism is that earning salvific merit in this life through good deeds gets one closer to heaven. The causal arrow runs from deeds in this world to rewards in the next. Protestantism bent the causal arrow so that salvation in the next world is foreshadowed by rewards in this world. This is an important shift that deserves careful, in-depth consideration, which, for purposes of continuity, we must defer until chapter 8.

The Godfather

What has come to be known in contemporary circles as the economics of religion is dominated more by Smith's paradigm than by Weber's. That is, the connection, if any, between economic development and forms of religion has taken a back seat to the specification of individual economic/religious behavior founded on the maximization of utility. The person most responsible for redirecting economics to all manner of extra-market activity is Gary Becker, who pioneered a utility-maximizing model of household behavior based on full-price notions of demand and supply. In a sustained flow of intellectual creativity, Becker applied economic analysis to such wide ranging and diverse topics as family, crime and punishment, addiction, marriage, fertility, altruism, egoism, and suicide.[31] Although religion is not one of the subjects that engaged Becker directly, the economics of religion, in its present form, may aptly be described as a "Beckerian" enterprise. In this enterprise, as in any academic endeavor, the results of investigation depend in large measure on the questions being asked.

Studies of Religious Participation
One of the first questions asked, by Corry Azzi and Ronald G. Ehrenberg,[32] and in somewhat different context later by Laurence R. Iannaccone,[33] concerned the determinants of religious participation. Azzi and Ehrenberg employed a multi-period model of household behavior and two data sets—one on statewide church membership and another based on a survey sample of church attendance—to test a number of relationships that concern sociologists: (1) male versus female participation in church-related activities; (2) the age distribution of church attendance; (3) relationship(s) between income and church attendance; and (4) demographic characteristics (black/white, urban/rural) of church attendance. Their model allows individuals to allocate their resources (time and goods) to both temporal and "afterlife" consumption. Afterlife consumption, heaven, eternal peace, communion with God, and so on, is a function of time engaged in religious activities during one's lifetime.[34] Their results tend to corroborate the work of sociologists in the field. They were able to explain, for example, why religions that are less time intensive grow faster in the United States than more time-intensive religions, by connecting membership in the latter to households with lower alternative time costs (lower wages imply a lower cost of engaging in non-wage activity). Azzi and Ehrenberg also found that religious participation rates rise with wealth; that higher wages (of both genders) reduce church attendance rates; that rural religious participation rates exceed

those in urban areas; that females have higher religious participation rates than males; and that male church attendance falls off significantly as men grow older (presumably due to health considerations). These results have been challenged by other investigators, either in whole (by D. H. Sullivan in 1985[35]), or in part (by Laurence R. Iannaccone in 1998[36]), but the study by Azzi and Ehrenberg had an important catalytic effect on further research.

Iannaccone extended Azzi and Ehrenberg's model to include religious human capital in the form of knowledge, familiarity with ritual and dogma, and other factors, suggesting that the service sold was something more than the promises of an afterlife.[37] Defining a specific stock or amount of religious experience that an individual has built up at any given time as a function of previous activities, Iannaccone acknowledged the possibility that religion can be a kind of addiction that can grow over time. In such circumstances, perhaps unsurprisingly, children tend to adopt the religion of their parents (e.g., "cradle Catholics"); religious switching takes place at relatively early ages and in belief systems similar to those in which early capital has been acquired (i.e., as religious capital is acquired with age, the cost of switching rises); and individuals tend to marry within their own religion, a result that was asserted by Becker at an earlier date.[38]

The operational premise established by these early investigations is that demand for religion is determined by the sacrifice of both time and goods. Becker confirmed that the value of time is a function of income, wealth, or wages, a result that is pivotal to understanding several key issues in the economics of religion, including such factors as individual choice of religions, interdenominational mobility, the nature of religious firms, and the nature of religious products or services.

One area of religious participation that has come under increasing scrutiny concerns the economics of cults. Not surprisingly, inspiration for this kind of analysis can also be drawn from Adam Smith, who believed that religious cults had the potential to create civil disorder and unrest. He clearly understood that membership in religious organizations had "club" effects—that is, that the utility a person receives from his consumption of a club good depends upon the number of other persons with whom he must share its benefits.[39] He provided a brilliantly intuitive example of self-interested self-regulation. Smith asserted that a "man of low condition" in a small community will regulate his behavior appropriately due to low information costs (i.e., everybody knows his business). By dint of moving to a city, the same person sinks into "obscurity and darkness" and becomes vulnerable to profligacy and vice. Seeking redemption and respectability, such a person may join a "small religious sect." Smith described the consequences as follows:

> He from that moment acquires a degree of consideration which he never had before. All his brother sectaries are, for the credit of the sect, interested to observe his conduct, and if he gives occasion to any scandal, if he deviates very much from those austere morals which they almost always require of one another, to punish him by what is always a very severe punishment, even where no civil effects attend it, expulsion or excommunication from the sect. In little religious sects, accordingly, the morals of the common people have been almost always remarkably regular and orderly; generally much more so than in the established church. The morals of those little sects, indeed, have frequently been rather disagreeably rigorous and unsocial.[40]

A key point of this passage is that in a religious sect the utility derived by any single member depends on, and affects, the utility of the other members. This proposition is also true of clubs.[41] A corollary of this is that sects and clubs inevitably face a "free-rider" problem—the prospect that some members will receive the benefits of membership without bearing proportionate costs.

The benefits to church or cult membership are both private (confined to the member) and public. The public benefits that Smith recognized take the form of a well-ordered society, open to the progress that is promised by innovation and science. These benefits can be circumvented by superstitious and irrational governments, as Smith recognized, which explains why he put so much emphasis on the organizational structure of religions and their relationships to the state.

Iannaccone argues that strictness is the mechanism used by religious sects to control the free-rider problem. He attempts to explain an apparent anomaly, at least to economists, namely why some people prefer religions that demand *greater sacrifice*, that is, why individuals might choose strictness over leniency. Iannaccone contends that because the cost of monitoring group utility-reducing behavior is high, religious sects turn to strictness as a means of controlling the free-rider problem.

It may be possible to demand of members some salient, stigmatizing behavior that inhibits participation or reduces productivity in alternative contexts: shaved heads, pink robes, or an isolated location does the job quite effectively.... Deviant norms thus mitigate the externality problems faced by religious groups. Distinctive diet, dress, grooming, and social customs constrain and often stigmatize members, making participation in alternative activities more costly. Potential members are forced to choose: participate fully or not at all. Paradoxically, those who remain find their welfare increased. It follows that perfectly rational people can be drawn to decidedly unconventional groups.[42]

This analysis rationalizes the use of certain screening mechanisms, such as one-time initiation costs and ongoing membership costs (e.g., "dietary restrictions, Sabbath laws, distinctive clothing, celibacy, geographic isolation, and the like"[43]). More recently, Eli Berman has extended this analysis to the behavior of terrorist extremists.[44] Though useful in a limited way, this avenue of research offers little to explain the operation of pervasive religions.[45] For example, Catholics within large community churches may easily escape scrutiny when they miss Sunday Mass. Likewise, financial contributions by members of large corporate churches are difficult to monitor. Free-rider problems in large churches remain intractable for the most part.

A major shortcoming of Iannaccone's work is its neglect of the nature of the product and the form of its demand. Sacrifice and stigma may explain how certain temporal benefits can accrue to a small group, but the fact remains that for many religious participants the demand for religion is primarily supernatural. Among Christian religions, the chief product *is* an afterlife. Theology as a blueprint for achieving a happy afterlife does matter. By rejecting Azzi and Ehrenberg's "afterlife consumption motive" Iannaccone assumes a demand function, but does not specify its form. In other words, he takes demand for granted. Moreover, within the constraints of his model, if the demand function were to be specified, it would only apply primarily to a club good with individuals' benefits determined by the number of adherents. Yet, as we argued above, and attempt to demonstrate below, there are both private and public good aspects to religion. A full-scale theory of demand for religion must take into account both aspects of this complicated product.

Once the promise of an afterlife is admitted to the analysis, the religious product becomes a kind of *credence* good. Credence goods require that certain types of assurances be given in order to satisfy purchasers[46] because the quality of the good in question cannot be determined either before or after the sale.[47] Actually, given time and/or resources expended, one could determine the quality of such "credence goods" as tax services, psychiatric counseling, transmission repair, home security systems, or marriage and family counseling—goods for which quality assurances or licensing are routinely given. The quality of transmission repair, for example, will be revealed over time as will that of tax services and marriage counseling. With regard to an afterlife (e.g., heaven, hell, nirvana), however, it is self-evident that the quality of the product is unknowable even with time and resources spent. Dead men tell no tales, even about what lies beyond this earthly vale of tears. Thus we go beyond the credence good characterization to characterize religion as a *meta-credence good*, because unlike some earthly credence goods (such as automotive repair or psychiatric counseling), verification cannot be achieved with time or resources spent. While, as we will see, some earthly warranties may be given by suppliers of religion—indeed, there may be huge investments in quality assurance claims—no church offers a money-back guarantee to a soul that is dissatisfied with his or her afterlife experience. This fact, however, does not seem to hinder an active market in religion that, in the United States alone, comes in thousands of different forms.

The credence-good nature of religion conforms to and may help explain some of the club aspects of religious practices, because the plausibility of a religion's claim to salvation is buttressed when others adhere to the same belief system. This interaction creates something like a superstar effect, as described by the late economist Sherwin Rosen,[48] meaning that positive benefits flow to those outside the group as well as within. However, this facet alone does not explain the initial or ultimate demand for religion. The complete and accurate specification of the demand and supply functions for religion poses the most intractable problem in the economics of religion. The issue is further complicated by the fact that in markets for Christian religions, assurances of eternal salvation rarely if ever make up the sole object of demand. Religion is in almost every case a complicated product that serves many different wants of demanders, including social services, political cohesion, access to business contacts, reduced information costs (e.g., with respect to dating and marriage), and so on. As a result, churches, as suppliers, are necessarily and incessantly engaged in establishing observable quality dimensions for their product.[49]

The critical nature of the product and the essence of product demand and product supply are major concerns of our inquiry. We look at markets not merely in the static sense of equilibration at a fixed point in time but also in the dynamic sense of how behavior, institutions, and outcomes change over time. What we find in the existing literature is that some studies amplify the demand side of the market to the neglect of the supply side, while others stress the supply side at the expense of demand. Nowhere is the nature of demand and supply nailed down in any precise fashion. What is needed is a cohesive and workable foundation for this most basic of market phenomena. As the economics of religion expands to embrace the work of more and more specialists, awareness of this important lacuna is starting to emerge. Thus, aware that religious pluralism can accommodate heterogeneous consumer preferences because not all demanders will desire the same theology or strictness, Kent D. Miller, a management scientist, maintains that economic theory must transcend Iannaccone's principle of strictness in order to understand religious organization.[50] Whereas Iannaccone recognizes resource commitments, he does not elaborate on the feasibility of extracting such commitments from diverse market participants. When the dynamic efficiency of markets is considered, product differentiation designed to satisfy heterogeneous demands must be a part of the organizational characteristics of religious markets. Thus, strictness is an outcome of religious adherence and organization, not a cause of it. According to Miller: "Differentiation can increase per capita organizational resources by exploiting switching costs across subcultures. Hence, a strategy of focused differentiation may result in more loyal participation, with loyalty expressed in terms of longevity of involvement as well as resource commitments."[51] In effect, Miller argues that a competitive process wherein degrees of strictness are perceived as outcomes creates efficient religious organizations.[52]

Whereas Iannaccone's strictness issue has been a lightening rod for several additional studies, other researchers have pursued different aspects of religious participation. For example, Brooks B. Hull and

Gerald F. Moran conducted empirical studies on religious participation in colonial churches of New England in general and Connecticut in particular.[53] Jody Lipford, Robert E. McCormick, and Robert D. Tollison explored the relationship between religious participation and crime.[54] Ian Smith,[55] Ian Smith, John W. Sawkins, and Paul T. Seaman,[56] and Ian Smith and John W. Sawkins[57] verified Adam Smith's proposition that connects market structure and church attendance, using national and international data. Jonathan Gruber modeled the impact of market density on religious participation and economic outcomes, concluding that higher religious densities lead to higher participation and to better outcomes involving income, education, and marital status.[58] As interesting and productive as these studies may be, the shadowy nature of the demand for religion haunts them all.

Studies in (New) Economic History

Whereas economic studies of religious participation focus on the recent past (i.e., newly generated data), "new" historical studies in the economics of religion emphasize the events of the (sometimes distant) past. Inasmuch as history provides a prologue to the future, we believe that the study of economic history holds great potential for contributing to our understanding of the economics of religion. History records the unfolding of events, which can be interpreted within different analytical frameworks. Although many past studies of church history have been sensitive to economic considerations, we are aware of none that attempt to interpret major historical movements within the framework of contemporary economics. This book is therefore an early foray into mostly uncharted waters. It is not without precedent, however.

The historical approach that we favor involves mining Adam Smith's fundamental insight that in the religious realm, organizational structure (i.e., what economics calls the theory of industrial organization) is a major determinant of individual and group behavior. Brooks B. Hull and Frederick Bold embarked on this path by modeling the church as a firm that maximizes profit under competitive conditions in order to maintain long-term survival.[59] In their joint work and in Hull's,[60] the church as firm took on the role of provider of social insurance,[61] promises of an afterlife, and other social and economic services. Hull and Bold concluded that church enforcement of property rights is a public good, but in contrast to the enforcement of property rights by the state, church authority can summon the supernatural enforcement mechanisms of heaven and hell. Hull maintains that this was a particularly important feature of the establishment of mendicant orders of the Roman Catholic Church at the beginning of the thirteenth century.[62] By their practice of poverty, itinerant monks added "quality assurance" to the products being sold by the church, which, in turn, promoted efficient property and financial rights within the emerging towns and cities. The invention of purgatory and the establishment of the threat of hell and damnation at the time of death helped establish and enforce efficient standards of behavior. At the same time, social goods, such as abbeys, monasteries, hospitals, and schools, were also added to the mix of things that make up the product of the church.

We extended the basic concept of the church as an economic firm in *Sacred Trust*, which was a compilation and extension of various particularized studies involving the organizational structure of the medieval church and its economic consequences. Because the medieval church was a quasi-monopolistic, bureaucratic firm, prospects for rent seeking (i.e., using the political or bureaucratic process to secure economic advantage)[63] was a major component of our investigation. Since then, we have broadened our reach to include analysis of the Protestant Reformation and the Catholic Counter-Reformation.[64] This book is yet another leg on an extended intellectual journey.

History holds that Christianity rose (against long odds) as a fledgling competitor in the faith market that was dominated by varieties of late Greek and Roman Gnosticism. After the tenth century, Christianity had so extended and consolidated its market power that it took on the form of a supranational government, with important implications for economic growth. We perceive that the medieval church was (rationally) as worldly as it was otherworldly, and that it developed a market for assurances of eternal salvation (and other elements of a complicated product) under extremely venal conditions. The medieval church sought to extract wealth from secular society and to dominate civil authority in a variety of ways: suppressing heresy through violence, regulating credit markets for its own benefit, and monopolizing religious doctrine and dogma. Moreover, as a kind of supranational government, the Roman Church clashed with secular rulers and administrations, with civil jurisdictions, feudal aristocrats, and virtually all other non-Church authorities. In general, an observable outcome of these clashes was either stimulation or protection of Church rents. That is, the Roman Church was a rent-seeking organization.[65]

The theory of rent seeking has undergone numerous emendations since its inception.[66] In terms of applying the theory to historical episodes and to historical institutions, no extensions have been more important than those integrating and illustrating the rent-seeking process to regulatory and institutional change. Economists George J. Stigler[67] and Sam Peltzman[68] designed an elaborate analytical apparatus for this purpose. They present a model that emphasizes marginal trade-offs by politician-regulators in an interest-group setting, accounting for both producers' and consumers' surplus distributions and redistributions. Rent seeking is the motivating factor of a process through which regulations appear and disappear. Seekers of regulation (i.e., any effective interest group) are willing to invest resources to get it, and regulations may come in many forms: taxes, tolls, regulated prices, quantity or quality restrictions, territorial limitations, and so on. Those injured by such economic controls, typically larger numbers of unorganized consumers, will invest up to the amount of their interest in preventing such regulation. The challenge faced by the politician-regulator (e.g., pope, monarch, dictator, legislator) is to balance the gains from favors granted to one group against the costs imposed on another.

By encouraging misallocation of resources (i.e., expenditures merely to obtain differential privilege), rent seeking becomes a theory of government and historico-institutional change. Over time rents and potential rents emerge through technological change that can support new regulations, deregulations, or a cycle of interventions. Ripe cultures for rent seeking are established by monarchy, dictatorship, and authoritarian rule of whatever kind, whether secular or religious. When the tools of modern industrial organization theory, public-choice theory, the microeconomics of information costs (including asymmetric information), and concepts of full price are wedded to it, rent seeking becomes an important tool for analyzing explicit and implicit markets, including those related to religion and, in the case of this book, the evolution of modern Christianity.

This new historical approach that seeks to bring culture within the purview of economic analysis is slowly gaining adherents. Economist Douglas Allen has developed a model that treats Christian churches as firms constrained by their theology.[69] Like all firms, churches must manage opportunistic behavior. As attempts are made to do so, a church finds that its organizational structure is determined by the transaction cost problems that arise in the production of its spiritual good. Allen attempts to test this theory by examining the history of the church and examining cases of church failures and successes. Economists Dieter Schmidtchen and Achim Mayer posit a model of the medieval church as a rent-seeking, franchise monopolist, and use game theory to demonstrate that friars were "licensed" to sell indulgences (i.e., dispensations from purgatory) in competition with parish priests.[70] (The latter, prior to the introduction of the mendicant friars, had exclusive territorial rights in the sale of indulgences.) Friars are here represented as raiders licensed by the pope to increase papal rents in the face of opportunistic behavior by the local clergy. Schmidtchen and Mayer maintain that in this way a profit-maximizing papacy could divert economic rents from the local level to the Vatican. In their game-theoretic model they show how the pope could exact greater profits by regulating the amount of indulgences sold by friars.[71]

But unlike economist Audrey Davidson's study of monasteries, which is supported by empirical evidence on the incentive-incompatibility problems faced by medieval monasteries,[72] Schmidtchen and Mayer do not provide any direct historical examination of contracts that would have the effects predicted by their theory. As a consequence, their claim remains unsubstantiated that the objective function of the pope was to contract with friars to exact maximum profits from the system. It is no less likely that the establishment in the thirteenth century of Franciscans, Dominicans, and other mendicant orders was a consequence of other, perhaps more overarching, goals of the papacy.[73]

Some writers have employed the rent-seeking paradigm in an attempt to explain selected features of religion, such as the institution of auricular confession within Catholicism. Economist Benito Arruñada views confession as a form of "moral enforcement," albeit one that involves a trade-off between specialization advantages and exchange costs.[74] This interesting approach offers insights into the possible function of confession, but it does not displace the fact that confession and price schedules were *not* designed for optimum deterrence, or that rent seeking riddled church policy during the high Middle Ages when the upstream church was clearly an input monopoly.[75] Auricular confession was one of several concomitant product developments introduced by the church in the twelfth and thirteenth centuries, including the invention of purgatory and the distinction between mortal and venial sin—a distinction that paved the way for commerce in indulgences.[76] Nevertheless, using contemporary data, Arruñada finds that increases in the frequency of confession are positively correlated with increases in cash giving and in-kind service, which lends credence to the premise that rent seeking remains a component of the modern Roman Catholic Church.[77]

Studies in Sociology and History
During the long hiatus in the economics of religion between Adam Smith and Gary Becker, sociologists and historians steadily and persistently enriched the field. Max Weber's provocative study appeared in German in 1904–1905 and was followed shortly thereafter by Emile Durkheim's *The Elementary Forms of Religious Life*.[78] Economist Werner Sombart and economic historian Richard H. Tawney erected counterarguments to Weber's celebrated thesis.[79] In the 1930s historians Henri Pirenne and Ernst Troeltsch explored the economic and social history of the church; and in the same decade historians William E. Lunt and Robert H. Snape published their respective investigations of papal and monastic finances.[80] Harvard professor and historian Raymond DeRoover analyzed medieval banking and finance, and jurist and historian John T. Noonan examined the role of usury in the doctrine of the medieval church.[81] Many other sociologists and historians contributed to the growing volume of literature on the social and economic history of the medieval church on such topics as church property, marriage, the doctrine of purgatory, heresy, the Inquisition, and the Crusades.

Reflecting the encroaching influence of economics, contemporary sociologists such as Andrew M. Greeley, Rodney Stark, and William Sims

Bainbridge have been studying the impact of secularization in religion and religious movements.[82] In an attempt to explain religion as an ubiquitous force of human behavior, these writers have explored various facets of religion such as cult formation, magic, fundamentalist revival, the evolution of the concepts of God and religion, and many other issues. Their efforts—especially in establishing the empirical nature of their inquiry—have bolstered the foundation of the economics of religion.[83] Even as they search for principles rooted in sociological premises (e.g., the social effects of power and its distribution), a growing number of contemporary sociologists have incorporated economic methodology into their studies.

Vital contributions have also been provided by scholars carrying on related areas of investigation. The careful exegesis and analysis of ancient and medieval texts by economist Odd I. Langholm concerning value, exchange, and usury are invaluable to historical inquiry into the economics of religion.[84] The same can be said of historical studies of medieval attitudes, such as avarice, which has been the subject of a complete survey by medievalist Richard Newhauser.[85] It would be impossible to fully understand religious competition in the early Middle Ages without this kind of rigorous foundation. Ironically, Newhauser found that the concept of avarice, as promulgated from the earliest Christian teachings through the Middle Ages, created a mindset foretelling the end of the world in the tenth century, but later used it to good effect by heretical sects to justify doctrines of liberalism and laissez faire in opposition to the authoritarianism of the Catholic Church.

Challenges Ahead

A meaningful survey of recent contributions to the economics of religion enables us to appreciate past accomplishments but also to grasp the challenges ahead. A daunting array of issues confronts investigators in this field. Should the objective be to explain religious participation, economic growth, or evolutionary change? Are answers best sought in models of individual or group behavior? Which is the most promising underlying premise of motivation: self-interest or public interest? Should the investigator strive for explanation or prediction? What is the precise nature of the product involved? And finally, how do forms of religion evolve over time in conformance with the principle of utility maximization?

Since choices have to be made, we consider it important to declare ours at the outset. Our goal is to explain institutional change using the tools of contemporary economics. Therefore, our analysis is firmly grounded in the neoclassical economic principle of self-interested behavior. We apply this principle to institutions in order to see how far the analysis can be stretched. Underlying this approach is the proposition that rational choice, exercised under particular constraints, creates and alters institutional arrangements such as contracts, property rights, and forms of government. In the case of religion, rational choice leads, over time, in the face of changing constraints, to altered doctrine, dogma, forms of worship, and, most important, forms of the product demanded and supplied. Religious institutions and the organizations they promote create incentives or establish costs and benefits that, for a time, govern economic activity. Thinking of churches as firms enables us to specify or observe a particular market structure, the degree of competition therein, managerial/organizational behavior, and a resulting pattern of rent distribution.

As economists Barro and McCleary warn, the most difficult inference problem in the social sciences involves the sorting out of directions of causation when using non-experimental data.[86] In our case, we want to know how changing constraints on individual behavior lead to institutional change. But we must recognize that institutional change may itself alter constraints on individual behavior. In other words, causation may run both ways. In the final analysis, the intractability of this problem may limit the validity of investigative findings. But it does not nullify the effort to find meaning in the historical record.

A related problem involves model specification and the division between endogenous and exogenous variables. (Endogenous variables are those brought within the framework of analysis; exogenous variables are those that are kept outside.) No social science can consider all aspects of a problem at once. According to standard economic method, problems must be stated in refutable fashion by limiting and identifying the major issue under investigation. This means that certain variables must be excluded from purview because not all factors in a theory can be considered endogenous.

It is common, for example, to place technology outside the standard economic model because factors that seem to drive technology are sporadic and somewhat random.[87] Throughout much of its history, economics treated all institutions as exogenous, a practice that has started to break down with the advent of the "new" economic history.[88]

The opening up of economic analysis to include institutions as endogenous factors in a theory of evolutionary change means that institutions that were traditionally considered beyond the reach of economics, including religion, may now be analyzed in a more scientific manner. Older studies that explored religion from spiritual, sociological, historical, or psychological perspectives may now be seen in a different light. Economic rationality can be seen to derive from either self-interest or public interest. In terms of religious markets, the former may be termed the *economic* hypothesis whereas the latter may be labeled the *spiritual* hypothesis. In the spiritual hypothesis, spiritual ends become a collective expression of the common good, and religious organizations motivated by the public interest would be expected to behave in conformity to this proposition. They would be expected to provide spiritual goods (e.g., marriage contracts) at marginal cost or at competitive rates. They would be expected to always enforce property rights for the common good. And, in Christian communities at least, they would be expected to maintain some level of austerity in terms of the riches, sex, and other "things of the world." Our reading of economic and religious history indicates that churches do not regularly behave in this way. By contrast, a private interest approach does not burden the economics of religion with any of these expectations, and seems to more closely describe historical events and facts.[89]

If the task of economic history is to explain the emergence, growth, or decline of institutions—religious or otherwise—and the economic and social impact of such change, then it would appear that the economic model of rational self-interest has much to offer. Of course, it is incumbent on those who choose a different model to bring forth persuasive evidence for the alternative.

The task we have set for ourselves in this book is to employ the tools of modern economics to develop a theory that explains pivotal events in history. This theory is framed with a view to collecting historical, sociological, and ideational evidence that is capable of illuminating refutable hypotheses. In all historical studies, evidence is a slippery concept. The kind of data that informs most contemporary economic studies is simply unavailable for distant periods of time. Almost always, anecdotal evidence must suffice and, even so, available material is often scant and of poor quality. These hindrances, however, do not preclude the presentation of an economic picture of particular historical episodes in the development of modern Christianity. Because this picture relies on a market-oriented framework, this project cannot begin to unfold fully until we identify certain foundational market aspects about the nature of the economic product called religion and its demand and supply characteristics, a task we turn to in the next chapter.

3

Religious Markets

I don't want realism. I'll tell you what I want. Magic!
—Blanche DuBois, in Tennessee Williams, *A Streetcar Named Desire*

In order to submit any kind of human behavior to formal economic analysis, three things are required, at a minimum, in addition to the axiom of rationality. The first is a clearly defined product (i.e., good, service, or intangible). The second is an operational notion of demand. The third is an operational notion of supply. Previous studies in the economics of religion generally come up short in one or more of these areas. Azzi and Ehrenberg, for example, model the consumption of "religion" as "afterlife consumption" or as "religious commodities," without specifying details about the precise nature and meaning of the product. Although he has written extensively in the field, Iannaccone has remarkably little to say about the nature of the product that we call religion. In our earlier work[1] we loosely defined the product as "assurances of salvation," but we did not probe very deeply into the nature or form of the product demanded and supplied in religious markets.

Among the pioneers in this field, Brooks B. Hull and Frederick Bold[2] have been most conscientious in attempting to identify economic determinants of religious participation based on the number of religious products, or forms of religion. But in all these studies, including our own, markets for the particular forms of religion are simply *assumed*. In this chapter and the next, we examine some of the reasons why these markets may be characterized as rational and why they emerge and evolve in particular forms at various times and places in ancient and contemporary societies. The point of this effort is to establish the existence of an ongoing market for religion founded on historical, psychological, and physiological phenomena that are capable of explaining determinants of the demand for and supply of religion in all human societies. The quest to formulate a rational demand for religion and to describe markets in religion is not entirely new. Sociologists Rodney Stark and Roger Finke apply an axiomatic, sociological approach to the rational choice of religion in order to develop an interesting model similar to that explained in this chapter.[3] A central difference between our analysis and theirs is that we attempt to set the theory of religious-form choice within the framework of economic theory. But whatever model is employed, it must be noted that the conclusions drawn from it are highly sensitive to definitions of religion, spirituality, magic, and belief.

Myth, Magic, Religion, and Survival

Belief in myth and magic is as old as sentient humanity. Many scholars have argued that some form of mythmaking is as integral to "being human" as are sex and food. Yet, the market for myth—most particularly the demand side of the market—is nebulous and complex. Although the economic approach espoused here does not require a complete comprehension of the characteristics of particular myths or magic, it is important to understand some fundamentals in order to arrive at a conception of demand for particular forms of religion.

The ambiguity and complexity of the demand for religion suggest that we rely on insights from many different fields of human behavior. Psychology, anthropology, sociology, philosophy, and psychiatry have all contributed to our understanding of the demand for religion. In developing the concept of demand for religion, at least in its earliest manifestations, it is difficult to distinguish among myth, magic, and religion. Over time, myth tends to morph into magic and magic into religion. Whether this is a kind of natural progression or evolution of ideas is beyond the scope of our analysis. We agree, however, with Stark and Finke that anthropologists have made key contributions to our understanding of primitive forms of myth, magic, and religion.[4]

The anthropologic view is that humans have a self-induced demand for myth that springs from the vagaries of human life and the persistent uncertainty about human origins and destinations. Cultural historian Joseph Campbell presents a natural history of gods and myths in which he ascribes myth to the human condition, strongly suggesting that belief in myth is "a primary, spontaneous device of childhood," whose "inevitability... is one of those universal characteristics of man that unite us in one family."[5] Campbell and many cultural anthropologists identify recurring themes and subjects in mythmaking such as creation, death and resurrection, virgin birth, and spiritual or dreamlike existence in another world. Anthropology, in sum, has established a long and involved history of the evolution of myth to magic to highly organized religions—a history that is important for understanding contemporary problems and analyses of religion.

Hunter-Gatherer Demands for Religion

Animism was a dominant force in the earliest of human societies. Animism is a term that has both narrow and broad definitions. In a narrow definition, animism is some attribution of conscious existence and other human characteristics to natural objects (e.g., a bison, bear, tree, or stone). Another narrowly defined form of animism consists of belief in devils or in ghosts, spiritual beings separable from their corporeal bodies. In a broader use of the term, an unspecified immaterial force motivates or animates the universe. This belief may be primitive in nature (e.g., gods demanding human sacrifice as propitiation for sunshine or crops) or sophisticated, relying on abstraction or philosophy as a condition for existence.[6]

The earliest humans of nomadic societies in Africa, Asia, and elsewhere had to devise a rationalization for the brute conditions of life and the struggle for survival. These early rationalizations took the form of myth, which was premised, at least in the standard anthropological formulation, on a desire to explain the obvious fact that humans are mortal and that their mortality is linked to an immediate everyday problem of survival. In effect early *Homo sapiens* (and possibly other species) sought methods of holding "existential terror" at bay—the threat of extinction in the face of the fundamental economic problem of finding and securing sustenance. Faced with persistent threats to survival, early humans in virtually all regions of the world created mystical cults and death rituals based on myths. There is amazing physical evidence of carved madonna-like figures and rituals surrounding death, even among Neanderthals. The earliest-known manifestations of religious services or totems mixed a concern for survival (the Madonna of the Dordogne), with semi-abstract art (the thirty-two-thousand-year-old Vogelherd ivory horse), and music (bone-flutes and whistles). Paleolithic hunters worshiped gods and images of gods that were thought to bring luck in the hunt and thus increase survival. Anthropologist Ian Tattersall speculates on the likelihood of "bear cults" circa 50,000 BCE among Neanderthals.[7] Moreover, it is well known that Neanderthals buried their dead as *Homo sapiens* do over ninety thousand years ago. Such practices are evidence of complex patterns of belief. After the social and economic transition to sedentary agriculture, the form of the gods changed to include corn gods, grain gods, mother goddesses, earth goddesses, and spirits of all kinds that dealt with the ongoing stress and toil of survival.

Animism dictated the natural contours of mythmaking among these early hunters because deer, bison, and other food sources were the keys to survival for (by then) omniviporous humans.[8] Even today animistic religions persist and sometimes dominate in countries that are still struggling with economic development, especially in Africa.

Agriculture and the Emergence of Religion

As early societies turned away from the nomadic existence required of hunting and gathering toward sedentary, agricultural life, individualistic forms of magic—the direct use of mechanisms to change nature or human behavior, such as spells, chants, amulets, etc.—gave way to more formal ritualized modes of behavior that began to resemble what we now call religion. Human survival was made somewhat less uncertain by the domestication of plants and animals. There are different (not always conflicting) explanations for the transition from nomadic hunter-gatherer societies to agriculture that occurred about twelve thousand to ten thousand years ago. Jared Diamond, in his popular book, *Guns, Germs, and Steel*,[9] attributes the transition to limited spatial availability of plants and animals that could be domesticated on an East-West axis. This plus the "horizontal configuration" of the Eurasian versus the

North-South America and African continents, at least to Diamond, explains the relative rates of early economic developments in these regions. Taking an approach that is complementary rather than exclusionary, Douglass North explains the major transitions of history in terms of changing property rights.[10] Either way, the transition had a decided impact on the forms of myth and magic that held sway in the new era.

We make no attempt here to distinguish between magic and religion. One line of thought holds that there is no distinction. Nevertheless, it is useful to consider how some distinctions have been made. Magic is sometimes characterized as any art that attempts to control or predict natural events, effects, or outcomes by appeal to supernatural forces. Magicians typically employ control mechanisms such as spells, incantations, amulets, potions, and objects such as paintings or effigies. Such magic was designed to heal the sick, punish an enemy, help find a lover, or directly affect some event (forestall bankruptcy or directly obtain a favor). Rodney Stark and Roger Finke declare that magic is "all efforts to manipulate supernatural forces to gain rewards (or avoid costs) without reference to a god or gods or to general explanations of existence."[11] In their view, magic is impersonal and does not generate extended or exclusive patterns of exchange. In magic there is no "system." There is no good reason, given this definition, that individuals cannot create their own system, that is, their own religion, unorganized though it may be. Like magic, religion appeals to supernatural forces (God, the Great Spirit, or Divine Mover), but most often implies an ongoing system of myths, beliefs, values, and practices drawn from a spiritual leader or body of moral principles.

The use of intermediaries in religious markets may have developed from the failure of magic to have empirical content, that is, to work in some predictable, demonstrable fashion. Andrew Newberg, Eugene D'Aquili, and Vince Rouse characterize religion in its crudest forms as attempts to influence powerful spirits with sacrificial gifts, noting, "The act of sacrifice is based upon the assumption of a contractual agreement between humans and the higher powers they believe in. This assumption is a defining characteristic of religion, and the component that lifts religion above the primitive level of magic."[12] The emphasis they place on the contractual agreement between humans and the higher powers is, we think, a fruitful one for exploring the basic product nature of religion.

Where religion is concerned, the contract is almost never explicit or precise. Hence, the mixture of magic and religion may have occurred very early in the development of *Homo sapiens*. Even in hunter-gatherer societies there is evidence of some kinds of propitiation or sacrifice to deal with the everyday necessity of survival. But it is generally believed that religion as an organized, propitiating force to obtain favors from powerful gods originated in settled agricultural societies. According to these definitions, neither magic nor religion has ever been absent from any known society. In early forms of religion, human or animal sacrifice, dance, art, music, and a myriad of other forms of propitiation were used to placate the gods.

In contemporary religions that employ organized forms of worship, it is faith, obedience to particular precepts, prayer, and monetary sacrifice that provide protection from harm, remission of sins, deliverance from devils, communication with the divine, and promises of eternal life. Some modern religions require detailed propitiation and intermediate steps to salvation while others ask less. But although the form of ritual may change, the tendency throughout history has been for humans to utilize myth, magic, and religion to try to control nature and the human mind—in other words, to relieve a universal existential dread. Some prehistoric ideas survived the transition to agrarian society, which created new forms of religious observance, which, in turn, gave way to contemporary forms of religion. Religion, broadly conceived to include magic and myth, sets boundaries to define individual and collective reality. These boundaries, observed by rites, rituals, sacrifices, and propitiations, stave off chaos, provide order in human life, and relieve human beings of the existential terror of sentient mortality.

Has Science Abolished Myth and Magic?

Religion, of course, is not the only form of relief from existential dread. Individuals may seek relief using philosophy, materialism, sex, drugs, or any of a number of palliatives, to varying effect. Protestant theologian

Reinhold Niebuhr (1892–1971) argued that in effect universal dread is both a determinant of religious behavior and an explanation for bellicosity in the world.[13] Whatever the release, this ubiquitous dread is the essential characteristic of all existence—from which a demand for release and religion spring. According to an ancient story, if there could only be one wish granted to humans from the gods, it would be "never to have been born." Magic and religion are in essence inventions to deal with human angst.

It is therefore self-evident that religion did not evolve independently of other human activities and achievements. Clearly art, music, and science were all intertwined in the early development of human life. The "spirit caves" of Lescaux depicting animals and people most likely had religious connotations. Prehistoric stone art of the kind found there may also have been positioned so that it had an "acoustic impact" on viewers. Science writer Fenella Saunders speculates that the sound of cloven-footed animals may have been replicated by early hunters by means of clapping or playing primitive musical instruments, thus suggesting that the spirits were talking to worshippers.[14]

In the realm of magic—where early man attempted to control nature, belief preceded knowledge. Survival demanded production and consumption of economic *and* spiritual goods, and when magic did not perform well, it gave way to other tactics. Formalized religion, a survival tactic wherein god or the gods could answer "yes" to human requests in exchange for propitiations, was thus invented. If sacrifices and propitiations did not get the desired results, the obvious answer was that there was not enough sacrifice, prayers, or monetary transfers. In this manner, the credence-good aspect of religion took on new dimensions. (Later, philosophy was one response to the degeneration of forms of earlier credence goods.) Religion bears a different relation to the sacred than magic, although magic has always remained a part of religion. Mexico is a case in point, where pre-Columbian myths coexist with Roman Catholicism. It is not considered any kind of contradiction in that country for a farmer's plow to be blessed by a priest in the morning and for the farmer to engage in some form of blood sacrifice in the evening, all with a view to improving the harvest. Historian Theodore R. Fehrenbach provides ample evidence that Christianity's conquest of the Central and South American Indians was a phenomenon that was more apparent than real.[15] Rather, attempts to replace indigenous, ancient forms of animism produced incredible hybrids of worship.

Science, rudimentary as it was, was also an early part of magic and religion. Herbal medicine was undoubtedly part of the shaman/priest's toolkit, as were hallucinogenic drugs. The substantial conjunction of science, magic, and religion in early societies lasted until the late Middle Ages in the West, after which empirical science and the scientific method gained ascendance. A more distinct separation of science and religion was ushered in by the emergence of Protestantism in the early sixteenth century. The cleavage was retarded in most of the countries remaining Roman Catholic. Only in more recent times have societies that were dominated by animistic forms of religion and worship begun to experience economic growth fueled by technology and science.

Eventually, for some at least, science became a religion. The breakdown of the conjunction of science and religion was called the "scientific revolution," sometimes interpreted as secularization; but empirical science was probably always part of human activity, as evidenced by early linkages between astronomy and the calendar. Nevertheless, everchanging boundaries between science and religion created different forms of religion. For most, the cruder forms of magic were expunged from worship and religion, although some forms of magic remained and persist, as we already noted in the case of Mexico. However, the more science explained, the more the credence good had to be altered, a development that can be observed through time. In a sense the history of science is a history of the forms of religion. As science expanded the scope of explainable phenomena, religion's sphere of explanation shrank. Since empirical science substitutes for magic and cruder forms of religion, one might think of the state of science as a constant or a parameter for *some* of the services of magic and religion (e.g., solar eclipses, rain, and disease). This does not mean, however, that fundamental existential dread has been quelled by science, nor does it suggest that certain forms of magic do not remain a part of religion. Even in extreme circumstances, such as religious persecution (e.g., ancient Rome, Nazi Germany, and the former Soviet Union), it has not been possible to raise the costs of particular forms of religious belief high enough to make them disappear altogether. Perhaps this is because there are other reasons for religion besides existential dread, but those other reasons remain mostly hidden from scholarly purview.

Neurological Origins of Myth and Religion?

One of the intriguing questions that has arisen in contemporary life is whether the demand for religion is acquired, as described by anthropologists, or whether human brains are hardwired to embrace magic and religion. Did human brains evolve in their earliest physiology to adopt magic and religion? Some scientists believe that religion, magic, and myth are part of the physiological makeup of human beings. Perhaps an early manifestation of this connection involved primitive, starving hunters who commonly hallucinated visions of their prey. Success in the hunt may then have been attributed to the vision, which may possibly have been augmented by its transcription into cave art, such as that found in Altimira or Lescaux. It is a growing claim by scientists and the popular press alike that biology buttresses moral behavior and the social utility of religion.[16] According to this view, the human brain evolved in a manner that enhanced the probabilities of individual and group survival. If valid, religion or magical systems may be part of that hardwiring.

Some neuroscientists argue that brain scans of subjects under conditions of spiritual unity (higher states of consciousness) show that neurological processes reveal a "universal reality that connects us to all that is."[17] This view is shared to some extent by Pascal Boyer who argues that what he calls "genetic survival" trumps "death-avoidance."[18] Religion is merely a "consequence or side effect of having the brains we have, which does not strike one as particularly dramatic."[19] In this view, God won't go away because spirituality is hardwired in the brain. Others see religion as an evolutionary adaptation. Those societies practicing religions that promote tribal cohesiveness—wherein, for example, parts of the mythology are to respect fire, avoid poisonous plants and animals, and so on—tend to possess higher survival qualities. Uniform rites and rituals may promote social cohesiveness and social peace as well.

Naturally, genetics also plays a part in survival, and genetic survival of early humans interacted with physical survival to produce modern man.[20]

According to Joseph Campbell, Carl Jung argued that there are inherited universal archetypes in the form of myths that explain remarkably similar ideas relating to myth, survival, and religion.[21] These myths of creation, seasons, weather, birth and death provide the substance of most early religions from around the world. Although details differ according to variations in culture, climate, and geography, general forms and ideas about myth are essentially constant. In sum, evolutionary biology and cognitive psychology are making contributions to our understanding of why religion has been, and continues to be, important and demanded in human life. However, whether God is some exogenous force independent of human beings or whether God is a product of evolution as an endogenous creation of the human brain vital to survival is somewhat beside the point of economic inquiry. A demand curve for magic and/or religion may be generated in either case.

What Is the Core Product of Religion?

The core product that is supplied by organized religion is information, but it is information of a peculiar sort. It is typical of any religion that the information supplied cannot be verified by experimental, empirical, or other scientific means. Hence, as we noted earlier, religion is a credence good. Moreover, the information provided may be used to satisfy wants on many different margins. For example, moral codes provide unity, social order, and stability. Hence, religion is a public good. Some religious doctrines provide personal solace for individual misfortunes or tragedies, as well as positive reinforcement for a virtuous life. Hence, religion is a private good. Churches offer opportunities for social interaction and mutual support. Hence, religion is a club good. Because the information imparted is capable of satisfying several, or all, of the above wants simultaneously, religion is a joint product. Economic theory is relatively efficient at analyzing any of these goods (credence, public, private, club, joint) in isolation, but not at dealing with a single good that combines all these features. Therefore investigation of religious markets has to proceed by identifying the dominant trait of the religious product and tailoring the analysis accordingly.

We may be able to deepen our understanding of the issues involved by drawing an analogy between a church and a cafeteria. Churches offer spiritual sustenance; cafeterias offer physical sustenance. Consumers in a cafeteria face a wide array of choices, and combine their individual selections in such a way as to satisfy their demand for food. Consumers of each form of religion face a wide array of information services, and pick and choose in a way that will satisfy their demand for spiritual food. But the demands of no two church members will necessarily be alike. It is much easier to analyze the demand for any single item of food than it is to analyze the demand for the composite entity called food. Likewise, it is much easier to analyze the demand for a unique aspect of religion than it is to analyze the demand for its composite identity. This requires extreme caution in using the notion of demand for religion: We are forced to define demand in as narrow a sense as possible.

In the previous section, we saw that anthropology and sociology alike advanced the idea that whatever its form, religion is a response to man's existential dread, or to the eternal questions regarding the meaning of life. One way of coping with existential dread is to establish the credibility of utility in life after death. A common theme of most religions, therefore, is the promise of an afterlife. So it seems reasonable, at least in certain instances, to represent the demand for religion as the demand for "assurance(s) of eternal salvation." This does not deny the other aspects that, bundled together, constitute the product, religion, but by holding these other aspects in abeyance, we can make headway in understanding the nature of religious market activity.

What we are claiming, albeit reluctantly, is that a technical, comprehensive demand function for religion is beyond the capability of contemporary economic science. But we believe that a demand function for a particular aspect of religion is a valid operational construct. Because all Christian religions accept the central premise of an afterlife, and arrange their organizational principles and informational services accordingly, it appears that the assurance of salvation makes up the core element of the product (service) offered by suppliers of religion. Obviously products differ from one form of religion (denomination) to another, so the demand for religion is really a demand for a particular *form* of religion derived from the nature of that form's assurances of salvation.

The premise that the core element of the demand for religion is assurances of salvation means that the market for religion operates in some respects like the market for insurance. In insurance markets higher levels of uncertainty increase the demand for insurance. But typically insurance companies are only willing to underwrite the risk associated with an objective frequency distribution of statistical probability. The principle of insurance is an application of "the law of large numbers." In a large group of trials the proportion of occurrences to non-occurrences of an event tends to be constant. It is uncertain that I will be involved in an automobile accident in the foreseeable future, but insurance companies are willing to insure my potential loss because they can calculate the frequency distribution of accidents involving numerous other drivers of my age, sex, education, and driving experience. Not all risks are insurable, however. The American economist Frank Knight (1885–1962) wrote, "The uncertainties which persist as causes of profit are those which are uninsurable because there is no objective measure of gain or loss."[22] The same could be said of salvation. No one has yet been able to calculate the frequency distribution of souls that go to heaven versus those that go to hell.

Insurance markets are also subject to the problem of moral hazard. A moral hazard is said to exist if one party to a transaction has an incentive to engage in behavior that is inimical to the interest of the other party. There is a moral hazard problem involved in federal deposit insurance of bank accounts, for example. Once a depositor knows that his deposits are "safe" up to the proscribed limit (currently $100,000 per account), he or she is unlikely to scrutinize or supervise the quality of bank management, which could encourage more risky behavior on the part of banks and lead to increased bank failures. In a similar vein, religious "insurance" may be an excuse for bad behavior. Under some interpretations of Catholic doctrine, for example, an eleventh-hour recantation could theoretically wipe out a life of crime. (This was said to be the case for Al Capone.) Another problem is that, under favorable and highly competitive conditions, there might be a race to the bottom of the moral heap, with competitions progressively lowering price for the product, and religion might not have much effect on behavior. These effects must be counterbalanced with the statistical evidence that shows that many religions are highly correlated with accepted societal norms. In the strictest sense, there is no moral hazard problem in the purchase of religious insurance, because unlike the insurance company, which cannot easily monitor the behavior of its customers, true believers think that God is omniscient. Hence, he knows every individual thought and action. There can be no unobserved free riding under these circumstances.

Political economists Kenneth Scheve and David Stasavage argue that religion and welfare-state spending are substitute mechanisms that insure individuals against adverse life events. As a result, individuals who are religious will prefer lower levels of social insurance than those who are not religious. Moreover, if the benefits of religion are subject to a network externality (each person derives greater satisfaction from religion when others are also religious), then multiple equilibria are possible across countries. High religiosity will coexist with low levels of social insurance in one equilibrium, whereas in another, low religiosity will coexist with high social insurance.[23] In their latest book, political scientists Ronald Inglehart and Pippa Norris also discuss the need for security, but they never clearly define what "security" means, which casts doubt on the causality between religion and security.[24]

In this study we focus chiefly on religion as a response to existential uncertainty in this world *and* the next, and on how individual demand is shaped as a consequence. Although it never disappears altogether, the degree of existential uncertainty that can be reduced by religion is related to the state of science, medicine, education, stability of governments and communities, age, and other factors. These factors affect the credibility of the claims of suppliers of religious services and may be thought of as demand "shifters" that propel markets toward a kind of spatial equilibrium over time. For example, the forms of religion demanded by people who live in dangerous, primitive worlds, or in societies where there are high levels of uncertainty, tend to be rule-oriented, ritualistic, and/or animistic.

As we come to appreciate the nature of religion as a credence good, we begin to understand many of the practices of Christianity that may otherwise appear either irrational or inefficient. Sellers of worldly credence goods often introduce various mechanisms to increase the quality assurance of their products: licensing, product warranties, money-back guarantees, brand reputation, and so forth. Purveyors of religion often do the same, but since the product itself is ambiguous, efforts to enhance quality are directed toward the agents of the marketplace. Priests, for example, are required to receive more education than the parishioners they serve in an attempt to make them better intermediaries between God and man. They are required, moreover, to invest heavily in theological capital. Priestly celibacy may also have been motivated in part by the perceived need to have God's intermediaries adhere to a higher set of rules of conduct and sacrifice.[25] Such strictures in fact preceded Christianity. Vestal virgins of Greek and Roman religions provided similar assurances. The building of cathedrals, often at enormous expenditure of human and physical resources, was an investment in nonsalvageable capital that may have been undertaken to raise the credibility of the church's product. Such structures and their lavish embellishments (e.g., marble statuary, stained glass, gold ornamentation) served as a kind of bond between the church and its members that the promises of heaven were genuine. Cathedrals were also a signal to potential entrants into the medieval religion market that the church intended to provide for all demanders.[26]

Product credence may also be established by particular forms of theology and the rituals that are attached to them. We have seen that religion is far from a homogeneous product. Many forms of Christianity exist at present in the United States, and even more forms have existed throughout the world. Credence may be attached to each form of religion by tailoring a combination of ritual and theology to fit the income and educational profiles of a church's potential customers.[27] Levels of education, which proxy the general state of science, also impact the faithful's degree of risk tolerance (the "fear factor"). A theology or ritual that does not quell existential dread will not be widely demanded. As the form of theology and ritual that people want changes over time, competing forms of religion arise to meet new demands of new generations and new societies. Other societies may stagnate in this respect. A highly intellectual form of religion based on informed, individual spirituality is probably unsustainable in a society like Haiti, for example, where the ubiquitous practice of voodoo reflects the mismatch of Catholicism's conservative theology and ritual with the customs and habits of an illiterate, poverty-stricken population attuned to more occult forms of worship.

Religion: Public Good or Private Good?

When we turn our attention to the question of religion as a public or a private good, we encounter different sets of issues. A private good is one that is easily divisible into parts that can be sold in a market so that it becomes the unique possession of the purchaser. By virtue of this unique possession—enforced by private property rights—the owner of the good can exclude others from the benefits that the good conveys. Hence, private goods are subject to the exclusion principle. An apple, for example, is a private good because its owner can exclude others from using it, and once it has been consumed, it cannot be used again. A pure public good is the opposite of a private good in the sense that it can be consumed by one person without reducing or excluding the benefits that other consumers enjoy. Unlike private goods, public goods are not subject to the exclusion principle. The classic example in economics is national defense. My benefit from national defense may not be the same as yours, but both of us may benefit simultaneously from like expenditures that we make to increase our safety and security.[28] If we regard Christianity as a creed rather than an organization, then we may consider religion to be a public good. But if we think of religion as a choice of form (e.g., Roman Catholic vs. Presbyterian), then we must regard religion essentially as a private good: My choice to be a practicing Roman Catholic precludes me from simultaneously being a practicing Presbyterian.

Organized communities of Christian believers typically coalesce around a form of ritual and organized system of belief, usually based on some kind of divine revelation. All religions supply joint products and some of those products are in the nature of public goods. Within a particular community, some of the goods are characterized by noncompeting (complementary) consumption. Within Catholicism, for example, contrition and indulgences are complementary means of increasing one's chance to go to heaven. In many religions, network externalities are created by membership. As Iannaccone noted, free riding is possible under such circumstances and some form of prescribed ritual is usually developed

as a tax for membership in certain cults or clubs.[29] There may be a continuum of individual religions that become more private as exclusion
becomes more feasible. Ultimately this depends on the definition that religion takes. Iannaccone's analysis of cults emphasizes excludability, but
confines itself to rather small religious communities where club-like conditions apply. However, larger religious communities and organizations
also produce public goods. During its ascendancy in the Middle Ages,
the Catholic Church generated public goods in the form of education,
aid to the poor, and a court system. Large religious communities also
confront the free-rider problem, but they typically deal with it by invok-
ing less extreme measures than those employed by cults or clubs. In set-
tings such as the medieval period, with its high risk of deprivation and
uncertainty of survival, rules and regulations concerning penance, forgiveness, and salvation/damnation logically became major parts of
Roman Catholicism. Many of these rules remain in effect today but are
less strictly enforced in developed nations compared to underdeveloped
ones. Inasmuch as church authorities cannot easily observe whether a
member goes to Mass every Sunday, missing Sunday Mass is proclaimed
a sin. Whether it is serious (mortal) or not (venial) depends on a number
of conditions. Moral relativism often results from political and economic
realities. Hence, in the "North" or developed world, missing Sunday
Mass is considered a less serious infraction than it is in the underdeveloped world, where conservative ritual and practice are demanded.

In some measure, the services supplied by organized religions are
purely private in nature. Religion may provide solace to a person who
has lost a loved one due to death. It may provide inner peace to someone
beset by personal difficulties. It may provide healing of a psychic (and
sometimes physical) nature to individuals in ill health. It may simply provide good karma in return for virtuous activity. Also, the accumulation
of religious capital, like the accumulation of human capital (e.g., education) provides highly individualized benefits as well as spillover effects
to society at large. In a sense, each person that seeks religion from an
organized church purchases an implied contract that contains obliga-
tions and expectations that, once fulfilled, result in passage to a utility-
maximizing afterlife.

A Qualified Statement of the Demand for Religion

Although it is circumscribed by the qualifications enumerated in the preceding section, our notion of the demand for particular forms of religion is sufficiently meaningful to inform many of the developments that have taken place in the evolution of Christianity. Central to our analysis is the characterization of religion as a Z-good. The Z-good is a device employed by Gary Becker in his seminal article on household production.[30] In Becker's formulation, households are both producing units (i.e., "small factories") and consuming units (i.e., utility-maximizers). As producers they combine time and market goods (inputs and outputs) to clean, feed, procreate and otherwise produce useful commodities. The final goods produced by a household are, in Becker's formulation, Z-goods. Examples of Z-goods are meals and clean clothes. The production of a meal requires time and effort to transform foodstuffs into a final product. Meat, eggs, fruit, vegetables, cheese, and spices may be considered outputs in certain consumer markets but become inputs in the production of a meal. In producing meals (vs. other household products) a household maximizes its utility subject to its production capabilities and its budget constraint. The solution of this maximization problem provides not only the household's demand for market goods but also its members' labor supplies to the market and to household production tasks.

Religion is a Z-good because whatever shape the final output takes (whether it be assurances of salvation, social solidarity, social insurance, business contacts and security, fellowship, etc.), religious services are produced by combining capital goods (physical and human), labor, and market goods. The resulting output is consumed in a utility-maximizing manner. Demand for this Z-good is a function of its full price, which amounts to resources sacrificed (including money and time) in order to participate in religious activity. As recognized by Azzi and Ehrenberg, there is an inverse relationship between money and time so that, other things being equal, in spatial equilibrium the form of religion chosen depends on the composition of its full price. Households with lower time values will supply greater amounts of time to religious participation than those with high time values, and vice versa.[31] In highly developed money economies, less ritualistic resource-oriented religions have evolved. In these circumstances the monetary component of price is large relative to the time input. The reverse is generally the case among low-income individuals or in low-income and primitive societies. Other things equal, the higher the full price of religion the lower the quantity demanded of it, *within certain parameters*. Depending on an individual's uncertainty profile and other determinants, a change in full price will have both income and substitution effects. A positive income effect results when the price of any consumable falls, thus raising the real income (or purchasing power) of the same level of expenditures. A negative substitution effect arises when the price of any consumable rises, thus encouraging the search for lower-priced substitutes. As incomes rise, both the income effect and the substitution effect work toward the adoption of time-saving religious practices. Religion thus becomes less formal, less time-intensive, and more money-intensive over time as economic growth proceeds. Hence, one testable proposition is that the length of church services should vary inversely with income. But we may also expect that at certain critical values individuals will alter the form of religion chosen (i.e., switch religions). Theoretically, we should be able to calculate and predict the "switch points" between forms of religion once we know the intensity of demand among participants.

Having robed our concept of demand for religion in appropriate qualifications, we may proceed to a more or less standard economic formulation. The demand for any given form of religion (Brand X) may be expressed as a function of its full price and a set of demand shifters. Demand shifters are determinants other than full price that tend to alter the quantity of religion consumed. Thus a stylized version of demand may be set forth in the following manner: The quantity demanded (i.e., number of adherents) of a particular form of religion will depend on its full price, the full price of its substitutes, household income (or wealth), members' tolerance for risk, and utility. We recognize that education may also be an important determinant, but exclude it here in the interest of simplicity—because income and education are highly correlated, we feel that the effects of education may already be captured in income. In a "tight" theoretical model containing both stocks and flows, the acquisition of "religious capital" through time, or an inherited stock of some particular religious form, would also be important in establishing a demand curve,[32] but we omit these complications, too, in order to keep the analysis as simple as possible. In this stylized formulation, full price is the sum of money prices (contributions and other monetary exactions) and the value of the time spent in attendance and on ritual. Thus a doubling of the tithe imposed by any church would (all else remaining the same) increase the full price of a particular form of religion and reduce the quantity demanded of it. By the same token, an increase in the wage rate of household members would increase the opportunity cost of time spent on religious participation.

Like any other demand curve, the demand for religion will shift rightward or leftward owing to a number of factors. A lowering of the full price of *another* form of religion (Brand Y) would, other things equal, reduce the entire demand curve for Brand X. An increase in the full price of one religion (Brand X)—which includes both money and time—will reduce the quantity demanded of Brand X. Suppose, for example, that the wage rate for an individual rises. This means that the value of time rises for her and the consumer will shift away from a time-intensive religion. But there is another effect as well when the wage rate changes—an income effect—and here we must confront the question of whether a religious good is normal or inferior (no pejorative context suggested). If income or wealth rises (or falls)—as it would with an increase (decrease) in the wage rate—and the quantity taken of the religious service (Brand X) declines (or rises), the good is said to be inferior in economic terms. The converse is true if religion is considered a normal good—a rise (fall) in income or wealth would increase (decrease) the quantity taken of Brand X consumed. If we use wage rates to proxy income, the literature suggests that there is a mild negative relationship between income and religious participation suggesting that religion generally is an inferior good. This result controls for bidirectional causality between the two. What we have is a contest between an income effect and a substitution effect. The data suggest that this substitution effect dominates any "pure" income effect that we cannot observe. It is probable that income effects differ across religions. Worldwide, Catholicism and Protestant fundamentalism are probably inferior goods, whereas liberal Protestantism and Judaism are likely normal goods. Identification of an income effect, however, is extremely difficult empirically and it may be that individuals substitute other inputs—monetary contributions—for participation as their incomes rise.

Most important perhaps, changes in risk tolerance will affect the position of the demand curve for a particular form of religion. Other things equal, the advent of war or terrorism will increase the demand for most forms of religion, as evidenced by an increase in church attendance during such circumstances. But there are many factors that affect an individual's risk profile. Stability of governments, the level of educational attainment, the state of scientific knowledge, and survivability conditions, for example, all will shift the demand for particular religious forms by altering an individual's perception of risk and fear of the unknown. In economics the demand curve is a logical consequence of the presumption of rational behavior. Thus we argue that religious behavior is as rational as any other kind of market behavior. Our final position is this: Churches produce various public and private goods. We are interested in one important private good: the doctrinal transaction (implied contract) between church and member regarding salvation. The operations of this market drive all of our analyses in the ensuing chapters. Church doctrine and practice are determined by the forces of supply and demand in this market. Of special significance is that fact that the church provides a service. Since services are nontradable and cannot be arbitraged or bought at a low price and sold at a higher one, this means that conditions are especially ripe in monopolistic religious markets for sellers to engage in price discrimination, provided consumers can be segmented into different demand classes. Price discrimination allows a seller producing religious outputs at the same cost to successfully sell the same item, or virtually the same item, at different prices to different customers.

Anecdotal Evidence of Market Forces at Work

We believe that the broad contours of history provide evidence for the view that people exhibit a demand for religion and that churches respond by supplying religious services. History tells us that when survival was most uncertain—as in primitive societies with low levels of science, education, and resources—the forms of religion demanded involved time-consuming rituals, cult-like behavior, and, eventually, club-like organizations (e.g., Freemasons or the Knights of Columbus). Existential dread was considerably higher before the establishment of secure property rights, stable governments, and the development of science. In such circumstances the full price of less rigid rival forms of religion is high and the net benefits to the individual are low for two reasons. The first is that liberal forms of religion do not quell fear sufficiently in the present life and do not raise expectations of the afterlife. The second is that they require more non-time resources. Net benefits of membership in these religious forms are therefore insufficient to induce adherents to break away from more rigid forms.

In societies with highly disparate income distributions, such as those of medieval Europe, survival fears and existential dread led to both more time-intensive religious activities by the lower-income population and higher monetary giving by the wealthy. During bouts of the Black Death (bubonic plague), flagellants went from city to city across Europe flogging each other as atonement for the sins that were perceived to be the cause of the disease. Art historian Henry Kraus maintains that funds to build cathedrals were more readily donated when the threat of plague was imminent.[33] Commenting on the incredibly harsh living conditions of populations in the Middle Ages, anthropologist Robert Scott argues that belief in supernatural forces and the desire for divine protection led people to seek protection and security in the arms of the Roman Catholic Church.[34] Like Kraus, Scott points out that the period when Gothic cathedral-building was at its peak coincided with the harshest living conditions in the West.

Other things equal, liberal creeds generally do not find large numbers of demanders in societies or communities where there is great poverty, little or no social order or cohesiveness, religious persecution, insecure property rights, and impoverished education and science. In these circumstances, cult-like religions, often emphasizing magic, voodoo, and fundamentalism, carry low prices relative to liberal creeds, because among low-income individuals time is a cheap, plentiful resource. Factors such as income, information, science, education and institutional stability act as demand shifters.[35] By affecting the terms of survival in the here and the hereafter, they alter the level of existential dread, causing some individuals to choose a different form of religion. Other writers have suggested that there is a relation between the trade-off of money and time committed to a religion and the amount of ritual contained in it,[36] but we have not yet seen the argument that the demand for ritual is also a function of the shifters that we have cited, such as the state of education and science, stability of government, security of property rights, and other factors.

It would appear that the rapid adoption of Christianity within the Roman Empire conforms to this argument. Rodney Stark estimates that in 100 AD the Christian percentage of the Roman population was 0.0126; whereas by 350 AD more than 56 percent were Christian, with growth occurring not only in Rome but also in the farther reaches of the Empire, such as Asia Minor, North Africa, and Egypt.[37] Disintegration of Roman economy and society meant a reduction in the net benefits of being a Roman citizen—safety, security, and life span were all adversely affected. Thus, the net benefits of loyalty to the Roman gods fell relative to the net benefits of joining the new Christian cult. The early and sometimes savage persecutions of Christians obviously reduced the gross benefits of joining the new religion, but in benefit-cost calculations it is always net benefits that matter. The acceptance of persecution and death by early Christians may have added credence to the product. At some point, therefore, as Christianity offered greater probability of survival and Roman gods offered less, the net benefits of switching must have risen accordingly. In a more contemporary vein, historian Philip Jenkins argues that a Christian revival of massive proportions is taking place in a way that pits southern hemisphere conservative Christians (chiefly in Latin America and Africa) against northern hemisphere liberal Christians (in Europe and the United States).[38] This phenomenon, not unlike the Protestant Reformation, seems to contradict the principles we have just set forth. The conservative revival emphasizes ritual, inflexible rules, and a return to the fundamentals of biblical teachings (much as Luther espoused in 1517). Jenkins maintains that traditional denominations of the North, such as Anglicans and Roman Catholics, have become too liberal in their policies regarding such matters as scriptural interpretation, the role of women, tolerance of homosexuals, and general deportment. He sees a new reformation coming from the South. While it is difficult to reject the factual outlines of his analysis, Jenkins does not consider that the full price of religious forms in the South might change with alterations in income, science, technology, and information costs. Such changes could create a liberal backlash in these countries.

Another potential challenge to the proposition that more people will generally prefer low-cost religions to high-cost religions is presented by thriving religions that seemingly run counter to the theory. Two examples of such religions are Hasidic Judaism and Mormonism. The average levels of education and income are relatively high in both religions. Additionally, both religions require large commitments of time and money, and therefore should be predictably small. But such is not the case. In fact, the Mormon religion is the fastest growing religion (in terms of members) in the United States. This anomaly may have unseen causes, but we emphasize as before that in the individual decision nexus, it is net benefits that matter. As it stands, the calculation of net benefits in these two religions is likely influenced by several important factors. Both have endured persecution—Hasidic Jews for several millennia, and Mormons for a considerably shorter time, but nevertheless from its inception as the Church of Jesus Christ of Latter-day Saints (LDS) in 1830.[39] Therefore, the benefits of cult or club-like behavior are high to members of both these religions. Where governments do not provide stable security of life or worship, highly insular, "defensive" religious forms may be expected. The near-exclusive dominance by Hasidic Jews of certain trades, such as diamond cutting and merchandising, may be a source of substantial benefits to members. The LDS Church exacts high sacrifices from its members: Every youth is expected to perform "hands-on" missionary work for several years, and a 10 percent tithe is rigidly enforced. Mormon businesses are known to be "clubbish" and selective in employment and in other forms of contracting. A deeper analysis of individual religions, in other words, may reveal that mitigating forces sweep away apparent anomalies. In the case of Hasidic Jews and Mormons, the apparently high full price of membership in their religions may be offset wholly or in part by special benefits that accrue to an aggressively and persistently persecuted community forced to establish enhanced survival mechanisms.

The demand for forms of religion is akin to the demand for relief from uncertainty. In the face of known and unchanging survival constraints, income, education, and risk tolerance, fewer customers will demand religions that carry a high full price and more customers will demand religions that carry a low full price. This is what an economist would call the *law of demand* for religion. It is a cause-effect relationship that holds under the express condition that certain non-price determinants do not change. But as the determinants, such as income or risk, change, the demand function shifts (hence the determinants are called "shifters") so that either more or less religion of a particular form is demanded. Forms selected will, in most cases, be affected by a demander's income, education, sex, age, degree of risk tolerance, and the sophistication of science. Thus a rational demand for particular forms of religion may be established by the usual standards of economic science. The distribution of adherents among forms of religion will also be related to the supply conditions under which forms of religion are allowed to emerge and expand. In other words, market structure matters.

Supply of Religious Services

Demanders of religion may also be suppliers of religion. Both suppliers and demanders are motivated in part by the immediacy of survival and/ or the persistence of existential dread, including fear of death. We have already seen that religion may be self-generated without the benefit (or encumbrance) of formal organizations (churches). But because we want to focus our investigation on the behavior of organizational entities, we will not dwell on self-generated religion in our treatment of the supply side of the market. The typical pattern of supply within religious institutions involves the use of intermediaries, or agents. The role of these agents has evolved over long periods of time and across various cultures. The shaman of early societies eventually gave way to the priest of later civilizations.

Joseph Campbell offers the following contrast between priest and shaman, both religious (supply) agents in a market framework: "The priest is the socially initiated, ceremonially inducted member of a recognized religious organization, where he holds a certain rank and functions as

the tenant of an office that was held by others before him, while the shaman is one who, as a consequence of a personal psychological crisis, has
gained a certain power of his own. The spiritual visitants who came to
him in vision had never been seen before by any other; they were his
particular familiars and protectors."[40] Unbound by organizational structure, shamans had more freedom of activity, but their role in hunter-
gatherer societies was difficult and precarious. According to E. Lucas
Bridges, son of a missionary to Tierra del Fuego, who wrote about native
Indians, "Medicine men ran great dangers. When persons in their prime
died from no visible cause, the 'family doctor' would often cast suspi-
cion, in an ambiguous way, on some rival necromancer. Frequently the
chief object of a raiding party...was to kill the medicine man of an
opposing group."[41] Despite their extensive powers to create myths and
inspire beliefs, shamans were in constant danger of being replaced by
those with stronger powers. Of course, as science developed, their influence waned. But in several important ways shamans and necromancers
in nomadic societies presaged the priests who were to come: (a) They
were the moderators of science and scientific belief and (b) They recognized that magic could be sold as a quid pro quo for their Z-good.
Both of these points have been confirmed by countless anthropological
studies—the first in an explicit way and the second in an implicit way.
Shamans were specialists. As Bridges notes, they preferred chant and
teaching to drudgery and work.[42] Thus they supplied their expertise in
return for sustenance by the community. In some early societies, such as
ancient Egypt, myth and religion were so integral to everyday life that
the lion's share of society's resources was devoted to maintenance of a
priestly class (with the god Pharaoh as its head).

The Transition from Magic to Religion
The nature and practice of magic and religion underwent a fundamental
change after settled agriculture replaced nomadic hunting and gathering
roughly twelve thousand years ago. Because sedentary agriculture produced an economic surplus, demanders of religion were able to support a permanent or quasi-permanent priesthood. As a result, exchange
between demanders of religion and the priests who acted as supply
agents grew more formal. There followed a predictable supply response:

a proliferation of gods and goddesses, most derived from the earliest mythologies. Gradually, over a long period of time, magic became disconnected from religion, though it could be argued that the break was neither final nor complete.

In the early temple societies, gods and goddesses were either assimilated from competing cults or created to meet a specific need. One god supposedly brought the rain that made crops grow; another brought the sun. Along the gulf coast of Mexico, Mayans prayed to the god Hurracan to spare them from violent storms (from which we derived the word "hurricane"). Single-purpose deities were common and as they grew in number, so did the amount of ritual surrounding their worship. In the case of ancient Egypt, distinct economic interest groups developed around gods and rituals. Egypt and other temple societies, such as such as those of Abyssinia, Babylonia, Mesopotamia, and pre-Columbian South America, tended to embrace religions that were highly authoritarian and monopolistic. Greek and Roman religions were more democratic but were no less disposed to violence in the form of blood sacrifice or in the form of religious persecution (as in the case of Christianity, which Rome considered primarily a political rather than a religious threat).

Suppliers of religion, whether ancient or modern, encounter the same basic problems as businesses. They must decide on the nature and quantity of services to produce and the price to charge. As with businesses, the solutions to these problems depend in part on the type of market structure within which a firm operates. Although the object remains the same—to maximize utility—the rules of competition differ from the rules of monopoly. Competition promotes consumer sovereignty, product innovation, and cost reduction—monopoly does not. Ironically, however, violence may be common to both: Competitors may resort to violence to gain market share; monopolists may engage in violent acts in order to maintain market share, or to prevent encroachment of new firms. The fact that religious organizations are nonprofit entities does not change the fundamental facts. Church-firms supply different things to different groups, attracting adherents and donors. In some cases, their leaders are enriched in the process, but even without economic gain religious leaders receive considerable perquisites in the form of power, status, and prestige.

In an attempt to bridge the gap between this world and the next, the priest in contemporary society defines the parameters of religious technology. This technology defines the contract between customer and supplier, specifying the duties, responsibilities, and expectations required of both parties. For some people this bridge is built on faith; for others it stands on science (e.g., secular humanists). But regardless of its foundation, such a bridge is generally conducive to order and stability in society. As guardian of a theology derived from higher authority, the priest also acts as keeper of the calendar.[43] However, because religion is a credence good, theology is eventually pressured by change—it is likely to be in a state of flux in societies that are economically and socially progressive. Supply agents must have a fallback position in the event temporal predictions fail. Generally that fallback position is to argue that *more* faith, sacrifice, repentance, or prayer is required, which effectively amounts to saying that quality comes at a price; that is, a higher full price will get you a higher quality of religion.

Despite the fact that societal and cultural idiosyncrasies shape particular beliefs, and the fact that technology alters religious content, the law of supply nevertheless applies in religious markets. Political and regulatory powers permitting, higher prices tend to bring more competitive suppliers into the market, other things being equal (including the state of scientific knowledge). Many early agriculturally-based temple societies, such as ancient Egypt, allowed competition between gods, but more advanced agricultural societies enforced monopoly conditions by means of political arrangements (as in ancient Babylonia or the medieval Roman Catholic Church). In the final analysis, market structure depends on economic *and* political considerations.

Is There a Tendency toward Monopoly (and Violence) in Religion?

One final issue involves both the demand and the supply of religion. If network externalities are present in religious participation (i.e., one derives satisfaction from one's religion in proportion to the number of others who belong), then credence may depend in a critical way on the number of believers in a particular form of religion.[44] This precept explains why some religions tend to be highly proselytizing; it also helps to explain why violence is often perpetrated in the name of religion.

Proselytizing religions engage in activities that privately advertise, cajole, and pressure nonmembers to join. Missionary activity by the Roman Catholic Church from the sixteenth century on is an example of proselytization. Jehovah's Witnesses and the Mormon Church are more recent examples of proselytizing religions. In some instances, the threat of reduced utility from loss of members to rival sects, or the very existence of large numbers of nonbelievers, may provoke open military action or brute force. The current threat of Muslim terrorist activity may derive in part from some extreme forms of this effect. Militant Muslims maintain that there are only two religions: Islam and everything else. All believers that are not Muslim are therefore considered infidels, and are not to be tolerated. History is replete with earlier examples as well. The Crusades of the twelfth through fourteenth centuries, ostensibly undertaken to rescue the Holy Land from infidels, was warfare in the name of one religious group against another. Religious wars (some of a highly local character) broke out all over Europe in the wake of the Protestant Reformation. Tensions between Catholics and Huguenots led to violent acts in sixteenth- and seventeenth-century France. Where one religion dominates a religious market, it is not uncommon to find violence as a byproduct of monopoly.

Importantly, religious tolerance and religious pluralism are functions of governmental form. Theocracy requires a marriage of political form and religion. In Egypt, the Pharaoh *was* a god, and worship and ritual form were dictated by the state. Constitutional forms of government have generally been openly or partially pluralistic. For example, the characterization of the United States as a Christian nation is, given the establishment clause, factually incorrect. The country contains a large number of Christians, but many other religious sects as well, not to mention a sizeable portion of the populace that claim "no religion." This does not mean that particular policy positions of a theological nature are not "democratically" foisted upon the general populace. For example, evangelical Christians, including some Roman Catholics, are increasingly attempting through the political process to assure that their theological views of science—on abortion, stem cell research, and other issues—are law for the entire society. Pushed to a limit, a marriage of church and state could result in a governmentally enforced theocracy, which would result in the destruction of constitutional protections of minorities. To be effective religious monopoly must carry enforcement mechanisms—the chief of which would be dictatorial governmental powers as in authoritarian or fascist states.

The history of world religions indicates a tendency for religious markets to be competitive in some instances and monopolistic in others. Egyptian religion was for the most part authoritarian and theocratic in nature, with very few exceptions (see chapter 4 for a discussion of one of them). Early Greek and Roman religions were pluralistic, but Christianity in its earliest form was monopolistic. However, it did not become an entrenched monopoly in Europe until it was endorsed by the Emperor Constantine in the fourth century. The "superstar" effect described by economist Sherwin Rosen[45] and employed by Iannaccone[46] suggests that there might be a tendency toward natural monopoly in religion. This effect is the result of a network externality whereby the utility derived from religion by each person is a function of the extent to which his or her religious beliefs are shared by others. As more adherents of a particular religion are brought together, therefore, the shared beliefs tend to crowd out alternative beliefs. The effect is not unlike the tendency in the business world for firms to conglomerate. Monopolies are difficult to sustain indefinitely, however, because their persistence requires extra-economic forces, such as political or military power as noted previously. However, the more successful a monopoly is in building economic surpluses, the stronger the incentive for rival firms to invade its market. Thus, schisms and other forms of market entry are to be expected in religious markets that are highly monopolistic. We investigate these consequences in chapter 5 with regard to the major religious upheaval of the late Middle Ages, the Protestant Reformation.

In a pluralistic society, political action on the part of some groups (e.g., evangelical Christians in the United States) may be viewed merely as a milder and more constrained form of this tendency to violence. Meanwhile, at the other end of the theological spectrum, where theologies are more elastic and self-determined (such as Buddhism and Hinduism), self-security and independence appear sufficient to maintain social peace. So it appears that fear tolerance and the degree of insecurity (both appearing to be partly functions of education and income) determine in large measure the particular sect or theology demanded. And, as a corollary of network externalities in religion tendencies toward violence, political action, or imposition of meddlesome preferences may emerge.

Thus, religious forms are both supplied and demanded, and markets, either competitive or monopolistic, are established. But religious markets, like those for types of automobiles or shoes, are not static. Religious markets are in constant flux for the reasons given in this chapter. The full price of religious forms and the demand determinants change as income, wealth, the price of competing religions, science, and many other economic and political factors change and evolve through time. Four episodic examples of this phenomenon are presented and examined in the next chapter.

4

Religious Form Change: Case Studies

From ghoulies and ghosties and long-
   leggety beasties
And things that go bump in the night,
   Good Lord, deliver us!
—Cornish prayer

An economic interpretation of religious form changes assumes that individuals choose particular forms in a rational manner as a function of
economic variables including the full price of membership and a number
of shifters. Before turning to an analysis of the form changes introduced
by Protestantism, we use four historical episodes—one ancient, two
medieval, and one modern—to show how the functioning of economic
markets may be used to analyze religious change. These episodes, while
quite disparate in time and distinct in character, provide the reader with
examples of a common theme—that the economic approach to religion
is capable of adding value to previous explanations of key changes in religious forms and doctrines. While distinct, we do not intend our examples to be a "grab bag." Each change focuses on a key alteration. The
examples we use all revolve around famous episodes: (1) the attempt by
the Pharoah Akhenaton (also known as Amenhotep IV) to bring monotheism to Egypt around 1350 BCE; (2) the reduction in information cost
to members of society and its impact on religious form initiated by the
invention of the printing press in the fifteenth century; (3) the change in
rules of fasting and abstinence, occurring in 1966, that released Roman
Catholics from the necessary obligation of abstaining from meat on Fridays; and (4) the full-price changes in doctrine and ritual created by the

medieval Roman Catholic Church that set the stage for the successful entry of Martin Luther and Protestantism in the sixteenth century.[1]

One of the most important sociological investigations into the emergence, growth, and decline of some of the forms of Christianity, for example, is that of Roger Finke and Rodney Stark in their *Churching of America, 1776–1990* and *Acts of Faith*.[2] Thus we begin our investigation of religious change by more fully considering the contrasting and complementary aspects between an econo-sociological theory and a theory based more fundamentally on modern microanalytic principles.

Religious Form Change: Melding Sociological and Economic Interpretations

Many modern sociologists assume, as do economists, that religion is rational behavior based on a weighing of costs and benefits and that a market analysis such as Adam Smith's helps explain the emergence and decline of particular churches and sects, that is, forms of religion. Finke and Stark argue, as we do, that religion is not on the wane, offering empirical evidence that stricter religions are on the rise in the United States. Distinguishing between sects and churches, they argue that more conservative sects tend to emerge when religious bodies become more "churchlike," dominated by the wealthy and more liberal members of congregations. Further, according to these authors, "Secularization is a self-limiting process that leads not to irreligion, but to revival ... As religious bodies become increasingly churchlike they not only lose their vigor but give rise to sects that revitalize the religious tradition in new organizations. ... the result is not a decline in religion, but only a decline in the fortunes of specific religious organizations, as they give way to new ones ... Sects arise to satisfy the needs of those less fortunate in pursuit of the world's goods."[3] Quoting Reinhold H. Niebuhr, who anticipated this view in 1929,[4] they note that religious revolts that created sects have been the products of the revolts of the poor and downtrodden—those in extreme misery who must resist life's "temptations" (that is, the temptations of the wealthy). Finke and Stark adopt Iannaccone's view in their discussion of why "mainline" denominations are in decline, arguing, "religious organizations are stronger to the degree that they impose significant costs in terms of sacrifice and even stigma upon their members."[5] The value, or benefits, of belonging to a religion is a positive function of the consumption costs in terms of sacrifice demanded. (Demand is a function of the conditions of supply in other words.) Mainline churches are becoming more liberal and sects peel off to become more conservative, offering higher utility to (and demanding greater sacrifice from) their customers. This argument seems to maintain that the consumption cost (price in terms of sacrifice) is a measure of value and that the higher the price, the greater the quantity demanded and the greater the utility provided.

Our own theory focusing on the economic demand for and costs of religion (see chapter 3) has elements in common with this econo-sociological approach to historical changes in Christianity. (We do not agree, however, that demand curves are positively sloped, which would occur if utility and price were positively related to each other.) It is indisputable, for example, that membership or attendance in conservative and evangelical denominations is growing relative to mainline denominations, although there may be some evidence that certain conservative sects in the United States are undergoing slowed growth. We go further, however, to argue that the underlying economic determinants of religious change must be added when assessing demand. Some features of the econo-sociological approach in the dynamics of religious change and religious forms find alternative explanations when such factors as income, full price, the state of scientific knowledge, and factors affecting the risk preferences of populations are included in the analysis. Consider two examples that will be amplified later in this book.

The Protestant Reformation was a response of mainly the wealthy—to whom Martin Luther had appeal and redress—to the full price charged by the Roman Catholic Church (as we discuss in detail in chapter 5). The simplification or total elimination of ritual together with a democratization ("every man a priest") of both doctrine and organizational changes giving Christians greater local autonomy most certainly lowered the full price of religion. The vigor of the earliest dissidents, moreover, together with their willingness to engage in armed conflict to protect the new Christian churches and sects, revealed a fundamental risk preference in contrast to adherents of a strict Roman Catholicism. This risk preference likely carried over into their choice of Protestantism with its emphasis on personal interpretations of the Bible and the simultaneous dispensation of the intricate skein of Roman rules to attain salvation. Early Protestant churches and sects were apparently able to provide enough credence in the forms of their products to maintain and gain adherents. Some did not make it (e.g., Zwingli in Geneva) mainly for political reasons, but humanism was increasingly reflected in new church doctrines and organizations. Further, the Peasants' Revolt (1524–1525), supported by extremely risk-preferring humanist sects, did not include a call for stricter, more rule-driven religion. Rather, it espoused an almost anarchistic simplification of ritual, one that was cheaper than the quasi-Roman forms preached by Luther.

Dynamic religious form changes in colonial and modern America also appear to run counter to the sociological theory of Finke and Stark. New forms of religion developing from strict indigenous Puritanism were most certainly functions of some of the economic variables we have identified as shifters. Early Unitarians, such as Ebenezer Gay (1696–1787) for example, emphasized love, forgiveness, and Christ's teachings rather than the fire, hell, and brimstone sold by the typical Puritan congregation. This religion married then-modern science with Calvinist teaching, producing a form of Protestantism that was more liberal, more attractive, and far less costly in a ritualistic sense. As religious historians David A. Rausch and Carl Hermann Voss note: "Unitarianism became the religion of the educated, the refined, the wealthy; and the leaders of society on the eastern seaboard in the early nineteenth century delighted in its insights."[6] In general, sects that chose to integrate science with Christian theology broke away from theologically more conservative, highly ritualistic mainline churches of early America. Using the simple cost-benefit theory of rational conduct, observations such as these would appear to imply that the high price of the stricter churches did not reflect the utility received from membership. This does not mean that the Finke-Stark theory that the growth of conservative, evangelical churches out of and exceeding mainline churches cannot be verified with evidence in certain cases, particularly in the post-Colonial era—only that the phenomena is demonstrably more complex than what they describe as suggested in the example of Unitarianism.

Modern examples also appear to cast doubt on the socioeconomic theory as a singular explanation. Recent breaks in mainline Protestant religions in the United States, whose overall growth has fallen as a percentage of the total, also raise questions about the sociological interpretation. While it is true, for example, that the Southern Baptist Convention, an ultraconservative branch of that church, disassociated itself from the World Baptist Conference for ostensibly being "too liberal," growth in that religion has also slowed and it is unclear which sect is breaking away from which sect. The evidence, according to statisticians Tom W. Smith and Seokho Kim, also seems to show a stark rise in the proportion of Americans with *no* religious preference or with those identifying themselves as "Christian" with no church membership whatsoever.[7]

Movement to sects or other churches—either more or less conservative or ritualized—simply indicates that a tipping point in full price has been reached or that one of the shifters has changed (income, the level of empirical scientific knowledge, or risk aversion). Finke and Stark are correct that a particular form or variant of religion will fit particular sets of demanders. They only fail to fill out the argument with economic content, including the conception of full price that includes the value of time spent in rituals. Breakaways from mainline churches are not only toward conservative sects as we will see later in chapter 9 of this book. Other things equal, there is a "time bias" in full price against highly ritualistic, dogmatic religions. Historically, moreover, forms or qualities of religious belief will respond to the incremental but continuous alterations in economic interests, technology, and science.

Other observers have offered valuable insights into the form or "product variety" offered in the religion market. Iannaccone relates the number of forms of religion to the debate over whether establishment or nonestablishment churches have higher attendance, finding that those countries with state-supported religion have significantly lower attendance rates than pluralistic nations. (His results depend in a critical way on eliminating Catholics from the sample.) Brooks B. Hull and Frederick Bold, using U.S. county data, conclude the opposite: "For religion, church members may benefit from *reducing* the variety of products."[8] Here the costs of variety exceed the benefits. There is a problem with this argument however. Over time, we have observed a marked increase in the number of Christian sects in the United States (by 2002 there were over 2,600 distinct types or varieties of religions in the United States, many of them Christian, as sorted by researchers[9]). If variety did not increase utility, this tremendous growth in variety would not be observed.

The econo-sociological theory does offer insight into what Stark and Finke call "niche switching" under major forms of religion (the example they use is Methodism).[10] Distinguishing among ultraliberal, liberal, moderate, conservative, strict and ultra-strict niches, Stark and Finke argue that demand shifts occur due to (what appear to be) income changes. They write: "Niche-switching is mildly related to status attainment, because, as already noted, higher-tension religion is more costly for the more privileged. People who have achieved a status well above the average level of their niche will tend to shift to a lower-tension faith. Conversely, the downwardly mobile will tend to switch toward higher tension. But keep in mind that these are not strong effects. Class is far from the primary determinate of religious preferences. Socialization is many times more important," according to these authors.[11] By contrast, our discussion of the demand for religion in chapter 3 emphasizes economic, rather than sociological determinants of demand, despite clear similarities in both approaches.

Demand and supply interactions for myth and religious services function in all societies igniting changes that will benefit some interests and interest groups and harm others. Forms of religion evolve over time but rarely disappear altogether. We turn our attention now to four historical episodes that illustrate this phenomenon.

Economic Interest Groups and Ancient Egyptian Religion

Temple societies with various forms of gods and priesthoods based on agrarian surpluses emerged in many geographic areas over the past ten thousand years and were inextricably involved with political structures (often with monopolies over violence).[12] In most of these societies an aristocracy prevailed but only with some kind of theocratic overlay in which the leader was either the messenger of the gods or the deity itself. One point seems to be overlooked however. Highly skewed or wide disparities in income distributions generally have a limit, and when the limit is reached the masses take over the government. However, stronger religious beliefs and observances have the effect of stretching the limits on the skew or lopsidedness in income distribution. In principle, it is testable whether the stronger the religious or magical hold on society, the more skewed the income distribution, but we eschew this question to ask, "How and why did these temple societies change gods over this long period?" We believe that the economic basis for choosing the religious forms described earlier helps explain these mythological evolutions, and we take an example from Egyptian history.[13]

The saga of the Egyptian pharaoh Akhenaton, who founded a form of monotheistic religion and moved the capital of Egypt from Thebes to Akhenaton (also called simply "Amarna" or in modern times "Tell el-Amarna"), is one of the strangest and most unique in the history of the ancient world. The ancient origins of Egyptian deities—numbering as many as two thousand—were as distant from Akhenaton's lifetime (c. 1391–1353 BCE) as Akhenaton is from our own.[14] The study of Egyptian religion and its pantheon of gods and their relation to magic is, of course, quite specialized.[15] But in keeping with our characterization of the demand and supply of religion, certain characteristics stand out:

• No gods were eliminated from the pantheon in a system that evolved into one in which particular deities achieved favor at times and were relegated to minor status at others;

• A general belief in a select coterie of major gods surrounding the ancient Egyptian creation and death myths dominated Egyptian mythology (e.g., Osiris, preparer of the dead) but not to the exclusion of multiple minor deities;

• Each city, as with the medieval Roman Catholic Church system of local saints across Europe, had a deity, some of which achieved highest prominence in the Egyptian pantheon—Ptah when pharaohs ruled from Memphis; Re, the sun god of Heliopolis; Amon in Thebes at the time of Akhenaton; and so on.

All cult gods had to be propitiated when in favor, and major priesthoods were supported by the Pharaoh-rulers who, in turn, were often dominated by a high priest and a priesthood of a particular cult. Such was the case by the time of the New Kingdom (1539–1070 BCE). Amon, god of Thebes and of humble beginnings, achieved ascendance as the chief god of all Egypt but not before a bitter rivalry between the priests of Amon (or Amun) and those of Re. As the Egyptian polity at Thebes prospered from conquests in the Near East and elsewhere, the priesthood of Amon and other related deities in the eighteenth and other dynasties flourished: "It was a heavy blow for the priests of Heliopolis. They found themselves compelled to sing the praises of the usurping deity of the south. Re, demoted, was considered merely one aspect of Amon now...its political power was gone."[16] The priests of Amon grew in power, clearly achieving the status of an economic interest group. According to historian Robert Silverberg, "The domain of Amon grew until it vied in splendor with that of Pharaoh himself. The king, forever under the necessity to honor priests or nobles with gifts, was unable to accumulate great wealth. What Amon received, though, Amon kept and never gave back. The god's store of gold grew from year to year. The most fertile fields of Egypt were farmed on Amon's behalf. Palm forests, fish-ponds, meadows, whole towns and villages, an army of scribes and soldiers and farmers, laborers and tradesmen—all this was Amon's, ruled over by a Theban high priest of awesome might."[17] By the time of Ramses III, after the restoration of Amon, the Egyptian temples and their priests controlled 720,000 acres of land, which was about 15 percent of cultivable land; about 80 percent of it (583,000 acres) was controlled by the priesthood of Amon.

The Emergence of Monotheism in Egypt

Although the great king Amenhotep III (1391–1353 BCE) supported these priestly perquisites, the Amon priesthood somehow lost its political power over the king, which set the stage for a "reformation" of sorts. As a result, the pharoah's son, Amenhotep IV (later known as Akhenaton), fomented the most complete break in the history of Egyptian mythology. This break included the establishment of a new deity, Aton, and a new capital city, Akhenaton.[18] While he did not displace Re, the sun god, Aton became the god of the sunrise and the sunset. As the one true god, he took on several roles that had been assumed by other deities, such as caretaker of the dead, a role formerly ascribed to Osiris. Moreover, in a shift not seen again until the advent of Judaism or Christianity, Aton presented himself as a loving god available to all without threat or force, a purveyor of earthly beauty, joy, and happiness, as well as a heaven in the hereafter. This new Egyptian monotheism had one agent and priest, Akhenaton.

The resulting disavowal of the Amon priesthood and of the other temples at Thebes had important economic consequences. As payments from the pharaoh were cut off, temples were abandoned, priests were reduced to beggary, and sacrileges committed against priests and holy places occurred with increasingly frequency. The priests of Amon scattered and their religious precepts were discredited. And priests were not the only interests groups that were adversely affected. The dramatic explanation of historian James Henry Breasted provides important insights into a whole chain of economic interests that were damaged by the establishment of Aton: "Groups of muttering priests, nursing implacable hatred, must have mingled their curses with the execration of whole communities of discontented tradesmen—bakers who no longer drew a livelihood from the sale of ceremonial cakes at the temple feasts; craftsmen who no longer sold amulets of the old gods at the temple gateway; hack sculptors whose statues of Osiris lay under piles of dust in many a tumbled-down studio; cemetery stone-cutters who found their tawdry tombstones with scenes from the Book of the Dead banished from the necropolis; scribes whose rolls of the same book, filled with the names of the old gods, or even if they bore the word god in the plural, were anathema."[19] As the sole mediator between the people and the distant and abstract god Aton, Akhenaton collected huge rents from the estimated thirty thousand to fifty thousand citizens of Akhetaten and all other parts of Egypt where Akhenaton imposed monotheism to lesser levels of success. Interest groups undoubtedly developed around Aton, but most accounts suggest that the support came primarily from the elite classes, especially those who depended on the king for support.

Just how Akhenaton was able to accomplish this substitution is an issue of some debate. The "gods shift" probably took place slowly at first. Since the king controlled the army, armed insurrection by the Amon priesthood was not possible. One analyst argues, "Most priests of Amun were royal appointments: even the wealth invested in the

Amun temples and nominally controlled by the priests may have remained at the royal disposal."[20] What is clear is that the move of perhaps no more than a total of eighteen to twenty years created economic suffering for the priesthoods of all gods other than Aton. Just as interest groups for and against privatizing social security in the United States battle for political supremacy, supporters and enemies of Aton and Akhenaten engaged in strategies to control the political-theocratic process.

Economic Interest Groups and Return to the Old Gods

The monotheism of Akhenaton did not and—given the technology of the times and its relation to belief and myth—could not survive Akhenaton's death. Two factors explain this, both stemming from developing economic interest groups. First, the masses rejected Aton as a single abstract god with one agent, the Pharoah. After Akhenaton's death, no corporeal form of the god existed. Much as the Roman Catholic Church has been unable to drive out voodoo and animism from exceedingly poor and nonscientific cultures (e.g., Haiti), belief in an abstract god did little to satisfy the demands of ordinary Egyptians. Science and technology had not advanced (and have not yet advanced) so as to eliminate the need for deities with forms and faces or, for that matter, with characteristics of magic and animistic mythologies to quell existential dread. Most important, the elimination of corporeal representations of Isis and Osiris, gods of benevolence and protection of the dead, and Re, the warrior sun god, were as necessary as accompaniments to a major deity as the saints and holy martyrs were to Christ in the development of Christianity. In short, given the state of science and the general form of religion demands, Akhenaton was unable to redefine monotheistic religion as an acceptable product. Relative full prices and the state of science and education meant that abstract, more philosophical religion could not have appealed to the people in general who demanded more ritual and animism. Breasted notes that when Aton ruled as a single god,

Actors and priestly mimes ... were driven away from the sacred groves on the days when they should have presented to the people the 'passion play,' and murmuring groups of pilgrims at Abydos who would have taken part in this drama of the life and death and resurrection of Osiris. Other interest groups were dispossessed: "physicians deprived of their whole stock in trade of exorcising ceremonies, employed with success since the days of the earliest kings, two thousand years before; ... peasants who feared to erect a rude image of Osiris in the field to drive away the typhonic demons of drought and famine; mothers soothing their babes at twilight and fearing to utter the sacred names and prayers learned in childhood, to drive away from their little ones the lurking demons of the dark."[21]

Demanders of religious services coalesced around the old gods and their priests and became an interest group supporting the restoration. And more important, mass consumers had a direct incentive to restore the many festivals, where work time abated and "free food" was provided for supplicants of the gods, much the same as in the medieval Roman Catholic festivals and feast days of Western Europe. Other, more subtle elements may have been involved. Akhenaton probably did not create a sufficient safety net around his monotheism. Most reports indicate that wealth became concentrated with the king's receipt of religious offerings and concentration of land. With a high full price of monotheism and Akhenaton's enforcement ending with his death, the tipping point for a return to the old gods was reached.

The return to Amon and the old gods occurred almost immediately after the death of Akhenaton. According to Robert Silverberg, Tutankhamen, Akhenaton's successor, returned to Amon, inducting "priests and prophets from the children of the nobles of their towns" with all of the property of the temples "doubled and tripled and quadrupled in silver and gold, lapis lazuli, every kind of costly stone, royal linen, white linen, fine linen, olive oil, gum, fat ... incense, myrrh, without limit to any good thing."[22] Quoting temple wall inscriptions, Breasted notes that Tutankhamen refers to himself as "the good ruler, who did excellent things for the father of all gods (Amon), who restored for him that which was in ruin as everlasting monuments."[23] The priests of Amon grew powerful and, in some of the succeeding dynasties, controlled the kingship of Egypt. The retreat from formless, abstract religion back to polytheism would not abate until the emergence, first, of Judaism and, later, Christianity. Judaism, originating in approximately 1000 BCE, advanced a one true God with consequences for not believing in that God and/or defying God. Christianity, which mimed to a large extent elements of temple religions, would also be changed by the scientific and knowledge revolutions of the late Middle Ages and the Renaissance. The important point is that economic interests and interest groups determined the direction and content of religion within a rationally-determined market of both suppliers and demanders.

Science and Technological Change: Shifts in the Form of Late Medieval Religion

Changes in religious or magical forms are created when alterations in science or other variables acting as shifters affect degrees of survival uncertainty or existential anxiety. Some examples are obvious—modern meteorology has reduced the demand for rain dances or rituals. Other examples include the well-known attempt by the medieval Roman Catholic Church to defend doctrinal orthodoxy and orthodox science, ultimately unsuccessfully, through condemnation of late medieval scientists, including John Hus (burned at Constance in 1415), Copernicus, Giordano Bruno (burned at Rome in 1600) and, most famous, Galileo Galilei. Indeed, the case of Galileo may be interpreted in interest-group terms. His most important and notable contribution was his *Dialogue Concerning the Two Chief World Systems—Ptolemaic and Copernican* in which he demonstrated the superiority of the theory of Copernicus that the earth revolved around the sun.[24] It was this book, the eternal cause célèbre for the necessity of free scientific inquiry, that was censured by the Inquisition. Galileo, reasonably early (in 1611) and under the clear influence of Copernicus, was convinced that the Aristotelean-Ptolomaic (A-P) view of the earth in relation to the universe was incorrect. The A-P universe was static, unalterable, and "incorruptible," as Galileo was taught by his Aristotelean-influenced Jesuit philosopher-teachers. But it was a group of teachers from this order, Jesuit astronomers supporting the Tychonic over the Copernican system and Dominican licensers, who formed interest groups in Rome, which were key to the eventual trial of Galileo. The shift from Italian printers in Venice and Rome to Protestant printers in Wittenberg and other Protestant areas was also at play in the prosecution of Galileo.[25] While interest group economics might be factually applied to these other episodes of religious repression, we focus on a fifteenth-century invention that was a prelude to the modern world having profound implications for the form of religion.

The printing press, based on the principle of movable type, was invented by Johannes Gutenberg in the middle of the fifteenth century. The rapid dissemination of printing had earthshaking implications for the course of civilization, virtually creating the foundation for widespread literacy, the development of a permanent and ongoing Renaissance in science, philosophy, and literature, and establishing the basis of the modern world. Less than seven decades after Gutenberg, the new science of printing paved the way for a new form of Christian religion. A plethora of early heresies, those of Wycliff, the Waldensians, and many others, emphasized church corruption, the sale of indulgences, and a church that had strayed from the aims of Jesus Christ, but it was only with Luther and Calvin that a reformation against Roman Catholicism was able to stick. Though not the sole cause—some Roman demanders switched due to high and discriminatory pricing schedules, for example—printing was for the first time available as a mass medium to publicize Church abuses. A growing but incomplete literacy in parts of Europe fostered this development, but early forms of printed etching and woodcut production even bridged these gaps. The lack of literacy was bridged by what later were termed "broadsides," pictures that told a story or provided messages of abuse.[26] Like the later examples of broadsides used for political purposes by Goya in Spain, Daumier in France, and Posada in Mexico, these early etchings were sometimes created by great artists such as Cranach the Elder and Albrecht Dürer.

Eisenstein notes that between 1517, when Luther published his Ninety-five Theses, and 1520, Luther's thirty publications sold over three hundred thousand copies in the vernacular.[27] Rejecting the Roman Catholic Church's monopoly on scriptural interpretation, Luther transferred this power to the individual.[28] The Church used the press to develop its objections to Luther and other Protestants and the resulting "pamphlet wars" between 1520 and 1525 made Luther a household name and the Reformation a reality. Historian Jean-François Gilmont noted that although the whole story of the emergence of Protestantism was not "justification by print alone," the great interaction between printing and the Reformation made the many emerging forms of Christianity possible.[29] These media wars between 1517 and the Peace of Augsberg (1555) and other "settlements" that established Protestantism in most of northern

Europe were clearly made possible by Gutenberg.[30] Eisenstein writes, "Heralded on all sides as a 'peaceful art,' Gutenberg's invention probably contributed more to destroying Christian concord and inflaming religious warfare than any of the so-called arts of war ever did. Much of the religious turbulence of the early modern era may be traced to the fact that the writings of church fathers and Scripture itself could not continue to be transmitted in traditional ways. As a sacred heritage, Christianity could be protected against most forms of change. As a heritage that was transmitted by texts and that involved the 'spreading of glad tidings,' Christianity was peculiarly vulnerable to the revolutionary effects of typography."[31] Clearly, the reduced information costs to increasingly literate ordinary citizens made possible by printing and the spread of literacy were able to make "everyman his own theologian." This new science of printing shifted religious forms in both content and number, permitting a less rule-driven and more individual and philosophically oriented group of Christian sects to emerge. Science, literacy, and education permitted a shift in religious forms.

Printing Technology and the Form of Religion

What effect did the printing revolution and the successful Protestant Reformation it helped engender have on the Roman Catholic Church? The Church fully understood the impact of literacy, the dissemination of printed books, and the secular frame of mind that they produced on its doctrinal monopoly. For many centuries the Church engaged in censorship of ideas and science that it deemed "heretical," including the Crusades at Albi, campaigns against all kinds of opponents (Jews and Muslims were often subject to interdict), and assaults against any threat to the economic interests of the church. Inquisitions were a product of the early medieval period. But the printed word and the literacy that it engendered was something else entirely. Book censorship and book burning became the main tools of the church to rid itself of heresy. Even before Luther, Calvin, and other Protestant reformers, the Church recognized the power of the printed word to challenge its interests. In Spain most particularly, repression of books and censorship of ideas were in full swing by 1490. More than six thousand volumes on sorcery and magic were burned in that year at Salamanca[32] along with Hebrew bibles and any other works deemed antithetical or critical of received Roman Catholic theology. The most virulent repressions of the Inquisition were practiced in Spain with the full approbation of the civil and royal governments. Books in Spanish but printed in Germany and elsewhere in northern Europe were being imported into Spain. Those caught in this trade could be imprisoned or tried for heresy. Permits to read books had to be acquired; bishops and papal inquisitors were the only people who could read without regulation.[33] In Italy, censorship of scientific writings and the printing of scientific and other writings were used as political devices to suppress church competitors of all kinds— writers, scientists, and booksellers for example. As Burman notes, book censorship had "the most disastrous effect...on the development of scientific thought in Italy; the lead which Italian scientists and philosophers had achieved during the Renaissance was truncated and never recovered."[34] Censorship and intellectual repression may have had much to do with the lack of progress in these countries in future centuries.

In 1520 Pope Leo X produced a Bull, an official papal directive that excommunicated Martin Luther, forbidding the printing, distribution, or possession of his writings.[35] An Index of Forbidden Books was concocted, first under the management of the Roman and Spanish Inquisitions and later consecrated under the "Congregation of the Holy Office," only to end in 1966. The index was an acknowledgment that free thought, unrestricted explorations of science using the scientific method, and individualism of any stripe would not be tolerated by the Roman Catholic Church, except under its own interpretive rules. An expanded Tridentine Index, established at the end of the Council of Trent in 1564, restricted the reading of the Bible in the vernacular to those who could obtain permission from an inquisitor or bishop.

All this did not alter the expansion of new forms of Christianity, which morphed into thousands of Christian church forms over ensuing centuries. The Council of Trent, often cited as the crown jewel of the Counter-Reformation, had little effect on the wholesale side of Church behavior—on the abuses of the upper levels of church authority (e.g., cardinals, pope, and curia) (see chapter 6). The Roman Catholic Church itself has been slow to restructure its positions on the censorship of science and individualism, with some change occurring only in the latter part of the twentieth century. The four thousand works listed in the 1945 Index included both works and authors, including those of Hume, Voltaire, Zola, Locke, Smith (*The Wealth of Nations*), Mill (*Principles of Political Economy*), Defoe, Gibbon, and other writers whose work constitutes a history of Western thought, literature, and philosophy. The Catholic Church's assault focused, and to a large extent continues to focus, on nineteenth- and twentieth-century liberalism and on individualism. While many prohibitions on published books have been deleted, the Church still reserves the right to censor books by Catholic authors submitted *before* publication, paying particular attention to those dealing with sensitive issues on priestly celibacy, the role of women, divorce, abortion, gay rights, and so on.[36] The form of contemporary Roman Catholicism has changed only slightly since the later Middle Ages, but the forms of Christianity underwent a sea change during the scientific-technological revolution. The unremitting fight against individualism and liberalism was in fact joined anew in the twentieth century by Cardinal Merry del Val. The association of the Inquisition with censorship ended in 1908, but the crusade against individualism and an individual's recourse to his or her own conscience continues to be a part of Roman Catholic rule making, now called the "Sacred Congregation for the Doctrine of the Faith." Philosophers and theologians teaching in Catholic schools and universities remain, under Pope Benedict XVI, subject to censorship by bishops and other church authorities, as do books published by Catholic authors relating to Catholicism.[37] The dangers that some see in "secularization" and individualism justify such activities. We simply note that printing technology was a shifter in that it encouraged and fostered the Protestant revolution against the Roman Catholic monopoly.

Interest Groups and Doctrinal Change: Eating Meat on Friday

Doctrinal change is often believed to be out of the purview of economic interests and, admittedly, there are many factors to consider. In some instances, however, economic interests and groups representing them help explain doctrinal change and changing religious proscriptions. For example, real reform in Roman Catholic Church doctrine was afoot during the late 1950s and 1960s during the reigns of Popes John XXIII and Paul VI. These institutional changes were promulgated first through the congregation of bishops assembled to oversee reform (Second Vatican Council, 1962–1965) and then through the particular reform policies of Pope Paul VI. On February 17, 1966, Paul issued an apostolic decree called *Paenitemini* that made extensive changes in church regulations on penance, including regulatory changes that ended centuries of specific rules on fasting and abstinence (Pope Paul VI, 1966). Abstinence from meat on Fridays had been a major Roman Catholic expression of penance since the third century. This abstinence was made mandatory by Pope Nicholas I in 851 and was continued until 1966 when it was changed by Paul VI. With the exception of several Fridays in Lent, Roman Catholics, at the discretion of local bishops, were no longer required to abstain from meat on at least forty-six Fridays of the year. Economically, the effects of the release of Catholics from the requirement were clear: The price of fish was lowered in the United States[38] and in many parts of the world due to a decline in demand. But economics may also help us go behind the narrow confines of effects to analyze the cause of the change.

An Evolving Power Structure

Collegiality characterized the Church of Peter and his successors for over one thousand years. This meant that bishops, including the Bishop of Rome—the Pope—were elected by the clerics and by the people through regional or national synods. In the early Church, the rank of Cardinal (which, like the Pope, is simply a bishop) was partly administrative and largely honorific. Papal election by a College of Cardinals, the current practice, did not begin until the twelfth century. Initially the College of Cardinals was constituted as follows:

25 priests in charge of Roman churches (*ordine dei preti*);

13 (later 19) deacons from Rome and vicinity (*ordine dei diaconi*);

7 bishops of dioceses close to Rome (*ordine dei vescovi*).

Also, in the twelfth century additional cardinals, from more distant lands, were added; but in the thirteenth and fourteenth centuries the number of cardinal electors seldom exceeded thirty because vacancies often remained unfilled.[39] A maximum number of cardinals was set at seventy by Pope Sixtus V in 1586. It was a limit that was not exceeded until the reigns of John XXIII and Paul VI, who vastly enlarged the active number of cardinals in the late 1950s and mid-1960s.

In examining the rule change in penance, it is important to note that with the exception of critical "matters of faith and morals," the Pope seldom reaches decisions without the advice and consent of the senate of cardinals (and/or its subset, the curia). It is important to understand that a large part of the Second Vatican Council was aimed at "internationalizing" the Church. That internationalization of church administration begun by Pope John XXIII was continued by his successor Paul VI, who ascended to the Papal throne at John's death in 1963. This movement included reform of the College of Cardinals and the curia and changes in the composition of the world's cardinals. Table 4.1, derived from the official *Papal Annual*, shows these changes between 1951 (during the pontificate of Pius XII) and 1966. During this fifteen-year period, the total membership in the College increased from fifty-two in 1951 to ninety-nine in 1966—far in excess of the maximum of seventy established in 1586. The "open window" of John XXIII and Paul VI resulted in an expansion in the total number of cardinals to 145 by 1973 (a trend of expansion that was continued by Pope John Paul II).

By the time of Paul VI's decision, the actual number of cardinals rose by forty-seven between 1951 and 1966 and by twenty-two in one year, 1965–1966. Membership from the third-world countries tripled between 1951 and 1966, with a full seventeen of these new third-world cardinalates being appointed between 1958 and 1965 by John XXIII and Paul VI. Of these third-world cardinals, eleven came from South and Central America and Africa.

Economics, World Food Production, and the Form of Penance

Were economic as well as spiritual motives at work in the process of institutional transformation of the Roman Catholic Church between the late 1950s and mid-1960s? We believe that the economic motive of the Church—that of wealth maximization—was conditioned by patterns of world food production and that economic facts might help explain the Church's decision to alter the rules respecting penance. Regional and

Table 4.1
Distribution of actual membership in the College of Cardinals by world region
and political bloc, 1951, 1965, and 1966

	1951	1965	1966
Regional distribution			
North America			
Canada	1	2	3
United States	4	5	5
South America, Central America (including Mexico)	7	13	14
Europe (excluding Italy)	15	21	27
Italy	19	26	29
Eastern Europe and the Soviet Union	3	3	7
Africa	0	1	4
Mid-East	1	1	4
East	1	4	5
Australia	1	1	1
TOTALS	52	77	99
Political distribution			
Western Bloc	44	55	65
Soviet and Eastern Bloc	3	3	7
Third World	9	19	27
TOTALS	52	77	99

Sources: Annuario Pontificio per l'Anno 1951 (Citta del Vaticano: Tipografia
Poliglotta Vaticana, 1951), 29–63; *Annuario Pontificio per l'Anno 1965* (Citta
del Vaticano: Tipografia Poliglotta Vaticana, 1965), 38–67; *Annuario Pontificio
per l'Anno 1966* (Citta del Vaticano: Tipografia Poliglotta Vaticana, 1966), 38–
89.

country-by-country economic interests in meat and fish are particularly
relevant in this regard. As table 4.2 shows, the decision reached by Paul
VI in *Poenitemini* is perfectly compatible with world fish and beef
production patterns between 1951 and 1966, the year of the decree. In
restructuring the College of Cardinals in such a way as to enhance the
representation of North America, South America, and Africa at the proportional expense of European representation, Paul in effect reduced the
power of Europe. The case for economic interests is even stronger when
the data is refined to a country-by-country level. Consider tables 4.3 and
4.4, which list the major meat and fish producers for the twenty countries in which meat or fish production is greatest relative to the country's

Table 4.2
Number of newly appointed cardinals, and beef and fish production (millions of metric tons) by continent, 1951–1966

	Number of new cardinals*	Fish production	Beef production	Fish/beef
North America	4	61.7	1,246	0.049
South America (including Central America and Mexico)	7	66.8	656	0.102
Europe	45	126.3	892	0.142
Africa	4	31.4	211	0.016
Asia	6	230.7	262	0.878

Sources: Annuario Pontificio per l'Anno 1965: 38–67; *Annuario Pontificio per l'Anno 1966*: 38–89; *Production Yearbook*, Food and Agriculture Organization of the United Nations, Rome, various issues; and *Yearbook of Fishery Statistics*, Food and Agriculture Organization of the United Nations, Rome, various issues.
* New cardinalates and replacements (1958–1965) created by Popes John XXIII and Paul VI, who were voting members of the college in 1965–1966.

gross national product (GNP). The number of new (and replacement) cardinals appointed between 1958 and 1966 are also given for each of the countries. While some anomalies exist, these tables provide striking evidence of a tilt in the College of Cardinals (at this period) toward meat producing and relatively Catholic nations and away from fish producing and relatively non-Catholic nations. It is natural to argue that the Pope would seek to provide once-and-for-all rents for producers in Catholic rather than non-Catholic nations, leading to permanent redistribution of wealth from non-Catholic nations to Catholic nations. In aggregate, the leading meat-producing nations received twice the number of appointments (twenty-four) than the fish-producing nations received (twelve).

Joint Products: Penance and the Price of Leather

Consider tables 4.3 and 4.4 even more closely. They show that meat and fish production both account for a relatively large part of GNP in Peru, Denmark, Taiwan, South Africa, the Netherlands, Canada, Spain, and Chile. (Spain is a special case, for reasons we discuss later in this

Table 4.3

Twenty major meat-producing countries (as percent of GNP), 1958; number of new and replacement cardinals in 1966 (by country) appointed, 1958–1966

Country (rank)	1,000 metric tons/$ billions GNP	Number of new cardinals (1958–1966)
1. Uruguay	274.1*	1
2. New Zealand	236.7	0
3. Argentina	179.8	0
4. Ireland	172.4	2
5. Denmark	168.0	0
6. Taiwan	145.4	0
7. Columbia	120.6*	1
8. Brazil	111.6	1
9. Australia	107.6	0
10. Peru	82.2	1
11. South Africa	75.2	1
12. Chile	74.9*	1
13. Netherlands	57.8	1
14. France	53.7	3
15. Spain	50.3	4
16. Mexico	48.8	1
17. West Germany	45.9	3
18. Belgium	45.0	3
19. Canada	40.7	1
20. Sweden	38.3	0
TOTAL		24

Sources: Meat production: *1961 Production Yearbook*, Vol. 15, Table 78B (Rome: Food and Agricultural Organization of the United Nations, 1962), 189–196; GNP: *Yearbook of National Accounts Statistics: 1966*, Table 7A (New York: United Nations, 1967), 725–729; *Annuario Pontificio per l'Anno 1966* (Citta del Vaticano: Tipografia Poliglotta Vaticana, 1966), 38–89.

* 1958 meat production data unavailable. Adjusted 1961 data used in calculating meat production.

Table 4.4
Twenty major fish-producing countries (as percent of GNP), 1958; number of
new and replacement cardinals in 1966 (by country) appointed, 1958–1966

Country (rank)	1,000 metric tons/$ billions GNP	Number of new cardinals (1958–1966)
1. Peru	500.1	1
2. Norway	399.7	0
3. Iceland	207.3	0
4. Japan	187.9	1
5. Korea	141.1	0
6. Denmark	130.1	0
7. Taiwan	127.1	0
8. Thailand	98.1	0
9. Philippines	87.6	1
10. Spain	81.7	4
11. Malaysia	68.1	0
12. South Africa	67.4	1
13. Pakistan	48.1	0
14. India	37.7	0
15. Netherlands	36.7	1
16. Kenya	36.6	0
17. Ceylon (Sri Lanka)	33.9	1
18. Indonesia	33.2	0
19. Canada	32.6	1
20. Chile	31.1	1
TOTAL		12

Sources: Fish production: *Yearbook of Fishery Statistics: 1965*, Vol. 21, Table
A1–2 (Rome: Food and Agricultural Organization of the United Nations,
1966), a6–a16; GNP: *Yearbook of National Accounts Statistics: 1966*, Table
7A (New York: United Nations, 1967), 725–729; *Annuario Pontificio per
l'Anno 1966* (Citta del Vaticano: Tipografia Poliglotta Vaticana, 1966), 38–39.

chapter.) We might presume that in these countries meat- and fish-producing interests cancel out, and that the clerics of these nations were "neutral" on the rule change from an economic perspective. From wealth-maximizing logic, Spanish cardinals may also be presumed to have been neutral, but for a different reason: Catholics in Spain had eaten meat on Fridays since 1089 as a consequence of a special dispensation granted for their victory over the Moors.[40] But there is another good economic reason why the Italians and the Spanish cardinals (in particular) did not resist the "no meat on Friday" rule change: the fact that leather is a joint product in production with beef.[41]

In an ingenious argument recognizing the joint production of beef and leather (hides), Mark Thornton shows that the Pope's decision to lift the ban on meat would also reduce the price of leather.[42] Both producers of leather goods (shoes, saddles, purses, furniture, and so on), who must buy hides as an input, and consumers of leather products benefit. Thus, Thornton suggests that the Pope's decision was good economics for leather-using and exporting regions, such as Italy and Spain, as well as for beef producers. Increased production of beef led to an increased supply of leather, which, given constant demand, reduced the price of leather as well. Thornton shows that the average annual production of bovine hides increased by 40.4 percent from 1961–1965 to 1979–1981 due to expanding beef production (both sheep and goatskin production increased as well). Along with the increased output came lower prices (about 25 percent).

In Italy, the footwear and apparel industry was highly significant—more than 6 percent in 1965 and 8.8 percent of total manufacturing in 1969. Italy's export of shoes alone produced 20 percent more revenue than the entire fishing industry. Although both Italy and Spain are beef producers, the imports of hides soared after the rule change. The Italians and the Spanish also have a comparative advantage in the creative abilities of designers and artisans for leather goods. As Thornton notes, "The Church stands to gain from such changes to the extent its members benefit from a lower price of leather and transfer a portion of their higher real incomes to the Church in the form of larger contributions."[43] While Spain had reasons for neutrality in the rule change (they were not bound by the rule), the Spanish cardinals also had economic incentives to support it. The powerful Italian branch of the College of Cardinals—a group that has had a disproportionate influence on Church policy until modern times—had the same incentives to support changing the laws of penance or at least to offer no resistance.

Naturally, the rule change is consistent with other motives. As indicated in the proceedings of the Second Vatican Council, poverty in the third world was a major concern of world bishops, especially those of the third world. Pope Paul VI probably already knew he was going to reaffirm the Church's position on birth control (*Humanitae Vitae* in 1968). The rule change placated the third-world cardinals and poor church members by giving them an expanded budget choice—that is, more protein source options for the hungry. Also there was an observable anomaly in the severity of punishment levied for breaking the laws of fast and abstinence. If it was a mortal sin, and in the same class as murder or rape, the relative cost of punishment in hell was the same, and marginal deterrence from sin was not obtained. Church membership would also suffer along with church wealth. This point was made by Bishop La Ravoire Morrow of India during the third session of Vatican Council II (October 1964) when he asked, "How can the men and women of our time understand that God is good if we continue to teach them that those who do not abstain on Fridays go to hell? They do not see any proportion between the Church's precepts and God's commandments. How can eating meat on Friday deserve the same punishment as committing adultery or murder? This causes the moral sense of people to become blunted and ecclesiastical authority to be despised."[44]

Finally there is some evidence that the rule, in the United States at least, was being ignored.[45] Like contemporary "cafeteria Catholics" who pick and choose areas of belief such as abortion, genetic cloning, or homosexuality (see chapter 9), Catholics in the United States simply chose not to follow the rule. It is perhaps significant that meatless Fridays were ended quickly in most U.S. dioceses in spite of the suggestion of Paul VI that it might be appropriate for wealthier developed nations to maintain the meat ban.[46] Thus, while many reasons may be adduced for the rule change on "meatless Fridays," there were economic (i.e., self-interested) considerations within the expanded College of Cardinals and those areas of the world that they oversee. According to Pope Paul VI, "The demands of various localities (make) it necessary to inculcate some special form of penitence in preference to others."[47] An examination of the relative production of meat and fish products and of the locales of leather production and use by region and country gives new meaning to the term "demands" used in Paul's papal decree. More broadly, this case points to the interesting possibility in modern interest group economics of including the discovery of motives underlying institutional change in one of the chief Christian religions in world history.

Changing Prices in the Medieval Roman Catholic Form of Religion

A general method for analyzing the economics of religion and changes in religious form was applied to the early medieval church in our earlier book *Sacred Trust* under conditions of Roman Catholic monopoly. After the twelfth century, Roman Catholicism (with only insignificant fringe competition from Jews and Moors) came to dominate large parts of Western Europe. The legal system of the Catholic Church, canon law, was beginning to supplant and eventually dominate civil law in (then) loosely organized states and other political entities. Ecclesiastical officials enacted laws respecting all aspects of the supply decision of such goods as assurances of eternal salvation, political support from the papacy and clergy, and social services of all kinds. Marriage, trade, and all manner of behavior were regulated in conjunction with the supply of these services. Kings, princes, and aristocrats of all kinds owed much of their power to the approbation of the Roman Catholic authorities who, with full complements of upstream or upper clerical levels (bishops, cardinals, pope) and downstream or lower-level agents (priests and monks), helped negotiate trade deals, wage wars, and maintain armies. The Roman Catholic Church, moreover, was immensely wealthy and was a huge landholder during the medieval period. The retail side of the church offering religious, medical, and social services of all kinds was also a primary source of revenues in addition to payments (taxes and other forms of rents) from monarchs, politicians, and the local religious establishments (monasteries, parish churches, etc.).

The organization of the church was that of a contemporary M-form corporation. The M-form corporation is an internal organization adopted in order to help avoid managerial problems of inefficiency. Responsibility for the firm's various activities—financial, production, marketing of products, and so on—is decentralized into operating divisions, each with their own managerial structures. Division heads typically report to a Chief Executive Officer (CEO). In the case of the Roman Catholic Church, the pope is the CEO, the curia and cardinals are upstream directors of various functions including a financial division collecting revenues called the papal camera (treasury), and a geographically dispersed downstream retail division, local bishops, parish priests, and monks of various orders "sell" products and services.[48] The primary role of the upstream church was to provide doctrine and dogma relating to the essential principles of membership (e.g., interpretations of the Holy texts) and to collect downstream rents. It established, with authority centralized in the Pope after the Council of Trent (1545–1563) but formalized only later in the nineteenth century, the often labyrinthine conditions for eternal salvation and the penalties for violating any of those conditions.

Downstream were the geographically dispersed purveyors of local Roman Catholicism. These included the regional mendicant and contemplative religious orders, monasteries (some of which were as much production units of agricultural and other goods as sellers of religious services), parish priests, and other local clergy. While rents were collected at all levels, primary revenues came from these retail agencies of the downstream church. Enforcement policies and assigned agents of the centralized Roman Catholic authorities were necessary to prevent opportunistic behavior in distant locales of the church.

Entry control was obviously necessary to maintain the strength of demand for the products of Roman Catholic monopoly. Misfeasors, when caught, were subject to severe punishments. Interdict, whereby the "sinner" could not have contact or truck with other Christians, was one form of punishment. Most severe was excommunication of the wrongdoer—a total separation from the body Catholic and a sentence of eternal damnation if repentance was not made. Heretics of all kinds (those who did not adhere to the main body of Catholic dogma and interpretations) were of course excommunicants, but many were also subject to violent death through the various holy wars or crusades of the Middle Ages. Later, even more virulent punishments were meted out to Protestants and other heretics through inquisitions in Spain, Rome, and elsewhere. These punishments may be seen as attempts to maintain monopoly.

Doctrinal manipulations were also used by the Roman Catholic Church to make its demand curve more inelastic and/or to shift it rightward. The conditions attached to the Church's chief product—assurances of eternal salvation—were manipulated throughout the Middle Ages in order to increase revenues and the number of demanders. Marriage markets, largely of secular and civil concern prior to the Church monopoly, were taken over by the Church with conditions attached to the simple contract respecting endogamy, presence of a priest, posting of bans, and so on. Regulations respecting divorce and marriage dissolution were intricate and varied with income and circumstances of petitioners. Such price discrimination manifestly increased the Church's rents over the medieval period. Another doctrine that was almost manipulated out of recognition was that respecting usury and "just price." When the church was a debtor, it seems, usury prohibitions were enforced, but not when it was a creditor. The same manipulations attended church rules respecting monastery tithes and taxes, the granting of indulgences, jubilee attendance, and benefices granted to bishops and cardinals. Such methods and practices of rent collection reached a limit in the sixteenth century precipitating the Protestant Reformation.

A theory of rational behavior permits an understanding of the church as an economic entity—one that benefited from increasing secularization of European society but one that recognized that science, technology, and humanism would ultimately weaken the kind and form of magic the church was selling. If belief in Christ and Christian principles were the main issue, it would be difficult to explain how Roman Christians issued crusades against other Catholics, the Eastern Orthodox Christian Church, or (later) Protestant Christians of all stripes. Moreover, the emergence of fierce censorship of all kinds in the sixteenth and earlier centuries is also difficult to understand (Galileo was a devout Catholic) except in an economic context, that is, the context of monopoly rent seeking by interest groups in the Church. Economists objectively viewing these policies and doctrines see them as examples of monopoly behavior and all that the model entails. If religious organizations, in this case the Roman Catholic Church, were acting solely in the public interest, they would behave as a "good government"—one that provides information, spiritual goods, and social goods to the faithful at competitive, that is, marginal cost. An economic examination of the behavior of the medieval church does not provide overwhelming support for this view. The emergence of Protestantism, which we analyze as rational economic behavior in chapter 5 and the reaction to entry in the form of a Counter-Reformation, discussed in chapter 6, further unhinges the public interest theory of Christian religious organizations.

Anthropology, history, and psychology provide essential keys to the characterization of market demand and supply in the economics of religion. In the present chapter we have focused on the impact that these elements have on the demand and supply of the forms of religion. Demand for the metacredence good is determined by full price and its proportions of time to resources, and by a set of shifters, including critical factors such as education levels, the state of science and, especially, by income and income distribution (which proxies other factors as well). Product credibility is determined within these parameters for given segments of the total market for magic and religion, given supply conditions as well. Credence, as we interpret it, is created in religious (or magical) products and forms through such factors as priestly celibacy, investments in non-salvageable capital, and specific theologies and rituals. Changes in full price will have both income and substitution effects, given an individual's uncertainty profile and the stock of shifters. Religious participation within a given form of religion will be affected given these parameters, but at critical values individuals will also alter the form of the religion chosen. Two examples in particular—the attempt by Akhenaton to institute monotheism in Egypt and the impact of a techno-scientific discovery (moveable type)—illustrate the impact of the determinants of the form of religion on religious change and evolution.

Income and substitution effects both favor the creation of time-saving religious practices as incomes rise. Religious forms and doctrines within forms thus tend to become less formal and less time-intensive and more money-intensive over time as the economy grows and science and technology expand. We have argued in this chapter that markets of some kind have and always will characterize magic and religion, and those markets, once products are understood, are amenable to economic analysis. We do not dispute any of the characterizations of the product of religion that have appeared heretofore in this literature on the economics of religion (see chapter 2). In this chapter we have attempted to more clearly delineate the nature of the product and how it changes form due to economic factors determining supply and demand. In chapter 5 and ensuing chapters we apply this analysis to a discussion of the historical declension of Christianity from the advent of Protestantism through the early modern period. In a final chapter—chapter 9—we suggest some implications of our study for the state of contemporary Christianity.

Appendix 4A: Preliminary Tests of Demands for Forms of Religion

Our hypothesis in chapter 4 is that both full-price elements and a set of independent variables help explain the demand curve for a particular form of religion as well as religious forms themselves. In order to support this hypothesis we offer two preliminary empirical tests of whether the form of religion is related to a particular set of variables that proxy full prices and other factors determining the form of religion. Our tests include two types of animistic religions or beliefs—time-intensive, third-world tribal forms of animism and less time-intensive forms of New Age spiritualism.

Our tests use a method called regression analysis, a tool that may not be familiar to many readers. Basically, any problem will contain numerous elements and the "real-world" data collected by the economist or analyst will not easily give up its truths concerning cause and effect. That is why a favorite tool of the economist is regression analysis. *Regression analysis* is an econometric tool commonly used by economists to gauge a relationship between a variable, called a dependent variable, and one independent variable or a set of independent variables that move "independently" and are associated with changes in the dependent variable. Consider, for example, the movement of tides. That movement may be associated with phases of the moon. But simply because we observe two variables moving together—*correlation* is the statistical term for that—the observation does not imply that one *causes* the other (e.g., that phases of the moon cause the movements of tides at the seashore). Correlation, in other words, does not necessarily imply causation. And also consider that many other variables may affect the course of tides—depth of the water, barometric pressure, wind speed, and so on. Economists use a tool called *multiple regression* in order to determine the manner (positive or negative) and the magnitude (how much) the dependent variable (e.g., tides) is affected by a set of independent variables (moon, water depth, and so on). Again, while correlation does not necessarily imply causation, the economic analyst can use fairly sophisticated statistical tools in order to gain confidence in the direction and magnitude of the effects of independent variable changes on the dependent variable of interest. In the following tests, we seek to find out how particular independent variables affect the incidence of animistic religions (our first dependent variable) and how another set of independent variables might explain the presence of psychics in forty-six U.S. states (our second dependent variable).

Animism and Ethno-Animism in an International Context

A preliminary test of whether income, education, and other variables influence religious choice using international data sets is possible. A country's religious status in terms of percentages and numbers belonging to thousands of particular religious forms is available in the *World Christian Encyclopedia*.[49] We used thirty-six nations with data for these independent variables available from among the poorest (lowest income) populations of the world and divided the countries into those designated 50 percent or more "animistic" or "ethno-animistic" and those with 50 percent or more of the population composed of "Muslim, Catholic, Hindu, Protestant, or Buddhist." This sample selection helps eliminate the sort of bias that would exist if higher income groups of countries were included. Animistic religions are largely tribal in nature, and correspond closely to those practiced in primitive societies. The countries selected in this manner are shown in table 4A.1 where 43 percent are designated animistic and 57 percent are "other."

In order to test our hypothesis that religious form is related to income and other variables, we regressed, using probit procedures and pooled data from six sample years (1970, 1975, 1980, 1985, 1990, and 1995;

Table 4A.1
Thirty-six third-world countries divided into those with Animist beliefs comprising more than 50 percent and others containing Muslin, Catholic, Hindu, Protestant, and Buddhist beliefs comprising more than 50 percent

Animist	Other
Benin	Burkina Faso
Cameroon	Burundi
Central African Republic	Chad
Ethiopia	Comoros
Gambia	Congo, The Democratic Republic
Ghana	Congo, The Republic
Kenya	Haiti
Madagascar	India
Malawi	Indonesia
Mozambique	Lesotho
Nigeria	Mali
Sierra Leone	Mauritania
Togo	Myanmar
Zambia	Nepal
Zimbabwe	Nicaragua
	Rwanda
	Senegal
	Solomon Islands
	Somalia
	Sudan
	Uganda

Source: David B. Barrett, George T. Kurian, and Todd M. Johnson, *World Christian Encyclopedia* (New York: Oxford University Press, 2001).

$n = 202$), a dependent variable **ANIM** (animistic religion dominant) where **ANIM** $= 0$ and other religions $= 1$, against three independent variables:

GDPGROWTH = annual GDP growth rates for the cross-section of countries;

EDP = level of primary education for males and females in the country;

POPF = number of females in the total population of the country.

Data for the independent variables were obtained from the *World Bank Group (Data and Statistics).*[50] Our test is of the form

$$\text{ANIM} = a + b_0(\textbf{GDPGROWT}) + b_1(\textbf{EDP}) + b_2(\textbf{POPF}) + e$$

Here we are attempting to determine the statistical impact of GDP growth, primary educational level, and the number of females in a population on the presence of high degrees of animism in a society (over 50 percent). We posit a behavioral model, common to the social sciences, where all of the independent variables are shifters to the extent that GDP growth proxies industrial development, a capital/labor ratio, and some "state of science." Note that GDP growth also provides a rough measure of the value of time in a given society as a part of full price. On both counts we expect a negative relation between **GDPGROWT** and the degree of animism and "magic" in a society. The higher the income growth rate, the higher the full price of time-consuming animistic religions and the fewer of them we expect. Likewise, as the levels of science and technology rise, less primitive forms of religion are chosen. The level of primary education, **EDP**, is expected to be negatively related to the degree of animism. Ritual and more magical forms of religion are expected to be chosen when lower levels of education are present. Finally, the number of females in a given population, **POPF**, is expected to be positively related to the selection of animistic religions. Since, in most of the societies represented in our test (table 4A.1), the level of female education is quite low and participation in market work is minimal, lower time costs and the role of women in religious education of children suggest the selection of more animistic forms of religion will vary directly with the number of females in the population. Further, virtually all Western studies consistently show female participation in all religious activities to be higher than that of males.

The statistical results, shown in table 4A.2, are encouraging. In this one-tailed test, typical of testing social science data of this kind, all variables are significant at reasonable levels. A one-tailed test is a statistical procedure for determining the confidence with which one can view a particular statistical result. It is based on a specific cause-and-effect relationship between two variables. From this test, it appears that the selection of animist forms of religion is inversely related to GDP growth, even when those societies are all low-income societies. Further, if this measure of income is viewed as a proxy for the value of time, it would appear that highly time-intensive religions are related to a low value of time.

Table 4A.2
Impact of income, education and female population on degree of animism, thirty-six countries (see table 4.1)

Dependent variable = ANIM

Independent variables	Coefficient	Statistical error	T-value
Constant	19.10497	7.0099	−2.725
GDPGROWT	−0.17144-01	0.1403	−1.222***
EDP	−0.10735-06	0.7383	−1.454**
POPF	0.37616	0.1381	2.722*

* = significant at 1 percent level; ** = significant at 7 percent level; *** = significant at 11 percent level (one-tailed test statistics).

The level of primary education, as expected, is negatively related to the selection of animistic forms of worship. Since survival of the race is perhaps more closely linked to females than to males, given biological imperatives (which might also explain higher participation rates generally among women), the higher the number of women in a population of tribal cultures, the higher the level of animism expected. Finally, since religious participation rates are highest among women, lower levels of female education signal more ritualistic religious participation.

Animism and more primitive forms of magic and religion are suggested by more agrarian (less urban) cultures. On this basis we would expect virtually all of these countries to be animistic. Obviously this is not the case, which suggests that other factors, such as those found in our simple regression, help explain the form of religion chosen.[51] It is also worth noting that in most of these countries, the level of governmental stability, property rights security, and age distributions of the population would also be supportive of animistic forms of religion. While many other specifications of our theory are testable in principle, we regard these results as broadly supportive.

State Psychics Test

There is a kind of paradox, at least in the case of the United States, that the establishment clause of the U.S. Constitution, along with the tremendous growth in scientific achievement and high income growth, is creating a kind of individualism in religious and spiritual beliefs. The paradox is that this development might well parallel that of Paleolithic hunters who, some anthropologists believe, espoused highly individualistic beliefs. This is evidenced by the multiplication of recognized sects and New Age forms of religion, some of them animistic in nature, in which the independence of individual beliefs becomes paramount. In the *Encyclopedia of American Religions*, 2,630 U.S. and Canadian religions are described and broken down into twenty-six groups or "families" of faiths.[52] The author finds, for example, in addition to the majority of Christian faiths, distinct groups of 325 Pentecostals and 224 Spiritualist, Psychic, and New Age groups. Distinctive forms of individualistic spiritualism are emerging in advanced countries. Where relative income levels are low or nonexistent (as in primitive nomadic hunting groups), religion was by all accounts a highly individualistic matter. In high-income, wealthy societies, where highly structured, time-consuming ritual is shunned, spiritual individualism again becomes a principal mode of keeping existential dread at bay.[53]

With these considerations in mind—that is, that forms of animism appeal to both low- and high-income individuals in high-income societies—we have constructed a test of the determinants of animistic practices in the United States. There is no reliable data source for psychics or New Age religions by state for the United States.[54] We have therefore constructed a data set of psychics, mediums, spiritual advisors, and "consultants" for the United States by surveying the Yellow Pages in these categories. Calculations were made for the three most populous cities in each state plus a random sample of five cities and towns with less than fifty thousand in population. From these data, psychics per ten thousand in population (**LPCC**) was calculated with complete data for each of forty-six states.[55] We regress variables against our constructed dependent variable—psychics per ten thousand in the population—and use an ordinary least squares (OLS) technique (in log form), a technique widely used in economics, social sciences, and other sciences as well. OLS is a basic statistical practice for testing the validity of some theory about the behavior of a particular variable. A variety of forms of the technique are used, but the central principle of OLS is called the Best Linear Unbiased Estimates, meaning that the regression technique fits the best possible relationship between the explanatory variables and the variable to be explained. In the case at hand, the following explanatory variables were regressed against our constructed dependent variable:

LINC = log of per capita state income for forty-six states;

LHSG = log of the high school graduation rate for each state;

LPCTHIS = log of the percentage of Hispanics in each state;

DCAP = a dummy variable for the state of California.

Our test equation is

$$\textbf{LPCC} = a_0 + b_1(\textbf{LINC}) + b_2(\textbf{LHSG}) + b_3(\textbf{LPCTHIS}) + b_4(\textbf{DCA}) + e$$

Expectations for the effect of income on the dependant variable, in contrast to the test on low-income countries, is positive since the form of animism practiced in the United States is generally distinguished by its lower time costs (for example, regular church service attendance is not a part of New Age practices). But since our dependent variable does not distinguish between New Age religions and more occult forms of animism, it may well be that for persons of low incomes, consumption of some of the more traditional forms of animism (e.g., Tarot cards and palmistry) will be inversely related to educational level. Thus we expect the income variable, **LINC**, to be positive on balance and the education variable, **LHSG**, to be negative. Finally, we have included two additional variables in our test, the percentage of Hispanics in each state and a dummy variable for the state of California. Hispanics have a long tradition, reaching back to pre-Columbian Indian heritage, of animistic beliefs. Further, most New Age and psychic movements have had their origins in the state of California. Both variables are expected to carry positive signs in our regression.

Regression results are provided in table 4A.3 and, in general, conform to expectations. Note that in the test results described in table 4A.3 we use a statistical procedure called a two-tailed test. A two-tailed test, in contrast to the one-tailed test used in our test of animist religions, is a procedure to evaluate a statistical regression that does not make a specific prediction about whether the cause-and-effect relation is positive or negative. (We may, of course, have expectations as to these relations). The data itself tells the story. In all tests the higher the percentage the

Table 4A.3
Impact of income, education, hispanic population on number of psychics, spiritual advisors, and mediums in forty-six U.S. states

Dependent variable = LPPC

Independent variables	Coefficient	Statistical error	T-value
Constant	−37.16574	11.893	−3.125
LINC	5.03145	1.1714	4.295*
LHSG	−2.99820	2.1598	−1.388
LPCTHIS	0.23868	0.1459	1.636*
DCAL	2.70567	0.98332	2.752*

Sources: Number of psychics by authors' calculations; all other variables, *Statistical Abstract of the United States,* 2002.
* indicates significance at 1 percent level (two-tailed test statistics).

level of significance, the more confidence we have in the results. It appears that income is positively and significantly related to the dependent variable, at least insofar as the latter measures less time-intensive New Age beliefs. At the same time the education variable is negatively, but insignificantly, related to the dependent variable signifying that at least certain types of animistic beliefs emerge from low-education (low-income) Americans. These results suggest some support for the interpretation that forms of animism and highly individualistic beliefs coexist among high- and low-income individuals in developed high-income societies. Finally our interpretation that Hispanic population and Californians support animistic forms of religion is given strong support in the regression results of table 4A.3. These two tests of the determinants of animism and the use of psychics, preliminary as they may be, appear to suggest that full price, income, education, and demand shifters in general have an enormous impact on the form of religion chosen in both less developed and more developed nations.

5

Economics of the Protestant Revolt

Rome, your avidity deludes you, and you shear too much wool from your sheep. So great is your avarice that you pardon sins for money.
—Félix Rocquain, *La Cour de Rome, et l'Esprit de Réforme avant Luther*, vol. 2

When land, like movables, is considered as the means only of subsistence and enjoyment, the natural law of succession divides it, like them, among all the children of the family.... But when land was considered as the means, not of subsistence merely, but of power and protection, it was thought better that it should descend undivided to one.
—Adam Smith, *The Wealth of Nations*

Readers who have persevered this far have been asked to consider that changes in the form of religion take place as rational decisions determined by comparisons of benefits and costs. Individuals demand a Z-good, religious services, for which they pay some full price (monetary and time costs) and receive some benefits. Demand for this Z-good is determined by a number of factors, including, but not limited to, income, education, and risk tolerance. In societies that allow plural religions to compete with each other, religious entrepreneurs adjust product characteristics to match different sets of demands and, in the process, sometimes create alternative forms of religion.

In this chapter we employ the economics of religion in order to deepen our understanding of the first major break in the Roman Catholic religious monopoly, the Protestant Reformation. Prior to the Protestant Reformation there had been numerous attempts to break into the medieval religious market dominated by Catholicism. But earlier attempts fomented by Christian "heretics" (e.g., the Gnostics and Cathars) were put down, often violently, by the Roman Catholic Church. So the issue that confronts us is as much a matter of timing as it is of substance. In order to explain why the Protestant Reformation occurred when it did, as well as why it did, we enlist the language and theory of economics. We treat the medieval Roman Catholic Church as a firm that provided religious and legal services and used its market power to extract rents from its customers. We assert that by the late Middle Ages the Catholic Church was pricing its product too high in full-price terms to dissuade market entry by rival Protestant churches, and we attempt to test this theory by comparing regions that remained Catholic to those that switched to Protestantism.

The extensive literature on the Protestant Reformation contains essentially three competing hypotheses. The first, advanced by Protestant theologians, maintains that the Catholic Church gradually lost influence because it became ethically and morally corrupt. The second, advanced by historians, asserts that circumstances forced the Catholic Church to take sides in a series of conflicts between emergent northern European states and emergent cities. Its side often lost, leading to the Catholic Church's gradual decline of influence and prestige. The third, advanced by economists, follows an argument originated by Adam Smith in 1776: It holds that state-supported religious monopolies behave inefficiently in many ways, thereby opening up the possibility of entry by more efficient competitors.

We first advanced the idea that rent extraction through the selling of spiritual services at very high prices had important historical consequences about a decade ago.[1] One major finding of our earlier research was that control by religious authorities of portions of the legal system provides market power that can be used to exclude rivals. Thus, we were able to refine Adam Smith's general argument regarding inefficiency of monopolies, and simultaneously support Iannaccone's contention that religious monopolies do a poor job of providing religious services. We achieved this by explicitly recognizing rent extraction in the Roman Catholic Church's administration of justice and in exercising its gatekeeper function (control of the keys to heaven). We now advance an additional argument, that if the religious monopoly overcharges, it risks two forms of entry: (1) the common citizenry may choose other dispensers of religious services; and (2) the civil authorities may seek a different provider of legal services. The Protestant Reformation may be seen, in part, as a manifestation of both forms of entry.

Our explanation of religious form change explores supply-side as well as demand-side factors affecting the timing and acceptance of the Protestant Reformation. We recognize that the Protestant Reformation was neither a singular nor a homogeneous event. In discussing it, therefore, we accept Max Weber's stylized version. According to Weber, "the complete elimination of salvation through Church and the sacraments (which was in Lutheranism by no means developed to its final conclusions), was what formed the absolutely decisive difference from Catholicism."[2] We argue that the medieval church extracted rents by practicing sophisticated forms of price discrimination and that this gave new encouragement to market entry by a rival "firm" offering a modified "product." Moreover, we seek to test this hypothesis as best we can with limited historical data. Our test rests on the premise that the medieval church was most likely to maintain its incumbent-monopoly position in less heterogeneous, semi-feudal, rent-seeking societies that were mostly dissipating rather than creating wealth, whereas Protestant entry was most likely to occur in emerging market-order societies that were creating wealth through expansion of profit opportunities.

Superficially our hypothesis may appear to resemble Weber's sociohistorical view which maintains that Protestantism emerged in areas of highest economic development, that is, those most favorable to a revolution in the Church. But Weber's thesis is closely linked to Calvinism, which, according to Richard H. Tawney, was seriously divided between its teachings and its practice (at least in England and Holland).[3] In these markets, interference in business and control of economic enterprise by state and church leaders was resisted by budding entrepreneurs and capitalists. According to Tawney, this desire for independence from traditional authority reflected Weber's true meaning of the "spirit of capitalism." Protestantism, in short, not only molded the social and economic order, but was molded by it. Our argument, in contrast, asserts that individuals, seeking higher net utility, opted for a lower cost, implicit contract.

In the Middle Ages rent-seeking societies were characterized by tradition-bound rules and practices that encouraged alliances between church, state, and aristocracy, and by a stable, concentrated distribution of wealth. The emerging market-order societies were characterized by the entrepreneurial spirit, and by increasing opportunities to participate in market activities and to earn profits. The resulting distribution of wealth was fluid and unstable, and increasingly heterogeneous with respect to social class and status. In this setting the Catholic Church's system of price discrimination induced many of the faithful to embrace a substitute religion.

An Economic Theory of Luther's Entry

Our economic theory of Protestant entry contains demand-side and supply-side elements. Demand-side elements explain the individual and collective choices to embrace or reject a new religion. Rational individuals will switch forms of religion if the benefits exceed the costs of doing so. Supply-side elements explain how and why an incumbent monopolist like the Roman Catholic Church could be successful in barring new entry into its religious market.

The Demand Side: High Full Prices in a Monopolistic Religious Market

Most medieval church historians agree that the sale of indulgences by the Catholic Church played a prominent role in encouraging competitive entry by competing religions. Indeed, the proximate cause of Martin Luther's successful challenge of prevailing authority is almost universally held to be the Catholic Church's record of abuses involving indulgences. In a somewhat wider view, we assert that part of the explanation for the rise, and ultimate success, of Protestantism was the attempt by the Catholic Church to extract rents associated with manifold doctrinal innovations, among them the interwoven doctrines of purgatory, penance, and indulgences.

As with any monopoly, the aim of the medieval church was to eliminate competition. It used various methods to accomplish this objective, including political and social pressures against unorthodox dissenters (i.e., heretics) within its ranks, as well as against rival sects, such as Judaism and Islam. It also denounced magic and superstition, which had been practiced from early pre-Christian times. The medieval church devised various means to deal with internal and external threats to its market dominance, such as excommunication, crusades, and inquisitions. But since it was always the prerogative of individuals to self-select among formal and informal belief systems, the Roman Catholic Church had to maintain the quality of its product in order to prevent slippage, and in the face of potential competition it was required to price its services so as to attract new customers. When quality deterioration resulted in a higher full price for its product, the papacy took steps to retain, attract, or regain members. It met some heretics on their own grounds. For example, when internal heresies protested the medieval church's policies of wealth aggrandizement in the face of grinding poverty of the masses, the church responded by forming mendicant orders, such as the Dominicans and Franciscans, which specialized in ministry to the poor. In another example of policy accommodation, the church reduced relative prices for certain services provided to members of the English Church, which had always been more independent of Rome than its European counterparts.

The chief price confronted by individual church members over the first millennium was imposed by the terms of an uncomplicated offer of redemption. Despite the fact that temporal punishments and other forms of penance were administered through the confessional, in which some sins or infractions were more serious than others, individual penitents exercised discrete choice between eternal salvation and eternal damnation. Before the doctrine of purgatory and its accoutrements, the medieval church did not offer a continuum of choices, certainly none with a holding tank—purgatory—before salvation was ultimately attained. The invention and formalization of a package of new doctrines around the eleventh and twelfth centuries, discussed more fully in the following section, fundamentally changed the nature of medieval church doctrine and hence the full price of the church's product. Taken together, the invention of purgatory, the distinction between venial and mortal sins, auricular confession, and, most importantly, the granting of indulgences, created a continuum of price-behavior choices by which individuals might attain the main religious product, spiritual redemption. In the medieval Catholic Church, redemption was to be attained by living a virtuous life and/or making expiation for sins. Catholic theology held

Full price

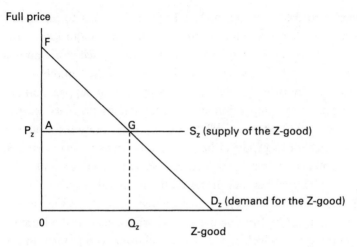

Figure 5.1
Demand and supply of Z-good

that by his death, Jesus bestowed the opportunity of redemption on all. Nevertheless, the actual achievement of redemption required conscious choices by the faithful. In effect, the choice offered to its members by the medieval church became continuous. Paradoxically, the doctrinal inventions referred to above initially lowered the price of sin (making them inconsistent with a public interest theory of church behavior), but they also created ever-expanding opportunities for rent extraction by raising the costs of redemption to church members.

In its role as gatekeeper of heaven, the medieval church engaged in activities akin to those that take place in a system of criminal justice. Although crime and sin are not the same, deterrence can be used against them similarly. Figure 5.1 depicts the demand for the Z-good religious services (D_z). It is negatively sloped and reflects the maximum demand price believers would be willing to pay for forgiveness. The invention of purgatory, the distinction between venial and mortal sins, and other innovations employed by the medieval church gave form to the demand function D_z. In contrast, the supply curve of forgiveness was dependent on the church's long-run costs of providing a belief structure. This included the costs of formulating doctrine, providing liturgy, establishing enforcement mechanisms in downstream church "firms" (e.g., confession), administering the sacraments, collecting relics, and so on. An equilibrium price of forgiveness, such as P_z, is consistent with this market view.

As in the case of the suppression of crime, some optimum may be reached,[4] such as Q_z in figure 5.1. For various reasons we do not believe that optimal deterrence was a major goal of the medieval church. Optimal deterrence means that punishment is levied in proportion to the severity of the crime or, in this case, sin. The instances of price discrimination described by the great ecclesiastical historian William E. Lunt suggest that the overriding goal of the medieval church was infra-marginal rent extraction, and that optimal deterrence—while perhaps a secondary goal—was subservient to the primary goal of rent extraction. While these two goals are not mutually exclusive, it should be noted that if the church achieved optimal deterrence, it would thereby undermine its revenue base from potential rents. Historical evidence suggests that the medieval church stood in the position of a nearly perfectly discriminating monopoly. The goal was to put all sinners on their demand curve for sin and forgiveness, thereby creating a situation in which maximum monopoly rents (in the amount of AFG in figure 5.1) could be collected. Optimal deterrence would have required the medieval church to set different prices for different sins, which, in fact, it did not do (see table 5.1 and the ensuing discussion). Instead, the church set different prices for different *customers*, based on their income. We hypothesize that overzealous price discrimination—fostered by ongoing doctrinal manipulations—led to the Protestant Reformation and the institution of a less costly pricing scheme, as well as the introduction of less restrictive conditions for salvation. At the same time, certain supply-side considerations allowed the Roman Catholic Church to maintain its power in some markets.

In some instances the implementation of price discriminatory schemes by the medieval church may have been accompanied by deterioration of church services. Of course this issue of reduced quality turns critically on how quality is defined. If "underprovision" of services means that the needs of the poor were neglected, we have found little evidence that this was the case. Historian Bronislaw Geremek distinguishes between "spiritual poverty," and "involuntary poverty."[5] The former is practiced by monks and hermits on a voluntary basis, whereas the latter is a result of inadequate resource endowments or economic inefficiency. The church always viewed the involuntary poor as objects of special charitable treatment (though malingerers and those who would not work were denounced by church and civil government alike). In medieval society, the deserving poor were cared for by both the church and the wealthy. Typically a third of the Roman Catholic Church's total "take" was given to the poor. But to a certain extent poverty and wealth were complementary in medieval society.[6] The poor in effect helped save the wealthy when the latter supported the former as an act of repentance for sins. Thus a sizable redistribution was sponsored by church doctrines and regulations, and the wealthy, in turn, supported church and papal interests. The poor thus provided a rationale for the existence of wealth. This, however, does not mean that the church underprovided services. Geremek notes that the models for the later provisions of social services were provided by Catholic charities. In the twelfth and thirteenth centuries, for example, hospitals and hospices were founded and administered by the church in France.[7] Further, while urbanization created an upsurge in poverty in the sixteenth and later centuries in Europe, a good deal of modern research shows that the medieval church actually provided important models for later Protestant innovations in the urban structuring of charitable and social services. Historian Brian S. Pullan shows that church activities in fourteenth and fifteenth century Renaissance Venice provided such a model.[8] Diminished quality provisions, though certainly possible and perhaps even expected in a monopoly without tradable shares or other forms of market discipline, might have the effect of pushing some individuals beyond their demand curves and possibly encouraging earlier entry into the market. It is recognized that quality diminution may take a number of forms, including personal and church aggrandizement, weak attempts to stimulate fervor and devotion among the faithful, or less liberal hospitality.[9] Further study will be required to identify such causes of increase in the full price of religion during the Middle Ages.

Supply-Side Elements: Taxing Wealth

The conditions necessary for the medieval church to enjoy continual success in maintaining its market dominance were the following: First, there had to be a large reserve of wealth to tap, which was the case in those societies where feudal institutions maintained a prosperous landed class, or other societal arrangements supported the concentration of wealth. Second, the prevailing wealth distribution had to be relatively stable in order to repay the Church's investment in information and to keep transaction costs associated with its pricing strategy relatively low. It was, for example, costly to establish, maintain, and change the price lists that provided the backbone of the Church's pricing strategy (which is elaborated on in table 5.1). Hence, the Church was interested in minimizing these costs as much as possible.

These two conditions were most easily met in tradition-bound, authoritarian societies in which the landed aristocracy typically engaged in rent-seeking rather than profit-seeking activities. In other words, the medieval church was most likely to preserve its incumbent monopoly status in semi-feudal societies that had a lot of low-income people (peasants) who were, at best, minor targets of the Church's discriminatory policies, and a strong landed class (nobility) which typically cut their own deals with the Church and routinely engaged in rent-seeking activity. By contrast, the medieval church found it difficult to continue its practice of price discrimination in societies that encouraged profit seeking by offering opportunities for increased market participation among less-favored economic classes. Where the power of the monarch was relatively weak and the ownership of property was widely dispersed, an ever-growing middle class was able to take advantage of new profit opportunities. The distribution of wealth in such societies was constantly changing, making it more difficult for the Church to engage in effective price discrimination. Societies in which political and economic power were decentralized rather than centralized therefore presented impediments to the ongoing profitability of the medieval church.

Price Discrimination in the Medieval Religion Market

The first prerequisite for a firm to practice price discrimination is the existence of monopoly power, which the Church had acquired by the Middle Ages. The medieval church took on the posture of a vertically integrated, dominant firm, capable of engaging in product innovation, differentiation, and development.[10] From the twelfth century on, it introduced doctrinal innovations that encouraged and facilitated the practice of price discrimination. Through these innovations, church managers were able to manipulate both the quality of their product (i.e., the solidarity of its redemptive promise), and the full price of membership in its spiritual body.

The second prerequisite for price discrimination is separable markets. Arbitrage means buying in one market for simultaneous sale in another. If arbitrage is possible, price discrimination will break down. Separation of markets is, of course, easier to achieve with services than with tangible products. The Church issued general rules and regulations respecting the redemption of souls, but local bishops, and especially parish priests, interpreted and applied these rules. The establishment of the requirement of auricular confession (ultimately mandated at least once a year for all church members) provided an efficient means of levying discriminatory tariffs on penitents. The intimate, small-scale nature of medieval towns and villages allowed priests to determine income profiles and other personal information about their parishioners.[11]

Finally, price discrimination requires the absence of available substitutes, and variations in the elasticity of demand across customers. Elasticity of demand refers to the intensity of wants. That different groups of customers had different demand elasticities is self-evident. The stronger one's belief in the afterlife, the more intense is the demand to achieve heaven. There were also strong social pressures to belong to the medieval church, especially for monarchs, aristocrats, and other people of wealth. The practice of papal investiture, which gave popes veto power over monarchs, meant that a good relation with the Church, at least formally, was often prerequisite to acceptance by the governed. Throughout the Middle Ages, the church and secular authorities were constantly vying for the upper hand. By 1516, French, Portuguese, and Spanish monarchs had complete control over the naming of Catholic bishops in their domains, so it was not always clear who controlled whom, but the pressure to belong to the church remained strong among the wealthy.

Social and economic pressures constrained the wealthy to few religious alternatives, but the poor had considerably more options, and therefore much higher demand elasticity. Their access to popular heresies (such as those found in southern France and Italy) and superstitions, especially those trailing the wake of the Black Death, created a number of substitutes that did not transfer across social strata to wealthier individuals. Equally evident in medieval society was the dearth of practical substitutes. Judaism was not a proselytizing religion, and, except for lingering Muslim influence in Spain, Islam was confined to the periphery of the European continent.

Successive doctrinal innovations quickened and intensified the practice of price discrimination by the medieval church, as indulgences, auricular confession, the dichotomy between moral and venial sins, and a number of other doctrinal practices provided more opportunities to extract rents from the faithful. One example involved opportunistic use of the usury doctrine. Since church doctrine treated usury as theft, confessors customarily withheld forgiveness until restitution was made. Often, the amount of restitution was based on the usurer's wealth. In the case of deathbed restitution, the Church took the money if the usurer was uncertain (*incerta*) about the identity of the wronged parties, which was a common occurrence.[12]

The explicit payment schedules for indulgences demonstrate the economic sophistication of the church managers. Product innovations of the Church were relatively new when it began to link price discrimination with indulgences to encourage participation in the Crusades. Gregory VIII was apparently the first pope to obtain money in this fashion, but his successors learned quickly. For example, in 1188 Pope Clement ordered the archbishop of Canterbury to command subsidies from the faithful for which the bishop "was empowered to grant them remission of sins proportioned to the 'quality of the person and the quantity of the subvention.'"[13] The collection and handling of monies from these partial indulgences became increasingly efficient throughout the twelfth century (beginning with Pope Innocent III). As the Middle Ages wore on, rent seeking through the sale of indulgences (for crusading and a variety of purposes) accelerated throughout Europe. Papal bulls countenanced differential pricing with regard to the granting of indulgences. Lunt describes a three-tiered system whereby the highest price was paid by the wealthy, an intermediate price by middle-class members, and a low price by the poor.[14] In Scotland a five-tier pricing schedule was imposed for the jubilee year of 1475.[15] New devices for collection and refined schedules were a hallmark of rent seeking in the later period. Pope Alexander VI (1492–1503) routinely directed papal agents to press the faithful for more "donations."

Papal agents also showed considerable sophistication in devising price-discriminatory schemes. For example, Jasper Ponce, the papal agent to England during the late fifteenth and early sixteenth centuries, developed a schedule of "gifts" for a plenary indulgence with three categories of givers (laymen owning substantial real property, laymen owning substantial movable property, and clergy owning substantial real property). Each category contained four to seven differentiated tariffs based on personal income.[16] Ponce and his deputies were given complete power for the absolution of *all* sins, mortal and venial, excepting only those committed directly against the papacy itself.[17] During the reign of Henry VII, the same principles were incorporated into the establishment of a "jubilee indulgence" in 1501. This last schedule is replicated below as table 5.1. This kind of evidence confirms that the medieval church was engaging in (second-degree) price discrimination. Economist Sam Peltzman has taught us that opportunities for increasing producer wealth through price discrimination are never fully exploited because complete exploitation would narrow the consumer base of the monopoly's constituency.[18] This was no less true in the Middle Ages, when the invention of purgatory made it easier for the medieval church to levy huge taxes on wealthy sinners, making Protestant entry easier, other things equal. But entry occurred on a selective basis, as we shall demonstrate momentarily.

There is, of course, no self-selection here—one's income or the real value of his property is determined a priori—but the monopolist sets out charges ex ante on finely graded income classes. Note that the wealthiest property owners were charged the highest amounts regardless of whether their property was fixed or movable. Moreover, clergy were not spared the indulgence tax—if anything, the tax was stiffer on prelates and monasteries. The rich paid dearly, and only the poorest escaped with payments geared to "their level of devotion," indicating a high degree of price discrimination.

While the schedule shown in table 5.1 was produced specifically for England, papal agents used a variety of taxes throughout Christendom. Judging from the papal records, fraud was common and malfeasance

Table 5.1
Papal bull establishing jubilee indulgences in England, 1501

Fixed property (tenements, rents, etc.)	Rates of levy
(all individuals earning above £2,000 per annum)	£3, 6s., 8d.
Fixed property (secular)	
£1,000–£2,000	£ 40s.
£400–£1,000	26s., 8d.
£200–£400	13s., 4d.
£100–£200	6s., 8d.
£40–£100	2s., 6d.
£20–£40	16d.
Fixed property (clergy)	
£2,000>	£10
£1,000–£2,000	10 marks
£500–£1,000	£3, 6s., 8d.
£200–£400	40s.
£100–£200	20s.
£40–£100	10s.
Fixed property > £40 plus movable property > £1,000	40s.
(secular)	
Movable property (secular)	
£400–£1,000	6s., 8d.
£200–£400	2s., 6d.
£20–£200	12d.
£0–£20	(level of devotion)

Source: William E. Lunt, *Papal Revenues in the Middle Ages*, vol. 2 (New York: Columbia University Press, 1934), 481–482.

was dealt with severely through excommunication. Typically, chests were installed in churches where the faithful might deposit offerings for the forgiveness of sins. Three different keys were required to open the chest: one was held by the bishop, another by the parish priest, and a third by a devout laymen.[19] Around 1512, wealthy banking families, such as the German Fuggars, became papal agents for the collection of indulgence receipts and other forms of taxes.[20] These agents had sweeping powers. The kind and severity of taxes multiplied as the Middle Ages wore on. Temporary levies became permanent, and many new taxes were imposed on the wealthiest church members. Church documents reveal that sons and grandsons of heretics had to pay up for the sins of their fathers, "compounded at least at 25 ducats if poor, otherwise, as much as can be had."[21] Vows and oaths were commuted on payment (except those relating to chastity or religious orders), the souls of deceased relatives could be extricated from purgatory for fees, and those leaving money or gifts for crusades "in their wills would receive an indulgence proportioned to the quality of their persons and the extent of their resources."[22]

Historians agree that the market for indulgences provided the church an important means of extracting wealth from the faithful. Another market that provided rent-seeking opportunities for the medieval church, although less emphasized by historians, is the marriage market. In the Middle Ages, the most prominent device for accumulating wealth, especially landed property, was the dynastic family. Marriages were arranged with this in mind. Endogamy regulations established who could marry within a kinship group, or degree of "blood." Marriage between brother and sister was a first-degree relation, between first cousins, a second-degree relation, and so forth. The medieval church found an opportunity to manipulate these regulations in its interest. It could extract higher payments from dynastic families by attaching "redemptive promises" to the marriage contract. Consanguinity exemptions were paid for by the wealthy, not the poor, who were permitted to plead *in forma pauperum*,[23] yet another manifestation of a high degree of price discrimination. The threat of excommunication for lying about one's income served as an enforcement mechanism. Marriages based on kinship as high as the seventh degree were prohibited, making it easy to find (or manufacture) an illegal tie. In his analysis of papal financial records, Lunt uncovered the fact that Maximillian, Duke of Austria and Burgundy, paid 2,250 ducats for a matrimonial dispensation, a considerable sum during the Middle Ages.[24] Strong evidence that exemptions for endogamy were routinely granted to the aristocracy for high prices or for political favors has also been presented by medieval historian Georges Duby[25] and by economists Audrey B. Davidson and Robert B. Ekelund Jr.[26] Differential punishments levied for these and other victimless crimes such as usury suggest again that neither optimal deterrence nor efficient punishment were immediate goals of church policy. Rent seeking rather than welfare maximization appears to have driven the Church's actions.

Protestant Entry

Through time, the Church continued to direct doctrine and practice to extract as much consumer surplus as possible from the faithful by implementing various second- and third-degree forms of discrimination. The Church, in short, manipulated both the quality and the full price of its product so as to put members on the margin of defection. Protestantism offered a cheaper, alternative path to salvation by eliminating the priest as middleman. The new religion held that personal salvation did not come from the institutional church but directly from the grace of God; hence the believer was saved by faith, which was considered, in turn, to be a gift from God. In its initial form Protestantism had fewer mechanisms through which its agents could extract rents, so that, in effect, it sold redemption much cheaper, even allowing for the seemingly random allocation of God's grace. This lower-cost alternative might be especially attractive to the wealthy, who saw the prospect of regaining some or all of their consumer surplus that the Catholic Church was taking from them.

Protestantism also repudiated the formalism and much of the complexity of Catholic dogma, as did all of the reform movements, whether espoused by Luther, Calvin, Zwingli, or others. This prospect of independence from the institutional church, with its plethora of rules and regulations, and the emphasis Protestantism bestowed on "in-kind" expenditures, such as "good works," instead of monetary payments, constituted a clean break with established religion. This break had its own attendant costs, but such costs may have been perceived as less burdensome than those imposed by the Catholic Church's strategy of price discrimination, which weighed more heavily over time, tending to drive certain believers to the brink of defection. The theology embodied in the new contract offered by Protestantism did not merely substitute an in-kind payment (e.g., "good works") for a monetary one (e.g., the purchase of indulgences). In the new religion the individual who is saved by faith (grace) would necessarily demonstrate that saving grace in the practice of good works. Most laymen probably thought they were earning salvation by good works, not just demonstrating their faith, but this is contrary to Protestant and traditional Christian doctrine. According to Weber, good works "are the technical means, not of purchasing salvation, but of getting rid of the fear of damnation. In this sense they are occasionally referred to as directly necessary for salvation. ... Thus the Calvinist ... himself creates his own salvation, or, as would be more correct, the conviction of it. But this creation cannot, as in Catholicism, consist in a gradual accumulation of good works to one's credit, but rather in a systematic self-control which at every moment stands before the inexorable alternative, chosen or damned."[27] In a further defining moment, Weber asserted, "There was no place [in Protestantism] for the very human Catholic cycle of sin, repentance, atonement, release, followed by renewed sin. Nor was there any balance of merit for a life as a whole which could be adjusted by temporal punishments or the Church's means of grace."[28]

Despite the obvious appeal of a simple, direct, and relatively inexpensive path to salvation, Protestantism did not meet with universal success. To understand the ability of the medieval church to maintain its incumbent monopoly status in the face of this new challenge, we look to the supply-side elements of our theory.

Rent Seeking versus Profit Seeking

Our theory predicts that, other things equal, rent-seeking societies would reject Protestantism, whereas profit-seeking societies would embrace it. How well does this theory hold up to the historical record? Did Catholicism eventually price its product so as to drive away large numbers of customers seeking redemption at a lower cost? Incomplete or unreliable data from an era so far removed in time make these questions difficult to resolve in any conclusive sense, but we have devised a two-stage test in an attempt to find evidential support of our theory. The first test treats the institutional practice of primogeniture as a proxy for income distribution. The second test correlates changes in city size (i.e., urban growth) to the practice of primogeniture in those countries where such laws existed.

It is clear that larger historical forces were at work than those that can be captured and made operational in a stylized theory such as ours. For example, economists Andrei Shleifer and Robert W. Vishny demonstrated that pre-industrial absolutist governments are associated with low economic growth.[29] We hypothesize that in a low-growth environment such as occurred in the Middle Ages, one means the Church could use to maintain its market hegemony was restrictive property laws. Feudal forms of property differ from capitalist forms of property. Some countries practiced primogeniture and some did not. Primogeniture was confined mostly to Europe and was practiced mainly among the upper classes, which were entrenched within a centralized power system. The intent of the law was ostensibly to concentrate wealth in the hands of few dynastic families, but by disinheriting younger children, it could also cause untold bitterness within the family. For these reasons, practice often diverged from the letter of the law.

In those societies that resisted an emergent market order, children were key to dynastic survival. Too many children, particularly adult males, strained and sometimes destroyed the resources of houses practicing partible inheritance. But too few children created even worse problems. Somewhere in the minds of medieval kings and princes always lurked the fear that they would not have a legitimate male heir. No one knew how many sons were needed for a line to survive. Statistical norms, if they existed, were not reliable. Child mortality rates were high. Royal inbreeding exacerbated the problem. The mortality of adult firstborns was always in doubt. Yet, primogeniture could induce landless sons to remain bachelors, thereby reducing the pool of eligible heirs. Dynastic families not only considered it a duty to have children but also to care for them, which meant not only providing nurture and basic education, but also launching them into the adult world with some measure of economic security, namely, mate and property.

Important to understanding rival entry into the religious market in the sixteenth century is the question of how primogeniture laws may have influenced individual decisions to embrace Protestantism and reject Catholicism. Cultural anthropologist Jack Goody maintained that the medieval church, as early as the sixth but definitively in the eleventh century, manipulated the marriage market and inheritance prospects in its own favor by limiting kinship claims to land and property.[30] The Church may have supported primogeniture for similar reasons. But we regard the following hypothesis as more persuasive.

Given its institutional milieu, the medieval church served as a kind of insurer, or employer of last resort, to the landed aristocracy. Younger sons could become retainers through ecclesiastical sinecure, a station that could be relinquished if the eldest son died. Moreover, female children could also find ready employment in the Church. As Historian P. Sutter Fichtner observed, "Catholics had a better way to enjoy the advantages of primogeniture, yet live with their consciences over the treatment of younger sons. They could still arrange appropriate livings for their offspring in the church."[31] Prince-bishops, which is what many of the nobility became, were assured that as high church officials they could maintain a lifestyle befitting their dynastic station. Ecclesiastical careers did not bar anyone from secular dynastic affairs, and even if they had, ecclesiastic nobles had little trouble returning to secular life. The medieval church, in other words, approved of primogeniture precisely because it promoted the kind of stability of wealth distribution that enabled it to successfully price-discriminate among certain members, and because it extended the Church's control over kinship, which was an ongoing concern in its constant battle with dynastic families for political and economic control. Simultaneously, the practice of primogeniture provided an incentive to the heads of dynastic families to remain within the system of established religious practice.

Primogeniture and Protestant Entry

As a preliminary test of this proposition, we gathered data on the principal entry points of Protestantism and compared the acceptance of the new religion with the conditions most likely to encourage its success or failure. Our stylized theory predicts that societies enforcing primogeniture would be most likely to remain Catholic, whereas those societies with more fluid property laws (and hence more opportunities for wealth enhancement by a larger strata of society) would find Protestantism more palatable. One possible drawback of this theory is that it treats primogeniture as exogenous, which may not have been the case. At this point, however, we do not have the historical wherewithal to construct a model that makes primogeniture fully endogenous.

Table 5.2 is replicated from a sociological study undertaken by Guy Swanson.[32] It shows the pattern of primogeniture in various European countries where Protestantism competed with Catholicism in the sixteenth and seventeenth centuries.

Table 5.2
Civil governments, religious choice and primogeniture

Society	Religion	Final settlement	Regime established	Primo-geniture
Austria	Catholic	1620	1521	Yes
Bavaria	Catholic	1564	1505	Yes
Berg-Jülich	Catholic	1614	1423	
Florence	Catholic		1282–1366	Yes
France	Catholic	1685	1460	Yes
Ireland	Catholic		1350	Yes
Poland	Catholic	1607	1490–1573	Yes
Portugal	Catholic		1490	Yes
Scottish Highlands	Catholic		Before 1400	Yes
Spain	Catholic		1492	Yes
Venice	Catholic		1297	Yes
Swiss Confederation				—
Fribourg	Catholic		1469	No
Lucerne	Catholic		1424	No
Schwyz	Catholic		1353	
Solothurn	Catholic	1533	1533	No
Unterwalden	Catholic		Before 1400	
Uri	Catholic		1373	
Zug	Catholic		1415	
Bohemia	Protestant	1593	1500	
Brandenburg-Prussia	Protestant	1613	1450–1500	No
Cleves-Mark	Protestant	1569	1480–1490	No
Denmark	Protestant	1536	1523	No
England	Protestant	1553	1400–1485	No
Geneva	Protestant	1536	1530	
Hesse	Protestant	1605	1500	No
Hungary	Protestant	1540	1500	No
Saxony	Protestant	1539	1425	No
Scottish Lowlands	Protestant	1560	1470–1490	Yes
Sweden	Protestant	1536	1523	No
Swiss Confederation				—
Appenzell	Protestant	1524	1513	No
Basle	Protestant	1528	1521	No
Bern	Protestant	1528	1500	No
Glarus	Protestant	1532	1387–1450	No
Schaffhausen	Protestant	1530	1411	
Zurich	Protestant	1525	1444–1519	
Transylvania	Protestant	1557	1541	
United Provinces	Protestant	1579	1579	
Würtemberg	Protestant	1535	1514	No

Source: Guy E. Swanson, *Religion and Regime* (Ann Arbor, Mich.: University of Michigan Press, 1967), 233–241.

The first column in table 5.2 shows the geopolitical divisions common to western Europe at about the time Protestantism emerged. Certain countries existing today were not united prior to 1700. Hence, Florence and Venice appear in table 5.2, but Italy does not. Likewise, Switzerland was not a unified country. It consisted of Geneva, on the one hand, and thirteen loosely confederated cantons, on the other. Certain Germanic principalities appear, but no unified Germany yet existed. The second column indicates whether each society remained Catholic or became Protestant. The date of final settlement is the year given by Swanson as the point at which the issue of religious choice was decided once and for all. The fourth column indicates the establishment date of the political regime in place at the time of final settlement. The final column indicates whether or not the regime enforced primogeniture or similar laws of entail.

It is difficult to get accurate data on all of the principalities involved, partly because controlling legislation is relevant only to a specific and limited time frame, and partly because the autonomy of several principalities eroded over time, and with it their geopolitical identities disappeared. Of the thirty-eight principalities in Swanson's study, we have been able to verify institutional practice on partible inheritance for roughly 70 percent of the regimes. We have been unable to find conclusive data on the rest. Nevertheless, these preliminary findings are interesting from several different perspectives. Among other things, they provide reasonable support for our thesis. They show that, by and large, those societies ruled by primogeniture remained Catholic, whereas those with partible inheritance laws embraced Protestantism.

The principalities that remained Catholic against the Protestant threat shared certain characteristics. For the most part, they were semi-feudal and tradition-bound. Austria, Bavaria, France, Spain, Portugal, Ireland, and the Italian city-states were rent-seeking societies, intent on preserving existing wealth, but hostile to the creation of new wealth because they limited access to land and to emergent market opportunities. The nobility in these societies was essentially parasitic, deriving their patronage from the monarch, who kept their powers in check. In some respects, Italy is a special case. Clearly, Venice and the other city-states, especially

Florence, prospered before and during the Renaissance. Nevertheless, because these cities, their governments, and their regulations were inextricably intertwined with papal interests, we categorize them as rent seeking in nature. The leading families of the Italian city-states had, for centuries, stood in a close financial position with the Church. Some families, like the Medicis, effectively inherited high offices of the Church, including the papacy itself. Italian business interests engaged in provisioning for the Crusades, banking for the Vatican,[33] and management of the papal cartel over Italy's alum mines.[34] It should be noted also that in Italy, as in France, a large number of nobles entered the Church, giving the landed interests disproportionate representation among the clergy. British historian John M. Roberts observed, "So large was the number of Lombard nobles entering the Church that it was inevitable that the Lombard families should be well represented in the higher ranks of the clergy."[35] And historian John McManners added, "For younger sons especially, the Church could serve as a system of luxurious outdoor relief."[36]

Austria and Bavaria were part of the far-flung Habsburg Empire, in which the Ottoman menace generated a strong desire to keep family estates intact. Unlike England, moreover, the Austrian nobility did not supplement their income by commercial or industrial ventures.[37] The gulf between the rich and the poor was perhaps widest in France, where the wealth of the nobility depended on the near-absolute power of the monarch. Spain and Portugal maintained centralized monarchies on the French pattern. Ireland's rigid land-tenure system worked to keep fortunes concentrated in few, mostly absentee, hands. Separate nobility classes existed in each of the Italian city-states, but all derived their wealth from land, which was preserved by the institution of primogeniture.

The lower half of table 5.2 shows the principalities that embraced Protestantism. In Bohemia the nobility had expelled the clergy from the Diet, and appropriated most of the wealth of the Church before the advent of Protestantism so that the Church was powerless in the face of the new religion.[38] Bohemia was the center of the Hussites, a sect devoted to the principle of Utraquism, the communion of the laity under the species of wine as well as bread, which in medieval times was officially reserved only for the Catholic clergy. In terms of heretical belief, it was a conservative movement. Nevertheless, in its desire to subordinate papal and conciliar authority to that of the Bible, it was recognized by Martin Luther as a significant prelude to the Protestant Reformation.

In Prussia and the German territories, as elsewhere in medieval times, the wealth of the nobility was based on land, but ancient custom sanctioned the right of each noble to apportion his private holdings at will among his sons, regardless of their order of birth. In the Middle Ages German principalities were characterized by weak emperors and fragmented politics. Germany was, moreover, distinctive for its developed urban life. Its land mass was covered by a dense network of almost two thousand towns, spread more or less uniformly across the countryside. These towns enjoyed a high degree of economic and political autonomy, and offered freer access to business opportunities than their counterparts in France or Italy.[39]

Scandinavia had a longstanding constitutional tradition that limited the power of the monarch. Land was valuable there not so much for the crops or livestock it could support but for the minerals that lay below ground. Land was not entailed, and there were few impediments to the transfer of lands held by the nobility. Moreover, it was extremely rare for the Swedish nobility to enter the Church. The Swedish aristocracy was mostly a working aristocracy of bureaucrats, soldiers, and sailors, whose livelihood depended on a good job and a fair promotion.[40]

England's experience with the Reformation was complex and atypical. So was its experience with primogeniture. Despite suggestions to the contrary,[41] modern historical research presents strong evidence that the institution of primogeniture was regularly thwarted from the time laws were first introduced by the Normans in the eleventh century.[42] (Neither Anglo-Saxon nor Germanic practices in England included primogeniture.) In the second half of the twelfth century, Henry II created a substantive land law with tenant rights reviewed by juries. Monarchical rent seeking, which produced fees for adjudication and returns from patronage, produced unforeseen consequences—the creation of property rights for tenants. Prior to King Henry's innovation, the lords were a party to the disputes over property, acting as both judge and jury. Henry separated title from lordly acceptance.[43] Even under feudal practice before Henry's reign, however, means of transferring property to another by tenant were underway; property transactions were merely disguised in feudal lingo.

A number of devices were developed throughout the Tudor era to avoid the effects of primogeniture. The English law, which eventually applied only in cases of intestacy and then only for real property,[44] could be at least partially avoided as early as the twelfth century through family arrangements that included planned marriages, *intervivos* gifts, and, most importantly, the use of wills. Studies explain how family wealth, minor children, and collaterals were protected through primogeniture-avoidance devices in the fourteenth and sixteenth centuries.[45] In fact, the legal history of English proprietors consists of a prolonged, multifaceted struggle between the common law rules of inheritance, which allowed for female inheritance in the absence of male heirs, and entails that (in part) opposed these rights. The English entail originated as a provision for younger children, providing a grant of land to a younger child upon his or her marriage, provided the marriage produced heirs. Many historians ignore this fact, and many more disregard its ambiguous character. Because entails specified the sex of those who stood to inherit, they provided a means of favoring one sex over the other. The statute of *De donis* (1285) gave permanence to entails that had formerly been temporary. Thus, entails could be used for two different, even contradictory, purposes. On the one hand, they could be used to distribute land to younger children. This supports our theory that entry occurred in areas where inheritance was partible. On the other hand, they could be used to keep land in the hands of male descendants, if not indefinitely, then through several generations. There is no comprehensive statistical evidence as to how entails were actually used, but as Adam Smith noted: "The common law of England...is said to abhor perpetuities, and they are accordingly more restricted there than in any other European country."[46]

Many legal artifices, such as the extremely complex doctrine of "uses," were developed to get around Norman feudal laws involving primogeniture, eventually culminating in the Statute of Wills (1540), which permitted all feudal tenants of the King or mense lords to transfer two-thirds of their lands by will.[47] Although Adam Smith recognized

England's ancient form of primogeniture as a reasonable policy for the lords' defense, he decried its effects in the Europe of his day. When he noted (as does economist Gary M. Becker[48]) that primogeniture "continues to be respected" and is "still likely to endure for many centuries," it is clear that he was speaking of continental Europe and not England.[49] By Smith's time, the rules of primogeniture were only applicable in intestacy and governed only a tiny portion of inheritances.[50] Historian Eileen Spring states: "With the Statute of Wills (in 1540) the common law rules of succession, long evaded in practice, were officially on the way to becoming default rules, rules that would apply only upon intestacy."[51] The growth of the use of wills and other devices, from the very beginnings of Norman rule, ensured that all children (including females) were generally included in inheritance and that wealth was being more widely dispersed than under strict observance of primogeniture.

The traditional view is that Henry VIII broke with the Catholic Church in response to a dynastic problem and, because of this, the English Reformation was more an act of state than in any other part of Europe apart from Scandinavia—the result of one man's obsessive quest for a male heir.[52] While this view and the probability that Henry wanted to expropriate the wealth of the church are certainly supported by the weight of history, the idea that religious entry was encouraged by high information costs imposed by ineffective primogeniture laws and resulting instability of wealth distribution is complementary. Despite the peculiarities of the English case, it nevertheless conforms to the general contours of our theory. By 1530, the Church of England was ripe for takeover and, in all likelihood, Henry VIII recognized this fact. Furthermore, there is evidence that Henry's confiscations of church property were made with relish. According to historian Alan Simpson, "Every class in England was involved in the immense exciting scramble for the confiscated property of the church."[53] In the end, the Reformation came to England for the same basic reason that it came to other parts of Europe: The Church's ability to maintain its discriminatory pricing system was being steadily eroded by the dispersion of wealth.

Finally, we note the bifurcated cases of Scotland and Switzerland. Scottish historian Julian Goodare attributes the success of the Reformation in the Scottish Lowlands to the ruinous taxation policies of James V, which forced bishops and monasteries to raise cash by alienating land through *feuing*, a method by which existing tenant farmers or other third parties could purchase the heritable rights to land, leaving the benefice holder with only the right to collect feudal dues fixed in perpetuity.[54] The heavy inflation of the sixteenth century left the benefice holders with ever-shrinking long-term revenues. After 1530, nobles and rulers imposed their kinsmen as commendators of the monasteries—secular heads that drew revenues from monastic enterprises without taking monastic vows. The monks were powerless to resist feuing and the creeping secularization that accompanied it. Thus, unlike in England, there was no dissolution of the monasteries in Scotland. They merely faded away, victims of the feuing movement which essentially revolutionized land tenure and launched a new class of small, independent proprietors.

In the Swiss Confederacy, a natural division of sorts existed between the rural and the urban cantons. The rural states were Appenzell, Glarus, Schwyz, Unterwalden, Uri, and Zug. The urban states were Basle, Bern, Fribourg, Lucerne, Schaffhausen, Solothurn, and Zurich. Geneva did not become part of the confederation until the nineteenth century, but its actions were affected during the Middle Ages by its Swiss neighbors. The strongest opposition to the Reformation came from Lucerne and the inner rural states, especially Schwyz, Unterwalden, Uri, and Zug. In the sixteenth century, Switzerland was within the orbit of what we now call South Germany, a region in which towns gained extensive rights of self-government, either as "imperial cities," which possessed liberties granted by the monarch, or "free cities," which possessed liberties granted by the bishops or other lords. The cities were centers of trade and manufacture, communication, and learned culture. They were treated with hostility by the nobles, who rightly saw the spread of confederation as a threat to their power. Largely infiltrated by the nobility, the Church allied itself with the nobles in seeking to repress confederation.[55] Hence, the cities were more likely to embrace Protestantism than the rural cantons, a pattern that eventually emerged, with one or two exceptions. During this time the political distinction in Switzerland between lay and ecclesiastical princes grew weaker because the major sees were becoming dependencies of the great families, giving rise to the complaint that the bishops were the cities' greatest foes. Historian Thomas A. Brady Jr.

wrote, "The forty-six bishops who sat in the Diet were commonly the cousins, uncles, nephews, and brothers of the lay princes in this great age of princely pluralists. No less than four sons of the Elector Palatine Philip (d. 1508), for example, became bishops, a record that their Bavarian cousins, the Margraves of Baden, the Wettins of Saxony, and the Hohenzollerns strove with considerable success to match."[56]

Urban Growth and Protestant Entry

In the previous section we argued that primogeniture is a reasonable proxy for income distribution in a medieval society. The predominant historical view, that the Protestant Reformation was basically an "urban phenomenon,"[57] offers another opportunity to test our theory. Inasmuch as city size and growth reflect exchange volume, and exchange volume reflects wider income distribution, a demonstrable link should exist between urban growth and the practice of primogeniture (a proxy for income distribution). In order to test this correlation we used the data base assembled by economic historians Paul Bairoch, Jean Bateau, and Pierre Chèvre[58] that was recently employed by Shleifer and Vishny to show that "absolutist" governments are associated with low economic growth (as measured by urban growth).[59] Our premise is that, if other things are equal, competition and capitalist exchange are hampered by primogeniture. If this premise is valid and if the relationships between Protestant entry and primogeniture laws are correct, partible inheritance should also be correlated to economic growth and city size.

In order to test this relationship, we analyzed the data between 1500 and 1650 collected by Bairoch, Bateau, and Chèvre. These two dates give us end-points for before and after the Protestant Reformation. The largest cities in 1500 were located in France and Italy; the smallest in Belgium and Germany. In 1500, primogeniture was practiced in twenty-eight of Europe's largest cities, and, of course, all were Catholic at that time. By 1650, seven cities in which primogeniture was practiced decreased in size, including five of the top ten largest cities in 1500, whereas only one city (Cologne) that did not practice primogeniture decreased in size. The cities that grew the most during the period were those in which primogeniture was not practiced and in which the Protestant Reformation made its greatest impact. In 1500 only three of the twenty-eight largest cities of Europe were in countries in which primogeniture was not practiced, but by 1650, ten such cities were among the largest. These ten were within the sphere of greatest influence of the Protestant Reformation—namely, the countries of Germany, Holland, Denmark, Belgium, and England. We do not suggest that these results are conclusive, but they are at least broadly consistent with the notion that inheritance laws may account, at least in part, for urban growth in the late Middle Ages.

If Protestant entry can be linked to primogeniture status, it presumably can also be related (along with other factors) to emergent markets in urban growth centers that were creating wealth through expansion of profit opportunities. One important result of this correlation is that it is consistent with the dominant historical view that the Protestant Reformation was an "urban phenomenon."[60] In short, rapidly growing towns, with dispersed and unstable wealth distributions, were ripe for Protestant entry. Those societies with more stable and concentrated income distributions were not, and they tended to remain Catholic.

Despite the axiomatic character of our argument that Protestant entry was facilitated by the instability of wealth distribution in countries where primogeniture either did not exist or was ineffective, we consider it significant that it accords with standard historical interpretations. In his essay confirming the substantial avoidance of primogeniture in England, legal historian George C. Broderick observed, "It is impossible not to connect the rapid growth and singular independence of the English gentry under the Tudors and Stuarts with the limitation of entails and freedom of alienation which characterised this remarkable period."[61] Long before the Reformation the yeoman class in England prospered and became a middle class of farmers and merchants. Historian Ralph V. Turner maintains that this process of maneuvering around restrictive property laws quickened as early as the thirteenth century, when nonaristocratic judges began changing feudal inheritance patterns in their own self-interest, thereby creating dispersion of property and an entrepreneurial spirit.[62] And George A. Holmes verifies the English nobility used "family arrangements" to control property in the fourteenth century and to avoid strict primogeniture laws when it was in their interest to do so.[63]

Market forces that encouraged entrepreneurial economic activity in England (which only nominally practiced primogeniture) had similar effects on the European continent where primogeniture was not the law. As noted previously, towns of the German and Swiss principalities were engaged vigorously in income- and wealth-generating activities. Bohemia was a robust entrepreneurial economy, styled as "the Nevada of Europe at the end of the Middle Ages" because of its mining industry, which attracted a large and transient population of foreigners.[64] By contrast, primogeniture encouraged the concentration of wealth and the stability of its distribution. The experience of the Italian city-state, Lombardy, provides a case in point. At the end of the seventeenth century the number of noble persons in Lombardy was around sixty-five hundred. The source of their wealth was land. The Lombard nobility was less than 1 percent of the total population of the province, but it owned nearly half the total landed property.[65] Wealth was preserved by the institutions of primogeniture and *fidecommessi*—a form of ecclesiastical mortmain, that is, a device used in wills to guarantee that property, especially land, could only be passed on to members of the same family or ecclesiastical community. Spain provides another example. The strength of the Spanish nobility lay in the sheer size of their estates. Historian Raymond Carr calculated that about a third of the cultivable land in medieval Spain was in the hands of four great houses.[66] The institution that kept a large proportion of the national wealth in the hands of the higher nobility was the *mayorazgo*, a law of entail that kept landed estates from ever being legally transferred. Lawyers' interpretations of the Laws of Toro (1505) consistently favored the growth of entail and guarded its strict nature.

Other historical episodes tell a similar story. The experience of Poland showed how political and religious interests cooperated (often by force of necessity) to preserve and maintain wealth. After 1370, Poland was ruled mostly by foreign kings. The nobility emerged under the early kings and princes in two groups. The Magnates, who formed the Prince's Council, ultimately developed into the Upper House of the Polish Parliament. From this class came the high officials of church and state, who aided the princes in the administration of the country. Below the magnates on the social and political scale were the *milites*, who originally formed the prince's army and frequently received land in return for military service. Together these two classes formed a large body of nobles. In the middle of the fifteenth century the king turned to the Polish nobility for money to fight the Teutonic Order, for which he gave, in return, a series of charters that gave the nobles considerable political influence in their local assemblies.[67] In sum, while we do not argue that primogeniture laws explain economic growth, there is a good deal of evidence that their observance helped to concentrate wealth and their avoidance helped to disperse wealth in England and in Europe.

This chapter advances the view that the Protestant Reformation was an economic phenomenon with roots in intertemporal benefits and costs to Catholic Church members and disaffected groups. Although we stress the economic aspects involved, our argument nevertheless conforms to the conventional wisdom. For centuries, historians and other observers have argued that the selling of indulgences produced the Protestant revolt. But the traditional historical argument has revolved around the ethical consequences and attendant moral corruption that such venality introduced. By contrast, our approach emphasizes the *economic* consequences of early, medieval, doctrinal innovations. Furthermore, we have added a supply side to the argument, which recognizes that the Catholic Church's viability was inextricably linked to the kind of societal and economic institutions that were extant at the time of the revolt. The medieval church controlled and manipulated doctrine and rules in order to increase its revenues. By the late Middle Ages, church doctrine involving purgatory, indulgence, confession, penance, and all of their attendant beliefs, had become so complex as to be unbelievable, especially at the high prices the Catholic Church was charging for redemption. One result was that benefits to church members were reduced by a church-directed policy of price discrimination that put believers on the margin of defection. The advent of Protestantism as a belief system meant that consumers seeking redemption could take a more direct, less expensive path to salvation. Protestantism made redemption cheaper, and it increased benefits to believers by reducing transaction costs.

In the Middle Ages, the successful entry of Protestant sects required a flatter pricing structure. Therefore, rather than introduce a whole new belief system, Protestant religions adopted Christ and core Christian teachings (e.g., the Bible), but simplified many of the details, and eliminated the temporal connections of the Catholic Church's belief structure. These doctrinal and organizational differences soon created a flood of new forms of Protestant Christianity, as we shall see momentarily. Before we embark on an economic analysis of evolving forms of Protestantism, however, we turn to the critical topic of how the Catholic Church was forced by new competition to adjust its policies. The so-called Counter Reformation produced changes in church doctrine and practice, with mixed degrees of success and failure.

6

The Counter-Reformation: Incumbent-Firm Reaction to Market Entry

It is to be desired that those who assume the episcopal office know what are their duties, and understand that they have been called not for their own convenience, not for riches or luxury, but to labors and cares for the glory of God.
—*The Canons and Decrees of the Council of Trent*

[Church] Reform... usually meant tightening up the rules for collecting money.
—Denys Hay, *The Church in Italy in the Fifteenth Century*

In chapter 5 we characterized the Protestant Reformation (1517–1555) as a form of market entry and showed that its success was a consequence of both demand-side and supply-side factors. As a dominant firm in its religious market, the Catholic Church was bound to respond to the market threat of rival entry. Historians refer to Catholicism's response as the "Counter-Reformation," or, alternatively, the "Catholic Reformation" (1555–1648).[1] We find that the Roman Catholic Church responded to rival entry in a way predicted by economic theory. After Protestantism gained a foothold in the religious market, the Catholic Church faced a residual demand curve that was composed of demanders who were less responsive to price than those that broke away. Consequently, it (1) lowered the average price of providing the Z-good "religious services"; (2) engaged in vigorous competition in certain contiguous areas; (3) attempted to raise rivals' marginal costs to move demanders back to Catholicism; and (4) tried to boost demand in its "retail" market, while simultaneously protecting and even intensifying its rent-seeking practices in its "wholesale" market. (By "retail" we mean direct sales to church customers, whereas by "wholesale" we refer to the structure of internal transactions of the institutional church, such as dealings between bishops and lower clergy.) In the final analysis, the Roman Catholic Church responded to Protestant entry and to the encroaching Age of Reason with lower full prices, with violence, and with nominal, rather than fundamental, doctrinal alterations.

An Economic Theory of the Counter-Reformation

Protestants invaded the medieval market for religion by launching a relatively simple strategy that owed its success in part to the economic excesses of the medieval Catholic Church. Protestant sects gained members by making all-or-none offers using an uncomplicated pricing scheme that substituted for the highly discriminatory prices of the dominant firm. They were aided by historical, mostly exogenous factors, such as the absence of institutional arrangements that concentrated wealth and the presence of others that dispersed it. Once entry occurred, the Catholic Church could be expected to react in typical fashion. Therefore the questions that are paramount from an economic point of view are the following ones: What were the effects of market entry on the incumbent firm? How did the medieval Catholic Church react to the new kinds of competition, doctrinally and otherwise?

By adding a few embellishments to the simple model introduced in chapter 5, we can clarify our theory of the Counter-Reformation and highlight the testable economic implications of Protestantism's entry into the medieval religious market. In figure 6.1, let AD represent the market demand for church services. The vertical axis represents the full price of religious participation, in the form of money and in-kind contributions for a Z-good that contains one large component that we have been calling "assurances of eternal salvation." MC_c and MC_p represent the marginal production cost of two religions, Catholicism and Protestantism, which, at least initially, are assumed equal to each other. Assume that the medieval Roman Catholic Church practiced perfect price discrimination before Protestant entry. Prior to entry the area under the demand curve above cost (ABC) represents potential consumer surplus. Under the circumstances of first-degree price discrimination, the entire consumer surplus is extracted, putting all consumers at the margin of defection. The largest donors of consumer surplus are those purchasers in

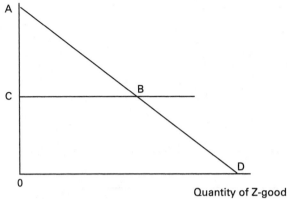

Figure 6.1
Christian religion market, c. 1517

the upper reaches of the demand curve. Under favorable conditions, entry takes place. Assume that Protestants enter as single-price monopolists charging P_p and selling Q_p of religious services, as shown in figure 6.2. For this analysis we assume that Protestantism entered the religion market as a rival monopoly-like firm charging a simple (but different) monopoly price. Its membership (entry) price was cheaper, but not free: A 10 percent "biblical" tithe took the place of the many exactions of the Roman Church. Protestant entry involved, indeed initially required, the use of political power to legitimize the new churches. In 1517 Martin Luther published his Ninety-five Theses. By 1530, after the failure of Emperor Charles V to restore Catholic orthodoxy in Germany, Lutheran princes united in a league against the Emperor and Catholic princes. The freedom and the very lives of Luther and Calvin depended on the protection of secular rulers but, as both discovered, political power can be used against particular religions as well. Nevertheless, both Calvin and Luther espoused action by civil authorities to police "idolatry, sacrilege, blasphemy and other public affronts to religion."[2] This meant oppression of Roman Catholicism ("popery") and Anabaptism, and other sectarian dissent within emerging Protestantism. Further, Luther's characterization of the polity was "the sword" and Calvin's was "the bridle." Around such theories, monopoly or quasi-monopoly religions formed in Scotland,

Full price of Z-good

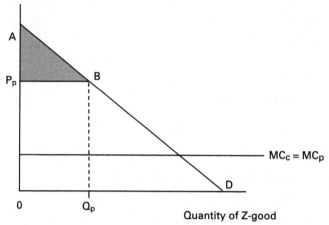

Figure 6.2
Protestant entry into Christian market

Scandinavia, more than half of Germany, large sections of the Netherlands and Switzerland, and areas of Central Europe. Henry VIII, of
course, declared religious monopoly in England as well.

Those demanders paying the largest amount of consumer surplus for
religious services—those in the upper reaches of the demand curve—
would tend to switch. Trades no longer take place at prices between A
and B. This means that OQ_p demanders will likely switch from Catholicism to Protestantism, leaving BD as the residual demand curve for Catholicism.[3] Whether the Catholic Church continues to price discriminate
or opts for a simple monopoly price, it is clear that average price will fall
in response to entry.[4] Note that this result would obtain whether the
Catholic Church continues to perfectly price discriminate along the residual demand curve or whether it chooses to charge a simple monopoly
price. A residual marginal revenue curve (not shown in figure 6.2) may
be drawn originating from point B. Simple monopoly price would be
established on the demand curve at the point of intersection between
MC_c (= MC_p) and the residual marginal revenue curve—at a point
lower than B, the Protestant entry price. This is the *first* testable implication of our theory.

A *second* testable implication is that competition will be most intense in the price region near P_p. Such competition might be expected even in areas that do not finally settle as Protestant. For example, some Spanish and French aristocrats located in the upper regions of demand curve AD may have wished to break away from the Catholic Church but were dissuaded from defecting by institutional impediments, such as primogeniture laws. Essentially, in areas where Catholics and Protestants were geographically contiguous, their prices and rent extractions would have been similar. This results because a Tiebout-like competition—where people "vote with their feet" in response to local economic policies—would have made these local economies quite alike in their characteristics. (For example, a similar interest rate would have prevailed.) In this case Catholic areas should exhibit the same economic growth and institutional characteristics as Protestant areas. This, of course, confounds an economic interpretation of the effect of Protestantism on economic growth, but we defer discussion of this topic to chapter 8.

A *third* testable implication is that, post-entry, the Catholic Church will attempt to extend its own demand curve by driving up the marginal cost of Protestant churches (MC_p in figure 6.2). In order to undertake this action, it must be cost-effective, that is, the marginal revenue of the action must be greater than the attendant marginal costs. For example, the organized suppression of defectors by Church-sponsored inquisitions must generate more revenue than costs. We expect more violence where the marginal product of violence is greater.

A *fourth* testable implication is that, as with any imperfectly competitive firm, the incumbent firm will try to develop policies that will shift BD to the right and make its demand more inelastic (e.g., advertising). Several strategies suggest themselves here: correcting abuses within the medieval Catholic Church; the development of alternative religious orders that are more resistant to corruption charges such as those leveled against the Catholic Church by Protestant reformers; and devoting more church resources to charitable endeavors or other means of social support.[5]

Did the medieval Catholic Church respond to Protestant entry by employing strategies that are predictable in light of the theory outlined above? We looked for evidence to support our thesis in the historical documents of the Reformation era and in the work of respected historians who have specialized in this field. Historical evidence shows that the medieval church responded to market entry on two different levels. On the retail side it took actions to raise and transform product demand, whereas on the wholesale side, the organizational structure of the Catholic Church acted as an impediment to meaningful reform.

Retail Adjustments by the Medieval Church

On the retail side, the medieval Catholic Church reacted to competitive entry as economic theory predicts. It attempted to lower price and improve the quality of its product so as to return disaffected customers to its fold. These reactionary attempts by the Catholic Church are documented in *The Canons and Decrees of the Council of Trent*. Between 1545 and 1563, the highest officials of the Catholic Church met in Ecumenical Council in the Austrian town of Trent, where it condemned the errors of the Protestant Reformation, made pronouncements on the justification of its own doctrines and practices, and established new measures of discipline.

Measures by the Incumbent Firm to Lower Its Retail Price

Many actions taken by the Council of Trent can readily be interpreted as attempts to lower the price, or increase the quality, of church services. We treat quality-raising measures as analogous to price reductions, which roughly comports with economic theory. The Council of Trent issued decrees concerning reforms in doctrine and practice, but we choose to concentrate on the practical reforms because this is what lay at the heart of the movement. The number of decrees on each subject of reform may be taken as a rough indication of the perceived severity of the problem by the fathers of the church (see table 6.1). The largest number of decrees was directed at reforming the rules of conduct of the episcopate, including the regulation of benefices.

The Council issued decrees limiting the conditions and number of benefices that each bishop could hold; establishing residency requirements for bishops and clergy; requiring bishops to exercise closer supervision over priests and monks; establishing minimum competency qualifications

Table 6.1
Decrees of the Council of Trent

Type of decree	Number of decrees
Regulation of benefices	19
Duties/authority of bishops	18
Governance of monasteries and convents	16
Competence of clergy	15
Duties/authority of clergy	12
Marriage regulations	8
Visitation requirements of bishops	5
Ownership of property by churchmen	5
Instruction of the faithful	5
Revenue sharing among churches	4
Residence requirements of bishops	4
Establishment/maintenance of churches	4
Measures to reduce simony	3
Rules against concubinage	2
Rules against nepotism	2
Rules of ordination	2
Election of bishops and cardinals	1

of clergy; renewing pious living precepts of priests, monks, and nuns; establishing procedural norms for the election of bishops and cardinals; and establishing penalties for concubinage and other public offenses.[6] The goal of these various decrees seems to have been, in the main, to establish a "kindler and gentler" clergy—a way of lowering the cost to the faithful of membership in the Catholic Church. This spirit comes through in the following passage from Session 13, Chapter 1:

The...holy Council of Trent, lawfully assembled in the Holy Ghost,...having in mind to decide some things that relate to the jurisdiction of bishops, in order that...they may the more willingly reside in the churches committed to them the more easily and conveniently they may be able to rule and keep in uprightness of life and of morals those subject to them, deems it appropriate in the first place to admonish them to bear in mind that they are shepherds and not oppressors and that they ought so to preside over those subject to them as not to lord it over them, but to love them as children and brethren and to strive by exhortation and admonition to deter them from what is unlawful, that they may not be obliged, should they transgress, to coerce them by due punishments. In regard to those, however, who should happen to sin through human frailty, that command of the Apostle is to be observed, that they reprove, entreat, rebuke them in all kindness and patience, since benevolence toward those to be corrected often effects more than severity, exhortation more than threat, and charity more than force.

Another problem that the Council of Trent addressed was financial abuse (the chief lightning rod for Luther's attack). Simony is the act of buying or selling things that are sacred or spiritual, a common practice in pre-Reformation times. In an apparent attempt to outlaw this practice and curb other financial abuses, the Council issued decrees prohibiting bishops from selling rights and offices; eliminating charges for selling certain church services (e.g., dispensations); prohibiting certain leases of church property; enjoining cardinals and prelates from enriching their families from the property of the church; abolishing the office of questor of alms (which was rife with abuse); requiring that clerics be compelled to pay what they owe; restricting abuse of wills and bequests by opportunistic clergy; and establishing restrictions on the conversions of benefices.[7] Through its general decrees, moreover, the church tried to institute quality control over the doctrine of purgatory and the veneration of sacred relics, and to abolish "all evil traffic" in indulgences.

Certain church reforms may be collected under the "advertising" rubric. In response to the Protestant threat, the Catholic Church sought to raise awareness of its members to the benefits of its product. The Council of Trent issued decrees establishing lectureships in Scripture and the liberal arts; imposing duties of preaching and teaching on the clergy; and providing detailed directions for the establishment of seminaries. Finally, the Catholic Church issued decrees to improve financial assistance to poor parishes; to soften some of its punishments, such as the use of excommunication; and to remove certain impediments to marriage, which had the effect of lowering transaction costs for the betrothed.[8]

Intense Competition around the Entrant's Price

The fact that competition was intense around entry price is demonstrable through a study of the geographic and spatial dimensions of religious competition in the sixteenth century. The kind of competition that concerns us is competition between Catholicism and the newly emergent Protestant religion(s). We recognize that competition *within* Catholicism, mainly in the Balkans, between the Roman Church and the Eastern Orthodox Church, existed for eight hundred years, but that is a separate issue from the one under examination here. With regard to rivalry between Catholicism and Protestantism, competition was more vigorous in contiguous areas where a Catholic region abutted a Protestant one. Religious competition was demonstrably more intense in Catholic Belgium (which borders Protestant Germany) than in Catholic Spain (which borders Catholic France or Catholic Portugal). Certain economic markets are not easily constrained by geographic boundaries. Hence, when Protestant countries eliminated usury prohibitions, interest rates in contiguous Catholic countries necessarily adjusted to the competitive market level.

In sixteenth-century Europe, practical boundaries were created by landscape rather than borders; where physical barriers were absent, people moved between different jurisdictions with considerable freedom. Boundaries in the contemporary sense were virtually nonexistent. With regard to France and Holland, for example, historian Andrew Pettegree noted: "Until the treaties of Madrid (1526) and Cambrai (1529) it was impossible to speak of a frontier between France and the Netherlands in any sense we would recognize. Fifty years later during the Wars of Religion citizens of both lands would continue to exploit the lack of controls or border markings to take themselves beyond the reach of trouble almost at will. In eastern and central Europe geographical borders between states were even more uncertain."[9] This geo-political reality could only serve to intensify the kind of competition for souls that the Reformation stimulated.

Measures by the Incumbent Firm to Raise Rivals' Costs

In certain respects, the medieval Catholic Church's reaction to Protestant entry was analogous to the reaction of business firms to regulated competition or to the tendency of special interests to seek protective trade legislation. In such cases, incumbent firms seek to protect their market power by raising rivals' costs. In the sixteenth century the rivals were, on the one hand, the new Protestant sects (Lutherans, Anglicans, Calvinists, etc.), and on the other, the new heretics from the scientific and artistic communities. The medieval Catholic Church viewed many Renaissance scientists and artists as dangerous threats to its authority and to the integrity of preserved scripture and established doctrine. Two prominent, historical episodes that demonstrate the incumbent-firm strategy of the Catholic Church were its conduct in the Thirty Years' War and the institution of the "Holy Office."

The Thirty Years' War   On becoming king, Ferdinand of Bohemia swore to uphold the right of Bohemian Protestants to practice their religion, but he reneged on his promise. The Bohemians reacted violently, accosting three Catholic officials and throwing them from a window into a dung heap. This episode, the so-called Defenestration of Prague, signaled the beginning of the Thirty Years' War, which eventually drew almost every European state into its orbit. The conflict became increasingly bloody as political and economic motives joined the religious motive of keeping Germany and other countries within the Protestant fold. Ferdinand sought to quell the rebellion by vigorously forcing Catholicism on the rebels. Historians Jerome Blum, Rondo Cameron, and Thomas G. Barnes report, "those who tried to keep their Protestant faith had to pay special heavy taxes and have soldiers quartered in their homes."[10] Ferdinand also confiscated lands of the Protestant nobility, retaking half of Bohemia. Alarmed by the gathering power of the Hapsburg dynasty, Sweden and (Catholic) Bourbon France entered the fray on the side of Protestantism. In the case of France, this showed how easily religion could be subjugated to politics. The last phase of the conflict (1635–1648) became a dynastic struggle between the Bourbons of France on the one hand and the Hapsburgs of Austria and Spain on the other. Eventually the 1648 Peace of Westphalia established the sovereignty of the German princes, signaling victory for German Protestantism and defeat for the Catholic Reformation (by quashing the imperial ambitions of the Hapsburgs in Germany).

The Holy Office   During the Council of Trent, the Vatican created a Holy Office (in 1559) to spearhead its repression and censorship of the new heretics. The chief form of repression was the Inquisition, and the main form of censorship was the Index of Forbidden Books. The use of inquisition by the Catholic Church was not new (having been invoked as early as the thirteenth century), but the practice took on new vigor after 1559 in response to the Protestant threat. Early inquisitions were directed at common heresies (e.g., Catharism, Waldensianism) and at Judaism and Islam. Later, Protestantism felt the heavy hand of the Inquisitors, whose broad powers included apprehension, detainment, minor punishments, torture, and even death.

As noted previously, the invention of movable type and the production of books in the middle of the fifteenth century posed a new threat to the Catholic Church's monopoly on matters of faith and morals. Most versions of early Protestantism extolled personal interpretations of Holy Scripture. The invention of printing reduced the price of books, including the Bible, and made them much more accessible to many more people. The Catholic Church reacted by imposing many kinds of censorship of literature, science, and art. Although the interrelationships between religion, science, and art are complex, the growth of science and the spirit of rationalism that accompanied it in the sixteenth century were often viewed as a challenge to the authority of the medieval church, which confronted this challenge by employing tools of censorship and repression. The Catholic Church eyed suspiciously the reintroduction of classical philosophy and the reawakening of classical aesthetics as pagan reincarnations as early as the thirteenth and fourteenth centuries. The invention of the printing press presented new opportunities for science and art as well as for the Church (to advertise, for example). In astronomy, the clashes in 1543 between orthodox ideas and the new theories of Copernicus, and, later, Galileo, were seen by the Catholic Church as direct challenges to its interpretation of Holy Scripture. Moreover, some of the most important art of the period, such as the work of Botticelli and (later) Caravaggio, reflected the melding of the rationalist spirit with traditional Christianity (or possibly a pagan interpretation of it). Art historians remain divided over the meaning of the imagery of Sandro Botticelli's *Primavera* (circa 1475–1478), for example. Ostensibly a secular work about springtime, its complex imagery has strongly suggested a pagan interpretation to some.

During the late fifteenth century, as the horrors of the Black Death receded into the past, Catholicism tempered its spirit of hellfire and damnation. Historian Robert Bireley acknowledges debate over the proposition that fear infiltrated late medieval Christianity wherein, as some authors contend, "fear of death, judgment, the end of the world, and Satan, permeated late medieval religion, provoking anxiety about salvation and an agitated spirit."[11] It is more likely that this feature of human life created a cyclical level of demand elasticity among the faithful. In short, the vagaries of human life were an exogenous feature of the demand for assurances of eternal salvation. During less perilous times, such as when the Black Death and other plagues waned during the later medieval period, demand became more elastic as death became less immediate, which allowed Christianity to be portrayed as a doctrine of God's mercy and love. Later, when Protestantism mounted a serious challenge to the Roman Catholic monopoly, repression and damnation returned to vogue. The emphasis on hell and damnation was, observationally, an attempt to make the demand for salvation more inelastic for Catholics. This changing spirit is also reflected in the art of the time, for example, Michelangelo's *Last Judgment* (1536–1541), which was undertaken as the initial wave of Reformation was overtaking many parts of Europe.

There is multicorrelation between the invention of printing, the emergence of Protestantism, and the ongoing development of science over this period. The best science of the day was often repressed by the Inquisition and the Index of Forbidden Books. The Roman Inquisition, in particular, targeted literature and science. In 1584 the Vatican placed the works of Giordano Bruno in the Index, specifically his book *On the Infinite Universe and World*—a work alleging intelligent life beyond the earth and advocating the unification of all religions. Bruno was betrayed to the Holy Office in 1591; nine years later Pope Clement XIII had him burned at the stake in Rome. The writings of Sir Thomas More were also added to the Index for a time (ironically, he was later canonized a saint by the same Church). The infamous episode of Galileo and the Church illustrates another case of scientific repression. Historian Edward Burman maintains that Galileo was punished less for his scientific statements than for his "offenses against the inquisition" and his challenge to orthodox Jesuit astronomers.[12] Lest we forget, the Roman Inquisition was equally harsh in its treatment of artists. The Venetian painter Paolo Veronese was hauled before the Roman Inquisition to defend his painting,

Feast in the House of Levi, in which he had placed dogs, dwarfs, a fool, a parrot, men with German weapons, and a man with a bleeding nose. Since such details were not mentioned in the biblical story of Levi the church regarded these extraneous elements as heretical. To placate the inquisitors Veronese reworked his canvas at his own expense, eliminating the offending elements. According to Sir Anthony Blunt, a noted authority on medieval and Renaissance art, "it is typical of the methods of the Counter-Reformation that the Inquisition in this case was satisfied with certain changes of detail which left the painting exactly as worldly in feeling as it was before."[13] Despite the infamy and persistent embarrassment to the Church of such episodes, the Roman Inquisition persisted until 1965, when the Holy Office was formally abolished in favor of the Congregation for the Doctrines of the Faith.

Outside Rome the Inquisition was focused on Protestantism at the borders of its influence. For example, near Trieste at the end of the sixteenth century, the Inquisition aimed at suppressing Lutheranism. Some of the most virulent inquisitions against Protestants were in Spain. Ships' crews, especially from England, were at extreme risk. According to Burman, "Henry Gottersum, the cook of the *Elizabeth* that anchored at Puerto de Santa Maria in 1574, was burned alive for admitting that he was a convinced Protestant."[14] Inquisitors seized cargoes, confiscated books, and arrested sailors, who were sentenced to the Spanish galleys for "religious crimes." The physical torture meted out by the Spanish Inquisition has been well documented. But the Inquisition employed mental torture as well, and was global in its reach. Speaking of French practice, Michel Foucault notes that the torture imposed by the Inquisition was "a regulated practice, obeying a well-defined procedure.... The first degree of torture was the sight of the instruments."[15] The ensuing degrees of torture employed an array of methods designed to break alleged heretics: the ordeal of water, the ordeal of fire, the *strappado* (victim lifted off ground with wrists tied behind back, then dropped), the wheel, the rack, and the *stivaletto* (pressurized boot torture). Torture, or even the prospect of torture, under a legal system that bestowed vast power on the Catholic Church, was a particularly vivid means of raising the cost of membership in a rival sect.

Measures by the Incumbent Firm to Enhance Demand

In order to counter entry by rivals, incumbent firms often seek to boost demand for their product and insure brand loyalty by advertising. Although the practice of advertising tends to follow the technology of the day, the concept is very old. There is evidence that the medieval Catholic Church recognized very early the necessity of advertising (and differentiating) its product. Early forms of advertising by the medieval church were both informative and persuasive. Preaching and instruction featured much advertising designed to inculcate brand loyalty. This seemed even more imperative in the wake of the Protestant Reformation. On June 17, 1546, the Council of Trent formalized its emphasis on advertising when it decreed that priests should "expound and interpret the Holy Scriptures, either personally if they are competent, otherwise by a competent substitute to be chosen by the[m]" and that money from church coffers be set aside, if necessary, for "instructors in sacred theology, the bishops, archbishops, primates, and other ecclesiastical superiors of those localities... who hold such prebend, benefice or income."[16] At the same session the Council exhorted "all bishops, archbishops, primates and all other prelates of the churches... to preach the holy Gospel of Jesus Christ."[17] The twenty-fourth session of the Council in 1563 likewise emphasized the preaching requirement of the clergy and compelled priests to advertise the efficacy of the sacraments.[18] Yet another way the medieval Catholic Church sought to clean up the retail side of its operations was by approving, supporting, and advertising new and (supposedly) less venal religious orders, such as the Jesuits, an order that specialized in preaching and education. In *The Founding of the Jesuits*, Michael Foss said, "The results of the Council of Trent were very pleasing, and very important, to the Jesuits. The universality of the Church and the primacy of the pope had been stressed. The need for the Church to become active, preaching and teaching, was acknowledged. The Jesuits' place in the Catholic structure, as noteworthy preachers and the possessors of the finest educational system in Europe, was secured."[19]

Reassertion of the celibacy rule was another means of shoring up demand for the Catholic product. The celibacy rule was instituted around the eleventh century as part of the move to concentrate and centralize powers of the papacy. By the sixteenth century, priestly celibacy had become lax if not blatantly ignored. A goodly number of priests that were outwardly celibate kept concubines on the side. The Council of Trent renewed prohibitions of marriage for priests and issued new condemnations of the practice of concubinage (see table 6.1). An economic justification for re-invoking the celibacy rule was to protect church wealth and property from alienation. Priests with children would, after all, have been especially apt to appropriate parish properties and revenues for their families, thus reducing Church wealth through inheritance. Given monitoring costs in the medieval context, a doctrine of celibacy minimized the risks of priests appropriating Church properties. However, we find it unlikely that this constituted the only justification. Before and after the Council of Trent, upper-level prelates routinely alienated church wealth by bequests to nonclerical relatives. Yet another justification for the reassertion of celibacy, especially at the retail level, was that sexual abstinence by priests added to the credence of the Church's product. If the official intermediaries between God and man were called to a greater sacrifice than the faithful, this somehow stamped a higher level of quality on the ultimate goal. Celibacy may therefore have been regarded as a type of warranty for demanders and potential demanders that the product was genuine.

Wholesale Adjustments by the Medieval Church

Whereas attempts by the Catholic Church to clean up its retail operations were transparent, its wholesale actions were much less so. Indeed, attempts to reform the wholesale side of the Church were ineffective. In order to understand this failure at the wholesale level, it is necessary to grasp the central characteristics of the administrative landscape of the medieval Catholic Church.

Two important changes in church organization occurred prior to the Protestant Reformation, and these changes were responsible in large measure for the outward failure of the Counter-Reformation. The first involved the centrality and primacy of the papacy, which shaped the medieval church's political and ecclesiastic policy. The second involved the progressive "Italianization" of the College of Cardinals, the curia, and the papacy itself, which eventually resulted in an Italian monopoly of the Vatican.

The Conciliar Form of Church Governance

According to most historians, papal dominance reached its apex during the papacy of Innocent III (1198–1216). At this time Rome became the center of the legal and religious machinery of the church, excising dominion over clergy and (often) dictating the policies of lay rulers.[20] The nadir of papal influence came about one hundred years later. Pressing his power, Innocent III's Fourth Lateran Council (1215) denied the authority of monarchs and other lay rulers to tax the clergy. But the economic strains of war were too much for most monarchs. By 1296 France and England were at war, both taxing church properties for war finance. Pope Boniface VIII issued a bull or official papal document (*Clericis Laicos*) that denied lay rulers absolute authority in their own kingdoms and cut off their access to church funds by taxation. When King Phillip IV of France resisted, Boniface planned to issue a decree of excommunication against him, but French mercenaries led a small army against the Pope, causing him to capitulate. (Boniface died a few weeks after, and two later popes renounced their authority over Phillip and France.[21])

After the thirteenth century, the monopoly structure of the papacy faced repeated challenges. In the Middle Ages the Holy See was an important city-state in world politics as well as a dominant-firm, global supplier of religious services. On the religious front, as we have seen, the Catholic Church confronted an ongoing spirit of religious reform throughout the medieval period. On the political front, it was wracked by the Great Schism of 1378, which led to competing claims on the papacy by French and Italian prelates, and the relocation of the papacy to Avignon for most of the fourteenth century. According to medieval historian Denys Hay, "The effects of the Schism were directly proportional to the structure of government and in Italy government in many areas was exceedingly divided, thus encouraging the popes to try to exercise their jurisdiction in ways that would be an embarrassment to their rivals."[22] Papal actions in France or Spain, for example, were intertwined with Italian interests, "as when Calixtus III [1455–1458] bargained Italian against Spanish bishropics and abbeys in an effort to cope with the hungry members of the Aragonese house and the appetites, only slightly less ravenous, of his own Borgia relatives."[23] Only when the rift was healed did the papacy return to Rome. The Great Schism had two prominent effects on the medieval Catholic Church. On the one hand it reawakened sentiment for the conciliar form of governance and, on the other, it ushered in a system of bribes and side payments by popes intent on maintaining power.

Re-establishment of the conciliar form of church governance—which had been the hallmark of the first millenium of church history—therefore received added impetus from internal strife within the medieval church. Before the looming threat of Protestantism appeared, religious reform movements emanated, in the main, from church councils. Indeed, the 1414 Council of Constance ended the Great Schism by reasserting the doctrine of conciliar supremacy. Denys Hay remarked, "The crisis of 1378 was a striking instance of the condition for which conciliarism...was a drastic remedy. The senior clergy who in 1414 faced the scandal of three popes accepted the notion that Christ's purposes were reflected in the whole church as represented in council."[24] However, sitting popes were not likely to give up their authority so easily and, in the end, the doctrine that popes were subject to properly convoked general church councils received little more than lip service. Despite a decree by the Council of Constance that church councils be called at regular intervals, Pope Martin V (1417–1431), as well as his successors, did everything they could to discourage them.[25] A conciliar form of church governance would have distributed ecclesiastic authority more evenly geographically and the power of the council would have been anterior to that of the pope, a prospect no papal monopolist or aspiring papal monopolist could be expected to embrace.

Catholic historian Brian Tierney identified two major problems relating to the limits and character of ecclesiastical authority over the period: one pertains to the nature of authority between the papacy and national governments and another deals with the internal governance of the church. These problems were interrelated: "The partisans of successive princes—of Frederick II, Philip the Fair, Lewis the Vabarian—all found it expedient to couple their claims on behalf of the secular power with appeals to the College of Cardinals or the General Council as embodying an authority superior to that of any individual Pope within the Church."[26]

Papal Bribes

Many different side payments were offered by the papacy in order to avoid calling councils that might weaken papal control over doctrine and over church revenues. Before the Reformation these side payments performed the dual functions of keeping the conciliarists at bay and forestalling defections by non-Italian nations, which favored conciliarism. Robert Bireley contends,

> Rulers, especially the French kings, used the threat of a council to extract concessions from the papacy. Louis XII called a council for Pisa in 1511 in an attempt to counter Pope Julius II's policy toward France in Italy, but the pope outmanoeuvred him. Pope Leo X, then, in the concordat of Bologna of 1516, yielded to Francis I the predominant voice in nearly all the major ecclesiastical appointments in the realm in exchange, in part, for the king's disavowal of conciliarism. Starting with Nicholas V (1447–1455), the popes concentrated increasingly on their role as rulers of an Italian state and were themselves elected from aristocratic Italian families.[27]

Medievalist C. M. D. Crowder claims, "By the time of the Great Schism the more influential monarchies of Christendom had established a practical understanding with the papacy for a rough and ready division of their conflicting interests of patronage. Nevertheless this was frequently achieved by contention and adjudication."[28] He further explains how the Roman Catholic Church granted concessions to France, England, and Germany in order to keep them in the fold, usually through formal agreements that conceded powers to civil authorities: "In a series of concordats the reforms which met their own demands were agreed with each of the French, English, and German nations. All were promised better representation among the cardinals. The French were given concessions chiefly from the burden of papal taxation.[29] The English obtained the promise of papal restraint in grants to monasteries, of exemption from episcopal jurisdiction, and of the appropriation of parish churches. The German concordat had many of the features of the other two, but claimed more explicitly a better representation in a reformed curia than Germans had enjoyed in the past."[30] Bribes of this sort did not prevent breakaways, as the Protestant Reformation demonstrated.

Indeed, the papacy seemed to make higher side payments to some countries as time went on, right up to Protestant entry. Thus, in the late fifteenth and early sixteenth centuries, the papacy did not intervene while England gradually converted papal taxation to royal taxation. Historian J. J. Scarisbrick calculated that the average tax collections from clerical operations in England between 1486 and 1534 resulted in £4,816 per year paid to Rome and £12,500 per year to the King. He concludes, "before the breach, Henry VII and his son were receiving well over two and half times the annual average of money paid to Rome."[31]

In many respects, the successes of the Protestant Reformation may be traced to a failure of side payments by the Catholic Church to achieve their desired effect in certain nations such as England, Germany, and parts of Switzerland and Scotland. Outside Italy, the pope's main interest was to suppress heresy, to keep rebellious nations within the fold of Catholicism, and, of course, to collect rents from downstream church organizations in as many countries as possible. The papacy and its bureaucracy needed revenues to fight wars (e.g., the French incursions into Italy) and to support massive building projects such as the construction of St. Peter's Basilica. These concerns set the stage for the "Italianization" and "Romanization" of the church as it strove to protect the papal monopoly and its declining revenues.

The Roman-Italian Response

The fifteenth century, which witnessed the dominance of French clergy on the one hand and the stirrings of "heretical" activity on the other, was pivotal. During this time the Vatican's response to internal and external events was to circle the wagons around Italy and, within Italy, around Rome. This process was underway when Luther first mounted his threat against Catholicism, and was still in evidence thirty years later when the Council of Trent began. Italian cardinals so dominated the Council of Trent that historian Michael Foss proclaims they were "so numerous that they were accused of bringing the Holy Spirit in their baggage train."[32] This dominance carried over to the selection of popes as well. Table 6.2 shows the extent of Italian dominance of papal conclaves (convocations to elect a pope) between 1431 and 1523.

Table 6.2
Italianization of the papacy before the Council of Trent

Date of conclave	Number of Italian cardinals present	Others	Percent of Italians	Election of
1431	6	6	50	Eugenius IV
1447	11	7	61	Nicholas V
1455	8	7	53	Calixtus III
1458	9	9	50	Pius II
1464	11	8	58	Paul II
1471	6	2	75	Sixtus IV
1484	21	4	84	Innocent VIII
1492	22	1	96	Alexander VI
1503	27	11	71	Julius II
1513	18	7	72	Leo X
1522	36	3	92	Adrian VI
1523	34	5	87	Clement VI

Source: Adapted from Denys Hay, *The Church in Italy in the Fifteenth Century* (Cambridge: Cambridge University Press, 1977), 38.

It can be seen that the Italianization of the Vatican was proceeding a century before Luther. As the papacy came increasingly under Italian control, it sought to maintain dominance not only by appointing a disproportionate number of Italians to the College of Cardinals but also by increasing the number of cardinals (by two-thirds between 1450 and 1500). The entire field of (thirteen) popes elected after Martin V, the first pontiff to take office after the Great Schism, was drawn from only nine Italian families. At the same time, the curia, which also expanded over this period, was increasingly made up of Italians. Denys Hay remarked that despite the "contraction of business" over this period, the size of the curia (papal government officials) grew to be between roughly 450 and 500 persons, "of which two-thirds were in the main departments of the *camera* [treasury], the *chancery* [judiciary] and the penitentiary and the *rota* [appellate court], the rest being in the *familia* [household] and the bodyguard, police and so forth."[33] Interestingly, the trend toward Italianization that began in the fifteenth century has continued to this day. Membership in the College of Cardinals, the governing body of the church, increased progressively to a maximum of seventy in 1586 (where it remained until increased further in the 1960s by Pope Paul VI). With the exception of John Paul II and Benedict XVI, all popes over the half-millennium since 1526 have been Italian. The only two non-Italians of the preceding century were Alexander VI (1492–1503), a Catalan, and Adrian VI (1522–1526), a Frenchman.

Despite the outward appearance of reform established by the Council of Trent, the Italian monopoly in Rome was reluctant to curtail its economic interests. Historian B. M. Hallman gives numerous examples of intensified rent-seeking by the princes of the Church in the sixteenth century.[34] These activities took the form of nepotism (use of sacred office to aggrandize one's family); simony (the purchase of sacred office); and other financial abuses, such as pluralism of benefices (possession of more than one sacred office) and alienation of property by last will and testament.

Rent Seeking by the Upstream Church after the Council of Trent

The evolution of the medieval Catholic Church from a quasi-conciliar body in the thirteenth and fourteenth centuries to a Roman-centered, Italian-dominated, papal monopoly was virtually complete by the time the Council of Trent was invoked. Thus, economic as well as spiritual power was concentrated in the hands of a tightly organized, geopolitically homogeneous circle of prelates in Rome. Despite the fact that the financial abuses of this body constituted the proximate cause of Luther's (and others') protests, the members of this circle were naturally eager to protect their economic interests, which centered on control of church property and revenues. One common abuse was nepotism. The official declarations of the Council of Trent took aim at some of the grossest abuses. A major decree[35] prohibited bishops and cardinals from "attempt[s] to enrich their relations or domestics from the revenues of the Church," and further forbade them from giving ecclesiastical properties, "which are from God," to relatives. However, such measures appear to have been mere window dressing. According to B. M. Hallman, not only did the papal monopoly not follow the admonitions of Trent, the post-Trent abuses flourished beyond previous levels.[36]

Popes of the sixteenth century often supported family and friends from the papal treasury. To cite one egregious instance: In a mere six-year pontificate, Pius IV distributed 334,000 gold *scudi*[37] from the papal treasury to members of his family, for various purposes unrelated to the provision of church services. Between 1561 and 1565 Pius IV gave 120,000 gold *scudi* to four nieces (mainly for dowries); 22,000 *scudi* to his nephews; 10,000 *scudi* to his brother; and more than 100,000 *scudi* to other relatives. On his deathbed in 1565 he gave 100,000 gold *scudi* to his nephew, Count Annibale d'Altemps, to whom he had also granted an annulment of marriage so that d'Altemps could marry Pius's niece, thirteen-year-old Ortensia Borromeo. We do not know if, or how, d'Altemps and his young bride were blood related, but the possibility raises numerous questions about dual standards for the privileged versus the faithful. Such practices persisted into the seventeenth century.[38] Robert Bireley writes, "the papacy took on features typical of the seventeenth-century European court, so exhibiting its consonance with the times. Despite attempts of other popes to do so, only at the end of the century, in 1692, did Innocent XII take effective measures against nepotism."[39] These practices were (weakly) defended by assertions that Italians were acting as the "good signore" by taking care of relatives, but there can be little doubt that nepotism dissipated the institutional revenues of the Church.

Another common abuse was simony. Popes and cardinals sold secular and honorary offices with new vigor after the Council of Trent. A popular device for raising money through the sale of offices involved the College of Knights, a papal creation that offered membership for a high admission fee. Pius IV created the largest college of all, the *Cavalieri Pii*, "in 1560, with a total of 535 offices [sold] at 500 *scudi* of gold each."[40] The buyer received an immediate elevation in social rank. The members who bought into these groups were often Italian bankers who were well connected with the Vatican. The interlocking of economic and spiritual power was so concentrated that by the end of the sixteenth century a mere nine Italian banking families dominated the entire College of Cardinals. Expanding the political and economic realm of the Papal States also required governors, administrators, and soldiers—thereby providing more patronage opportunities for the pope. Cardinals divided these offices up as so much booty, and "by 1550 it was customary that each cardinal should possess at least one," which could be sold to the highest bidder.[41]

There were other financial abuses as well. A major element of Luther's attack on the church focused on "property crimes"—that is, personal aggrandizement by the alienation of church property and wealth to individual benefit. In short, Luther attacked the Church as an instrument of rent seeking. But while some prelates recognized the problems within the Church and supported reforms that promised to reverse the swelling tide of protest, the property crimes denounced by reformers continued unabated after Protestant entry occurred. Thus, as Hallman points out, the abuses cited by Luther in his *Address to the Nobility of the German Nation* (1520) were practically the same as those cited by Pope Paul III's reform commission of 1537.[42] Entrenched in their religious fiefdom, the Cardinals ignored exhortations by the Council of Trent against long-term rentals of church property. In 1616, "twenty four of the thirty abbeys belonging to Cardinal Scipione Borghese were rented out," and by the end of the century long-term rentals and other alienations in return for present income were common.[43]

One way of alienating church property was by last will and testament. Hallman explains:

> The money disappeared permanently into the coffers of private families ... as luxuries increased in Rome, so too did the sums of money churchmen were allowed to bequeath.... The incomes of our ecclesiastical *rentiers* [property and stock holders] were being diverted into the hands of lay *rentiers*, who were transforming the social fabric of Italy by buying their way into the nobility.... As for last wills and testaments, they, like rental agreements, pensions, and other practices, became so customary that they were sanctioned by canon law. The privilege of bequeathing church money ... now accompanies the red hat [elevation to cardinal rank] as a matter of course.[44]

Another common practice ostensibly outlawed by the Council of Trent was the holding of multiple benefices by a single bishop or cardinal. The secular meaning of *benefice* is a feudal estate in land. In ecclesiastical parlance, it is a form of preferment (e.g., endowment) that provides a living for a prelate. By holding multiple benefices, high church clerics were opportunistically usurping resources of the church for their own use. The possession of multiple benefices meant that cardinals and bishops were, in effect, always absent from some of their spiritual charges, since they could not be in residence simultaneously in more than one place. Once more, the admonitions of Trent were disregarded. Calculating the incidence of multiple benefices held by cardinals and bishops before Trent, Hallman found that approximately 90 percent of the prelates were "double-dipping" or worse. Cardinal Farnese, Vice Chancellor of the Roman Catholic Church during the convocation of the Council of Trent, for example, held no less than sixty-four separate benefices simultaneously. Comparable data during the post-Trent period are more difficult to come by, but Hallman comments, "the years of reform did nothing to alter the practice of gathering together packages of benefices and conferring them as a whole . . . If anything this practice probably increased with the years. And when vacancies were in short supply 'expectative graces' were granted."[45]

The weight of historical research on the subject demonstrates that the wholesale side of the medieval church not only resisted actual and effective reform in the wake of the Protestant Reformation; it succeeded in conducting "business as usual," shielded from view by the cloak of secrecy that enshrouded the Vatican. Patronage, nepotism, and simony all intensified, made possible by the re-monopolization of the Roman-Italian Church after the Great Schism of the fourteenth century. While some in the Catholic Church recognized the need for genuine reforms on the wholesale side, the serpentine Roman bureaucracy, entrenched in its power for at least a century before the Council of Trent, defied actual reform at the wholesale level of church organization.

The Protestant Reformation can be understood as a reaction to perceived abuses at the retail and wholesale levels of the Catholic Church, whereas the Roman Catholic Counter-Reformation may be viewed as an incumbent monopoly firm's response to entry, either actual or threatened, by a rival firm. In the wake of the Protestant Reformation the average price of the Z-good (i.e., religious services or assurances of salvation) was lowered because the Catholic Church could no longer practice price discrimination in the upper reaches of the demand curve. As expected, it engaged in vigorous competition with new entrants to retain members and prevent defections to the new religion. To be sure, the resort to violence and repression to increase the cost to individuals of defecting is not what one would expect from the stewards of a religion based on Christian principles of love and forgiveness. Expectations notwithstanding, it is clear that the Catholic Church tried to maintain, and even increase, demand for its services in the face of Protestant entry.

Clearly, to stay in business the Roman Catholic Church could not simply re-institute strictness (which, as we noted in an earlier chapter, only works in small, club-like organizations). It had to increase benefits to religious orders while lowering costs to the public. Tridentine reforms, many of which involved greater form than substance, allowed the institutional Church to present an appearance of cleaning up abuses at the retail level of church organization, and this may have been sufficient in some regions of Europe to maintain memberships in the Catholic Church and to prevent further attrition. Also, certain of the retail products of the church that dealt with social services flourished before and after the Protestant Reformation and the Catholic Counter-Reformation. Between the twelfth and fourteenth centuries the Catholic Church's activities provided models for Protestant charitable organizations.[46] The reforms introduced at the wholesale level, however, had almost no salutary effect on the faithful.

We speculate that the probable result of the Counter-Reformation was to lower the price of membership in the Catholic Church, at least modestly. The overall effect on economic efficiency is unclear, however, because the Church attempted to support demand by increasing non-price competition as well. This involved considerable use of organizational resources. Both before and after the Protestant Reformation the Roman papal apparatus found it necessary to make side payments to church and state officials in other countries to keep them in the fold. Indeed, the Reformation may be viewed in part as a consequence of the failure of side payments to keep certain countries beholden to the Italian cartel. But in the end, the side payments bestowed on governmental and church interests were insufficient to maintain the hegemony of the Catholic Church's monopoly. Concessions, including financial concessions, made to French monarchs such as Francis II and to aristocrats in several nations appear to bear this out. These concessions were insufficient in amount and distribution to bring Protestant nations, such as England and Germany, back into the fold.

In the final analysis, the Catholic Church's response to Protestantism, in practice as well as appearance, failed to clean up the wholesale side of church operations or to broaden participation in the Catholic version of Christian religion. The "sins of the fathers," in the form of blatant venality, must have been obvious to Protestants and Catholics alike. Rampant abuses of church property continued at ever-increasing levels in the sixteenth century. A part—perhaps a large part—of the failure of the Counter-Reformation to re-establish a universal church must be placed at the door of the organizational defects that allowed such venality to continue. The concentration of wealth and power by the Pope in Rome, the centralization of the Roman Catholic Church, and the establishment of an Italian "club" as its administrative bureaucracy help explain the success of Protestantism at this juncture of history.

7

The Establishment and Evolution of Protestantism

How many different masters will the next century follow? The confusion will reach new heights. None of them will be willing to be governed by the opinion or authority of the others. Each will want to set up as his own *rabbi*...And what terrible scandals there will be! What excesses! The best course would be for the princes to avert such evils by means of a council. But the Papists would avoid this: they are so afraid of the light.
—Martin Luther, *Letters of Martin Luther*

The general argument of the preceding chapters is that Protestantism was a form of competitive action taken in a market that was previously monopolistic. As in economics, competition in religion has advantages. Adam Smith recognized that sixteenth-century Protestants helped promote a supply-side revolution that amounted to a massive tax cut in terms of money and time committed to salvation seeking. The full price of church membership fell for those who embraced the Protestant faith: Time costs were reduced by leaner rituals and less ornate churches; the cost of practicing one's faith was lowered by the elimination of middlemen; and the monetary cost of securing indulgences was eliminated. Protestantism gained a foothold in the religious market by offering a new product, but the nature of the new product was not fixed for all time at its entry point. Whereas Catholicism aspired to be an all-embracing, unambiguous faith with universal appeal, Protestantism ushered in heterogeneity and diversity, evolving in response to local customs, values, and politics, as well as measures taken by the Roman Catholic Church to counteract its entry. Eventually these different brands of Protestantism would come into conflict with each other.

In the previous two chapters we described in fairly general terms the process of new-firm (Protestant) entry and dominant-firm (Catholic) reaction. In this chapter we focus on the subsequent development of Protestantism after it gained a foothold in the religious market. We wish to accomplish three major objectives. First, to establish an economic theory capable of explaining the evolution of the many forms of Christianity that Protestantism spawned. Our theory focuses on the evolution of the characteristics of these forms and on spatial competition as a determinant of market structure. Second, to particularize, mainly in economic terms, the initial governance systems (theological and organizational) of the various forms of Protestantism that were demanded and supplied in the period following Luther's break with Rome in 1517. Finally, to develop a brief analysis of the export of Christian religion and the competitive conflicts that took place as a result of European Christian market expansion.

A Theory of the Evolution of Protestantism

Our fundamental premise is that religion can be understood from an economic perspective, which means that it can be analyzed within the context of a market. In the market for Christian religions the theory of form change is informed by two main economic precepts: (1) a model of product characteristics and (2) the principles of locational competition.

Product Differentiation and Form Change under Protestantism

Because markets exist for the exchange of products, the nature of a product is central to market analysis. Compared to traditional economic theory, contemporary economics offers a sophisticated view of product in which the essence of any good is defined by the bundle of utility-creating characteristics that customers want and are willing to pay for.[1] Hence, a loaf of bread purchased at a convenience store must be seen not merely as bread, but as bread plus convenience. In other words, the customer is willing to pay a price that reflects his or her utility from consuming the bread, and a premium that reflects the utility of time saved at a convenience store as opposed to a supermarket.

Bread is not a complicated product, yet economists readily acknowledge that it involves other dimensions (time, location, etc.) that are capable of conveying utility. Many products are more complicated, thus dramatizing the basic point. An automobile is a complicated consumer product that combines characteristics that appeal to a person's demand for transportation, fashion, prestige, status, and so forth. Even within the same product group (e.g., automobiles), different characteristics are combined in different ways to attract consumers' interests and, ultimately, to clinch a sale. From an economic perspective, religion is a complicated product, entailing as it does characteristics of morality, security, acceptance, status, society, and so forth. We earlier characterized this product, in the language of Gary Becker, as a Z-good.

The history of religion from the sixteenth century to the present is a history of ever-changing faiths, each seeking out a peculiar niche in a vast religious market. In a few instances this was accomplished by monarchs, such as, for example, in England and Scandinavia. More often it was accomplished by religious entrepreneurs—Luther, Zwingli, Calvin, Knox, and so forth. As entrepreneurs they assigned different characteristics to the product (e.g., articles of faith or organization) in an attempt to satisfy potential demanders; they did this at some risk to themselves, since no one can foresee perfectly the extent of demand for a new product. From an economic perspective, this development is entirely predictable—it illustrates perfectly the unfolding of the competitive market process, a chief element of which is the theory of product differentiation. We may therefore think of Christianity as a product that evolved from its monolithic state before the Reformation to a differentiated product within a product group after. Within this product group, different denominations—or forms of religion—emerged over time to satisfy the various consumer groups who demanded different bundles of (religious) characteristics. In this way, economics predicts that once market entry was successfully achieved, Protestantism would eventually produce different denominations that appealed to different groups of consumers.

The fact that religion is a complex product (combining elements of public good, private good, credence good, club good, etc.) does not change the basic contours of the analysis we suggest. Protestantism began as an effort to reform a monopoly religion. The economic consequences of this action established a system of beliefs and membership services that was comparable to the monopoly product of the Catholic Church but entailed a lower price. The demand price was lower because consumers no longer had to bear the onus of confession, penance, good works, high taxes, and (for some) price discrimination. The supply price was lower because the new churches and the new rituals were less elaborate, requiring less initial capital and less ongoing maintenance. Both products promised salvation, but whereas the Catholic Church had so complicated its doctrinal product through rent seeking and other opportunistic behavior as to make it expensive, if not unbelievable, Protestantism presented a simplified doctrinal product that was considerably cheaper to sell and to buy.

The cost savings to buyers and sellers can be found in the theological and organizational changes that defined the new churches, as we will soon see. Some people, for example, may derive comfort from a doctrine that justifies faith by grace alone, whereas others may get utility from voting, and would therefore, other things equal, be attracted to a particular organizational form of church that allowed its members greater participation in decision making. Competition between churches can be expected to move along these margins (theological and organizational), as well as along many other margins too numerous to mention here.

In religious markets as we know them, it is inevitable that theology and organization become intertwined. All Christian religions, Catholic as well as Protestant, seek to find a scriptural basis for both their doctrines and their organization. In economics, organization is an important consideration in assessing the efficiency of outcomes, but when speaking of Christianity, it is necessary to recognize that form often follows doctrine. Roman Catholics have used the scriptural text in which Christ entrusts to Peter the "keys of the kingdom" to establish the primacy of the pope. But this was not always the case. Before the end of the first millennium, the early Catholic Church adhered to a congregational form, which eventually and gradually gave way first to an episcopal (consistory) form, and only later to the most authoritarian/hierarchical form known to any religious institution. Protestants interpret Christ's adjuration differently; they see it as the assignment of a mission to solicit and gather up a community of believers. The Protestant structure for realizing this goal can, and does, take on different organizational forms.

In chapter 5 we described a process whereby doctrinal manipulations by the medieval church steadily raised the price of membership, creating an opportunity for new entry based on a more attractive, lower-priced product. In chapter 6 we argued that the dominant-firm reaction—represented by doctrinal changes legislated by the Council of Trent (i.e., the Counter-Reformation)—had the effect of reducing the full price of some church services; but in the main, the Catholic Church continued to alienate its customers by persisting in various kinds of rent seeking. All of this took place within an organizational form that remained highly centralized and authoritative after the papacy consolidated its power around AD 1100. Because Luther bucked the authority of the old Catholic Church, it is tempting to conclude that organization was the toehold allowing Protestants entry into the religious market—but this is belied by the fact that emergent Protestant churches embraced different forms of organization, almost from the very start. It is therefore clear that the doctrinal imperative of justification by faith alone—the core unifying principle of Protestantism—can be realized under alternative forms of church governance. Hence it makes sense to treat organizational form as merely another competitive margin to be exploited in the quest for customers.

Spatial Competition and Organizational Form

This issue of the rational basis for selection of church governance among the reformed churches of Europe in the sixteenth century has not attracted much attention. Yet there is a pattern of selection that can be explained by economic theory. In religious markets that were contiguous and in which the central government was relatively weak, Protestant churches adopted more democratic (i.e., congregational) governance structures; but in isolated or sheltered markets where central government was strong, Protestant churches embraced episcopal forms of government in which bishops exercised authority. In Germany and Switzerland the authority of the central government was too weak to enforce religious conformity and avoid civil wars. The Netherlands was a federation of largely independent states, each ruled by its own representative estates. These countries were in close proximity to each other, so churches competed actively for members and were therefore forced to be more user friendly. What we observe here is the same principle we encountered in chapter 6, namely that competition was keener in contiguous or near-contiguous markets because proximity of various suppliers of religion forces them to be more competitive. This assertion is implicitly corroborated by some historians—for example, after noting how liturgy and ritual became marks of identity separating different Protestant religions, historian Bodo Nischan observes: "Concurrently there had occurred another subtle but important shift in the way Lutherans were treating church usages, *notably in regions where they were vying with Calvinists for people's confessional loyalty.* Some of the very same liturgical practices which earlier critics of the interim had condemned as 'Catholicising', many followers of the Augsburg Confession were now defending as a useful prophylactic against Reformed and other sacramentarian perversions."[2]

Denmark and Sweden were elective monarchies that placed significant restrictions on royal power. Though more isolated, its citizens nevertheless expected a measure of shared governance. Thus we find that the countries of Germany, Holland, Switzerland, Denmark, Sweden, and their dependencies adopted the congregational form of church governance, in keeping with their political/economic circumstances.

In England the outcome was opposite. Before the civil wars of the 1640s, English (Stuart) monarchs held extensive powers, and England was cut off from the Continent by physical and ideological boundaries. The central government was strong and entrenched. Not surprisingly, the English church adopted the episcopal form of governance. It fit the mold of the existing regime, and there was little pressure on the state to make the new religion user-friendly. In sum, Episcopalianism was the face of the Protestant Reformation in England, whereas Congregationalism was the face of the Reformation in Europe.

New Characteristics of Christianity: Theological Change

Catholicism offered a metacredence good that interjected complex and complicated intermediaries between God and the faithful; it also claimed exclusive rights to define the conditions of salvation for all Christians. By contrast, Protestantism—in its original form as well as in the numerous splinter groups that subsequently developed—contained an essential simplification, which was that Christ was the only intermediary between man and God. Protestants hold that God's word is revealed in the Bible, which can be read and interpreted by each and every individual without the intervention of priest or cleric. Luther stripped the belief system down to the Apostle's Creed, the Ten Commandments, and the Lord's Prayer, along with three sacraments: baptism, the Eucharist, and penance. Not all reform sects agreed on the nature and scope of doctrine, but the essential principle of "no intermediary except Christ" was common to all Protestant variations of belief. "Every man a priest" is more than a catch phrase, for Protestants believe that neither priest (in the conventional sense) nor pope is necessary to interpret the conditions of salvation. This fundamental idea—the elimination of intermediaries between God and man—is central to understanding the evolution of Christianity in its various Protestant forms.

Luther's initial and fundamental change in the religious product led to ever-changing belief systems that varied from the evangelical, ultraconservative (sometimes literal) interpretations of the Holy Bible to extremely individualistic interpretations. The principal early Protestant denominations were Lutheran, Calvinist (i.e., Reformed Protestant), and Anglican. Almost immediately factions arose between and within these churches that placed the members of each on the "left" and on the "right." On this development, historian Steven Ozment declares:

The division within Protestant ranks that is so striking to us today began almost immediately with the Reformation's initial success. Luther nailed his famous theses to the door of Castle Church in Wittenberg on 31 October 1517, and before a decade had passed he faced determined Anabaptist, Spiritualist, and Zwinglian competitors. Each took inspiration from his movement, while at the same time decrying its corruption and declaring independence from it. Here began the unending line of would-be reformers of the Reformation, who have ever since confronted the original and later versions of Protestantism with their own, allegedly truer interpretations of Holy Scripture.[3]

Thus Christianity, a religious product that had been monopolized for more than a millennium, eventually splintered into myriad consumer products offering various kinds of appeal to diverse consumer groups.

While individual precepts differed among all sects—Anabaptists did not believe in infant baptism, for example—the idea that each Christian was, to a greater or lesser degree, a unique individual capable of directing his own salvation was the essential revolutionary change of Protestantism. Some of the defining characteristics of both sixteenth- and seventeenth-century Protestantism included the following:

• Justification by faith alone: Good works (acts of Christian charity, devotion, etc.) offer no guarantee of salvation. Salvation can only be assured through a deep-seated and unwavering faith in the divinity and mercy of Christ.

• Scriptural authority: The word of God is revealed in the Bible, which is the supreme authority in all spiritual matters. The word of man, expressed through the teachings of the Catholic Church, is flawed and imperfect.

• Priesthood of all believers: Every believer, lay or clerical, can and should have a personal relationship with God. The priest was stripped of his role as special intermediary between God and man. The Bible should be made available to all believers in their own language. Since priests no longer have a special role, they need not be bound by special rules, such as celibacy.

• Fewer sacraments: Luther confined sacraments to only those outward signs that were personally instituted by Christ, which included baptism and the Eucharist, but excluded confirmation, penance, matrimony, ordination, and extreme unction.

• Denial of transubstantiation: Luther and others denied that eucharistic bread and wine are actually transformed into Christ's body and blood.

While differences existed on many minor points of doctrine (e.g., existence of the Trinity, adoration of saints, number of sacraments, predestination), a major difference between Protestant religions that was of economic consequence concerned forms of organization.

New Characteristics of Christianity: Organizational Change

Early forms of the new Christianity were characterized by different organizational schemata that were either adapted from, or reactions to, (1) the hierarchical and authoritarian form of organization employed by the Roman Catholic Church, and (2) the political environment in which the reformers found themselves. The early Reformed Church took one of two forms: congregational, or episcopal. The former represented a more dramatic break with orthodox Christianity than the latter. In the episcopal form, bishops govern, and they are appointed by a higher authority within the church. After the Reformation, some churches (e.g., Anglicanism) continued to uphold the Roman Catholic principle of apostolic succession, whereas some (e.g., Lutheranism) did not. But all episcopal forms maintained the special role of the bishop. This system is hierarchical, centralized, and in some manifestations (e.g., Roman Catholic), authoritarian. In the congregational or presbyterian model articulated by Calvin and Knox, church government is exercised by ministers and elders who are usually elected along lines that loosely conform to representative democracy. The congregational system is the form favored by Calvinists, Presbyterians, Puritans, and Congregationalists, to name a few. Interestingly, advocates of both administrative models strove to find anticipations of their organizational views in Holy Scripture, with varying degrees of success. In our reading of Scripture, we find no support for the superiority of one form of church organization over another. Christ's declaration, "Thou art Peter and upon this rock I shall build my church," is open to diverse and ambiguous interpretation, for example.

Separation of church and state is a relatively modern idea, associated more with the United States than with Europe. The concept was generally not part of the intellectual toolkit of the religious reformers of the sixteenth and seventeenth centuries. The Reformed Churches varied in terms of their official connection with the state as well as their organizational structure. What we are looking for in the history of the early Reformation are indications that the choice of organizational form by each of the Reformed Churches followed a rational pattern or underlying theory of action. We initiate this search by a brief review of the major early currents of the religious Reform Movement. For reasons that will become obvious as we progress, we have divided this survey into developments on the Continent versus companion developments in England.

Protestantism on the Continent and in Scotland

The structure of government in the different Reformed Churches assumed different form depending on contrasting economic, political, and geographic circumstances. The Reformation was born in Europe and spread most rapidly on that continent. As it moved out from Germany, Luther's influence quickly infiltrated Switzerland, the Netherlands, Scotland, and Scandinavia.

Luther (1483–1546) and Lutheranism   In the sixteenth century, church and commonwealth frequently clashed in cities or towns that enjoyed privileges granted by a strong secular ruler. In pre-Reformation Copenhagen, for example, city leaders were painfully aware that about a third of the houses and land within the city walls were owned by the Church and so exempt from taxes. The consequent limit on the municipal revenue prevented geographical and economic expansion.[4] In some cases, the bishop was also a duke, so secular authorities were unable to exert their independence. Moreover, conflicts between churches were not always "pure clashes between the laity and the clergy; they might really be struggles between cities and the nobility beyond their walls, or between different interest groups within a ruling caste."[5] A religious reformer in such a milieu could easily get caught on the wrong side of a power struggle. Indeed, powerful forces initially opposed Luther, seeing him as a threat to entrenched authority. Therefore, Luther had to be careful to align himself with the right protectors, which he did by adopting a more moderate stance than some of his contemporaries.

Following his personal interpretation of the Bible, Luther held that political institutions were ordained by God and that good Christians owed allegiance to constituted authority. Luther was a pragmatist, aware of the emerging strength of local democracies, which demanded social cooperation in civil affairs. Thus he took a moderate position in support of preference-based Christianity and individual interpretation of the Bible, but in opposition to the policies of such radical Protestant sects as the Anabaptists, Spiritualists, and Zwinglians, who leaned toward theocracy. Luther maintained that civil government should enforce Christian morality (i.e., the Ten Commandments) in their application of laws, but should not slip into theocracy. Ultimately he won out over more radical sects, possibly because of the political ramifications of their destabilizing ideas. The princes of Europe did not want a highly skewed income distribution to lead to revolutions and revolt. Luther's moderate position on the role of (reformed) religion and its interface with the political structure was obviously more appealing to the powers of the day. Church historian Diarmaid MacCulloch attests to the pragmatism of the early reformers: "With the trend in late medieval central Europe for local secular rulers to take more and more power and responsibility away from leading churchmen, it was not surprising that the first reformers in the 1520s looked to princes rather than to bishops or abbots to undertake a new round of reforms in the Church, or that much of the Reformation continued to develop with the assumption that the godly prince was the natural agent of religious revolution."[6] Of course, any such alliance of religious and secular interests strikes at the heart of the North American sensibility of separation of church and state, but the New World doctrine was born out of the desperation of religious persecution after the Reformation had become a fait accompli. Separation of church and state was not central to the original spirit of religious reform known as the Reformation.

Luther's condemnation of the Peasants' Revolt of 1524–1525, Europe's largest and most widespread popular uprising before the French Revolution of 1879, distanced him from the radical sects and undoubtedly cemented his relation with Saxon rulers. Chief among the radicals were the Anabaptists, the first insurgents against Luther. They espoused a system of socialist mysticism, defended by Thomas Müntzer, a one-time protégé of Luther. Anabaptism offered a completely different view of society, state, and Christianity. Based roughly on the earlier dualist philosophies of the Albegensian and Cathari groups, the Anabaptists denounced infant baptism and modeled all Christians as self-purified "saints." Echoing earlier intellectual and social revolts against Roman Catholicism, they extolled the poor and proclaimed all civil, secular, and state affairs as evil. Calling Luther the "pope of Wittenberg," the Anabaptists set up a popular theocracy in Mühlhausen and fomented the Peasants' Revolt of 1524–1525. Luther denounced this popular uprising against what he perceived to be "constituted authority," a move that obviously endeared him to the nobles. Even at this early date, the dissenting Protestants defended their right to choose their own pastors to instruct them in the faith of their choice.

The term "peasant" in this context is misleading, because it describes the kind of self-reliant families from which Luther, Zwingli, and so many other clergy had come. The conflict, like so many of that era, arose from landlords' attempts to impose legal and financial burdens on their tenant farmers. However, the Reformation injected an extra pressure point because it challenged the authority of the churches and monasteries, many of which were landlords in the dispute. Both Catholic and Protestant princes put down the Peasants' Revolt, which constituted a threat to their wealth and status. Luther's stance cost him sympathy with the lower classes but he gained much political support for his movement from Protestant princes who were able to invoke the new religion in efforts to secularize (confiscate) the property of the Catholic Church. As historian Emile Leonard demonstrated, Luther himself stood between the authoritarian organization of the Catholic Church on the one hand and the "anarchy" of forced wealth redistributions by civil authorities on the other.[7]

Despite the political advantage that Luther gained by his opposition to the Peasants' Revolt, it is nevertheless surprising to find a supposedly enlightened religious leader endorsing violent action against those who would destabilize society. Not surprisingly, Luther found justification in Scripture, notably St. Paul's Epistle to the Romans: "Let anyone who can, smite, slay and stab, secretly or openly, remembering that nothing can be more poisonous, hurtful or devilish than a rebel" (Romans 13:1). Diarmaid MacCulloch claims that Luther, the acknowledged champion of the ordinary Christian, was transformed into an apologist for official savagery for two reasons: his deep disappointment at the untrammeled course of evangelical reformation, and his uneasy and unspoken knowledge that without *his* reformation the events of 1524–1525 would never have happened.[8]

As if this wasn't enough, shortly into his new ministry Luther became embroiled in constant battle with the "humanists" (personified by Erasmus as well as the anarchistic theocrats). Beset on many sides, Luther took the middle ground between theocracy and anarchy. His theology was uncomplicated and calculated to have widespread appeal: A simple catechism of the Lord's Prayer, the Ten Commandments, and the Apostle's Creed were necessary for the ignorant, but within general guidelines each local church would minister to the needs of parishioners. His ideas quickly spread northward, to areas of Europe receptive to his message.

Huldrych Zwingli (1484–1531): Humanist Reformation at Zurich As Luther anticipated, early Protestants were unable to maintain a single identity. The unity of the new movement was threatened by a major rift between Luther and Zwingli over the doctrine of the Eucharist. An effort at Augsberg to reunite the whole Church failed, but in the spirit of unification, the Protestants produced the Augsberg Confession, a document that established the theological foundation for a new branch of Christendom, which soon took on the name of Lutheranism. Over the next four decades the Confession also became the basis for other statements of faith that did not strictly adhere to Lutheran lines.

The split between Luther and Zwingli produced two early versions of Protestant history and religion. Whereas Luther focused on the future (i.e., the Christ who is to come), Zwingli concentrated entirely on the past. Zwingli constructed a historical identity that stressed the unity of church and civic society; its appeal was directed toward the urban, burgher class, and it offered little to the numerically superior rural population. Historian Bruce Gordon claims that Zwingli's construction of Protestant history promoted "a view of the Swiss past which may have made sense to anti-Hapsburg sentiments, but the Zwinglian historical identity failed as a polemical tool to make the Reformation acceptable to most of the Swiss Confederate states. It was a tendentious creation too clearly aligned with the hegemonic interests of Zurich."[9]

On the doctrinal front, as boundaries and beliefs became clarified, one branch of the new Protestantism retained the name "Lutheran" and the other came to be known as "Reformed" Protestantism. Even though both versions accepted the central doctrine of justification by faith, the Reformed branch was distinguished mainly by its lack of deference to Luther and its alignment with Zwingli and Zürich. In Zwingli, political and religious ambitions overlapped. Swiss cantons became increasingly divided in the 1520s between those who accepted the evangelical message of Reformed Protestantism and those who remained loyal to the Catholic Church. Zwingli encouraged the new evangelical communities to come together in a political alliance, with the idea of maneuvering reformists and traditionalists toward religious reform. In his zeal to accomplish this holy mission, Zwingli waged war against the Catholic communities of Switzerland in the summer of 1529. The outcome was a compromise peace, the chief element of which was that each parish or village was given the right to choose, by majority of male inhabitants, which religion to adopt. The religious and political significance of this development was summarized by Diarmaid MacCulloch:

Majority voting was a new idea in communities that had previously made decisions by reaching consensus; it was also an obviously useful device for overcoming traditionalist minority obstruction. Zwingli extended the principle by organizing territorial assemblies, including both clergy and lay delegates who would make common decisions on worship for the parishes of each territory. He thus created the first evangelical church synods, which in many later, more fully developed Reformed systems formed part of a tiered structure of such decision-making bodies, some alternatively called presbyteries. This was a precedent of huge significance, not just for Reformed Churches throughout the world but for the shape of western political life generally. Often the English point complacently at their "mother of parliaments" as the source of western democratic ideals. They forget that by modern standards there was nothing especially democratic about their parliamentary system for most of its history; whereas the synodical, representative form of government in the Reformed Church established hierarchy in society. The synodical model was of particular importance when after 1776 the leadership in the fledgling United States of America drew on its own experience of Reformed Churches in creating its new forms of government.[10]

Zwingli's overreaching attempts to impose the Reformation by force in Switzerland ended abruptly when he was cut down and butchered by a Catholic army that rose up against his economic blockade against the Catholic Inner States of Switzerland. His impact might have died with him but for Heinrich Bullinger's successful attempt to return the Zwinglian Church to stability. An able and patient priest, Bullinger remained true to Zwingli's legacy even as he quietly modified its troublesome aspects. Refraining from political involvement, Bullinger tried to heal divisions between the followers of Zwingli and Luther. His most durable contribution lay in developing one aspect of Zwinglian theology that provided a unifying force—the idea of the covenant. According to Diarmaid MacCulloch, "The idea that God made demands of his chosen people in a covenant was attractive to Reformed Protestants because it offered a solution to a great problem posed by Luther's doctrine of justification by faith, namely, how to persuade people to be moral beings if God had already marked them for salvation without any effort on their part."[11]

John Calvin (1509–1564) and Calvinism   After Zwingli's untimely death, Calvin—who was never ordained a priest or minister in any church—became the leader of the Reform Movement. Unlike Luther, he took a precise and detailed interest in how the church should be structured. His ideas struck a harmonic chord in the city of Geneva. Geneva gave him the opportunity to try out his new ideas because the city's ruling elite wanted to maintain such a structure under its control. Martin Luther taught that God looks after what goes on in the world in two distinct ways. On the one hand, God provides governments for basic social order; on the other hand, God provides the church to proclaim the Gospel. The business of government is to preserve and protect society, and the business of the church is to share God's grace and to remind Christians of their responsibility to their neighbors. This became known as the "two-kingdoms" theory, designed to reinforce mutual responsibilities between church and state. Calvin applied this theory to good effect by structuring the Genevan church so as to function hand in glove with the city government. From Martin Bucer, the leading reformer in the German city of Strasbourg, Calvin borrowed the premise that the New Testament established four functions of ministry: pastors, doctors, elders, and deacons. Pastors carried out the general ministry of the laity exercised by medieval priests and bishops; doctors were responsible for teaching at all levels (including scholarly investigations of the Bible); elders exercised disciplinary functions; and deacons supervised and administered almsgiving.

Calvin succeeded in Geneva where Bucer had failed in Strasbourg. He set up a church governmental apparatus that operated citywide, so that under his influence Geneva approached a theocracy. From 1541, governing councils in Geneva stood alongside the system that Calvin had created for the Church—city councils had some say in choosing the elders of the Church but did not interfere directly in the selection of pastors.

As a result the Genevan pastoral ministry became a self-perpetuating body. Diarmaid MacCulloch explains the contrast in governing style between Calvin and Luther: "[Calvin's system] was a far cry from the clerical ministry simultaneously evolving in Luther's Germany, [being] effectively a wing of the bureaucracy of princes or city councils, and chosen by them as they would choose their other officers. It was in fact much more like the high clericalism of the old western Church."[12] Ironically, the church structure that arose from the peculiar political circumstances of Geneva was copied all over Europe wherever Calvin's independent form of the Church was admired, even though the same political circumstances did not exist in all those places.

As Calvin was consolidating his position in Geneva in the 1550s, he became more outspoken in his rejection of Luther's doctrine of the Eucharist, insisting that the sacramental bread and wine had mere symbolic significance. Lutherans retained the liturgical trappings of the traditional Mass, which suggested to the Reformed "an understanding of the Eucharist which was, to put it simply, papal and magical rather than evangelical."[13] As a consequence, the division between Lutheran and non-Lutheran Protestants, manifest decades earlier in the controversy leading up to the Augsberg Confession, hardened into doctrinal warfare, and dashed the hopes of earlier reformists that a real reunion could be accomplished. In fact, from the middle of the fifteenth century on, division reigned not merely between Catholics and non-Catholics but between Lutherans and non-Lutherans as well. Moreover, in the clash between Catholics and non-Catholics, Protestants demonstrated that they could be bloodthirsty as well. This was especially true in England, where in the decade between 1581 and 1590, 78 priests and 25 laypeople were executed. More executions occurred in the following years: 53 priests and 35 laypeople between 1590 and 1603; and 70 more priests between 1601 and 1680. "In fact," notes MacCulloch, "England judicially murdered more Roman Catholics than any other country in Europe, which puts English pride in national tolerance in an interesting perspective."[14]

As a consequence of this religious divide, Calvin's name came to be associated with the whole of Reformed Protestant theology and practice, so much so that the blanket term *Calvinism* was applied to a wide range of Reformed Churches. Aside from the fact that Calvin himself would not have approved of this, it obscures the fact that there were many currents within the Reformed Protestant world to seek leadership elsewhere. Calvin's doctrine of predestination proved to be a particular sticking point. The idea that some fixed number of souls would be saved by God's grace did not sit well with some, especially the merchants. Calvinism therefore spawned alternatives offering a softer version of predestination and, structurally speaking, resembling a more labor-managed form of local church organization.

John Knox (1505–1572) and Reformation in Scotland   Whereas in England the Reformation was directed at every turn by the Crown, the Scottish Reformation was grounded in a rebellion against God's anointed monarch. Queen Mary arrived from France as Scotland's new monarch in 1560 after the death of her young husband, François II. Inexperienced in politics, she quickly made a mess of things, alienating Protestant politicians who had tried to remain loyal to her. Her misrule led to civil war, resulting in a series of Protestant and pro-English regimes. Steering the national revolution against Queen Mary was John Knox, a protégé of Calvin's who admired the Geneva Church.

The Lutheran character of the Reformation evaporated quickly in Scotland, leaving the path open to the Reformed Protestants. With the backing of Scotland's lesser nobility, Knox and his cohorts prevailed in the Scottish Parliament. The outcome was legislation that created a radically new Protestant Church, the Kirk. Establishment of the Scottish Kirk was part of a shrewd political deal that set up a national church polity allowing the Kirk to coexist alongside a ghost of the old Catholic Church system. This allowed for the "repatriation" of the old Church's officeholders, who continued to draw two-thirds of their former revenues even if they did not take an active role in the new Church—which, of course, many did. The result was a more orderly, less violent, transfer of religious power from old to new.

Knox was, according to MacCulloch, "an anglicized and comparatively moderate Calvinist" who envisioned a broadly based Protestantism accepting of the bishopric and allowing a strong role for the secular power in church affairs.[15] However, after his death this vision was supplanted by a more doctrinaire presbyterianism that asserted equality among ministers in the Kirk and independence of political authority. The modern Presbyterian Church stems from this post-Knoxian development.

Protestantism in Scandinavia   In Scandinavia, as elsewhere in northern Europe, the spread of Protestantism was made possible by the enthusiasm of the government for the movement, probably because it promised increased independence from Rome. Within two decades of Luther's break with the old Church, the Reformation was established in Scandinavia by peaceful means. The political map of Scandinavia was different in the sixteenth century. The strong kingdoms were Denmark and Sweden. Norway and Iceland were dependencies of Denmark; Finland was dependent on Sweden. Outside Germany, Scandinavia is the only area in which Lutheranism became the official state religion. The monarchs of Denmark and Sweden themselves sponsored the reform movement, and broke completely with the papacy.

In Sweden, the path of the Reformation superficially resembles the English experience. In both cases, the Reformation was led by the king himself and the wealth of the Church was confiscated. In some ways, however, the Swedish case was a better example of naked economic opportunism. Gustavus Vasa, the elected king of Sweden after the deposition of the tyrant Christian II, needed funds to run his kingdom, and the Church provided a ready source of great wealth. Assisted by brothers Olaus and Laurentius Petri, Vasa advocated the adoption of Lutheranism as the state religion. The Catholic authorities in Sweden saw that they would have to cut a deal with the king, so they agreed to support him politically and financially if he would leave the Catholic faith and its liturgy alone. Gustavus agreed. At that time, most Swedes still favored the Catholic Church. But in his bid to make his kingdom financially secure, Gustavus gradually maneuvered the Catholic Church into a corner. Swedish Catholics appealed to Rome, but the popes could do little to help. Italy was too far away.

By action of the Swedish Diet in 1529, the Church was turned into a national institution, its estates were confiscated by the crown, and the Protestant Reformation was introduced in several stages. After the reformers published the Bible and other books in Swedish, the Swedes came to prefer Reformation doctrines.[16] But except in Stockholm, the Reformation in Sweden was never a popular movement. It was imposed from above.

The Reformation was more of a popular movement in Denmark than it was in Sweden. But here, as well, the impetus came from the king. The successor to Christian II was Frederick I, who, upon his coronation, promised to persecute the Lutherans in Denmark. Instead, it was during his reign (1523–1533) that the Catholic Church in Denmark was destroyed. From 1526 on, Danish bishops were confirmed by the king, and never after did they seek papal confirmation. In major cities, such as Copenhagen, reformers gained the upper hand, with the complicity of the king. Throughout Denmark the monasteries gradually disappeared and churches were destroyed with the king's permission.

A brief interregnum followed upon the death of Frederick I in 1533. His son and likely successor, Christian III, was a devout Lutheran, which prevented his election to the throne by a council whose majority was Catholic. Three years later, Christian III acceded to the throne after successfully repelling a German invasion with the help of Gustav Vasa. Strapped for cash, as had been his ally, Vasa, Christian turned to the Church to help finance his kingdom. When the bishops proved reluctant to help, he had them arrested and imprisoned, and appropriated their property. Eventually, the churchmen were released, but the property and positions were never restored; the action was accepted by the laity because the bishops had not been popular. In 1536 a national assembly held in Copenhagen abolished the authority of the Roman Catholic bishops throughout Denmark and its subject lands, thus officially signaling the downfall of the old Church. Within two decades of Luther's break with Rome, Lutheranism reigned supreme in Scandinavia. However, as in England, the Reformation in Scandinavia was less the product of religious entrepreneurs than of monarchical aspirations.

Protestantism in England   In the sixteenth century, England was a country of exceptional conditions, both civil and religious. Compared to developments on the Continent, the shape of the Protestant Reformation in England was determined by circumstances that are sufficiently peculiar to warrant separate treatment. On the Continent, the new religion was embraced in countries that were more or less contiguous (e.g., Germany, Holland, Switzerland). As a result, the market in Europe for different religions was broader, and competition was keener between Protestant sects. As an island kingdom, England was physically isolated from Europe, and its isolation made it easier for a powerful monarch such as Henry VIII (1491–1547) to control the religious market.

Henry's quarrel was not with traditional religion but with the pope. In fact, Henry was repulsed by Luther and he initially wholeheartedly supported the Catholic Church's campaign against him. Henry's difficulties with the papacy began in the late 1520s, when he sought annulment of his marriage to Catherine of Aragon, who had failed to produce a male heir to the throne. The Vatican, already enraged with the English over their refusal to help defend Europe against the Turks, obstructed the annulment. Henry was goaded by the Vatican's stance into finding an alternative strategy for accomplishing what he (and God) wanted. He mobilized a team of theological experts to tackle the problem. The result was his sudden awareness of an ancient truth: that he was Supreme Head of the Church within his dominions. Henry got his way by merely putting his own authority above that of the Church. Having no particular interest in administering a state religion, he delegated his new royal supremacy over English religion to his ambitious minister, Cromwell, who seized the opportunity to plunder the churches and monasteries in order to enrich the kingdom. In the final analysis, England took Church property but did not reject its organizational form. It maintained its traditional threefold ministry of bishop, priest, and deacon, thus clinging to the old episcopal structure of the Catholic Church from which it broke away. Eventually, this distinctively British form of Protestantism assumed the name of Anglicanism.

Henry no doubt welcomed the resulting wealth that he derived from his nationalization of the Catholic Church in England, and he seemed indifferent to the consequential elimination of much of traditional religion that resulted from his confiscation of Church property. But the nationalization of religion, like the nationalization of industry, requires an investment of economic resources and produces economic consequences. For one thing, it establishes a future risk premium that can impede the actions of future religious entrepreneurs and retard the flow of future investment in religion. If assets can be nationalized (confiscated) under one monarchy, they can be under future monarchies as well. It also alters the flow of monetary rewards and employment patterns for participants in the old and new regimes.[17]

The Dissenters, or Nonconformists By the time King James ascended to the English throne in 1603, the Church of England was dominant, but it was also regarded by many religious leaders as static. A younger generation of Protestant clergy was frustrated by the intransigence of the bishops, who resisted change. This younger generation coalesced into a minority group that came to be known as Puritans, a new sect that saw episcopacy as part of the problem. The obvious solution was to replace the episcopacy with a presbyterian system.

Puritans became increasingly disenchanted with liturgical approaches to God, and more convinced that preaching was the only way in which ordinary Christians could receive God's truth. Calvin said as much, though not as forcefully as the Puritans. Despite lack of theological controversy, the Puritans eventually separated from the national Church of England. To put it simply, Puritan separatism was about organizational structure, not religious or devotional issues. Nevertheless, their resistance to episcopal and secular rule resulted in increasingly intensified attacks by conformist authority. To escape the threat of persecution, and to establish a purer version of Protestant Europe, English Puritans eventually sailed across the Atlantic to settle in the New World.

The conflicts engendered within the Church of England by those who refused to conform to the requirements of an established church were a major factor leading to the English civil war. After the victory of the Puritan party in that war, other nonconformist sects gained a stronger foothold. But the restoration of the English monarchy in 1660 also brought the restoration of the episcopacy, and repressive legislation against the Puritans. By requiring episcopal ordination of all ministers, the Act of Uniformity (1662) made a distinct split between conformists and nonconformists inevitable. As a result, nearly two thousand English clergymen left the established church, marking the beginning of significant nonconformity in England. Within short order, dissenting denominations were formed by Presbyterians, Congregationalists, Baptists, Quakers, Methodists, and Unitarians.

Some historians consider the British Nonconformists to be an extremely important factor in the Industrial Revolution. Dissenters found themselves barred from public employment and university education at Oxford and Cambridge by a series of Test Acts in the 1660s and 1670s. As a consequence, they became active in manufacturing, and Unitarians in particular established dissenting academies as alternatives to university education. The new academies stressed mathematics and the sciences—disciplines that contributed to the development of manufacturing technologies. Although the Dissenters were excluded from government circles, they were considered to be fellow Protestants by many middle-class businessmen and financiers. They therefore had access to capital which the most enterprising of these sects could direct—almost by necessity—to technologies created in the wake of the scientific revolution of the seventeenth century.

Foreign Markets vs. Domestic Markets

As markets mature, more and more attention comes to be lavished on production for export. By the sixteenth century, the mature market for Christianity was in western Europe and the British Isles. Europe achieved this status even before the Reformation percolated. Therefore, in tracing the history of the export market for religion, we must start from pre-Reformation times. What we find in the case of religion is that foreign markets are developed primarily by two mechanisms: emigration and missions.

The Export of Protestantism after the Reformation
Reformation Protestants engaged in practically no missionary activity outside their home market (Europe) before the eighteenth century. They were too busy fighting Catholic forces in the struggle to survive, or quarreling among themselves in their quest for identity. As Protestantism became established throughout Europe, and the inevitable process of product differentiation proceeded apace, the field was opened for various forms of religious outreach.

By far the most important overseas market for Protestantism was the New World, and the chief form of expansion into that market was through emigration. Because the monopolizing spirit of Protestantism was greatest in England, it is not surprising that the first major wave of emigrants came from that country. In the New World, religious groups like the Pilgrims and the Puritans not only found more freedom to worship, they also began to proliferate in freedom's soil. Oddly enough, the Puritans championed individual freedom within their ranks but were intolerant of opposing creeds. Still, they could not establish a monopoly religion in a country as vast and resourceful as North America. Moreover, the new nation that we now call the United States enshrined religious toleration in its constitution and, over the next three centuries, in an ongoing process of product differentiation, spawned and nurtured many new branches of Reformed Protestantism. Having been erected on the twin pillars of individual and religious freedom, America became an important laboratory in a bold new experiment of religious pluralism. Many of the new denominations derived their substance and structure from one of the major Protestant churches of northern Europe.

The Character of U.S. Protestantism

Table 7.1 provides a summary view of major churches in the United States, showing several distinguishing characteristics of faith and structure. While practically all the new faiths were Bible-centered, a few maintained a higher authority in the figure of God himself. Quakers, for example, believe that Christ holds authority over the Bible.

To describe a faith as "eucharistic" means that it accords a prominent place to the Lord's Supper in its doctrinal base; "episcopal" refers to a hierarchic administration (i.e., bishops) not based on principles of representative democracy; "congregational" refers to an organizational structure that allows leaders to be chosen by election or other democratic process.

Table 7.1 makes no attempt to be complete or comprehensive. The number of non-traditional religious sects and denominations in the United States and in the world has continued to proliferate to the present day, but there is little point in scrutinizing every doctrinal or organizational peculiarity. Nor should this table be interpreted in a rigid fashion,

Table 7.1
Major Protestant churches in the United States

Church	Doctrine		Organization	
	Bible-centered	Eucharistic	Episcopal	Congregational
Adventists	X	X		X
Baptists	X	X		X
Church of God	X		X	X
Congregational Christian	X			X
Episcopal (Anglican)	X	X	X	
Friends (Quakers)				X
Lutheran	X	X		X
Mennonite	X	X		X
Methodist	X	X	X	
Mormon	X		X	
Moravian	X		X	
Pentecostal	X		X	
Presbyterian	X			X
Unitarian				X

because it is difficult to put some churches into precise categories on matters of doctrine or organization. Nevertheless, it serves to illustrate, at a glance, the general process of product differentiation that manifested itself in the establishment of churches once the market was opened by successful market penetration in the sixteenth century. The fact that it took decades, and in some cases centuries, for new "products" to emerge is of no particular consequence, because intermittent and ongoing product differentiation is to be expected in any market as long as that market remains viable.

With respect to church governance we find, for the most part, the same forces at work here as before. Churches that adopted the episcopal form in Europe maintained that form in the United States; for the most part, so did their offshoots. Methodism, for example, derived from the Anglican Church. Its founder, John Wesley, was a high Anglican prelate before he broke away from that staid institution to establish his new church. His disagreement, however, apparently did not extend to the matter of church governance. Moravians and Methodists were intertwined early on (Wesley is said to have derived his inspiration from a pious group of Moravians he met while aboard ship en route to the American colonies in 1736). The Moravian emphasis on conversion and holiness became and remains central to Methodism. Pentecostalism is a broad term that describes a large number of revivalist sects in the United States, most of which come out of Methodist or Baptist backgrounds. These churches have a tendency to preserve the governance structure of their root institution. The Mormons have had the most tempestuous history of any church in the United States. Attacked by angry mobs and by U.S. Army troops, they sought protection through isolation in the Utah desert, where they built a religious empire that defied the odds and became one of the fastest growing denominations in the United States. It is controversial to categorize the Mormon Church as Protestant, but we do so here in the interest of drawing meaningful generalizations rather than adhering to categorical precision. The Mormon religion appeals to people who yearn for discipline and are willing to grant loyalty to strong, centralized authority. This church influences every phase of the lives of its members, providing education, recreation, employment, and relief in illness or poverty. The Church of God is the name given to at least two hundred independent religious bodies in the United States, making it difficult to characterize in exact terms. Some of these churches elect leadership; some appoint.

Given the economic and political history of the United States, it was perhaps inevitable that even those American Protestant churches that organized around the episcopal system would nevertheless succumb over time to democratizing influences. The Episcopal Church in the United States is somewhat more democratic than the Anglican Church from which it derived. This merely affirms the fact that churches must respond to the market environment in which they operate as well as the demands of their (local) customers.

Financing Protestantism

There is, unfortunately, a scarcity of exact information on how the evolving variants of Protestantism were financed. Conventional wisdom is that local churches depended mostly on biblical tithing by members.

Where redistributive organizations such as synods did not exist, many congregational churches had to live by their own receipts. These churches, as Adam Smith suggested, most closely tended to the demands of members. Other organizational structures, such as the episcopal form, created methods of redistribution from wealthier parishes to poorer ones. In all forms, the biblical tithe of 10 percent of a member's income was held up as the ideal. In reality, that ideal was probably seldom met, with the prominent exception of the Mormon Church.

It appears from existing evidence that churches had to be innovative in their search for funds to cover expenses. Church historian David Hempton, for example, discusses the vagaries of the financing of Methodist churches in the post-Colonial period (up to 1830) in the United States. There seems to have been a trend away from volunteerism and egalitarianism in financing to a situation in which demands were met on a more structured basis.[18] More structure meant that congregations had to cater to the practical reality of financing religion by appealing to donors on the basis of what would get them to give. Appeal had to be made and influence given to the wealthier members of particular churches. Practices that worked in medieval times, such as naming aspects of the church (pews, stained-glass windows, etc.) for large donors, were often invoked.

While many churches, especially evangelical churches, depended on tithing, others showed signs of entrepreneurship in devising innovative finance mechanisms. In a discussion of the finances of a Dutch Reformed church—the First Church of Albany, New York—economists Robin Klay and John Lunn present a picture of church finance in the first half of the nineteenth century.[19] As might be expected, the ability of the church to cover expenses and finance new projects was a function of the economic conditions in Albany and in the economy in general. Early funding methods included land rentals and sales (ostensibly from purchases and gifts) and special collections to address shortfalls. Clearly, relying on the weekly donations of a "grateful laity" did not work. Voluntary tithing schemes are typically subject to the free-rider problem. By 1857 the First Church had sold all of the land it owned and was forced to develop more structure to pay for its activities, which included foreign and domestic missions, poor relief, education, publications, and so on.

Some activities were paid for by special assessments, such as the minister's salary (an exaction called *domine gelt*). One example that indicates the privileged position that its ministers enjoyed is in 1854, the board of Albany's Dutch Reformed church voted for a 25 percent increase in the minister's annual salary—from $2,000 to $2,500 at a time when the annual average earnings of nonfarm employees was $363. In the church's financial reorganization, weekly donations were structured and pew rents, a critically important form of revenue, were doubled. Pew rents, often accompanied by "naming opportunities," were a preferred method of support for all kinds of churches, including Roman Catholic churches, well into the twentieth century. Klay and Lunn report that as much as 88 percent of the operating budget of the First Church of Albany was covered by such rents.[20]

Pew rents gave religious entrepreneurs a method of practicing price discrimination. Financial statistics for the Twickenham United Reformed Church (in London) show that until 1911, regular members of the morning congregation rented specific seats on a "quarterly rental" scheme.[21] The cost of this reserved seating depended on the proximity to the pulpit, organ, and choir. Seats furthest away cost two shillings and sixpence (12.5p), whereas those closest cost 5 shillings (25p). Intermediate prices were charged for seats in between. It is important to note that these rates were "suggested" and had to be reserved through a church official. In 1910, pew rents at the Twickenham church covered 25 percent of its annual expenditure, with Sunday collections and donations covering 50 percent, and bazaars and similar efforts covering the remaining 25 percent. If all seats had been paid for in the amount suggested, the take on pew rents would have doubled. The high costs of monitoring and administering the pew rent system was one factor, and the non-egalitarian flavor of the discriminatory scheme was another.

The pew rental scheme to raise revenue, common in both Protestant and Roman Catholic churches well into the twentieth century, is a case of second-degree price discrimination. Here sellers (in this case local churches) create different qualities of products or services to maximize profits (or to meet a particular level of expenditures). Consumers are then free to sort themselves according to their demand for the created quality class differences. This differs from third-degree price discrimination, in which consumers are preclassified by external characteristics (age, income, location, and so on). While it might be expected that higher income parishioners would take the highest price seats, this is not necessarily the case. Status seekers, or others who want "to be seen" at services are willing to pay higher prices. Thus "egalitarian principles" may have supplemented the argument that pew rents were costly to collect or difficult to devise. In fact, the Twickenham church in London abandoned the pew scheme (and the use of bazaars) in 1911, switching to a system in which "each contributor has a private form sent to him in the first instance and is asked to say in confidence the total amount that he or she is prepared to contribute weekly toewards [sic] support of the church. The amount would be enclosed each week in an envelope to be placed in the collection plate at one of the Sunday services."[22] The abandonment of pew rentals appears to have begun by mid-twentieth century, but the practice was still a major financing device of both Protestant and Roman Catholic churches in the nineteenth and part of the twentieth centuries in the United States and in England.

Economic theory tells us that successful entry into a previously monopolized market is often achieved by offering lower prices to customers of the incumbent monopoly firm. The Protestant Reformation accomplished exactly that. The opening up of religious markets introduced competition among churches in the sixteenth century, and led to an ongoing process of product differentiation. This epochal transformation had a number of important possible effects. Chapter 8 examines a controversial effect: the impact of Protestantism on economic growth and capitalism. In the final chapter we consider another effect: the ongoing evolution of forms of Christianity made possible by the competitive process that the Protestant Reformation engendered.

8

Catholicism, Protestantism, and Economic Performance

Christianity is an idea, and as such is indestructible and immortal, like every idea.
—Heinrich Heine, *History of Religion and Philosophy in Germany*

Economists are quite naturally interested in the effects of ideology on economic performance, and because religion is arguably the most powerful ideological force of human experience, it is understandable that economic analysis would extend to the role of religion in explaining economic growth and development. The most famous study linking economics and religion so far is claimed by sociology, even though it was undertaken by an author with no formal training in the subject. Max Weber was employed as an economist and trained as a lawyer, but he wrote one of the most widely read studies in the history of sociology: *The Protestant Ethic and the Spirit of Capitalism*, a book frequently misinterpreted and often criticized, but, above all, a classic.[1]

Broadly stated, Weber's argument suggests that because Calvinist ethics support wealth accumulation, Protestants' marginal propensity to save increased and exceeded that of Catholics, so that capital accumulation and economic growth occurred more rapidly in Protestant regions of western Europe. In contrast, Catholicism retarded economic growth in large measure because of its (supposedly) socialistic view of wealth and its maintenance of usury prohibitions and other repressive measures. Weber's approach to capital accumulation is preference-based: It holds that the advent of Protestantism and its precepts changed *tastes* in favor of work versus leisure and saving versus consumption. This is clearly a demand-side argument for it emphasizes the fact that "saving for salvation," together with individual responsibility and initiative, means increased investment over time with economic growth a chief result.

We have no quarrel with the demand-side-preferences approach to Weber, but it may not go far enough. This chapter attempts to break new ground by offering a supplementary supply-side economic explanation for relative economic development in areas that became Protestant after the Reformation. Tastes changed, in other words, but so did constraints. The Reformation freed up resources such as saving, capital, and labor supply that could be directed to productive uses in the first half of the sixteenth century. We believe that both demand- and supply-side factors affected the timing and extent of Protestant entry. The average price of religious services was reduced, thereby releasing capital, increasing investment, and inducing growth. Reduced price came in the form of lower direct and indirect costs of religious activity. Specifically, the Protestant creed emphasized simple customs and worship rituals, and eliminated festivals, feast days, and pilgrimages, which freed up labor for economically productive activity. These factors stimulated economic growth.

Growth in Protestant areas was also premised on the failure of the Counter-Reformation to reclaim lost territory. Protestant entry freed up resources that were available for growth-promoting investments in the areas that embraced Protestantism. Our argument is that, in part, economic growth was made possible by the entry of new denominations offering many kinds of religious services at lower costs to consumers than those offered by the Roman Catholic Church. The consumer surplus released made investments in capital possible and, in Protestant areas, economic growth was stimulated. Additionally, the Protestant creed eliminated costly ceremonies and practices. Finally, one of the chief criticisms of Weber's hypothesis (or the naïve version of it, at least) is that it is falsified by demonstrable economic growth in countries that remained Catholic, such as Hungary or Belgium. A supply-side economic perspective demonstrates that growth in such countries was quite predictable.

Thus we reexamine the Weberian hypothesis by adding elements heretofore excluded from the discussion of the impact of religion on economic development. After outlining Weber's hypothesis, we present a theory of the possible impact of the release of physical and human resources made possible by Protestantism. While we make no strong inferences concerning the impact of the new form of Christian religion on economic growth, the addition of supply-side elements establishes a new perspective from which Max Weber's famous thesis may be evaluated.

Max Weber Revisited

Weber's analysis of the relationship between religion and economic development placed more emphasis on broad religious imperatives than on the specific injunctions that each particular religion might impose on economic behavior.[2] Hence he wrote of a singular "Protestant ethic," even though as we saw in the previous chapter Protestantism is a fractured and fragmented set of religions, each with its own code of beliefs, doctrines, and practices. His project aimed at establishing a link between this Protestant ethic and the "spirit" of capitalism, but it also sought an explanation for why Western civilization proved to be such fertile ground for the Industrial Revolution and the growth of modern capitalism. As such, Weber's study did not confine itself to religious factors, although he elevated religion to a position of dominance, especially in the long run.[3] The Protestant ethic is derived from fundamental religious principles, yet it is both secular and worldly. It includes, perhaps even produces, an *economic* ethic—"the earning of more and more money combined with the strict avoidance of all spontaneous enjoyment of life."[4]

For Weber, the *spirit* of capitalism is antecedent to the *emergence* of capitalism, and it is derived from the Protestant ethic. Nowhere in his study does Weber define "the spirit of capitalism," but he conveys its meaning in terms of Benjamin Franklin's homespun philosophy concerning the utility of virtue: "Honesty is useful because it assures credit; so are punctuality, industry, frugality, and that is the reason they are virtues. . . . According to Franklin, those virtues, like all others, are only in so far virtues as they are actually useful to the individual, and the surrogate of mere appearance is always sufficient when it accomplishes the end in view."[5]

Within this ethic, making money is not only the highest good, it is a *duty*, one which is closely connected with the religious idea of a *calling*: "The earning of money within the modern economic order is, so long as it is done legally, the result and the expression of virtue and proficiency in a calling."[6] In other words, economic success is a measure of individual virtue. It is this idea that sets Weber's analysis apart—he limits its acceptance to western Europe and America, but he was well aware that "capitalism existed in China, India, Babylon, in the Classic World and in the Middle Ages. But in all these cases...this particular ethos was lacking."[7]

Despite popular and naïve perversions of Weber's thesis, it is important to note that he did not claim that the Protestant ethic alone was sufficient to bring about the capitalist system—in other words, religion did not *cause* capitalism. Nor did he champion the extreme position that modern capitalism would not have come into being without the Protestant ethic. Rather, Weber maintained the intermediate position that the Protestant ethic significantly fostered and accelerated the development of Western capitalism. As noted previously, he was well aware that forms of capitalism existed prior to the Reformation. But he was equally aware that only in western Europe and America did capitalism evolve in such a way as to encourage an Industrial Revolution and an industrial society.[8] For Weber, therefore, there was something special about Western capitalism *after* the Reformation. He found that special factor in the Protestant work ethic and its strong element of asceticism.

The most basic aspect of Protestantism is its doctrine of salvation. Salvation is attained by faith alone, but Protestantism advocates forms of human behavior that are pleasing to God, such as good works. Luther, in particular, decisively altered the (pre-Reformation) Christian conception of good works by prescribing the fulfillment of duties in worldly affairs as the highest form which the moral activity of the individual could assume.[9] Calvin complicated matters by adding the doctrine of predestination. Under Calvin's influence, good works became an objective and reliable sign of grace, so that those who practiced them could thereby assuage their doubts and allay their fears. Hence, good works became not so much a toll on the highway to heaven but rather the means of getting rid of the fear of damnation.[10] It is easy to see how the combination of Lutheran virtue and Calvinist asceticism yielded an ethos that stimulated entrepreneurs and artisans alike to achieve economic success in their respective spheres. This ethic was a dramatic shift from the Christian ethic of pre-Reformation times. But being preference-based in origin, it postulated a demand-driven course of action: The advent of Protestantism and its precepts changed tastes in favor of work versus leisure and saving versus consumption. In Weber's own words, "We are interested in...the influence of those psychological sanctions which, originating in religious belief and the practice of religion, gave a direction to practical conduct and held the individual to it."[11] The relation to the modern theory of individuals using inputs to obtain more "ultimate" commodities is apparent. Our argument follows economists George J. Stigler and Gary S. Becker in that we seek an explanation of the impact of Protestantism that stresses resource availability.[12] This is what we mean when we refer to our approach as a "supply-side" or constraint-driven theory. We are aware, of course, that the postulated changes in tastes by Weber for more work and more investment impacted on the supply-side of these economies. But to Weber's demand-side theory we offer a complementary theory that stresses the supply side of economic behavior and brings more balance to the historical connection between religion and economic growth.

The Supply Side and Growth in Post-Reformation Europe

As we saw in previous chapters, the Reformation began a process of multiple-firm entry into a monopoly religious market in the sixteenth century. This process reduced the average price of religious services, thereby releasing capital from religious uses so that it could be redirected toward secular ends, the effect of which was to induce economic growth. Growth in Protestant areas was, of course, also premised on the failure of the Counter-Reformation to reclaim markets that it had lost to the new entrants. Rather than view the connection between religion and economic development in (Weberian) macroeconomic terms (i.e., a change in the labor supply or savings function of Protestants versus Catholics), we take a microeconomic approach that focuses on the effects of changes in individual and group consumer surplus. Our argument is that, in part, economic growth was made possible by the entry of new denominations offering religious services to consumers at costs lower than those offered by the Catholic Church. The consumer surplus released by this price reduction made it possible to invest in nonreligious capital, which had the effect of stimulating economic growth. We recognize that one of the chief criticisms of Weber's hypothesis (or the naïve version of it at least) is that it is disproven by demonstrable economic growth in countries that remained *Catholic*, such as Hungary or Belgium. A supply-side economic perspective casts a different light on this argument, as we shall see.

It is important to note here that a steady stream of rents flowed to Rome as the Pope and his bureaucracy maintained their monopoly with entry-and-competition-deterring programs such as the Crusades, assaults on heresies, inquisitions, and witch hunts. Protestant entry produced three important effects: (1) a reduction in the amount of resources flowing to the Roman Catholic Church from the demand side for religious services; (2) a reduction in the cost inflation created by rents, both "voluntary" and forced, gathered to finance massive church investments in cathedrals throughout Europe in the twelfth and thirteenth centuries, and (3) competition between contiguous Protestant and Catholic regions resulting in greater economic development in these Catholic regions.

Price Discrimination and Protestant Entry

In contrast to the naïve version of Weber's (demand-side) thesis, there are testable implications of the supply-side theory of Protestant entry. To underscore the testable economic implications of entry into the medieval religious market, recall our simple model from chapter 6. In figure 8.1 let AD represent the market demand for church services. MC_c and MC_p represent the marginal production cost of two religions, Catholicism and Protestantism, which, at least initially, are assumed equal to each other. The fact that the demand curve for religious services has a negative slope is unexceptionable. The cost function is related to the provision of inputs in the supply of religious services.

Assume that the medieval Roman Catholic Church practiced perfect price discrimination before Protestant entry. The entire area (ABC) under the demand curve prior to entry therefore represents potential consumers' surplus. Under these circumstances, the largest "donors" of consumer

Price of religious services

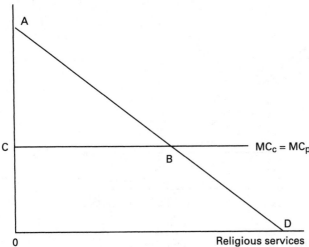

Figure 8.1
The market for religious services

surplus were those consumers in the upper reaches of the demand curve. Note that with perfect price discrimination, all consumers are on the margin of defection.

Under favorable conditions, entry takes place. Assume that Protestants enter as single-price monopolists charging P_p and selling Q_p of religious services, as shown in figure 8.2. Those demanders paying the largest amount of consumer surplus for religious services (those in the upper reaches of the demand curve) would tend to switch. This means that OQ_p demanders will likely switch from Catholicism to Protestantism, leaving BD as the residual demand curve for Catholicism.[13] If the Catholic Church continues to price discriminate along the residual demand curve, the average price falls in response to entry. There would be no trades at prices AB for Catholic religious services after Protestant entry. If the Church opts for a simple monopoly price after entry, price would also fall for Catholic religious services.[14]

Let us assume that Protestant churches entered the religion market as rival monopoly-like firms charging a simple (but different) monopoly price. Their membership (entry) price was cheaper, but not free—a 10

Price of religious services

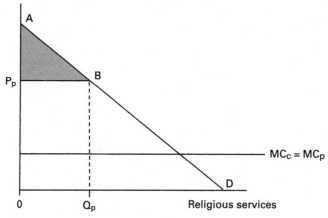

Figure 8.2
Perfect price discrimination and Protestant entry

percent "biblical" tithe took the place of the many exactions of the Roman Church. In particular, the Protestant price was "cheaper" for those formerly Catholic demanders previously located along AB of the demand curve. Actually, the resulting Protestant price was higher than the resulting Catholic price(s) after entry under either perfect discrimination or simple monopoly. In a way, the Protestants cherry-picked the market for religious services by luring away those for whom religion offered the most consumer surplus. This is another testable part of our theory. Given the realities of medieval life, Protestant entry involved, indeed initially required, the use of political power to legitimize the new religions. In 1517 Luther published his Ninety-five Theses. By 1530, after the failure of Emperor Charles V to restore Catholic orthodoxy in Germany, Lutheran princes formed a league united against the Emperor and Catholic princes. The freedom and the very lives of Luther and Calvin depended on the protection of secular rulers but, as both discovered, political power can be used against particular religions as well. Nevertheless, both Calvin and Luther espoused action by civil authorities to police "idolatry, sacrilege, blasphemy and other public affronts to religion."[15] This meant oppression of Roman Catholicism ("popery") and Anabaptism and other sectarian dissent within emerging Protestantism.

Further, Luther's characterization of the polity was "the sword," and Calvin's was "the bridle." Around these ideas, monopoly or quasi-monopoly religions formed in Scotland, Scandinavia, more than half of Germany, large sections of the Netherlands and Switzerland, and areas of central Europe. Henry VIII, of course, declared religious monopoly in England as well. After Protestant entry, however, these monopoly religions had to be comparatively efficient to ward off potential entrants in an obviously more competitive market for takeovers. The critical point is that the "savings" in consumer surplus from entry (triangle ABP_p in figure 8.2, a measure of the net gain by Protestant entrants) became available to support economic growth. This "supply-side" theory, which emphasizes the impact of the redirection of resources toward economic growth, has testable implications.

The Economic Role of Cathedral Building

The conventional model of the decline in rent seeking occasioned by Protestant entry into the religion market is, however, understated (by, for example, the area ABP_p in figure 8.2). In order to appreciate this we must note that medieval economic development in Europe usually occurred most dramatically in cities that contained major churches or cathedrals. The great era of cathedral building in Europe was between 1140 and 1280, but the tendency of cathedrals to promote local expenditures persisted for many centuries. These spiritual temples were financed by contributions that were sometimes voluntary and sometimes forced. Understandably, there was intense local competition for cathedral sites. The glory and legitimacy of monarchs—which over this period owed more to the support of the papacy and their largely political representatives (the bishops of a region) than to the feudal aristocracy—depended on church support, in large measure because bishops were at the very top of the feudal hierarchy. According to medieval historian Georges Duby these "prelate-businessmen...owned the best lands and enormous barns which the tithes exacted at each harvest filled to repletion. They levied taxes on urban fairs and markets and part of the profits from trade and agriculture found its way into their coffers.... [T]he social order of the time was so constructed that peasants and middle class were expected and enjoined to deliver a large part of their earnings to the military and ecclesiastical authorities."[16] While some such "donations" were, in view of redemption, "voluntary," many were not. The forced nature of such contributions is revealed in periodic revolts against bishops who pushed taxation too far. Duby reports that in 1233, infuriated by the exactions of an earlier prelate, the bishop of Reims's flock rose up against him and forced him to close down the work yards for a time and to dismiss the masons and sculptors in his service.[17] Although contributions might appear to be "voluntary," the amount of "forced demand" is debatable.

The competition between bishops, as head politicians of medieval towns, was fierce. Duby's account of the building of the cathedral at Saint-Denis emphasizes this point:

From the stained-glass windows of Saint-Denis stemmed, in the mid-twelfth century, those of Chartres, Bourges, and Angers, all of them cathedrals; from its column-statues those of Chartres, Le Mans and Bourges. The architectural innovations of Saint-Denis were followed up between 1155 and 1180 at Noyon, Laon, Senlis, Paris and Soissons, all in the lineage of the cathedrals of Neustria.[18]

In much of Europe, moreover, the local religious bureaucracy such as the bishops' canons were becoming de facto entrepreneurs by selling commodities such as wheat and wine produced in their regions, and marketing the (in-kind) tithes they received. As Duby notes, "The bourgeois was known to be well off and the Church authorities deliberately squeezed him, confiscating on occasion his casks of wine and bale goods. Thus a large part of [the Church's] wealth was drained off from a section of the population that was steadily becoming larger and more affluent."[19]

Locational competition for cathedrals was by no means fueled only by ecclesiastical interests. A new cathedral—and later the quantity and quality of its relic collection—attracted demanders and industry to particular towns. Communes of workers and businessmen marketed their cathedrals as spiritual guardians over industries and trades. Indeed, in order to do business in the medieval economy, one had to be member of and participant in the Roman Catholic religion. Heretics and non-payers (including Jews) were subject to excommunication, interdict, or other less humane punishments. The church devised a method of punishing usurers. For example, a deathbed confession of usury was levied with a punishment of payment to those injured. That is, if the guilty knew who he or she had wronged, the money (*certa*) went to the injured. If, as was often the case, the guilty was not certain about the injured party, the money (*incerta*) went to the church. Merchants who contributed to cathedral finance derived enormous benefits:

> The status of being a "man" of the Church ensured certain privileges and exemptions from customs tariffs, of whose value the local merchants were fully conscious. This was one of the reasons why the merchant class regarded this splendid monument, on which they prided themselves and which they had adorned, as theirs. At Amiens the dealers in the dyes used for textiles felt that their renown was enhanced, if indirectly, by the beauties of the cathedral; at Chartres each of the guilds insisted on having its own stained-glass window. Huge sums of money were spent on these edifices... [which] justified the opulence of the city and increased its fame.[20]

Thus, far from simply being a place of worship, the medieval cathedral was a multipurpose structure with some of the characteristics of the modern commercial mall, union hall, court house, and amusement park.

Competition, in medieval times and in our own, almost always has a locational component. Urban centers with cathedrals vied fiercely for relics and works of art to adorn their churches.[21] In the manner of modern sports stadiums, medieval cities engaged in a kind of spatial competition for ever grander cathedrals that inflated the costs of providing religious services of all kinds, including assurances of eternal salvation. In this as in all economic matters, the true cost of the cathedral was the opportunity cost of resources used in its construction and maintenance—the opportunity cost of stone masons, artists, and saver-investors whose human and physical capital resources were directed to the provision of religious services. By de-emphasizing cathedrals, Protestantism thus reduced a second kind of rent seeking. Figure 8.3 represents the cost inflation from cathedral building. MC_{rs} lies above MC_c, indicating that the cost inflation from spatially competitive cathedral building lies above the true competitive cost. As figure 8.3 reveals, the Protestant Reformation not only reduced rent seeking on the demand side of the church provision of services, but reduced rent seeking on the supply side of cathedral building as well, releasing EBCF in resources for private investment. Note that this is in addition to the freed up consumer surplus indicated earlier in figure 8.1.

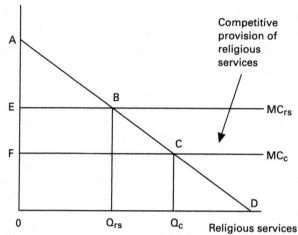

Price of religious services

Figure 8.3
Rent seeking due to spatial competition in cathedral building

The Intensity of Protestant-Catholic Competition at the Borders of Influence

Yet another important (and testable) implication suggested by figure 8.2 is that price competition will be most intense around the value P_p. Such competition may be expected even in areas that do not finally settle as Protestant. In 1956 economic geographer Charles M. Tiebout constructed a multi-jurisdictional model in which independent local governments offer a wide variety of expenditure and tax policies, and perfectly mobile consumers reveal their preferences for local public goods through their choice of residential community.[22] In other words, Tiebout argued that consumers "vote with their feet." Making allowances for differences in the economics and technology of transportation, this premise is applicable to medieval times as well. Members of different religions can be expected to move from one "tax jurisdiction" to another—for example, from a Catholic region to a Protestant region—and as they do, the economic characteristics of the two regions come closer together. Therefore, Catholic regions that are contiguous to Protestant regions should eventually exhibit similar institutional characteristics (e.g., interest rates) and growth patterns. This phenomenon is neither addressed nor explained by Weber's thesis.

Evidence for the Supply-Side View

We looked for evidence that Protestant entry into the European religious market unleashed resources previously dedicated to production of religious services in a number of quarters: cathedral building, architectural/ liturgical reforms, local labor markets, and religious pilgrimages. We warn that conclusive evidence is elusive; nevertheless, a provisional analysis is possible.

The Opportunity Costs of Cathedral Building

The great cathedral-building craze had run its course in western Europe by the fifteenth century, but it set the tone and tenor of medieval Christian worship for centuries to come. Despite serious attempts by economic historians, it is difficult to gauge the economic effects of cathedrals for several reasons. For one, they were multipurpose facilities that contributed to community as well as spirituality. People gathered at cathedrals for prayer, funerals, marriages, and festivities. Local guilds, magistrates, and municipal officials met there, giving the cathedral the role of town hall as well as church. Actors sometimes staged plays in cathedrals, and a certain amount of commercial activity also transpired there.[23] For another, their construction took place over long periods of time. For example, Canterbury Cathedral took 343 years from start to finish, of which less than half the time was spent in actual construction.[24]

The exact amount of resources used in the construction of cathedrals cannot be directly calculated, but a good deal of anecdotal evidence suggests that the opportunity costs were massive. Although cathedral building in England between 1100 and 1400 involved, on average, less than half of 1 percent of the adult male population annually, almost 9,500 ecclesiastical buildings, such as abbeys, cathedrals, and parish churches, were constructed in England and Wales during the medieval period.[25] By contrast, if we assume that the same labor technology was used to build equivalent-sized structures, France used eighteen times as much labor input in cathedral building over the same interval.[26] Medieval architectural historian Jean Gimpel claimed that more stone was cut in France between 1050 and 1350 than during the entire history of Egypt.[27] Even though capital markets were rudimentary in the Middle Ages, the building of religious structures on the scale described by these authors meant that resources responded to a kind of spiritual investment demand and that the consequence was that scarce capital was directed toward religious buildings rather than traditional infrastructure, such as roads and bridges, or education and technology.

Sociologist Robert A. Scott provides some provisional calculations of resource costs regarding parts of Westminster Abbey and Salisbury Cathedral. Scott calculates that the addition to Westminster Abbey undertaken by English King Henry III in the thirteenth century cost £45,000 in the currency of the day, at a time when the annual income during Henry's entire reign was only £35,000. On the basis of hod-carrier wage rates, then and now, Scott further estimates that each gothic cathedral or similar great church would cost hundreds of millions of pounds in today's currency.[28] Estimates like these, though far from conclusive, provide indirect evidence of huge opportunity costs of building cathedrals and churches. If secular economic growth quickened after the spate of cathedral building ran its course, as Max Weber asserts, it might have done so in part because of the reallocation of resources from cathedrals to traditional social/economic infrastructure.

An argument of this nature naturally assumes that the cathedral-based economy was on or near its production-possibilities frontier. Therefore our conclusion contrasts markedly with a Keynesian interpretation of cathedral building. Economist Virginia Lee Owen argues that cathedral building was comparable to the WPA projects of the American New Deal in that, she calculates, 2.5 percent of the European labor force was engaged in cathedral building between 1200 and 1328, presumably with appropriate income multipliers.[29] City size data does not substantiate that result, but even if it did, we reject the Keynesian macroeconomic premise that it does not matter what is produced as long as resources are used to produce something. Others have shown that there is a deadweight loss associated with resources used in monopoly-inspired rent seeking; in such cases, output would rise even if the resources were idled or retuned to underemployed uses. To be sure, medieval craftsmen and resources could have been used building fences around commons rather than building cathedrals.

Despite the difficulty of estimating the economic effects of cathedrals, it is clear that medieval Catholicism emphasized large-scale, extravagant structures over small-scale, simple ones. For example, the enormous cathedral at Amiens covered an area of about 84,000 square feet and contained a volume of 260,000 to 300,000 cubic yards. It is estimated that the historic cathedral at Chartres contained a volume in excess of 300,000 cubic yards. Economic resources have alternative uses. Therefore, by rejecting the extravagance of church buildings—however they were financed—Protestantism made it possible for such resources to be directed toward more secular, market-oriented activities. In addition, it is quite possible that cathedrals acted as signaling devices to potential entrants, including Protestants ultimately, that the Church was willing to establish excess capacity in order to deter entry of new religions (a point we embellish in appendix 8A to this chapter).

Reforms in Architecture, Liturgy, Custom, and Practice

Protestantism introduced ascetic changes in the function of churches as well as in their design and construction. During the Reformation, Catholic churches were stripped of statuary, paintings, and traditional symbols. New churches were designed as meetinghouses, harking back to early Christianity when believers met in each other's homes. Architecture, having lost its ability to signify the sacred, became merely functional, providing for the assembly's material or practical needs. The concepts of the church as auditorium and theater-in-the-round derive from early Calvinist buildings, which were designed to enable people to more easily see and hear the preacher. Destruction of altar, tabernacle, and sanctuary was commonplace, and often the altar was replaced as the focal point by a pulpit or baptismal font. This minimalist aesthetic, with its theological proscriptions against images and symbols, has continued to characterize Protestantism to the present time.

The contrast between pre-Reformation churches and post-Reformation churches was made more dramatic by the fact that Catholic churches continued to incorporate artistic embellishments into their structure and ceremony, even after the Reformation gained a foothold. According to one account:

While the Protestants in their Hebraic zeal, smashed all the graven images they could find, starting with the decapitation and mutilation of the statue of the Blessed Mother in Paris on Pentecost Sunday 1528, Baroque princes and prelates outdid themselves in producing new ever more glorious works of art. A wonderful example of this contrast between the Baroque and bourgeois spirit is the jewel encrusted statue of St. George...which cost the Catholic kings of Bavaria 300,000 florins, more than enough money to field a whole army. Crafted in 1587 it measures only 12 by 20 inches, but, it is encrusted with 36 large diamonds of 40 carats, 2,613 small diamonds, 130 emeralds, 430 rubies, 32 large pearls, etc. all set in pure gold. This little treasure was not created just to be beautiful but as a token symbol of Bavaria as St. George slaying the dragon of Protestantism in order to save Holy Mother Church.[30]

A poignant example of the lingering effects of Protestant asceticism can be found in Strasbourg, a city whose nationality shifted back and forth between Germany and France for centuries. The toweringly beautiful and elaborate cathedral of this city was built as a glorious shrine to Catholicism in the Middle Ages, but when the city became Protestant in the sixteenth century, the interior was shorn of its elaborateness. In an effort to make the church less Catholic, Protestants "removed large numbers of tombstones and figures of saints and of the Virgin...and more than forty altars disappeared. The resulting starkness, even gloom, still persists today."[31]

Another example of Protestant frugality can be found in the episodic history of religious reform in England. In terms of the number and quality of its church goods and the richness and luxury of its collection of vestments, Holy Trinity Church at Dartford was one of the richest churches in pre-Reformation Kent. But the simplicity of the reformed church services under Edward VI and Elizabeth made the use of these expensive goods and vestments unnecessary. The 1552 inventory shows that Holy Trinity church possessed four silver-gilt chalices, and one of these weighed more than twenty-six ounces. In total the church plate weighed in at over three hundred ounces of silver.[32] Church vestments were made from rich fabrics such as velvet, satin, and silk, and embroidered with gold. Eventually, the Dartford Priory was dissolved, and its wealth confiscated by civil authorities.

Protestant liturgy in the sixteenth and seventeenth centuries also reflected the new asceticism of the reformers. A key principle of the Reformation was its refutation of sacramentality, which brought about a reduction or loss of liturgical sensibility. Within a short time after the beginning of the Reformation, many Protestant denominations rejected strict liturgical worship and adopted different practices.[33] As a consequence, Protestantism has a very limited liturgical tradition and a small body of liturgical music, in keeping with its newly defined theology and doctrine.[34] This contrast between Catholic extravagance and Protestant frugality extends also to matters of religious dress, both liturgical and ministerial. The different editions of The Book of Common Prayer (the Anglican liturgical book) attest to sixteenth-century reforms and the rising power of seventeenth-century Puritanism as forces that provoked a decline in the use of vestments in church liturgies. It was in fact the struggle to change the liturgics of Protestantism that caused many of the new sects to move toward Puritanism by making worship an intellectual experience with little or no ceremonial form. In sum, practically everything about the Protestant religion was simpler and cheaper.[35]

Effect of Protestant Reforms on Local Labor Markets

In addition to the effects on church and worship, the Reformation also had a potential supply-side impact on local labor markets. Catholic tradition specified a large number of religious festivals, feast days, and pilgrimages to honor saints and historical religious events. Ironically, despite its condemnation of "pagan" festivals based on seasons or nature, the Roman Catholic Church replaced pagan practice with Christianized festivals and holy days. Town and monastery communities typically championed particular (often minor) saints, who were regularly entreated to bestow special favors on the faithful.[36] Proper observance of feast days and holy days in commemoration of saints and historical events required church attendance, feasting, and celebration—which required time off of work. This religious, social, and economic observance and its consequences were described by historian Hutton Webster:

As the Roman passion for holidays and their attendant spectacles increased, we find the number of days devoted to them rising from sixty-six in the reign of Augustus to eighty-seven in that of Tiberius, and, under Marcus Aurelius, to a hundred and thirty-five. [At the end of the Roman empire, the number was even larger, perhaps reaching 175–200 days per year].... Many of the holy days in the religious calendar of Christendom were borrowed ... from the public festivals of ancient paganism. This must be the chief reason for the observance of so many non-working days during the Middle Ages. Their number was largely reduced in Protestant Europe as the result of the Reformation, which did away with the majority of saints' days.[37]

Of course, one must not confuse labor input with labor output. Historians are divided on the question of whether Protestant reforms increased the number of work days in medieval Europe. Regional variance is a persistent complicating factor. On the one hand, economic historian Earl J. Hamilton claimed, "In the sixteenth and seventeenth centuries Protestantism afforded little relief from the plethora of religious holidays that afflicted most Catholic countries. Puritans prohibited markets on Saturdays, Sundays and Mondays. Numerous church services were held during the week."[38] On the other hand, Vatican historian Eamon Duffy puts the number of feast days in England at between forty and fifty, noting, in addition to regional variance:

The observance and the status of holy days were much contested issues, since holy days were also holidays. Workers sought to secure days free from secular toil, landowners and employers sought to extract the maximum work from their tenants or employees, and a particular bone of contention was the question of whether servants or lords should bear the expense of the loss of a day's work involved in each feast.... This trend achieved its starkest and most drastic expression after the break with Rome, when in 1536 the Crown abolished most of the local and national *festa ferianda* ... on the grounds that the excessive numbers of holidays were impoverishing the people by hindering agriculture.[39]

While there is some dispute over the effects of increased labor input upon aggregate output in *particular* areas,[40] it appears most likely that growth ensued in Protestant areas. Clearly, feast days created a reduced average workweek when Europe was under Catholic monopoly. Combined with other medieval Roman Catholic practices, the four or five day medieval workweek[41] suggests that the emergence of Protestantism gave a boost to productivity and output. Weber failed to recognize this and other supply-side aspects of the religious reforms embraced by Protestantism. Indeed, a study of contemporary practice that restricts itself to only the major *Christian-related* festivals by country reveals that those countries remaining predominately Catholic retain a significantly larger number of general saint and feast days than those that became largely Protestant.[42]

Years of Pilgrimage

Another potential effect on hours worked was the religious pilgrimage, a commonplace of medieval Christianity. In England, the abolition of pilgrimages by Henry VIII deprived some merchants and workers of their livelihood, particularly those involved in the manufacture and sale of pilgrimage souvenirs. But structural changes in employment are inherent in any dynamic economy, and are eventually corrected as labor and capital are reallocated to other sectors of the economy. Despite some short-run dislocations in local economies, therefore, the long-term effect of capital and labor reallocations to secular uses would likely prove beneficial to economic development. But how does one measure pre- and post-Reformation pilgrimage activity? A reasonable proxy might be the number of religious shrines established throughout Europe before and after the Reformation.

Table 8.1 catalogs the total current number of shrines by country or region across Europe. There is a clear and substantial difference between the number of religious shrines in Catholic versus Protestant countries today. More revealing is the establishment data about these shrines, which shows a substantial decline in shrines formed in the post-Reformation period, and almost complete cessation in Protestant regions. Table 8.2 shows the distribution through time of the 4,049 shrines that could be dated. More than 50 percent of European shrines were created prior to 1530 in Catholic Europe while 32 percent were created in the post-Reformation era, the vast majority of them considered to be "minor" shrines.

Available evidence suggests that the related practices of building shrines and making pilgrimages stopped almost completely in Protestant countries in the post-Reformation era. Cultural geographers Mary Lee Nolan and Sidney Nolan argue that "the dramatic 1530s low point in the cult-formation cycle corresponds closely with the beginnings of the Protestant Reformation," but that this low point "was short lived in regions that remained Catholic."[43] Indeed, the encouragement of shrines and pilgrimages was part of the Catholic Church's Counter-Reformation

Table 8.1
European shrines

Country	Number
Italy	1,194
France	1,034
Spain	1,014
West Germany	938
Austria	925
Portugal	332
Switzerland	283
Belgium/Luxembourg	151
Ireland	135
United Kingdom	86
Netherlands	48
Sweden	5
Denmark	3
Finland and Norway	2
TOTAL	6,150

Source: Mary Lee Nolan and Sidney Nolan, *Christian Pilgrimage in Modern Western Europe* (Chapel Hill: University of North Carolina Press, 1989), 5.

Table 8.2
Shrine formation

Period	Number of dated shrines	Percent of dated shrines
Christian (Roman Catholic), 699–1529	2,171	53.6
Post-Reformation, 1530–1779	1,308	32.3
Modern, 1780–1980	570	14.1
TOTALS	4,049	100.0

Source: Mary Lee Nolan and Sidney Nolan, *Christian Pilgrimage in Modern Western Europe* (Chapel Hill: University of North Carolina Press, 1989), 87, Table 4.1.

effort to prevent further defections from the Church and/or to lure defectors back.

In sum, religious festivals, pilgrimages, and holy days, while undoubtedly conveying utility to those participating (many from the working or indigent classes), meant a withdrawal of work effort. Protestant countries eliminated or severely restricted such Roman Catholic practices, a development applauded by seventeenth- and eighteenth-century writers as diverse as William Penn and Richard Cantillon. Seventeenth-century Quakers decisively rejected such practices, condemning cults of saints and festivals in their honor. William Penn declared, "It helps persons of mean substance to improve their small stocks that they may not expend their dear earning and hard-gotten wages upon...May games...and the like folly and intemperance."[44] Richard Cantillon, perhaps the most able predecessor of Adam Smith, was even more explicit about the issue: "Experience shews that the Countries which have embraced Protestantism and have neither Monks nor Mendicants have become visibly more powerful. They have also the advantage of having suppressed a great number of Holy Days when no work is done in Roman Catholic countries and which diminish the labour of the People by about an eighth part of the year."[45] It is interesting to note that Cantillon's estimate is consistent with Duffy's estimate of forty to fifty feast days a year. Thus, even as contemporary economic historians are grappling with the circumstances and consequences of work lost due to medieval holy days, festivals, and pilgrimages, ancient and modern sources agree that Protestant reforms encouraged an increase in the aggregate supply of work effort, a supply-side aspect missing from Weber's thesis.

Can Weber's Thesis Be Rehabilitated?

In view of the severe criticism that has surrounded Weber's thesis, attempts to rehabilitate it have been few and far between. We have argued that Weber's theory may be made more robust by the addition of supply-side elements to what is a predominantly demand-side theory. For example, there is an aspect of Weber's theory that seems to fly in the face of historical fact: economic development was not confined to

Protestant regions but experienced by Catholic regions as well. The most pointed—and least answered—criticism comes from Swedish economic historian Kurt Samuelsson, as summarized by Jacques Delacroix: "Amsterdam's wealth was centered on Catholic families; the economically advanced German Rhineland is more Catholic than Protestant; all-Catholic Belgium was the second country to industrialize, ahead of a good half-dozen Protestant entities."[46]

Supply-side elements provide some insights into this discrepancy. Whereas Catholic areas that were isolated (e.g., Spain, Portugal, and Italy) did not progress quickly to capitalism, those areas contiguous to countries that became Protestant bumped up against vibrant economic activities and were forced to respond in order to remain competitive. For example, merchants in Catholic countries were forced to borrow at market interest rates once Protestantism eliminated usury constraints. Moreover, it was not the German cities of the Rhineland that were growing and becoming centers of market activities; the most prosperous and growing German cities in the post-Reformation period (i.e., Danzig, Leiden, Hamburg, Nuremberg, Cologne, and Berlin) lay outside the Rhineland. Furthermore, while two cities in Belgium were among the largest in Europe in 1500 (Ghent and Bruges), Ghent declined in size and Bruges disappeared from the list in 1650. Bruges suffered adverse geographical consequences because it gradually receded farther and farther from the sea, depriving it of its vital seaport status. Belgium, of course, shares borders with both Protestant Germany and the Netherlands. In short, Weber's hypothesis is not denied by the fact that *certain* Catholic countries grew more or less simultaneously with the Protestant nations. A close examination of the evidence suggests a plausible reason for this coincidence.

In addition, the development of religious tourism in the "two Germanys" in the post-Reformation period suggests another kind of border competition.[47] By offering more religious shrines as pilgrimage destinations Catholic southern Germany competed with Protestant northern Germany for tourists in the immediate post-Reformation period (1530–1779). Whereas northern Germany held 6 percent of the total number of religious shrines in Europe, Southern Germany laid claim to 48 percent. This suggests that as part of its Counter-Reformation effort, the Roman

Catholic Church attempted to lure former church members back to its fold in part by offering fewer workdays as an inducement.

While it appears that possibilities exist for making Weber's thesis more robust, in the end, whether or not it can be rehabilitated is difficult to determine. The fundamental problems remain, especially the endogeneity problem—namely, in which direction does causality run? Did Protestantism encourage economic development or did economic development encourage Protestantism? Data limitations and other difficulties of framing and executing reasonable empirical tests appear daunting, given the realities of elapsed time. Despite these problems, and lack of success in dispensing them, the broader notion that religion and economic development are somehow connected has continued to intrigue economists and sociologists alike.

Religion and Economic Growth: Beyond Weber

Some economists refuse to be deterred by the intractability of religion to quantitative studies of growth and development. Robin Grier undertook a cross-national study of former colonies in Latin America in search of the elusive connection between religion and economic development, and found that (1) the growth rate of Protestantism is positively and significantly correlated with real GDP growth; (2) the level of Protestantism is significantly related to real per capita growth; and (3) former colonies steeped in the Catholic tradition (French and Spanish) performed significantly worse, on average, than former British colonies. Nevertheless, she rejected these results as verification of Weber: "Contrary to the Weberian hypothesis... my results show that religion is not the sole determinant of differential development and growth... Controlling for the level and growth rate of Protestantism does not eliminate the gap between the three sets of former colonies. As Weber's critics have pointed out, Protestantism seems to be only one of many factors which determine economic progress."[48]

Robert Barro and Rachel McCleary also used a cross-country panel of data to test whether there is a correlation between religion and economic development. They found that measures of religiosity are positively related to education, negatively related to urbanization, and positively related to the presence of children. At the same time, increased life expectancy tends to be negatively related to church attendance but positively related to religious beliefs (especially heaven and hell). Treating church attendance as a measure of inputs to the religious sector, and religious beliefs as a measure of outputs, they conjecture that on the one hand increased church attendance signifies more resources used up by the religion sector, with less attendant economic growth, and on the other hand, that religious beliefs stimulate growth because they help to sustain aspects of individual behavior that enhance productivity. While this last point is certainly Weberian in spirit, Barro and McCleary make no attempt to defend the core Weberian thesis.[49]

Although these recent studies do not confirm or deny Weber's hypothesis, they nevertheless demonstrate abiding interest in the key relationship between religion and economic activity. Moreover, recent studies tend to follow Weber's macroeconomic orientation, which might be appropriate to contemporary availability of data. But *historical* research aimed at finding a causal connection that runs in the Weberian (macroeconomic) mode has been hampered by the fact that aggregate quantitative indicators of economic prosperity are extremely scarce for earlier epochs. Two ideas currently vie for supremacy in historical empirical research. Economists J. Bradford DeLong and Andrei Shleifer focus on city size as an indicator of economic growth[50]; Daron Acemoglu, Simon H. Johnson, and James A. Robinson focus on urbanization rates as an indicator of economic growth.[51] Both approaches emanate from, and build upon, a data set constructed by Paul Bairoch, Jean Bateau, and Pierre Chèvre.[52] Neither DeLong and Shleifer nor Acemoglu, Johnson, and Robinson examine the relation between religion and economic development, but each suggest a parallel approach to the problems involved in discovering a plausible connection.

City Size as a Proxy for Economic Prosperity
DeLong and Shleifer use city size as a measure of economic prosperity in their test of the relationship between political institutions and economic growth in the pre-industrial era.[53] They find that slow economic growth in the eight hundred years prior to the Industrial Revolution was associated with absolutist governments, whereas republican governments were

more conducive to growth. The affinity of such correlation to the connection between religion and growth is strong, because the medieval Roman Catholic Church, by virtue of its central place in daily life and its monopoly position among institutional religions, functioned in many respects like an absolutist government. What, if anything, does the data on city size tell us about the (possible) connection between religion and economic growth after the Protestant Reformation?

In the year 1500, virtually all countries and cities in Europe were Roman Catholic. By 1650, large portions of Europe had become Protestant. By investigating changes in city size over this interval we might be able to infer something about the impact of Protestant religions on the emergence of market economies. The results, however, are inconclusive. At the dawn of the Reformation, only three cities that subsequently became Protestant were in the top thirty cities, ranked by population (i.e., London, Nuremberg, and Cologne). Over the next 150 years, eight "Protestant" cities made it into the top thirty. By 1650 the proportion of Europe's largest cities that were Catholic was reduced by approximately half, a ratio that remained the same in 1800.

Table 8.3 shows the thirty largest cities (by population) in Europe and their rates of population growth in three long intervals: 1500–1650, 1650–1800, and 1500–1800. While most cities grew over these three periods, some declined in population, and some dropped out of the top thirty as time elapsed. Newcomers to the top thirty list in 1650 included Amsterdam, Madrid, Vienna, Copenhagen, Antwerp, Brussels, Danzig, Leiden, and Hamburg—all except Brussels and Madrid were Protestant cities. Between 1500 and 1650, seventeen of the thirty largest cities in 1500 experienced positive average annual population growth rates. Of these seventeen, all but two, London and Nuremburg, were Catholic cities.

Table 8.4 shows the average annual population growth rates between 1500 and 1650 for the subset of the thirty largest European cities in 1500 that experienced positive growth rates. The four cities that experienced the most rapid increase in population were Marseille, London, Naples, and Lisbon. Except for London, these cities were Catholic, but they were also important seaports. Acemoglu, Johnson, and Robinson, for example, found that coastal cities grew at different rates after 1500: "Atlantic ports grew much faster than other European cities while

Table 8.3
The thirty largest cities in Europe by population in 1500 and population growth, 1500–1650, 1650–1800, and 1500–1800

City	Rank 1500	1650	1800	Average annual compound growth rate (%) 1500–1650	1650–1800	1500–1800
Paris	1	1	2	0.3843	0.2125	0.2984
Naples	2	3	3	0.5854	0.2403	0.4127
Milan	3	6	13	0.1216	0.0786	0.1001
Venice	4	5	12	0.2246	−0.0096	0.1074
Granada	5	14		0.0000		
Prague	6	26	30	−0.2241	0.2795	0.0274
Lisbon	7	4	7	0.5591	0.1751	0.3669
Tours	8					
Genoa	9	17	21	0.0656	0.2275	0.1466
Ghent	10	30		−0.2121		
Florence	11	12	25	0.1980	0.0603	0.1291
Palermo	12	10	11	0.3994	0.2246	0.3119
Rome	13	8	10	0.4632	0.2202	0.3416
Bordeaux	14		20			0.2177
Lyon	15	21	15	0.1216	0.3988	0.2601
Orleans	16					
London	17	2	1	1.3057	0.6665	0.9535
Bologna	18	18		0.1542		
Verona	19					
Brescia	20					
Cologne	21	27		−0.0785		
Seville	22	11	19	0.3843	0.1216	0.2529
Marseille	23	15	17	1.8465	0.2447	0.2698
Malaga	24					
Valencia	25	25	26	0.1163	0.3138	0.2150
Ferrara	26					
Rouen	27	22	27	0.2707	0.1920	0.2313
Cremona	28					
Nuremburg	29	29		0.0342		
Bruges	30					

Source: J. B. DeLong and Andrei Shleifer, "Princes and Merchants: European City Growth before the Industrial Revolution," *Journal of Law and Economics* 36 (1993): 671–702, Table 1.

Table 8.4
European cities with positive population growth rates, 1500–1650

City	Rank by size		Average annual growth rate
	1500	1650	1500–1650
Marseille	23	15	1.8465%
London	17	2	1.3057%
Naples	2	3	0.5854%
Lisbon	7	4	0.5591%
Rome	13	8	0.4632%
Palermo	12	10	0.3994%
Paris	1	1	0.3843%
Seville	22	11	0.3843%
Rouen	27	22	0.2707%
Venice	4	5	0.2246%
Florence	11	12	0.1980%
Bologna	18	18	0.1542%
Lyon	15	21	0.1216%
Milan	3	6	0.1216%
Valencia	25	25	0.1163%
Genoa	9	17	0.0656%
Nuremburg	29	29	0.0342%

Source: J. B. DeLong and Andrei Shleifer, "Princes and Merchants: European City Growth before the Industrial Revolution," *Journal of Law and Economics* 36 (1993): 671–702, Table 1.

Mediterranean ports grew at similar rates to inland cities."[54] As dramatic as London's growth was during this period, Marseille's was 41 percent greater. It would appear from this data, therefore, that while religion may be a force contributing to economic prosperity, it is clearly not the only one.

Urbanization Rates as a Proxy for Economic Prosperity
Acemoglu, Johnson, and Robinson used urbanization rates as a proxy for economic prosperity in their study of European economic development between 1500 and 1850. They define urbanization as the percentage of people living in urban areas, and treat this concept as a proxy for GDP per capita.[55] Their study concluded that Atlantic trading cities

played a central role in the growth of western Europe after 1500. In their estimation, the pattern of evidence "weighs against theories that emphasize the continuity between pre-1500 and post-1500 European growth and link the rise of Europe to certain distinctive European characteristics, such as culture, religion, geography, or features of the European state system."[56] Their data on urbanization and GDP per capita is presented by country rather than by city, and embraces several continents. We narrowed the scope of their data for our purposes to include northern, western, and central Europe. We excluded from our purview Lithuania (modern Russia) and countries that were primarily Muslim (e.g., the Ottoman Empire). This left us with nineteen European countries in our truncated data set. We classified each country by dominant religion (projecting backward to circa 1600), and calculated the average, annual compound rates of growth in per capita GDP over three intervals: 1500–1600, 1600–1700, and 1500–1700. The presumption is that if there was a Protestant effect on growth, most of the results would have been produced in the first century of reform, 1500–1600. However, our calculations show longer-term growth rates as well, from which other inferences might be made.

Table 8.5 shows average, annual compound rates of growth in per-capita GDP for the nations of northern, western, and central Europe by selected intervals, calculated using the data assembled by Acemoglu, Johnson, and Robinson. By 1600, Protestantism had made serious inroads into approximately 40 percent of the countries involved (marked by the letter "P" in table 8.5). But the record of economic growth for these countries over the ensuing periods is mixed. Table 8.6 shows the rank order of countries, by selected periods, in terms of growth in per-capita GDP. At the extremes, the two countries that grew most rapidly between 1500 and 1700, the Netherlands and England, were within the Protestant orbit; the most Catholic country in all of Europe, Italy, did not grow at all during the same period. The Catholic countries on the Iberian Peninsula, Spain and Portugal, grew relatively quickly between 1500 and 1600, but faltered badly afterward. Switzerland and the Scandinavian countries grew at relatively high, steady rates throughout the two centuries after the appearance of Protestantism. Switzerland, a country of divided religious loyalties, was also a relatively strong performer

Table 8.5
Country growth rates in per capita GDP, Europe, 1500–1600, 1600–1700, and 1500–1700

Country	Religion	Average annual compound growth (%)		
		1500–1600	1600–1700	1500–1700
Austria	C	0.1689	0.1711	0.1700
Belgium	C	0.1093	0.1589	0.1341
Czech Republic	C	0.1689	0.1711	0.1700
Denmark	P	0.1704	0.1719	0.1712
England	P	0.3144	0.2984	0.3064
Finland	P	0.1721	0.1706	0.1714
France	C	0.1458	0.1592	0.1525
Germany	P	0.1393	0.1404	0.1399
Greece	C	0.1106	0.0925	0.1016
Hungary	C	0.1106	0.0925	0.1016
Ireland	C	0.1564	0.1508	0.1536
Italy	C	0.0000	0.0000	0.0000
Netherlands	P	0.5975	0.4343	0.5159
Norway	P	0.1720	0.1692	0.1706
Poland	C	0.1106	0.0925	0.1016
Portugal	C	0.2016	0.0997	0.1506
Spain	C	0.2545	0.0000	0.1272
Sweden	P	0.1704	0.1705	0.1704
Switzerland	P	0.1707	0.1710	0.1709

Source: Daron Acemoglu, S. H. Johnson, and J. A. Robinson, "The Rise of Europe: Atlantic Trade, Institutional Change, and Economic Growth," MIT Department of Economics Working Paper No. 02-43, MIT Sloan Working Paper No. 4269-02, 2002, Appendix Table 2, available at http: ssrn.com/abstract-355880.

over the two centuries. France, a predominantly Catholic country, remained in the middle of the pack throughout. These ambiguous results do not provide strong evidence of a correlation between religion and economic development, but neither do they deny any such correlation.

Is It Time for a Paradigm Shift?

Recent research grounded more firmly in microeconomic than macroeconomic analysis suggests that Weber may have been right but for

Table 8.6
Countries ranked by growth rates, Europe, 1500–1600, 1600–1700, and 1500–1700

	Rank by growth rate		
Country	1500–1600	1600–1700	1500–1700
Netherlands	1	1	1
England	2	2	2
Spain	3	15	14
Portugal	4	13	11
Finland	5	6	3
Norway	6	8	6
Switzerland	7	5	5
Denmark	8	3	4
Sweden	8	7	7
Austria	9	4	8
Czech Republic	9	4	8
Ireland	10	11	9
France	11	9	10
Germany	12	12	12
Greece	13	14	15
Hungary	13	14	15
Poland	13	14	15
Belgium	14	10	13
Italy	15	15	16

Source: Daron Acemoglu, S. H. Johnson, and J. A. Robinson, "The Rise of Europe: Atlantic Trade, Institutional Change, and Economic Growth," MIT Department of Economics Working Paper No. 02-43, MIT Sloan Working Paper No. 4269-02, 2002, Appendix Table 2, available at http: ssrn.com/abstract-355880.

the wrong reason. Economists Ulrich Blum and Leonard Dudley reject Weber's core idea that the economic success of Protestant Europe in the pre-industrial period was due to a tendency of individual Protestants to work harder and save more than individual Catholics. Nevertheless, they advocate a "small-world" formulation based on Weber's thesis: They contend that Protestantism changed the *relative costs* of defaulting on business contracts in a way that stimulated economic development. Using noncooperative game theory as a frame for their hypothesis, Blum and Dudley[57] make the following arguments:

• The Catholic sacrament of penance resulted in a low cost of defection from contractual relationships, because pardon could always be readily obtained with the intervention of a priest, provided the sinner perform certain acts of reparation.

• By rejecting the sacrament of penance, dissenting Protestant denominations raised the subjective cost of defection. For Calvinists, any defection weakened the individual's conviction that he was predestined to be saved. Although predestination was not an article of faith in the other ascetic Protestant denominations, the dogma had a wide influence.[58]

• Protestantism therefore had the result of lowering the probability of default in a one-time game of exchange—this widened the network of market relationships for individual traders far beyond the limited number of people whose defection(s) could be punished in repeated transactions. According to Blum and Dudley, "If Weber's argument is correct, ascetic Protestantism lowered ... [the hedonic] cost [of cooperation] by abolishing the sacrament of penance. No longer was there an institutionally certified pardon for defection in contractual agreements. Instead, the individual was obliged to adjust his daily behavior so as to dispel doubt that he would be saved. To cooperate with others became an unavoidable moral obligation."[59]

• As the number of adherents increased, Protestants thereby created important *network externalities* (benefits from joining a group of similar believers) for each other.

• Unlike their Catholic counterparts, Protestant merchants were able to take advantage of the new arbitrage opportunities available in cities bordering on the Atlantic. This required that a wide range of information be made available in Protestant printing centers but this information was not available in Catholic centers.

• These growth effects were positively related to proximity to London, the financial and commercial hub of a new hierarchical structure of international economic institutions.

Using population growth rates as a proxy for real-wage growth, Blum and Dudley provide empirical evidence that by 1750 the Protestant cities of northern Europe achieved greater economic integration while the Catholic cities of southern Europe did not—a reversal of the conditions in 1500. In effect, northern Europe was restructured within two centuries of the appearance of Protestantism so as to favor rapid, low-cost communication; southern Europe stagnated in this respect. Their statistical tests lead Blum and Dudley to reject standard, neoclassical, human-capital growth theory as an explanation of differential European economic development in the pre-industrial era. They also point to the importance of information networks for explaining why some economies grow faster than others. They conclude that Weber's emphasis on cultural evolution in early modern Europe, when suitably reformulated in terms of contemporary economics, offers a possible explanation for divergent growth patterns in certain regions.

Blum and Dudley's empirical results are interesting but not conclusive. The robustness of their model depends on the simultaneous interaction of several significant variables besides religion, such as capital, network effects, and so forth. The precise causal relationship between religion and economic development in the pre-industrial era remains a matter of conjecture. Contemporary studies point in different directions. On the one hand, DeLong and Shleifer make a strong case for political regimes as a determinant of economic development in the pre-industrial era; on the other, Acemoglu, Johnson, and Robinson make an equally strong case for Atlantic trade. But the study by Blum and Dudley marks a kind of departure of sorts from the traditional approach to Weber's core question. Rather than focus on the behavior of individuals, as Weber did in his approach to cultural evolution, they focus on the behavior of groups in order to uncover network effects. Network effects are important, but group activity is the cumulative result of individual behavior, so this shift of paradigm is more apparent than real. More dramatic is the shift of emphasis toward the economic effects on individual and group behavior of alterations in relative price that are induced by institutional change. The interpretation of economic history on these grounds is not new—it was pioneered by economists Douglass North and Robert P. Thomas[60] and a number of others. But its deep penetration into the economics of religion has not yet occurred. Pursuing this topic in the same spirit of analysis may uncover novel insights that are otherwise beyond the reach of contemporary studies.

There is a substantial supply-side element to Weber's celebrated thesis that remains relatively unexplored. Over a century after the first appearance of his cultural thesis, Weber's grip on economists' imaginations remains strong. This is particularly true among development economists, who are determined to sort out the relative roles on economic development of economic resources, culture, and politics.[61] But major obstacles persist. As Danish economist Martin Paldam (2001, 384) states, "The relations between economic development, culture [and] religion... are surely complex, involving 'grand historical dynamics' far exceeding the possibilities of 'normal' empirical research."[62] In particular, historical studies that rely on a macroeconomic approach are hampered by the scarcity of adequate measures of economic prosperity and reliable sources of aggregate data. Studies that focus on the microeconomic aspects of institutional change, though less prevalent, also face serious challenges, but may offer promising outcomes in terms of understanding key historical transformations. We have attempted to sketch out some of these possible microanalytic implications of Weber's famous idea. In the next and final chapter we apply economic analysis, and specifically, the models discussed in this book, to a number of contemporary issues and problems affecting the form of modern Christianity.

Appendix 8A: Cathedrals as Signaling and Entry-Deterring Devices

We have, in this chapter, discussed with the use of anecdotal evidence, the opportunity cost of cathedral building. Whatever the costs—and they were substantial in some estimates—it is clear that medieval Catholicism emphasized extravagance and grandeur over the far simpler architectural forms of later Protestantism. In this appendix we attempt to shed light on the economic role of cathedrals in the market for religion. We argue that Protestant entry was not simply the result of mistakes by the Catholic Church, which, as well as being untestable theory, suggests that they did not employ rational methods to prevent Protestants and heretics of various kinds from entering the market. Rather the Church anticipated entry and was able to prevent it in certain parts of Europe—*those areas where success was most promising*. First we present a brief review of the economic role of the cathedral. Next we consider the possibility that cathedral building may have been an example of limit pricing (an artificially low price to deter entry) in the market for Christian religion— a strategy that had both retarded entry in general and impeded it over large areas of Europe. We argue, finally, with preliminary statistical support, that some facts conform to the limit-pricing hypothesis.

Cathedrals and Economic Development

What was the role of the medieval cathedral? One hypothesis says that these elegant landmarks were in part a vehicle for local economic development. The great cathedrals of the Middle Ages entailed massive expenditures of capital and labor as we noted in this chapter. Many were built on the ruins of earlier structures, or were extensions of existing churches. The enormous cathedral at Amiens, with an area of about 84,000 square feet, could house the entire population of the town (about ten thousand inhabitants). Most cathedral cities contained numerous parish churches, but many cathedrals were built to hold all or a greater number of the citizens of the town.[63] The nave of many cathedrals alone could serve as a place for guilds to meet, degrees to be conferred, and goods to be bought and sold.[64] The role of the medieval cathedral was multifaceted, with religious observance and ritual mixed with civil and commercial interests.

In fact, the medieval cathedral is a metaphor for all kinds of Roman Catholic investments—in liturgy, relics, dress, "feast days," festivals, and so on, features we analyze in this chapter. This suggests that there may be a link between the magnitude of a cathedral, the size of its host city, and economic development. Ideally, we would formulate some functional relationship that treats city growth as the dependent variable and cathedral size plus demographic factors as explanatory variables. While there are no extant data on the actual discounted cost of medieval cathedrals, anecdotal evidence does exist. Using scaled designs provided by Mitchell (1968), in table 8A.1 we establish the size of particular cathedrals in some of the top thirty cities of Europe measured by population between 1050 and 1800, taken from the authoritative study of Bairoch, Bateau, and Chèvre.[65]

Despite the very limited nature of our sample, it does not appear that the massive investments in cathedrals had much of an effect on city growth during or even after the Middle Ages. In many cases, construction of a cathedral took decades or even centuries to complete. One might conclude from table 8A.1 that the construction of the cathedral at

Table 8A.1
Cathedrals and economic growth

Cathedral city	Size (area in square feet) and dates constructed (approximate)	City growth (measured by inclusion in top 30 European cities in population 1050–1650)
Laon	57,000; (1160–1230)	Eighteenth largest in 1050; eliminated afterward
Amiens	70,000; (1220–1290)	Not on list
Reims	91,250; (1201–1427)	Not on list
Paris (and environs) Nôtre Dame/ Chartres	60,000; (1163–1250) 75,000 (1134–1220)	Grew from twenty-fifth in 1050 to second largest in 1200, remaining the first or second largest city until 1800
Bourges	79,200; (1199–1265)	Not on list (looted by Hugenots in May 1562)
Rouen	(unavailable); (1150–1509)	Not on list until 1330 at twenty-fifth, varying between twenty-seventh and twenty-second through 1800
Burgos (Spain)	64,600; (1221–1568)	Not on list
Ely	70,000; (1083–1348)	Not on list
Salisbury	72,600 (1220–1334)	Not on list
Canterbury	55,000 (1096–1497)	Not on list
Strasbourg	35,000; (1190–1439)	Not on list. Became Protestant in 1561. Reverted to Catholicism in 1681

Sources: Ann Mitchell, *Cathedrals of Europe* (Feltham, UK: Hamlyn, 1968); P. Bairoch, J. Bateau, and P. Chevre, *La Population des villes europeenes 800–1850: Banque de donnees et analyse sommaire des résultats* (Geneva: Librairie Droz, 1988). We include Chartres alongside Nôtre Dame because of its proximity to Paris. In the regressions below we use an alternative value of 46,000 square feet for Ely, as reported in Paul Johnson, *British Cathedrals* (New York: Morrow, 1980).

Laon may have actually reduced growth. In the case of Rouen (made famous in the painting series by Monet), continuous construction between the late twelfth and sixteenth centuries may have had a positive effect on growth, but verification of this prospect would require deeper studies of factors peculiar to that city. The two great French cathedrals of Nôtre Dame and Chartres for, which construction began in the twelfth century, could hardly have raised Paris to the second largest city in Europe by 1200, but they might have contributed to that result. Clearly, for eight of the eleven cities in table 8A.1, either a negative correlation or no correlation exists. This does not mean that the wealth or income of cathedral-city citizens and businesses were not enhanced over this period. It only suggests that cathedral building does not appear to have a positive effect on city growth, if growth is measured by city population size. Certainly, the quantity and quality of relics must have been big commercial draws for both ecclesiastical contributions and business for the town's merchants.

Obviously, these massive investments in cathedrals generated opportunity costs in terms of alternative investments foregone. An illustration of the magnitude of these investments is given by architectural historian Julius Baum in his account on the Church of Our Lady in Munich: "An indulgence from Pope Sixtus IV in 1479 resulted in so heavy an influx of funds that not only was the church finally completed...but sufficient money was left over to purchase gilt cloth from Venice for vestments."[66] Forced investments in ever-grander and taller cathedrals across the European continent meant less capital flowing toward the development of infrastructure and technology. But if, as it appears, long-term economic development did not follow cathedral building, what was the Catholic Church's rationale in directing and supporting these projects?

Cathedrals as Limit-Pricing Devices

Throughout the medieval period right up to the Protestant Reformation, there was attempted entry in parts of the areas dominated by the Western church. Heresies abounded in many areas—Gnosticism and Waldensian heresies, dissenters emerging within the structure of Christian religion (Savonarola), and heresies arising from an emerging scientific state of mind were all present. The Church responded vigorously to attempted entry with policies ranging from outright war (the Crusades), to inquisitions that long preceded the emergence of Protestantism, to other forms of religious sanctions such as excommunication and interdict.[67] Indeed, the emergence of religious orders such as the Franciscans and the Dominicans were aimed at addressing the entry possibilities of those advocating a more "Christ-like" church that ministered to the poor and sick. Generally, then, the Church engaged in a policy of raising entry costs to would-be entrants. Heresy—as defined by the Church—could be paid for with one's life. But there was another economic strategy available to the Church in forestalling or preventing entry—limit pricing.

Limit pricing is defined as follows: "A firm is limit pricing if it sets its price and output so that there is not enough demand left for another firm to enter the market profitably."[68] The key to limit pricing is that the incumbent firm must convince potential entrants that it will produce the same output (e.g., Q_i in figure 8A.1) regardless of entry. Assuming the market is being served by the incumbent at an existing price, p_0, the new firm will face residual demand curve, D_R, upon entry. The incumbent firm must convince the entrant that in will "overproduce" if necessary to drive down the price to a point that denies profit to the entrant (i.e., p_1, where the entrant's residual demand curve is tangent to industry average cost, AC). However, this course is not very plausible because

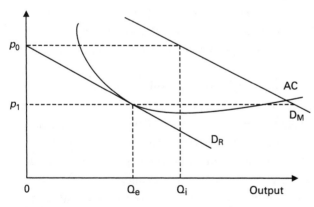

Figure 8A.1
Cathedral construction as a form of limit pricing

according to the incumbent's demand curve, D_M, price p_1 yields average revenue below average cost. Therefore the outcome depends on the credibility of the incumbent firm in making such a threat. With a credible threat the incumbent can reap monopoly rents in the interim. The usual channels used by the incumbent firm to signal its commitment are huge physical plants and long-term contracts. However, if entry occurs, the entrant will prove that the incumbent cannot sustain the output Q_i, and thus price will not fall by much, making the entry profitable and presumably encouraging more entry.

We suggest that an economic reason that the Catholic Church built huge cathedrals was to signal to potential entrants its commitment to maintaining market share or even increasing it. In addition to many functional by-products (guild meeting halls, and so on) they created, cathedrals were also *signaling devices of brand name capital* as described by Benjamin Klein and Keith Leffler.[69] The import of the signal was to indicate to prospective entrants (Protestants and others) that excess capacity existed for Roman Catholic religion and membership. (The corporate headquarters of large corporations—such as the Transamerica building in San Francisco—may provide evidence that the business is here to stay, for example.) In this way, firms, including the Roman Catholic Church, invest in brand name capital to create a "grandeur effect." Unquestionably, this strategy worked for a long period of time prior to the Protestant entry. The pre-Protestant heretics were unsuccessful despite the fact that there were repeated attempts at entry right up to the Reformation. But Protestant entry proved that in certain locales entry into the religious market was profitable, a fact that encouraged more entry.

Protestant entry can be seen in part as a result of the failure of rational policies to prevent entry. At some point someone was going to test the hypothesis of profitable entry and find it viable. In the interim, the Church was behaving rationally in deterring entry by investing in excess capacity. According to a model of limit entry pricing, the Catholic Church failed to convince the potential entrant (Luther) that it could sustain Q_i. Why did such a policy fail to convince potential entrants at the time that it did? It may be that the monopoly Roman Catholic Church had become so large and locationally diverse that is was unable to effectively monitor the signaling of all of its agents. But the theory of limit pricing, outlined above, suggests that the leader of entry at this time estimated that the Catholic signals were unenforceable and that it was an economically plausible policy to call the Church's bluff. Additionally, he was willing to accept the potential personal costs (death).

Entry was not a surprise to the Church, and it most certainly did not willingly allow Protestants to enter the Christian religious market. Rather the Church exhibited rational expectations, investing less in excess capacity in areas where entry was likely to succeed in spite of its efforts. It was too costly to fight entry in particular locations, so the incumbent firm chose to retreat from those locations and concentrate on others. Note that our argument is unaffected by the fact that the great period of cathedral building originated in the twelfth century; actual construction took place more or less continuously for centuries (see table 8A.1), and it helped deter entry from a number of heretical forms. Other entry-limiting devices were of course used by the Church, including repression and murder. Hundreds of thousands of people were tried, condemned, relieved of property, or killed. Witchcraft, in addition to more formal heresies, was severely condemned, with thousands murdered between 1300 and 1499 alone.[70]

Ours is a signaling theory, whereby actions taken are not taken for the sake of their direct results, but to inform prospective rivals or competitors. Fund raising and work on cathedrals was part of the entry deterrence strategy. We hypothesize that in the face of entry, the Catholic Church found it less costly to give up some locations to the Protestants than to fight. The testable implication here is that the pattern of investment in cathedrals reflects the Church's expectations in this regard. Our model also conjectures that once a successful entry occurs, more entry is encouraged; this is definitely the case today in the United States, where the religious market is becoming a competitive world in which everyone can follow the religion they want.

Constructing an Empirical Test

Naturally, constructing an empirical test of the proposition that cathedral building was an entry-limiting device created by the Church is difficult at these distances in time and data availability. We believe nonetheless that some preliminary evidence might be assembled. Sociologist Guy E. Swanson provides the dates and countries of "final settlement"—that is, the date and place where particular locations either converted to Protestantism or remained Roman Catholic.[71] We use a simpler form of a dependent variable—whether a country remained Catholic or converted to a Protestant form of religion irrespective of the date that they settled in our empirical test.

In terms of the independent variable, several variables might capture the concept of a cathedral's "capacity"—the ground plan area (measured in square feet) and/or the interior height (in feet). Our source of information is not systematic; it is a glimmering of data presented by Paul Johnson, who reports height and square-footage data on cathedrals in Britain and elsewhere on the continent of Europe. These data are reported in table 8A.2. We do not know of any systematic collection of data on the dimensions of cathedrals.

We note that the height of cathedrals is as critical in measuring "awe and grandeur" capital as is the actual capacity of a church. We believe that height is relevant, in other words. As Johnson notes:

Table 8A.2
Height and square footage of selected medieval cathedrals

Internal height (from pavement to apex of vault)			
Old St. Paul's	103	Cologne	155
Westminster	103	Beauvais	154
York	102	Bologna	150
Gloucester	86	Amiens	144
Salisbury	84	Bourges	117
Lincoln	82	Chartres	106
Ground area (square feet)			
Old St. Paul's	72,460	Seville	150,000
York	63,800	Milan	92,000
Lincoln	57,200	Saragossa	80,000
Winchester	53,480	Amiens	70,000
Ely	46,000	Cluny	66,000
Westminster	46,000	Toledo	66,000

Source: Paul Johnson, *British Cathedrals* (New York: Morrow, 1980), 19.

The cathedrals were almost out of scale with their times; it is impossible for us to conceive the extent to which, in a literal sense, they loomed large in the lives and vision of medieval people, reducing all else (including themselves) to insignificance and providing inescapable and ocular evidence of the power of majesty of God. They were awesome and overwhelming.[73]

These structures, which gave "ocular evidence" of the power of God, also provided evidence of the power of God's only recognized representative on earth during medieval times—the Roman Catholic Church. Thus, in addition to square feet as a measure of physical capacity, some "magisterial quotient" in terms of height and decoration is relevant to perceptions of potential entrants. We use height as a simple measure of this factor.

Some simple regressions can be performed with our data. The dependent variable is **CATH**, a dummy variable which takes the value of 1 if the country remained Catholic and 0 if the country converted to Protestantism. There are two explanatory variables: **HIGHFT** is the height in feet of cathedrals in the country and **GROUNDFT** is the ground plan area in square feet. Using OLS (defined in appendix 4A), we obtain the following results. Both coefficients are positive and significant at better than the .01 level, as shown below in tables 8A.3 and 8A.4.

The coefficients on area and height are significant in both regressions and are consistent with larger cathedrals acting as an entry barrier. Overall, the regressions explain more than 60 percent of the variation in

Table 8A.3
Heightft

CATH	Coef.	t	P > |t|
HIGHFT	.0154346	4.66	0.001
CONS	−1.282697	−3.26	0.009

R-squared = 0.6843   Number of obs. = 12

Table 8A.4
Groundft

CATH	Coef.	t	P > |t|
GROUNDFT	.0000285	3.55	0.007
CONS	−1.322844	−2.52	0.036

R-squared = 0.6120   Number of obs. = 12

height and size in this sample. We also ran more sophisticated regressions models, and although we do not have sufficient data for these exercises, we continue to find positive signs on these variables.

Our data for Protestant cathedrals is British and that for Catholic cathedrals is European. Supplementing this data with data for other Protestant cities in Britain and elsewhere with more modest cathedrals would strengthen our results.

There are cases, such as Germany and Switzerland, for example, in which the entire country or area did not change its religion. Parts of these countries clearly remained Catholic. Our theory would predict that those areas or regions that became Protestant would contain smaller and shorter Catholic churches. Unfortunately, our data does not permit such an analysis since we have no Swiss churches and only one German church (Cologne) in our data set.

Finally, we present a visual picture of our results in figure 8A.2. There, the Catholic and Protestant cathedral heights in feet are plotted, clearly

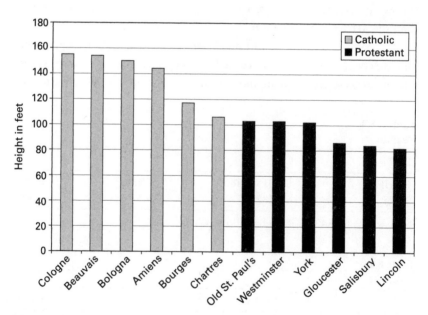

Figure 8A.2
Height of selected British and European cathedrals

showing the effect we postulate. Areas with higher cathedrals, represented by gray columns, all remained Roman Catholic. Thus, we suggest that while medieval cathedrals served many purposes and, indeed, were some of the greatest technical achievements of their time, they served a rational economic purpose as well. Protestant entry into the market for Christian religion finally materialized in the early sixteenth century. The Roman Catholic Church did not make a mistake in failing to forestall entry. Indeed, we argue that the Church made a conscious rational effort to do so. By supplying excess capacity and "awe and grandeur" capital in the form of medieval cathedrals, the Church attempted to signal potential entrants that entry would be unsuccessful. For a number of reasons, some of them relating to the pricing structure of Roman Catholic Church services, the attempt to forestall entry for longer was unsuccessful. Cathedral building in certain locales was, as we have argued with some preliminary evidence, one reason why some areas of Europe remained Catholic and others were lost to Protestantism, as well as a reason that Protestant entry did not materialize until 1518 and after.

9

The Competitive Revolution in Christianity

If ecumenism is successful, it will surely produce the return of a Torquemada and the relighting of the faggots.
—Anonymous

I have seen the moment of my greatness
Flicker,
And I have seen the eternal Footman hold
My coat, and snicker,
And in short, I was afraid.
—T. S. Eliot, *The Love Song of J. Alfred Prufrock*

This book presents a microeconomic and institutional analysis of the form change in religion with particular emphasis on the Protestant Reformation. We argue that a broad theory of monopoly and competitive entry helps explain the crisis of the medieval Roman Catholic Church—successful regional Protestant entry in the sixteenth century—and the market responses of the Church in the Counter-Reformation in the same and ensuing centuries. Our theory of how forms of religion are determined by particular variables and mutate given changes in those variables and in exogenous forces help describe some economic details of Protestant entry and the course of Protestantism after the Reformation. The fundamental change in religious product made possible by individualized interpretation of Holy Scripture within the Protestant nexus of thought created the possibility of truly competitive markets in Christian religious products and services.

We are now in a position to suggest how our central thesis of fundamental religious market change might be applied to some important historical and contemporary issues and problems of Christianity. First, we use our theory of the evolution of Christianity to explain the array of product choices available in contemporary societies. Our argument is that form is a function of the full price of religion together with a set of shifters such as income and risk profile. Two-way causation may exist, but we focus on the effects of the shifters (e.g., income, risk) on religious form rather than the impact of cultural factors on the shifters. Here we provide a discussion of the determinants of particular forms of Christianity in the United States. Second, we discuss the importance of the competitive innovations introduced by the Reformation and the market responses of Roman Catholicism for some critical issues in *contemporary* Christianity. These issues include the so-called divide between the "Northern" and "Southern" (developed vs. undeveloped nations) versions of Christian belief, the ecumenical movement, and particular liberal-conservative issues that divide Christians (gay issues, married priests, abortion, biological issues). In a concluding section we offer an institutional cum microeconomic analysis of the evolution and course of modern Christianity.

Understanding Contemporary Developments in Forms of Christianity

A demand curve for some particular form of religion may be expressed as a function of the full price of that form, the price of substitutes, income, and risk preference as explained in chapter 3. Full price of participation in any religion is composed of the money costs of membership and the time costs associated with a particular religion and its rituals. Risk preference is a positive function of such variables as an individual's stock of education, the level of government stability, and one's health; it is a negative function of an individual's age. Studies consistently show an increase in religious participation with age (up to a point, due, ostensibly, to increasing infirmity). In addition to these determinants, forms of religion change through time given political constraints on the freedom to develop religion. When new or alternative forms of religion develop within a monopoly structure—such as Gnosticism or Albigensianism in the Middle Ages—they may be repulsed or driven underground as "heresies." Other competitive tactics were used. When confronted with the ideas of Saints Francis and Dominic—particularly the idea that the Roman Catholic Church should be less concerned with wealth acquisition and more concerned with ministering to the poor, an idea that was treated as heresy by some popes of the Middle Ages—the papacy sought to bring in church orders devoted to such pursuits. The Church, under competitive pressures at certain times, saw these orders as weapons in their confrontation with heretics such as the Gnostics who held similar beliefs. Importantly, after being "bought out" by an apparent change in Roman Catholic Church policy, both Franciscans and Dominicans evolved into less extreme adherents of a life of poverty than their respective founders. Such doctrinal divisions and their repair by Protestant sects undoubtedly took place in other cases over the history of Protestantism.

Sustained entry in the religion market finally occurred in the sixteenth century when Protestantism emerged under political and military constraints that were amenable to believers of that general variant of Christianity. But the chief doctrinal innovation of Protestantism—establishment of a general belief that only Christ and Scripture stood between man and God—was the central element that permitted Christian forms of religion to develop into the thousands of forms that exist today. These new and emerging forms began as soon as biblical interpretation was thrown open to competitive interpretation. Even under Protestantism, however, some of the emerging sects espousing socialism or anarchy—that is, those most at variance with existing political structures—were crushed or became nomadic. Others such as Baptists or Puritans, some of whom arrived in North America after some intermediate migrations in the Netherlands, were, after initial periods of suppression and relocation, quite successful.

Two points must be emphasized. First, it was the ability to produce a credible claim to a "true interpretation" of Scripture that was necessary but not sufficient to the Roman Catholic monopoly of religious form in the Middle Ages. Sufficiency required the power, either religious or civil, to crush would-be opponents. Once this doctrinal monopoly met successful challenge, the door was forever opened to competitive forms of religion, each claiming to be the true variation on Holy Scripture. Second, it is critical to note that the *process* of Christianity is preference-driven, as ritual and interpretive variations are fashioned and re-fashioned by demanders when underlying factors and conditions, including full prices, change. Generally speaking, as argued in preceding chapters, lower risk preference will produce more conservative, ritualistic, and rule-driven forms of Christianity.

Religions laden with time-consuming ritual and dogmatic performance standards act as partial but incomplete substitutes for scientific knowledge, education, stable politics, and rational-empirical thought systems, such as those promulgated in the Enlightenment. Other things equal, higher and higher full prices, created by rising wages or incomes, ultimately create tipping points where individuals move to other forms or develop new and generally accepted forms of Christianity. Forms may also change when factors other than full price are altered. Greater political or social instability, or new forms of science and scientific explanation of phenomena will, other things equal, produce a demand for new or different forms of religious belief. Politics allowing, religious forms will morph into those demanded, maximizing the utility of believer-participants. Individuals may sometimes become both suppliers and demanders of some of these forms and call themselves Christian. We believe that self-created Christianity was operative in the early and high Middle Ages—as the Roman church crushed heretics and as Protestants finally entered the market—and that it is even routine today under the nonestablishment clauses that operate in most countries of the world.

Causation

There is plentiful suggestion in both anthropological and psychological literature that some mythological, magical belief system is self-induced as spontaneous operations of the psyche for each and every sentient individual. It is through an individual's definitions of "chaos" and "spirit" that reality is defined. Our focus has been almost exclusively on the forms of Christianity in subduing chaos. We have argued that Christianity in all of its variants is one example of that human trait and that economic variables determine the form of all religious products. But there is naturally a problem of causality and identification of the endogenous variable(s). Our analysis, as revealed in the discussion of the Weberian hypothesis (chapter 8), focuses on the central interpretive problem. Do economic variables determine forms of Christianity (or more general forms of religion) or does a specific form of Christianity (or religion generally) determine economic growth and income rates? In very general and largely anecdotal tests in chapter 3, we argued that economic variables have a clear impact on general kinds of religion chosen. But, clearly, both hypotheses could be correct and religion and economic growth could be endogenous and interrelated (the most likely and correct scenario). Some of the most interesting studies in this area have been conducted by Robert J. Barro[1] and Barro and Rachel M. McCleary.[2] For example, Barro and McCleary, using a twenty-year survey of church attendance and a variety of religious beliefs by the *International Social Survey Programme* and other sources, show generally that religiosity declines with economic growth, that church attendance and religious beliefs are positively related to education in advanced countries (thereby negating one interpretation of the secularization hypothesis), and that religiosity is negatively related to urbanization.[3] A major conclusion of this study is that belief is positively related but church attendance is negatively related to economic growth. It is the level of belief relative to attendance (the "productivity" of the religious sector) that is a positive determinant of economic performance.

Little empirical work has been done, however, on how forms of Christianity affect economic growth. An exception that includes one non-Christian form is a study of the impact forms of Christian religion have on growth in U.S. states. In pooled regressions from the years 1952, 1971, and 1980, economists William C. Heath, Melissa S. Waters, and John Keith Watson estimate the impact of four religions—Catholicism, Judaism, liberal Protestantism, and fundamentalist Protestantism—on state per capita income.[4] Including control variables for each state, they find that both fundamentalist and Catholic versions of Christianity exert negative and significant influences on per capita income over this period, with fundamentalism producing the most extreme decrease. Larger Jewish populations exerted a strongly positive influence on per capita state income after 1952 and liberal Protestantism had a positive (but statistically insignificant) impact. Naturally, such studies may be biased due to simultaneity problems. After estimating income levels and religious membership jointly, Waters, Heath, and Watson find the same results as those obtained in single-equation models. Fundamentalists "engender attitudes which inhibit economic activity...[by supporting] a religiously appropriate environment [that] results in legislative prohibitions on the production and/or consumption of goods and services."[5] Moreover, there is growing evidence that creativity and growth are enhanced in areas of the United States where social tolerance is the norm.[6] Creativity and growth decrease at national levels when scientific research is limited or thwarted by evangelically inspired legislation against, for example, certain scientific procedures such as embryonic manipulation.

In this final chapter we explore, both historically and empirically, the hypothesis that economic and other variables may determine religious form. We are certainly not the first to suggest this. It has long been maintained in sociological literature that types of religious belief are quite sensitive to income and education. For example, more fundamentalist (Pentecostal) sects—those promising more direct rules and instructions for divine assistance or retribution—appeal to low-education, low-income groups.[7] Latin America is experiencing a conversion to those types of religion in preference to or in addition to traditional Catholicism, which itself is becoming more conservative for those Christians. For its part, Roman Catholicism has responded by maintaining and enforcing rigid forms of the rigorous precepts of that religion in order to compete with hardline evangelical sects, as discussed later in this chapter, and to maintain credence in its product. The point is that there is a clear interrelationship between economic variables and the form of the religious product. First, consider how this might be interpreted within the historical context of the evolution of Christianity during and after the Protestant Reformation.

The Evolution of Christianity

We have advanced the view that modern microeconomic theory provides insight into the development of Christianity. In the remainder of this chapter we seek to present anecdotal and empirical evidence that economic variables explain the evolution of forms of Christian religion— their emergence, disappearance, fracture and cohesion, and policy positions—from the Protestant Reformation to the present. We further argue that these considerations, together with an infusion of modern neo-institutional economics, point to some interesting possibilities for the future of Christianity.

Protestantism, Catholic Response, and Contemporary Organization

Protestantism evolved in organization, doctrine, and ritual form from the very beginning and it is important to review these changes in variety. Some Protestants adopted the Roman Catholic episcopal form of governance and organization while others were more democratic in form (the presbyter form). Luther preached adherence to the Ten Commandments, the Apostle's Creed, and the Lord's Prayer with three sacraments, but the real cohesion of all Protestantism was a belief that Christ and the Bible as the word of God were the only intermediaries between man and God. Human conscience, enlightened by the reading of Scripture—available to average individuals as well as scholars—was the guide. Salvation was achieved only through God's grace, man's faith in that grace, and good works, not through some mechanical system of sin, penance, absolution, sin (etc.) in a highly complex doctrinal and organizational bureaucracy. But this is where agreement ended for many Protestants. Before Luther's movement was even a decade old, competing sects emphasizing alternative organizational structures and doctrinal principles emerged, with the Lutherans and Episcopalians on one (episcopal) side, and the Calvinists and many of the quasi-Lutheran offshoots in German-Swiss protest on the other (presbyterian) side.

Many of these developments and demands for alternative forms of Christian worship may be identified as economically motivated and as responsive to particular political situations (which, of course, affected risk preference). Like the early Waldensian and Gnostic heretics against Roman Catholicism, humanist reformers such as Ulrich Zwingli and Philipp Melanchthon, basing their theological ideas on the great humanist Erasmus, often used theology to support an economic position. Demands for many of these early forms were premised on the advancing science and knowledge of the day as well.

Splits in the doctrinal and organizational form were a constant feature of Protestantism adopted in England—tentatively by Henry VIII and more fully by his daughter Elizabeth I. Henry's break with the Roman Catholic Church was basically political, and he remained essentially

Catholic in outlook (though he profited by the confiscation of the monasteries and church property). Elizabeth, on the other hand, issued a revised Book of Common Prayer, the Supremacy Act of 1559, and Thirty-nine Articles of Anglicanism in 1563 rejecting purgatory, papacy, and relic worship among other rules. Almost immediately both the organizational and doctrinal forms of *English* Protestantism were challenged by various forms of "Puritans" and eclectics of all kinds. John Wesley, who had been a High Church Anglican prelate, founded the Methodist movement, which moved to North America and became a foundation of the Pentecostal movement.[8] Thomas Cartwright (1535–1603) called for a Presbyterian, democratic form of the election of pastors, no kneeling in services, and the abolition of "popish" offices (bishops, archbishops, etc.)—a Calvinist orientation. Self-determination in the selection of local pastors was also the foundation of English Congregationalism (founded by Henry Jacob, 1563–1624). These sects were developed within the confines of the Church of England,[9] but Separatist Congregationalists, advocating stricter Calvinism and baptism by immersion, developed a new form of religion in 1633—a form that evolved into Baptism. These "Puritans" met with various levels of acceptance (most fully under Cromwell between 1653 and 1658), but high-cost persecutions and imprisonments led them on odysseys to Protestant enclaves in Europe and, in 1620, to North America aboard the *Mayflower*.

Once in North America, so-called separatists and nonseparatists from the Church of England joined forces, successfully establishing Congregationalism in parts of Massachusetts, New Hampshire, and Connecticut. (It is said that they did well by doing good.) The Puritans were something of a contradiction—advocating individual freedom for themselves while at the same time practicing religious intolerance of others. Survival was often the primary issue in the often hostile conditions the group found themselves, so risk aversion must have been affected, creating stricter and more conservative forms of worship, ritual, and theology. Education was emphasized (to read and profit from the Bible) by Puritans as were some enlightenment ideas. According to historians David A. Rausch and Carl Hermann Voss, "To the Puritans, theology crowned a pyramid built upon the liberal arts. This included history, literary enterprises, and science. Later on, Puritans were personally involved in the scientific enterprise. Cotton Mather (1663–1728) wrote America's first treatise on medicine."[10] However sophisticated the Puritans were, their repressive and highly priced attempt to institute God's kingdom on earth created other forms of Protestantism. Roger Williams (1603–1684), for one, was expelled from the Massachusetts Bay Colony in the 1630s for rejecting the Puritan theocracy. The tipping point was reached by the interference of civil government in church affairs, and Williams moved to Rhode Island to form (what is regarded as) the first Baptist church in the United States.

These separatist movements, indeed a flowering of them, along with the migration of numerous other sects from Europe (French Huguenots, Lutherans, Quakers, Roman Catholics, and so on) broke the Puritan monopoly, leading to a religious pluralism that found its way into the American Revolution foundation documents (the establishment clause in particular) by the late eighteenth century.

Changing forms of Christianity was solely a Protestant enterprise. As suggested in chapter 6, Catholicism in the Tridentine (post–Council of Trent) period was doctrinally not very different from the Church in the pre-Protestant period. In all essentials, the Church remains the same today. While the conclave at Trent did eliminate or attempt to clean up some practices (for example, priestly concubinage and indulgence abuses at the retail level), it reaffirmed celibacy for priests and maintained a system of indulgences. While it tried to outlaw multiple benefices and alienation of church funds from bishops and other prelates to relatives, it achieved very little success for several centuries after Trent. We view the maintenance of doctrinal stability in the face of entry as a means of maintaining credence in the product of Roman Catholicism and as an attempt to shore up the central part of the monopoly. But however the Roman Catholic Church changed in terms of expansion or policies toward Protestants, the central core of its dogma and doctrine remained and still remain unchanged.

While core doctrine was maintained after Trent, the *organizational* form of the contemporary Church did later evolve. But the development of organizational authoritarianism on the part of the pope—as opposed to the shared authority with bishops over ecclesiastical appointments and other policy and doctrinal issues—took centuries to establish.

Tumultuous relations between European polities and the papacy over the nineteenth century, including political balkanization in parts of Europe and the loss of Papal States in Italy, led to a Council of Bishops in 1870 (the First Vatican Council). Political forces in some nations (e.g., France) had even led to a desire for national Catholic churches. The response in 1871 was to grant the pope absolute authority over doctrine and administration of the Roman Catholic Church, and to declare him infallible in matters of faith and morals. In describing the course of subsequent events, John Cornwell, Director of the Science and Human Dimension Project at Cambridge University, writes, "By the first decade of the twentieth century, however, the concept of papal inerrancy and primacy was becoming blurred. A legal and bureaucratic instrument had transformed the dogma into an ideology of papal power unprecedented in the long history of the Church of Rome."[11] On this foundation, an edifice of canon law was built to give the pope absolute authority in a sharply pyramidal church. This was accompanied by attacks on secularization, the renaming of the Inquisition as the Congregation for the Propagation of the Faith to maintain "doctrinal purity," and a general assault on capitalism as the progenitor of secularization. Gone were the primacy of conscience and the distribution of authority among bishops of the Church. The Second Vatican Council, invoked by Pope John XXIII in 1960, attempted to modernize the Church by allowing Mass to be said in the vernacular, granting more power to the laity, reforming the liturgy, and (supposedly) placing greater emphasis on a conciliar form of Church governance. This modernization effort was soon tempered by John XXIII's successor, Pope Paul VI, who advocated a return to traditional doctrine and organization. The backward drift to traditional authority was continued by Paul VI's successor, Pope John Paul II, and by his successor, Benedict XVI, who was elected pope in 2005 upon the death of Pope John Paul II. Diarmaid MacCulloch described John Paul II as one of the most powerful persons ever to occupy the throne of Peter, but added a cautionary note. According to MacCulloch, "[John Paul II's] aim was a confident reaffirmation of a version of the Counter-Reformation, replaying many themes of obedience and dogmatic certainty that would have been familiar to Carlo Borromeo or the early seventeenth-century Jesuit advisers of the Habsburgs and Wittelsbachs. The weakness of this variety of Catholicism has been that it has continued to take the Enlightenment to be its enemy, and has sought to exclude or silence those Catholics who take a different view."[12] In a book by John Paul II, published shortly before his death in 2005, the pope lamented that he had not imposed enough discipline on the Church. John Paul II's policies have found a sympathetic successor in Benedict XVI. Cardinal Joseph Ratzinger, who became Benedict XVI, was in fact in charge of maintaining doctrinal purity as head of the Congregation for the Propagation of the Faith, the renamed Inquisition. In this role he routinely denied priests the right to teach theology (Father Charles Curran is a famous case from the United States). Upon taking the pontificate, Benedict XVI quickly reaffirmed the fact that "inerrancy" on the part of doctrinal teachings would not be tolerated (the editor of the largest Jesuit publication in the world was relieved of his duties). Top-down management, with little feedback on doctrine or organization from lower-level prelates or members, characterizes the contemporary Roman Catholic Church.

Thus, the fundamental lines of belief and organization have been drawn between Catholics and all of the forms of Protestantism and they remain so today. But the forms and shades of belief within these major Christian sects continue to evolve as exemplified by the myriad policies associated with those varieties of Christianity. Before examining some of these policies within the context of the historical evolution of Christian religion, consider some preliminary empirical evidence on the impact of religious forms of Christianity in the United States.

Economic Variables and Forms of Christian Belief: Anecdotal Evidence

Nowhere, perhaps, has the evolution of Christian forms of religion been more pronounced than in the United States. Studies of the myriad varieties of Christian belief reveal an amazing evolution. They are, according to our view, evolving in response to full-price changes and a panoply of shifters that affect the stringency of doctrine demanded and the extent of ritual that will quell risk and anxiety ("chaos" relievers). First consider some estimates of the number of organized Christian sects available to demanders in the United States alone.

A number of estimates of U.S. churches generally and Christian churches in particular have been made. We present evidence based on two of them. Historian Frank S. Mead and religion professor Samuel S. Hill report thirty-three major organized Christian denominations operating in the United States.[13] Of these, there are about 184 formal subdivisions of these major sects, each with an alternative theology and ritual that can be labeled formally "Christian." How do we explain these alternative and evolving forms of Christianity—forms that have appeared and disappeared over the centuries since the Protestant Reformation? Fundamental microeconomic theory suggests that these forms emerge as the full price of membership—a price that includes adherence to a particular theology linked with particular ritual changes through time, given some state of science, education, and other shifters that create a state of risk preference.

Just as the rising full price of being Roman Catholic in the early sixteenth century led to a general breakaway by Martin Luther and a number of reformers, more subtle differences in the full price of membership in a particular form of modern Christianity leads to new forms of the Christian religion. A number of economic phenomena will change the full price of a particular theological-ritualistic form of Christianity. Ritual can affect full price. As we saw in chapter 8, for example, feast holidays of the Roman Catholic Church were manipulated (increased) in the post-Reformation period to attract adherents from Protestantism in areas where Catholics and Protestants were in close proximity. Price competition may be augmented and accompanied by change in cultural shifters to produce changes in the form of Christianity and belief structure. In the past decade, for example, a theological split in the largest non-Catholic denomination in the United States—the Southern Baptist Convention or SBC (one of the nineteen listed in table 9.1)—created a distinct wing of that organization. (The adjective "Southern" arose over the issue of slavery in May 1845, although racism was formally renounced in 1995.)

Internecine factionalism began in the Southern Baptist Convention in 1978. The highly conservative leadership (which is currently maintained) passed reaffirmations that the role of pastor was limited to males, affirming the primacy of husbands over wives in the household—all based on the "inerrancy of Scripture."[14] In 2000, while stopping short of an official breakaway, a group of one hundred representatives from fifteen

Table 9.1
Organized Christian churches and major subdivisions in the United States

Adventist	5	Mennonite	11
Baptist	19	Methodist	12
Brethern and Pietist	11	Orthodox and Oriental	14
Catholic	7	Orthodox	
Christian Churches (Stone-Campbell Movement)	5	Pentecostal	25
		Presbyterian	9
Church of Christ Scientist	1	Reformed	6
Church of God and Saints of God	1	Salvation Army	3
Community Churches, International Council	1	Schwenkfelder	1
		Triumph the Church and Kingdom of God in Christ	1
Congregational Churches	3		
Divine Science	1	Unitarian Universalist Association	1
Episcopal/Anglican	7		
Friends (Quakers)	4	Unity School of Christianity and Association of Unity Churches	1
Fundamentalist/Bible	11		
Holiness Churches	8		
Hutterian Brethren	1	Universalist Fellowship of Metropolitan Community Churches	1
Jehovah's Witness	1		
Latter Day Saints (Mormons)	4		
Lutheran	8	Worldwide Church of God	1
		TOTAL	184

Source: Frank S. Mead and Samuel S. Hill, *Handbook of Denominations in the United States*, 11th ed. (Nashville: Abingdon Press, 2001).

states met in Atlanta, Georgia, to adopt adherence to a "Network of Mainstream Baptists," rejecting fundamentalist domination over what they labeled "Baptist beliefs and practices." Clearly, the state of culture and science—not to mention the increased opportunity costs to women, chiefly in the form of new and better employment and income prospects—had changed the full price of Southern Baptist theology and ritual. The price of the package offered by conservative Southern Baptists was clearly too high for some. The result, while still "fundamentalist" in general orientation, is a de facto new form of Christian religion. (One might hazard a prediction, testable in principle, that the incomes and educations of these traditional Baptists are higher than their conservative Southern Baptist counterparts.) Further pronouncements of the mother body of the SBC with regard to scriptural interpretation may well lead to a formal schism (or schisms) within that body. Close investigation of the mutations of other forms of theology and ritual from the principal churches developed since the Protestant Reformation would yield similar interpretations. Importantly, form changes—due to the nature of the shifting agents—can be toward either liberal or conservative theologies or rituals.

Religion researcher J. Gordon Melton takes an even broader perspective of the multifaceted face of modern Christianity. His *Encyclopedia of American Religions*[15] is in its seventh edition and encompasses a survey of both Christian and "all-other" religious *families* operating in the United States. These "other" religions include such diverse belief systems as the many kinds of Middle Eastern religions, as well as "Magick," Ancient Wisdom, Spiritualist, Psychic, New Age, and so on. All in all, Melton found more than 2,500 distinct primary religious bodies within nineteen families of American religions. According to Melton, the member bodies of each family share a common heritage, theology (in its broadest sense), and lifestyle. We are particularly interested in the Christian families that constitute ten of the nineteen families and more than half the approximately 2,500 churches identified by Melton, but his broader reach and its implications for the economic study of religion will be discussed later in the chapter.

Clearly, the mere count of Christian churches is open to dispute. We make no attempt to present Melton's particular accounting, but his tally of one family of belief is instructive. In the "Pietist-Methodist" family, Melton finds four Pietist churches and thirty-three separate Methodist denominations (with the United Methodist Church the largest subgroup by far). Eighteen are labeled "Non-Episcopal Methodist," with seven "Black Methodist," three "German Methodist," and four "British Methodist." This number, of course, contrasts with the twelve subgroups listed in table 9.1. The long and tortuous evolution of Methodism from its origins with John Wesley in England in the eighteenth century to its many manifestations in the United States is recounted in some detail by Melton.[16] Like modern religious mergers and divisions, Methodism in the United States underwent multiple transitions and separations. Exogenous events such as the Revolutionary War, the abolition movement, disputes over the morality of war, controversy regarding episcopal versus decentralized local control, doctrinal divisions within the "holiness movement," and many other events changed relative prices creating different combinations of doctrinal foundations, policy interpretations, and organizational forms, that is, different forms of Methodist Christianity.

The same process of merger and schism (from a particular church's creed and organization) that affected Methodists occurred with virtually all other denominations. This is also true of Catholicism. There was a long-standing split between traditional Western Roman Catholics and Eastern Orthodox doctrine and ritual (the latter did not and does not recognize the pope as the infallible head of Christian Catholicism).

Melton maintains that religious families have stayed together due to basic commonalities despite the mutations (which create different full prices) that have occurred due to doctrinal or ritualistic differences or, more recently, the creation of liberal and conservative wings of many major denominations. A specific example will clarify this view. Melton argues,

For fundamentalists and for the Protestant churches, especially those which follow John Calvin's Reformed theology, the features distinguishing them from each other are their thought world. They hold divergent views on these topics in particular: sacrament, ecclesiology, the sovereignty of God, perfection, and the nature of the end of time. But even where there is agreement, sharing a thought world does not necessarily mean holding identical views. Rather, it means sharing some beliefs which set the context for constant debate over specifics.[17]

In our view, each of these variants carries a different full price for a particular form of religion—that is, of doctrine, ritual, policy, and organization. (As we will see, such differences, when extreme, may create serious divisions among families of religions.) The fact that a whole spectrum of beliefs exists from what might be termed "liberal" to "conservative" within some particular religion (Methodist, Presbyterian, Roman Catholic) creates many difficulties for a researcher trying to discover the determinants of particular forms of religion. There are, for example, liberal Baptists and conservative Episcopalians.

In our view, differences in fundamental beliefs—if that means fundamental differences in theology or scriptural doctrine—are to be interpreted as economic factors that create differences in full price. It is certainly true that, from the beginning of the Protestant Reformation, there have been many such theological differences between Christian sects. Some have rejected belief in the Trinity (seeing this as polytheism), the divinity of Christ (many Unitarians do not accept the theology), some or all of the sacraments (seven for the Roman Catholics, two or three—generally baptism and Holy Communion—for mainline Protestant churches, none for the now defunct Zwinglians and Anabaptists). Transubstantiation is a belief of Roman Catholics that the act of consecration creates the *actual* not the *symbolic* recreation of the body and blood of Christ. (Some writers, e.g., Diarmaid MacCulloch,[18] see transubstantiation as a retained element of magic in Roman Catholicism.)

All manner of biblical interpretational differences are held by the various Christian religious forms, and all have retreated to Scripture to justify their own interpretations and beliefs. Importantly, differences in ritual accompany theological or doctrinal differences within these forms. Some rituals (e.g., Mormons, cults, Pentecostals, Evangelicals) carry high time prices and often require service, plain dress, no makeup for women, revivals, born again rituals, and snake and "tongues" ceremonies. Others demand far less of members. The former lend credence to the particular forms of Christian product demanded and, as we have already emphasized, these forms are in constant flux owing to the shifting fit between demander profiles and the particular forms of doctrine and theology supplied by alternative firms. Ideally, one might be able to formulate a test of our basic theory concerning the determinants of the multiple forms of Christian religions, if families of believers (Lutherans) are represented by enough common belief that they are able to encompass both liberal and conservative forms of the general religion. The term "Lutheran" might then be used to represent a unified form of religion. It might be possible to group religions as "fundamentalist" or "traditionalist" with respect to general theology and ritual, but the gross number of Episcopalians or Lutherans or Baptists cannot capture a particular form of belief. Empirical estimations along these lines would be difficult since simple attendance or membership figures for, say, Methodists, cannot actually capture particular forms such as liberal, moderate, or conservative Methodists for whom the full price of religion, including combinations of doctrine and ritual, might be significantly different. Thus, while there are general families of belief, there appears to be as much difference within as between them. Contemporary changes in the many forms of Christianity rest not so much on fundamental tenets (the Ten Commandments, the Apostle's Creed, etc.), but on interpretations of these tenets for a modern world in which science, technology, culture, and other factors are undergoing rapid and continuous change.

Competitive Christianity: An Economic Approach to Contemporary Issues

We have argued throughout this book that standard modern microeconomic theory has much to contribute to an understanding of the historical changes in the forms of Christianity. We now go further to maintain that our economic model of the Christian church may help inform some of the current debates in the status of contemporary Christianity. Despite Melton's claim that more fundamental changes (such as formal schism) in religious families seldom occur due to a basic commonality of belief, it appears that a number of contemporary issues—policy-oriented interpretations of church doctrine in the face of scientific, cultural, or income changes or differences—may put that view to the test. The basic issue, as has always been the case since the Protestant Reformation or even the beginning of Christianity, is the matter of interpretation. In this critical matter, especially regarding the translation of scriptural writings into contemporary church or public policy, there is as much difference within denominational families as between them, as the following examples reveal.

Liberal-Conservative Issues

If we are correct that a multiplicity of forms of Christianity exist and are an economic function of income, education, factors affecting risk preference, and other shifters, a number of features of modern religion become understandable. Ecumenism, a movement that began in modern times during the Catholic Church's Second Vatican Council, becomes a distant and unreachable goal. For the same reason that Methodism's multiple sects are unable to come to agreement on some doctrines and policies, it is unlikely that more general agreement can be reached. As Melton notes, "Family traditions remain very much alive, and attempts to unite groups across those family lines in either liberal or conservative Protestant churches have failed time and again because of strong-held denominational differences."[19] In his view, ecumenism is unreachable due to metafundamental doctrinal differences. In an economic interpretation, something like the instability of cartels is at work. The income, educational, and risk profiles of members would not be expected to be the same under such a large umbrella as, for example, traditional Protestants or conservative Protestants. Forms will differ reflecting the underlying economic profile of believers and their tolerance for risk, just as individuals purchase different quantities and qualities of insurance based on similar variables. We argued in chapter 3 that the demand-side tendency to monopoly created by network effects is counterbalanced by the inherent problems of the instability of cartels. The reason that a full-fledged ecumenical Christianity is an unreachable goal explains why, in microcosms of particular Christian denominations, we *expect* division and, in the limit, schisms.

Particularly important shifters may be identified as affecting the evolution of modern Christianity. Perhaps the most critical issues facing modern Christianity—mainline denominations and the sects or churches that evolve or separate from them—are policies associated with doctrine or dogma, such as the sexual or life issues discussed below. Doctrinal differences may not be as important as the *interpretation* of doctrine or policy prescriptions. First, consider the decline in participation (attendance) rates in the largest mainline church in the United States and Europe— the Roman Catholic Church. Many observers, among them sociologists, note this development and attribute it to the reduction of stringency in the requirements of Catholicism that were brought about in 1960 by the Second Vatican Council. Since then, according to Finke and Stark, the reduction in attendance and the number of priests, nuns, brothers, and seminarians was the twofold result of the liberalizations of Vatican II and the issuance of an unpopular encyclical on birth control *Humanae Vitae*, promulgated by Pope Paul VI in 1968. Finke and Stark claim, "The distinctive sacrifices and stigmas of being Catholic were abandoned (without replacement) by the reforms of Vatican II. Recent declines in the vigor of American Catholicism reflect one more cycle of the sect-church process whereby a faith becomes a mainline body and then begins to wilt."[20] Unfortunately this argument will not bear scrutiny from a broader economic perspective. The changes wrought by the Second Vatican Council were entirely "cosmetic" (see the previous discussion) while the pre-Enlightenment, pre-scientific doctrines that continued to be promulgated have become etched in stone and even extended, especially in the papacy of Pope John Paul II and his successor Pope Benedict XVI. None of the core beliefs and practices of the church have changed. The Aristotelian-Aquinas theory of natural law remains the basis of Church views on life and sexual issues. Priestly celibacy, the secondary role of women, and the role of gay people in the church remain precisely the same. Indeed, as revealed by the policies of John Paul II and Benedict XVI regarding a centralized church espousing conservative values and new levels of censorship, the Church is clearly becoming more (not less) Tridentine in nature. It was not the lowering of price that led to Catholic religious defections in the United States, as argued by Finke and Stark and by Iannaccone,[21] measured in terms of attendance. The full price of being a Roman Catholic has not declined. Rather it was the *increasing* price of *official* membership in the Roman church on sexual and other issues in the face of improving incomes, education, and scientific knowledge that is causing defections to more liberal religions, to self-generated religion, and to less participation by attendance measures. It may also be said, in the context of economic theory, that the Roman Catholic Church is facing a credence problem due to the emergence of clear empirical science in areas such as sex and reproduction. Further, while celibacy remains the rule, emphatically reaffirmed by Popes John Paul II and Benedict XVI, it no longer provides the credence value that it once did. For U.S. Catholics the child abuse crisis by priests has probably dramatically reduced the belief that celibacy is a necessary condition for the priesthood. Additional credibility problems have been engendered by the widespread belief among Catholics that those guilty of enabling this abuse—bishops and other higher-ups—have not (save one bishop) and will not be made accountable for their poor administration.

The North-South Divide

The doctrinal split within Roman Catholicism and other Christian sects explained by historian Philip Jenkins is between what he calls the North (U.S. and Europe) and the South (third-world countries in the Southern hemisphere).[22] Indeed, denominational splits between Christian churches and sects within the United States and other advanced countries over doctrine are of a lesser order of magnitude than in the less developed world. And, as an economic theory of religious form predicts, this is also to be expected. High income societies, sophisticated in science and technology, are undergoing, in evolutionary fashion, changes in the forms of religion and belief systems. Where religious tolerance and forms are constitutionally protected, splintering within particular religions is expected. But fundamentalist, rule-oriented, highly ritualistic, and/or time-intensive forms of religion and magic are inversely related to income and level of scientific and economic development. Religions, including evangelical Christian forms in the underdeveloped world, espouse medieval values against those of the advanced liberal nations, and they are growing rapidly. What is the reason for this growth?

Clearly, many of the nations of the underdeveloped world are plagued by unstable governments and property rights encouraging a substitution of the security of religion for political security. The historically high concentration and participation rate of Roman Catholics in the Spanish and Portuguese colonies of South and Central America is evidence of this phenomenon. Low incomes, poverty, disease, low life expectancy, and a host of other factors all create an extreme risk aversion to liberal and highly abstract forms of Christianity. The security and joint products of ritualistic behavior permit such people to quell anxiety and risk. Low employment levels and wage rates reduce the opportunity cost and value of time. Other things being equal, the full price of participation in rule-driven and ritualistic religions is low to these low-income, poorly educated, and highly risk-averse individuals. This is especially so in underdeveloped environments where political instability and uncertain property rights exist.

The movement to religious evangelical conservatism in Pentecostal and Roman Catholic forms has been emblematic of Latin American Christianity. Political scientist Anthony Gill, for example, argues quite cogently that competitive pressures on the Roman Catholic Church in Latin America led to particular policies on the part of the bishops toward authoritarian regimes. He argues, correctly in our view, that in a sample of twelve Latin countries "progressive" Catholicism in Latin America, especially among the poor, is the product of competition with fundamentalist (Pentecostal) sects and animistic cults.[23] So-called liberation theology is prevalent where this competition exists and is absent where it does not. In countries without serious competition for Catholicism, bishops and the Church are generally far more amenable to military dictators and authoritarian regimes. Closer to our own theory of religious form, it is important to note that conservative Latin American religions focus on community—local support groups that concentrate on the needs of families and on political ends. While views on marriage are evolving in Peru, for example, matching similar changes in advanced nations,[24] the presence of political instability in countries such as El Salvador has provided great impetus to conservative forms of religion, as our theory predicts. According to researcher Illeana Gomez, "For both Pentecostals and Catholics in San Francisco Gotera, religion has provided continuity in the face of the fragmentation produced by the civil war and its aftershocks. Religious practice has helped maintain and re-create a background of common experiences and bonds though which the local population, especially young people, can construct personal and collective identities, loyalties, and commitments."[25] These conservative movements have formed in the face of political repression and in particular places have underpinned liberation and pluralistic political movements. Political difficulties in such countries as Nicaragua and El Salvador are perhaps extreme examples of how religious forms respond to risk determinants, but the combination of poverty and low levels of education throughout Latin America helps explain the growth of ritualistic Catholicism and conservative-evangelical sects on that continent and in other less developed parts of the world. Naturally, many forms of these general religions have developed depending on local circumstances.

Examples of this phenomenon are plentiful and fascinating. The many forms of religious practice by Latin Americans, Mexicans, and Native Americans of the U.S. American Southwest, especially those combining a Spanish version of Roman Catholicism with magic and spiritualistic rituals, fit well within the theory. Those in poverty are often close to the survival constraint. While the stock of formal religious capital may be Roman Catholic, more immediate and empirical services are often needed. Reference and practice often conform to even earlier religious

influences, such as those of pre-Columbian societies. The rituals surrounding the Day of the Dead (November 2), for example, clearly combine Christian and pre-Columbian ritual. In Mexico and in the American
Southwest, the use of *milagros* are common. Believers deposit small
(usually metal) replicas of particular body parts afflicted with a malady
(e.g., arms, feet, heart) in the churches in hopes of receiving healing
from God or by the intercession of a saint. Literally meaning "miracles,"
milagros are part of the North American Spanish culture. Many other
offerings and supplications are made for specific purposes (e.g., candles
for finding a lover) or for warding off evil spirits.

Economic development in these low-income regions can be expected
to have predictable effects on the forms of religion chosen and the
evangelical-fundamentalist forms are growing, including an extremely
conservative Roman Catholicism.[26] How much economic growth and
how long it will take to affect changes is problematical, however. While
the enhanced scientific prospects for human survival in the advanced
parts of the world help reduce the human dread and uncertainty associated with mortality, these problems have not disappeared for large segments of humanity. Ramifications for mainline Christian churches due
to the North-South divide may be dramatic and enduring if trends
continue.

Secularization, Politics, and Science

In general, the conclusion of sociologists that secularization has not substituted for religion is completely correct in our view. In their book *Acts
of Faith* Stark and Finke, for example, devote an entire chapter to "Secularization RIP."[27] If we stick to a definition of religion as "organization" and measure it by attendance or membership, this may not be so.
In the National Opinion Survey of religion, the fastest growth is "no religion." Further, the category "no religion" is growing fastest among the
young in the United States. However, when "religion" includes other
measures of spirituality, we would argue that religion is simply taking
other forms, which would ostensibly support the views of Stark and
Finke. For their part, Roman Catholic social scientists (and apologists)
see no problem reconciling "progress" with Roman Catholic teachings,[28]
suggesting that doctrinally Catholic thinkers are supportive of growth.

But when the demand and supply for the thousands of forms of religion and the *definition* of religion are considered, one could go even further. Surveys showing that natural scientists do not have vastly different church attendance rates than the general population (although those of social scientists are lower) appear to provide some evidence that scientists are not enemies of religion. The development of science in the area of embryonic stem cell research, condemned by the Roman Catholic Church and by particular polities (the United States), will probably not have much of an effect on belief in God, spirituality, or an afterlife. The religious condemnation of these potential but possibly major scientific advances hinges almost entirely on pre-scientific notions of natural law and definitions of "life." In this, Thomas Aquinas, who adapted the teleological natural law view of Aristotle to Christian theology, casts a long if weakening shadow. In Christian terms, this animistic view asserts that "life" is the "purpose" and "end" of existence. Thus, all life is sacred and must be protected no matter the circumstance. Birth control hinders the "natural" end of sex, life begins when cells meet (no abortion) and cannot be ended "unnaturally" (as in capital punishment or euthanasia). There is no room for interpretation or compromise here, but this view is becoming increasingly irrelevant in view of scientific advances calling it into question.

Few issues in the realm of pure science have garnered more attention than the theory of evolution. Darwinian evolution, the foundation of modern biology, is at the root of the debate. A biology of natural selection with a common ancestor and random changes are at the heart of most accounts of evolutionary theory. This gargantuan breakthrough in science was accompanied by the discovery of DNA and the biochemical "book of life." The neo-Enlightenment support in theory and evidence for Darwinian principles has never been accepted by the evangelical Christian Right. They have fought tooth and nail—from the Scopes trial to contemporary attempts to suppress the teaching of evolution in U.S. schools—to maintain a particular and literal interpretation of Biblical creation (some providing an exact *date* using the Gregorian calendar).

A debate, largely self-constructed by evangelical groups in the United States, has centered around new Bible-based theories involving "intelligent design"—the idea that some unseen mover has guided evolution.

These Christians believe that this view challenges scientifically accepted versions of Darwinism. In intelligent design, some kind of divine intervenor is necessary to explain the complex skein of life on earth and its development. This theory has been viewed as a more sophisticated Christian response to evolutionary science than biblical creationism.

Other contemporary developments make the issue even more serpentine. The Roman Catholic Church, which always had been claiming that Darwinian evolution was not incompatible with Christian faith, has now sought to redefine its teachings. Although Pope John Paul II stated in a 1996 address that the scientific argument and evidence for evolution was growing stronger and that the scientific revolution was God-given, the election of Benedict XVI in 2005 casts doubt on the Church's position. Christoph Schönborn, Cardinal Archbishop of Vienna, has sought to set up an antithesis between what he calls theories of a "neo-Darwinian provenance which explicitly deny to divine providence any truly causal role in the development of life in the universe."[29] He cites "overwhelming evidence for purpose and design found in modern science." There is no such "evidence," however, unless one invents it. In other words, science has nothing to say one way or the other about whether natural selection or random DNA changes are divinely inspired. They are such only if one believes they are. Creationists, who argue that Darwinian evolution is "only a theory," which may only be taught alongside biblical creation or intelligent design scenarios, simply hope to dismantle science and its methods. There is a fundamental area of conflict between Christians who argue that reason and science are compatible with faith and those who would use every tool—political tools are currently in favor—to suppress science and its methods as "anti-Christian." The creationists were dealt a severe blow in December 2005 by a federal judge's ruling declaring that the teaching of intelligent design in the public schools of Dover, Pennsylvania, was unconstitutional. The ruling, while not binding in other jurisdictions, has served as a warning in other bastions of creationist thought (such as in Ohio and Utah). The religiously inspired "culture wars" in the United States continue, however, and evolution is only one area of conflict.

Theologians and certainly scientists differ greatly on the issue of when life begins, which has been a lightening rod for Roman Catholic and fundamentalist-conservative churches in the United States. Success of stem cell research to cure human maladies such as Parkinson's disease, diabetes, and cancer will simply lead to ignoring Church prohibitions on such matters, as has been the case with the science that has given women (and now men) the ability to control reproduction. The ability to clone humans, fast becoming a reality, is yet another amazing feat of science that will find a place in human societies, as will the ability to develop human beings *outside* the womb. Evolutionists point out that extra-uterine reproduction would only be an extension of human development from one-celled animals, through egg layers, through marsupial reproduction, and through intra-uterine cell developments. There are no reasons, a priori, to believe that such scientific or "secular" advances will make fundamental religious, spiritual, or Christian beliefs obsolete. These developments will not prevent death or the risk and anxiety that accompany it.

Such scientific advances, unstoppable in the long run, have captured the attention of Christian sects around the world, especially in advanced countries, with important short-run political effects. Short-run effects on scientific policies have generated a massive resistance on the part of fundamentalist-conservative Christians in the United States. A few examples will suffice. Opposition to stem cell research wherein human embryonic stem cell lines—which are strings of identical cells—created in test tubes has been vociferous in the United States among Roman Catholics and other fundamentalist sects.[30] The uproar by these types of Christians over stem cell research joins that concerning other life issues such as abortion and gay rights. Politicians are naturally divided over these issues, but some Christian sects have attempted to influence the political process, threatening to cross the line between separation of church and state. Over the 1990s electoral cycles, fundamentalist churches (e.g., the Southern Baptist Convention) were warned by the Internal Revenue Service to cease distributing "voter cards," which was considered undue political influence. In the 2004 political race a subgroup of Roman Catholic bishops warned political candidates (and church members) that they would not be able to legitimately receive the sacrament of Holy Communion while supporting abortion, gay rights, or stem cell research. Clearly, the policies associated with religious forms—often derivative of more fundamental church doctrine or dogma—are expressed in the political arena. Tax exempt status may be endangered, however, when lines between political advocacy and "preaching Christianity" are crossed.

Self-Generated or "Cafeteria" Christianity and Spirituality

Perhaps the central problem with virtually all arguments concerning Christianity and the secularization hypothesis is that they miss the mark when based on statements concerning church membership or attendance records. As noted in chapter 1 of this book, religion, at least for many, is an extremely personal exercise. As one noted Nobel Prize-winning economist, James J. Heckman, put it, "There will always be a market for good answers to important social questions. This is my way of following my father's advice of being independent and developing an independent reputation and my way of avoiding appeals to authority in any form—whether mathematical or divine—that motivated my early break with organized religion."[31]

Most dictionary definitions of religion are far broader than those rooted in institutional context as we noted in the introduction to this book. Dictionary definitions suggest that belief and reverence to a supernatural creator in either organized institutional or personal fashion defines religion. Accurately counting believers when religion is defined in terms of some metric such as attendance or membership in a sect is problematic. Italy, for example, the country with the largest percentage of Roman Catholics, has the lowest church attendance record of major industrialized nations of the world. Many observers argue that the establishment of state religions reduces attendance[32] while constitutional protections have the opposite effect. It may be that the quasi-state sponsorship of Roman Catholicism in Italy has created Adam Smith's "poor preaching"—wherein preachers within a state-sponsored religion become lax—although we have no evidence of it. It is perfectly likely that many Christians give up an institutionalized form of religion to find or develop one which matches their demand profile. These religions may be Christian or based in other areas of thought. Christianity, like all other varieties of spirituality, may be self-generated, that is, self-supplied and self-demanded, and it likely always has been. Christian religious individualists have existed in all times. Consider, for example, the post-

Impressionist painter Paul Gauguin who said, in writing to his friend the symbolist painter Odilon Redon in September 1890, "I have a picture in my head of...*a star*; when seeing it in my cabin in Tahiti, I will not, I promise you, dream of death, but on the contrary, of eternal life, not death in life but life in death. In Europe, this death with its snake's tail is conceivable, but in Tahiti, it has to be seen with roots that come back as flowers."[33] Gauguin was in fact keenly interested in the spirituality of the South Sea islanders he painted, titling his works accordingly (e.g., *Spirit of the Dead Watching, Day of the Evil Spirit, Eternal Night, Day of the God*, and many others). Gauguin's personal spirituality was a unique combination of (French) European Roman Catholicism and the mysticism and magic of the Tahitians, overtly revealed in some of his most famous works (e.g., *Ia Orana Maria* [Hail Mary]).

Trends in religious affiliation in the United States are revealing about self-generated religion generally and Christianity specifically. Researchers Tom W. Smith and Seokho Kim, drawing from general social surveys conducted by the National Opinion Research Center at the University of Chicago, show that (depending on how some groups such as Mormons are counted) the Protestant majority will soon become a minority in the United States.[34] Most interesting from the perspective of organized religion is that those individuals having no religion climbed dramatically from 9 percent in 1992 to 14 percent in 2002. This particular trend is expected to continue, since, among those born after 1980, 27 percent claimed to have no religion. A category label of just "Christian" that did not exist in the 1970s was added to the survey, and has undergone significant growth since 1990. In the 1990–1996 period, 0.8 percent of Americans labeled themselves just "Christian," but that number had grown to 2.3 percent in 2002. Similar growth occurred in the self-labeled category "Inter- or Non-denominational," growing steadily from only 0.1 percent of Americans in the 1972–1978 period to 1.1 percent in 2002. Those labeling themselves "no religion" may well mean "no organized religion" in these kinds of surveys. A good deal of anecdotal evidence suggests that statistics such as these mean that some kind of self-induced spirituality, including Christian forms or beliefs, may be growing rapidly in the developed world, as suggested in the psychics test contained in appendix 4A.

We might label this development "cafeteria-style Christianity," where certain tenets of spirituality are accepted and others are rejected. "Salvation" or relief from existential angst is, in these systems, possible without religious institutions and institutional constraints. Individuals who pick and choose their spiritual beliefs probably existed in all ages, but one expects to find more of them in periods of rapid and dramatic scientific advance. The term "cafeteria-style" has often been applied to Roman Catholics as well. According to journalist Cathy Lynn Grossman, a 2002 National Opinion Research sampling of the 64 million American Roman Catholics found some very surprising results. Ninety percent of them approved of abortion for some or any reason, with only 10 percent totally opposed to it. Seventy-one percent favored capital punishment; 37 percent believe that homosexuality is "not wrong at all"; 67 percent favored euthanasia (mercy killing); and 64 percent thought that birth control devices should be available to teens even if parents do not approve. (For alternative statistics on some of these issues, see table 9.2 below.) Fully 95 percent of married American Catholics practice birth control.[35] These "cafeteria Catholics" are clearly Christian but they do not accept all of the policy tenets of the Church, which, officially, has taken the hardest line on these matters. If obedience to conscience rather than dogmatically imposed rules determines the achievement of the final product of religion or spirituality in a Christian sense, Christianity may be far more ubiquitous than suggested in membership or attendance measures.[36] A continued movement toward individualized Christianity and other individualized belief systems may be expected as Christian doctrine/dogma continues to conflict with ever-changing science and economic variables. Another consideration is the rapid emergence of New Age religions, some of them founded on Christian principles. This altered metaphysical vision, some of it created out of a rejection of organized religion (Christian and otherwise) and out of the emergence of science and its inability to answer ultimate questions of origin and destination, often combines elements of Western and Eastern religion and science. These highly individualized concoctions often consist of alternative visions based on Christian principles or Christian forebears (e.g., Joan of Arc, who heard "voices," or Joseph Smith, who channeled with the Angel Moroni). While they are extremely diverse and numerous,[37] they represent an attempted bridge between emerging science and traditional forms of religion.

Sex, Life Issues, and Schism

The greatest disputes within mainline Protestant denominations and the Roman Catholic Church, as well as between Christians in both the advanced and third world, relate to that most fundamental of human activities—matters related to sex and procreation. These developments have led and could possibly lead in a number of instances to schism, since belief in doctrinal interpretations of sex and life issues are undergoing fundamental changes in some mainline churches, including the Baptist, Episcopal, and Roman Catholic churches. Historical interpretations of the Bible and biblical criticism by scholars and theologians are the source of some of the most painful conflicts. A central doctrinal and interpretive issue is homosexuality. As Diarmaid MacCulloch points out, "Despite much well-intentioned theological fancy footwork to the contrary, it is difficult to see the Bible as expressing anything else but disapproval of homosexual activity, let alone having any conception of a homosexual identity. The only alternatives are either to try to cleave to patterns of life and assumptions set out in the Bible, or to say that in this, as in much else, the Bible is simply wrong."[38] (The New Testament's anti-Semitism and its clear acceptance of slavery as part of society are two examples.) The Bible offers numerous examples, preposterous by contemporary standards, of obsolete prohibitions—some made ridiculous by science. Abstracts from Exodus and Leviticus alone—from which the famous prohibition that "homosexuality is an abomination" is drawn—offer interesting examples. In Leviticus 15:19–24, sex with a woman while she is in her period of "menstrual uncleanliness" is another abomination; in Leviticus 19:19, two crops cannot be planted in the same field; in Exodus 35:2, death is the sentence for working on the Sabbath; in Leviticus 25:44, slavery of both sexes is permitted so long as they are from "neighboring nations" (Mexico and Canada?), and so on. The question is clear: Who is to interpret the Bible on these moral issues and how is it to be interpreted?

Some mainline denominations in the United States are beginning to ordain openly gay clergy, bless same-sex unions, and ordain women clergy. Some churches that do at least one of these in one form or another are the Evangelical Lutheran Church, the African Methodist Episcopal Church, Assemblies of God, the Presbyterian Church USA, the Episcopal Church, the American Baptist Church, and the United Church of Christ.[39] Even in traditional Roman Catholic universities, at least according to one study, students' opinions become more liberal over four years of college with respect to legal abortion, premarital sex, and same-sex marriages.[40] Civil marriage as opposed to civil marriage "with benefit of religious clergy" is on the rise in the United States, increasing from 30 percent of marriages in 1980 to 40 percent in 2001. Further, opinions on whether gay and lesbian couples should be allowed the same legal rights as married couples are also changing, with favorable and unfavorable opinions divided equally according to a U.S. survey in 2003.[41]

Such developments have prompted a counter-missionary movement among mainline churches, who send conservative, fundamentalist missionaries from third-world branches of these churches to U.S. communities, especially low-income communities, to proselytize. Schisms, formal or informal, within large families or groups of religions occur regularly. These developments are affecting the unity and potential unity of three major Christian sects: Baptists, Anglicans, and Roman Catholics.

Baptists   In June 2004 the Southern Baptist Convention voted to secede from the World Baptist Alliance, a global federation of Baptist denominations, the latter being "too liberal" with respect to the role of women and other policies. The SBC was instrumental in forming the global alliance of churches one hundred years ago. That alliance is a federation of 46 million Baptists in 211 denominations (SBC membership was 16.3 million in 2004). The schism, provoked by the increasing conservatism of the SBC sect over the past twenty-five years, is emblematic of the disputes over attitudes and policies toward homosexuals. The SBC believed that particular churches in the Baptist association, in particular the American Baptist Churches sect, were altering the "inerrancy of the Bible" and that some were becoming "gay friendly congregations."[42] The conservatives also required seminary professors and missionaries to sign fidelity oaths to particular interpretations of scripture in order to keep their jobs.

Potentially important, however, is the fact that growth rates in the SBC have been lagging since the conservative-evangelical takeover. The Associated Baptist Press, a publishing arm of the moderate wing of the Baptist Church, estimates that there has been an enormous slowdown since the conservative coup in 1978–1979 with membership increasing 22 percent since then and 64 percent during the previous quarter of the century.[43] Baptisms in the SBC are at half the rate they were in 1954 and the constituency is aging rapidly—an ominous sign since younger members (and certainly potential members) hold far more liberal beliefs on the nature of science, doctrine, and policy.

Anglicans   The ordination of a gay Episcopal bishop in the United States in August 2003 has created a potential schism within doctrinal Episcopalians and the Anglican Church.[44] Conservative sects within the United States and especially those in less developed nations (where the religion is thriving) have threatened and continue to threaten a split in the Anglican Communion. There are in fact a significantly larger number of members of the Anglican Communion in Africa than there are in England. The natural question is whether the Anglican Communion is headed toward schism. Anglicans in North America have pushed the boundaries of their church's doctrine. In addition to the controversial ordination of a gay bishop, Episcopal clergy in the United States perform blessings (i.e., pseudo-marriages) for same-sex couples. The Episcopal Church of Canada has affirmed the integrity and sanctity of gay and lesbian relationships. Conservative Episcopal parishes, particularly in the American Midwest and the South, began attempting to reassert conservative values by moving to jurisdictions of conservative bishops. In 2004 a kind of moratorium was reached whereby the American Episcopal Church appeared to agree to cease consecrating gay bishops (but not priests). By 2006, however, that agreement appeared to be breaking down with the prospect of ordination of a gay bishop in California. Individual priests, moreover, remain free to conduct same-sex blessings. Such policies and prospective actions continue to enrage conservative parishes in the United States as well as Anglican affiliates in the third-world countries of Africa, Asia, and Latin America. By March 2006, the move toward schism picked up steam as more than three dozen American parishes (out of approximately 7,200 with 2.4 million members) affiliated with non-American members of the Anglican Communion in Uganda, Rwanda, and Brazil. In addition, twenty-two out of the thirty-eight branches of the worldwide church have broken off relations with the American Episcopal Church.[45] While belief in the sanctity of same-sex relations is not required for salvation in the American Church, the drive to schism by conservatives in the United States and Europe, as well as in the third world appears inevitable leading to a North-South split as described earlier in this chapter.

These developments are predictable, at least broadly, within the context of our theory: Growing tolerance ushered in by a change in scientific knowledge—many scientists and psychiatrists argue that homosexuality is not a choice and in fact may be genetic in origin—is altering religious forms in a rational economic manner. The Universal Fellowship of Metropolitan Community Churches, founded in 1970, with a membership of about fifty thousand in three hundred churches (in 1998), ministers to lesbians, gays, but also to heterosexuals. It professes "traditional Christian theology on such doctrines as Scripture, the Trinity, and the sacraments."[46] On the other side of the ledger, conservative fundamentalist Southern Baptists (for example) make no attempt to disguise or soft-pedal their own particular interpretation of the Bible's view on homosexuality. In 2004, the sect proposed the withdrawal of church investments in Carnival cruise ships since they offered a "gay cruise," and urged members to withdraw students from Southern public schools due to instruction in sex education that included discussion of the "homosexual life style." In 1997 the SBC approved a boycott of the Walt Disney Company for permitting "gay days" in its parks and for providing domestic benefits to its gay and lesbian employees. The boycott was lifted in June of 2005 without a response from Disney. (SBC officials claimed that they had cost the Disney Company hundreds of millions of dollars—a purported fact that did not prevent Disney stock values from rising between 1997 and 2005.)

The likely makeup of SBC membership is traditional Christians who have left churches in response to the full price and other economic factors of membership. Despite this evidence, and growing civil acceptance of marriage unions and other forms of contracts, traditional Episcopalians, along with Southern Baptists and a number of other conservative Christian churches, continue to condemn homosexuality and particularly the establishment of full rights for homosexuals. In the terms we have used, a shifter is altering the demands for particular forms of religion. If the determinants of the demand for religious forms in terms of both doctrine and organization that we describe in this book are correct, schism into new forms of Anglican-Episcopalianism may be predicted.

Roman Catholics We have, in this chapter, suggested some reasons why the Roman Catholic Church may be ripe for schism. A pyramidal form of organization and primal papal authority on structure and doctrinal interpretation exists for the entire church, including the North and South, and developed and less developed areas of the world. Conditions of doctrinal supply are the same everywhere, but demand conditions for particular forms of Christianity (in this case with a Roman Catholic flavor) differ greatly depending on demand determinants. The chief subjects of these differences are related to sex and life issues. The situation in the developed world (the North) vis-à-vis the less developed world is clearly suggested in table 9.2, tabulated by the *World Values Survey*. Among Roman Catholics, percentages of respondents from seven nations who say that abortion, divorce, homosexuality, and euthanasia are never justifiable reveal the gap. Attitudes toward these matters are drastically more liberal in developed countries (represented in the table by the United States, Spain, and Germany) than those in less developed nations (Argentina, Venezuela, the Philippines, and Mexico). In general, U.S. Catholics are more liberal than Catholics worldwide and are even more liberal than the average U.S. population on divorce and gay issues.

The drop in Catholic populations in the United States, measured in terms of the number of priests and the number of Catholics attending Mass on a regular basis, is yet another symptom of growing demands for something other than hardline Catholicism. It is estimated that the number of diocesan and religious-order priests fell by 22 percent and that the number of parishes dropped by 3 percent nationwide. And, over an eighteen-year period, the percentage of Catholics claiming to attend weekly Mass has declined from 44 percent in 1987 to 33 percent in 2005.[47]

Table 9.2
"North" and "South" values among world Catholics (percentages responding that the following are "never justifiable")

	Abortion	Divorce	Homo-sexuality	Euthanasia
Catholic population				
United States	37%	7%	20%	31%
Spain	27%	11%	13%	21%
Germany	37%	16%	18%	28%
Argentina	66%	24%	39%	48%
Venezuela	71%	29%	63%	55%
Philippines	51%	40%	26%	45%
Mexico	67%	38%	49%	56%
Worldwide	46%	26%	51%	43%
General population				
United States	30%	8%	32%	24%
Worldwide	44%	26%	56%	44%

Source: The *World Values Survey*. Available online at www.worldvaluessurvey.org/services/index.html.

A number of explanations have been given for these phenomena: Population trends from cities to suburbs, the lack of managerial skills on the part of prelates, the child abuse crisis within the Church, and so on. But these trends are of long standing and it would appear that time-cost increases with income increases, together with advances in education, science, and technology—the shifters—are at the base of these sea changes in developed-world Roman Catholicism. Most of these shifters relate to life issues and to sex. Embryonic research enabling the creation of new colonies of stem cells creates the possibility for addressing conditions such as spinal cord injuries, juvenile diabetes, congenital immune deficiencies, Alzheimer's disease, and cancer. On the matter of sex, startling discoveries that reveal that instinctive behaviors of sexual choice can be specified and triggered by genetic programs such as those that determine eye color and other human traits.[48] These kind of phenomena may be creating a foundation for disbelief in rigid Roman Catholic Church teachings. For the Church's part, at least given the pronouncements of Benedict XVI, John Paul II's successor, genetic research, divorce, artificial birth control, trial marriages, and free-style unions, with homosexual unions leading the way, have all been loudly and roundly condemned. Again, the stage for schism in the Catholic Church is set. Mounting evidence that doctrinal interpretations of sex and life issues do not comport with scientific knowledge will likely cause either a change in interpretation (as in the case of slavery or knowledge concerning indigenous populations[49]) or will engender new Catholic forms of religion through schismatic activity. Maintenance of the traditional proscriptions by the papacy may create a smaller but more tightly organized church which, according to some, would make a more attractive product in the religious market place. One problem is that this better defined product will only find demanders in the poorer and less developed regions of the world and among low-income, low-education demanders in the advanced world. As Anthony Gill has pointed out, intense competition from non-Catholic evangelicals is taking members from the Roman Catholic Church in the third world, possibly due to the tight proscription against birth control by the Catholic Church.[50]

The probability of schism is augmented by the organizational structure of the Church that, due to the reaffirmed rules of canon law as revised early in the twentieth century, admits only an absolutist pyramidal structure of the Roman Catholic Church. Pronouncements by Pope Benedict XVI reaffirming the Church's stance on hot-button issues also signals a foundation for schism as well as a good deal of confusion. Almost immediately after his installment in 2005, Benedict affirmed policies that would bar gay men with deep-rooted homosexual tendencies or those who supported a gay "lifestyle" from entering seminaries. Self-restraint is no longer sufficient for would-be priests. "Transitory" gay men may be admitted to seminaries, however, and the new directives do not apply to existing priests, bishops, or cardinals, and it does not distinguish between homosexuals and pedophiles. For now, the schismatic trend among both mainstream and fundamentalist denominations will likely continue along liberal-conservative lines. It is important to recognize that this split is *not* over doctrine or organization per se, but over the interpretation and political implications drawn from Scripture or precedent within particular denominations. It is even more important to recognize that heresy and schism, in and of themselves, are not to be discouraged even if that would be possible. As French poet, critic, and essayist André

Suarès (1868–1948) noted, "Heresy is the lifeblood of religions. It is faith that begets heretics. There are no heresies in a dead religion."[51] Stated in economic terms, heresy and schism will be constant factors in emerging Christianity because heterogeneous demands for new forms are functions of factors—income, education, or science—that are in constant flux. Our economic theory of the determinants of religious form predicts that there will be further (and perhaps more serious) schisms within these religious organizations as incomes, educational attainment, and scientific knowledge all increase. This result, in a sense, is the outcome of the expansion of the scientific, cultural, and economic revolutions of the sixteenth and seventeenth centuries. It will also be interesting to observe how religious forms change in the third world as incomes, education, and political conditions advance.

Conclusion: Competition in Religious Markets

Far from disappearing into the unholy mists of science, godless sectarianism, and secular humanism, religion and magic have never been more prevalent than in modern society. According to some estimates of American experience, admittedly self-reported, 96 percent believe in God, 71 percent in an afterlife, and 75 percent in some kind of heaven. Weekly church attendance rates are higher in the United States than in most countries of the world.[52] Further, if the number of palm readers, TV mediums, and fortune tellers are any indication, forms of religion, magic, and mysticism also proliferate. In the United States alone, there are more than 2,500 distinct types or varieties of religions. Like it or not, modern economics has extended into this new and crucial domain of social behavior. The economics of religion uses the principle of rational behavior as well as interest-group analysis, public choice analysis, industrial organization analysis, and the theory of clubs to develop and evaluate the following propositions:

• Religion as the rational behavior of individuals may be expressed in terms of the supply and demand for varieties of Christianity.

• The principles of monopoly, competition, and market entry provide insights into critical episodes in the evolution of Christian religions.

• The Protestant Reformation may be depicted as lower full price entry into the market for Christian beliefs; the lower price was both monetary and doctrinal in nature.

• The Roman Catholic response was perfectly analogous to that predicted by the theory of industrial organization, attempting to regain market share by (some) reforms of the retail side of the church but maintaining a doctrinal monopoly of interpretation, by the simultaneous imposition of violent repression, and by the establishment of missions in what has become the third world.

• The subsequent development of Protestantism was predictable in that the essence of the breakaway was the elimination of intermediaries of doctrinal interpretation, opening the door to the competitive evolution of thousands of forms of Christian belief.

• In addition to the doctrinal monopoly maintained at the Council of Trent and at the First Vatican Council in 1871, which proclaimed the Pope infallible in matters of faith and morality, subsequent developments have led to a pyramidal structure of Roman Catholic Church organization.

• The traditional Weberian view of the emergence of capitalism as based on altered preferences may be supplemented with an economic argument emphasizing the cost savings from the supply side of all Protestant sects (with the possible exception of the Episcopal version).

• The economic principles of competitive entry, full price, and supply and demand for forms of religion set in motion by the Protestant Reformation and its aftermath may offer insights into current practices and policies of contemporary religious forms; and these policies may lead to emerging schisms in a number of denominations—splits that produce continuous product development in the market for Christian religion.

More than one hundred years ago (1898), the economist-anthropologist Thorstein Veblen (1857–1929) argued broadly that what he called "ceremonial institutions" (government, the church, property rights structures) were unique to a particular form of science and technology ("technological institutions"). His argument created a kind of evolutionary theory based on Darwinian precepts—as invention, labor technology, and hard science evolved, ceremonial institutions such as religion did also. Our theory and the analysis of historians and sociologists are similar to Veblen's in some important respects.[53] Clearly, the Enlightenment and the scientific world that it ushered in overturned long-established beliefs concerning the operation of the world and humankind's place in the universe. These changes helped create an acceptance of a religion (Protestantism) that was less rule-based, less ritualistic, and had less dogmatic certainty concerning the interpretation of Holy Scripture. But, if we are correct, even extreme advances in science have not and will not fully alleviate metaphysical dread for the great mass of humanity.

There is what appears to be an innate demand for the services of magic, religion, and spiritual experience. This may be hardwired for individuals due to evolutionary factors. The anthropological and psychological literature clearly suggest that some mythological system is self-induced as a "spontaneous operation of the psyche" for each and every sentient individual. Indeed it is through an individual's definition of chaos and a development of a means of keeping it at bay that the dimensions of reality are defined. This means that, so long as this problem exists, religion, magic, spiritual, and philosophical activity will be a permanent part of human societies. Despite the skepticism that sometimes challenges religious markets, evidence is that such markets are thriving. They are thriving even where temporal survival constraints are less binding (e.g., in the United States). Existential terror will not disappear no matter how far science takes *Homo sapiens*.

Modern science *will* alter the *forms* of religion but it will never be a perfect substitute for religion. Modern science, particularly the biological revolutions responsible for birth control, test tube babies, the possibility of a "gay gene," cloning, and so on, will ultimately affect the form of theology as Veblen would have predicted. But a *modern microeconomics must be imposed on the Veblenian dynamic* for the evolution of religious forms to be fully understood. High income societies, sophisticated in science and technology, are undergoing evolutionary changes in the forms of religion, its interpretations, and rituals. It is perhaps worth remembering that the Roman Catholic and other Christian churches initially rejected and then later accepted all manner of technological advances: the printing press, vaccination, dissection and autopsy of human bodies, organ transplants, and so on. Cloning, woman priests and ministers, married priests, gay clergy, gay civil rights, and many other issues are all candidates for debate and resolution within particular forms of Christian religion today. Where religious tolerance and forms are constitutionally protected, splintering within particular religions due to acceptance of progress on sex and life issues is expected and those expectations are being realized. But fundamentalist, time-intensive forms of religion and magic are inversely related to income and level of scientific and economic development. A movement away from fundamentalism in the third world and the less developed parts of the advanced world may come at some point.

While the prospects for human survival in the advanced parts of the world help reduce human dread and the uncertainty associated with existence, this is not the case for large segments of humanity. For all societies, due to the intimate connection between psychology and economics, markets for magic and religion of some form will continue to exist. The great historian Arnold Toynbee, in a somewhat romanticized statement, put it this way: "No human soul can pass through This Life without being challenged to grapple with the mystery of the Universe. If the distinctively human impulse of curiosity does not bring us to the point, experience will drive us to it—above all, the experience of Suffering."[54] But, as usual, William Shakespeare has the brilliant final word concerning the fate of human existence. In what are regarded as some of his last written lines in his final play, he considered play writing in particular and human existence in general. In the words he gave Prospero in *The Tempest* (Act 4, Scene 1), Shakespeare mused, "We are such stuff as dreams are made on; and our little life is rounded with a sleep." For such eternal and immutable reasons, markets for magic and religion of all forms, including Christianity, are here to stay.

Our research not only accepts this general proposition, but adds that the course of Christianity and its continuous evolution cannot be fully understood outside the context of Adam Smith's conception of economics and competition. All great and important revolutions in the course of humanity have been supply-side revolutions. The agricultural revolution of approximately 10,000 BCE, the Industrial Revolution that carried on the wave of Enlightenment science and scientific methods, and the digital-biological revolution currently underway are examples of watersheds in human progress. No less a watershed is the competitive revolution in Christianity unleashed by the successful entry of Protestant competitors in the sixteenth century. Just as free and open competition increases the utility to consumers of goods and services, the open and extremely competitive market for Christian and other religious products and product forms creates a variety that maximizes satisfaction for individuals whose demand for such services is limitless and, as Shakespeare knew, is a matter of eternal concern and curiosity for all.

Notes

1 Religion, Church, and Economics

1. *The Spectator* (June 3, 2005). http://www.spectator.co.uk/article_archive.php?id=6201&issue=2005-06-04.

2. In Robert B. Ekelund Jr., Robert F. Hébert, Robert D. Tollison, Gary M. Anderson, and Audrey B. Davidson, *Sacred Trust: The Medieval Church as an Economic Firm* (New York: Oxford University Press, 1996).

3. Damian Thompson, *The Spectator* (June 3, 2005).

4. According to the *Christian Science Monitor*, the top ten organized religions in the world are Christianity, Islam, Hinduism, Buddhism, Sikhism, Judaism, B'haism, Confucianism, Jainism, and Shintoism (http://www.adherents.com/misc/rel_by_adh_CSM.html). Of these, Christianity claims about one-third of all adherents, even allowing for the presence of 'nonreligious' groups (e.g., agnostics, atheists, secular humanists, etc.), some of whom are theistic, though not religious.

5. Chapter 2 devotes considerable space to Smith's pioneer efforts in this regard.

6. Corry Azzi and Ronald G. Ehrenberg, "Household Allocation of Time and Church Attendance," *Journal of Political Economy* 83, no. 1 (1975): 27–56.

7. Some representative works are: V. Smith, "The Primitive Hunter Culture, Pleistocene Extinction, and the Rise of Agriculture," *Journal of Political Economy* 83 (August 1975): 727–755; Richard W. Ault, Robert B. Ekelund, Jr., and Robert D. Tollison, "The Pope and the Price of Meat: A Public Choice Perspective," *Kyklos* 40 (1987): 399–413; Brooks B. Hull, "Religion, Afterlife, and Property Rights in the High Middle Ages," *Studies in Economic Analysis* 12 (1989): 3–21. Brooks B. Hull and Frederick Bold, "Towards an Economic Theory of the Church," *International Journal of Social Economics* 16 (1989): 5–15; Robert B. Ekelund Jr., Robert F. Hébert, and Robert D. Tollison, "An Economic Model of the Medieval Church: Usury as a Form of Rent Seeking," *Journal of Law, Economics, and Organization* 5 (Fall 1989): 307–331; Robert B. Ekelund Jr., Robert F. Hébert, and Robert D. Tollison, "The Economics of Sin and Redemption: Purgatory as a Market-Pull Innovation?" *Journal of*

Economic Behavior and Organization 19 (September 1992): 1–15; Roger Finke and Rodney Stark, *The Churching of America, 1776–1990: Winners and Losers in Our Religious Economy* (New Brunswick, N.J.: Rutgers University Press, 1992); Laurence R. Iannaccone, "Sacrifice and Stigma: Reducing Free Riding in Cults, Communes, and Other Collectives," *Journal of Political Economy* 100, no. 2 (1992): 271–292; Laurence R. Iannaccone, "Introduction to the Economics of Religion," *Journal of Economic Literature* 36 (September 1998): 1465–1495; Ian Tattersall, *The Last Neanderthal: The Rise, Success, and Mysterious Extinction of Our Closest Human Relatives* (New York: Macmillan, 1995); Andrew Newberg, Eugene D'Aquili, and Vince Rause, *Why God Won't Go Away: Brain Science and Biology of Belief* (New York: Ballantine Books, 2001); Matthew Alper, *The "God" Part of the Brain: A Scientific Interpretation of Human Spirituality and God* (New York: Rogue Press, 2001); Robert J. Barro and Rachel M. McCleary, "Religion and Political Economy in an International Panel," working paper, Harvard University, May 2002.

8. Although commonplace among economists, these terms may be unfamiliar to some readers. We therefore define them fully in the course of our discussion, at the point of their initial application. These terms are also defined in the glossary.

9. Ekelund et al., *Sacred Trust.*

10. William Campbell, "Review of *Sacred Trust: The Medieval Church as an Economic Firm*," *The Bulletin of Association of Christian Economists* (Fall 1997): 27.

11. Campbell, "Review of *Sacred Trust*," 27.

12. For an opposing view on this issue, see John Wells, "Review of *Sacred Trust: The Medieval Church as an Economic Firm*," *Journal of Markets and Morality* 1, no. 1 (1998): 99–100.

13. *American Heritage Dictionary*, 3rd ed., emphasis added.

14. Barro and McCleary, "Religion and Political Economy in an International Panel."

15. If religion or personal spirituality are regarded as a psychological phenomena (or parts of a set of phenomena) to keep "existential chaos at bay, it may be that not only are there no atheists in foxholes," as some observers would have it, "but that there are no atheists anywhere." We do not push this point, however.

16. See http://www.icpsr.umich.edu:8080/GSS/rnd1998/merged/cdbk/.

2   The Economics of Religion

1. Ronald Coase, "The Nature of the Firm," *Economica* 4 (November 1937): 386–405.

2. Adam Smith, *An Inquiry into the Nature and Causes of the Wealth of Nations*, vol. 2, ed. R. H. Campbell and A. S. Skinner (Oxford: Oxford University Press, [1776] 1976), 760.

3. Smith, *The Wealth of Nations*, 789–790.

4. Smith, *The Wealth of Nations*, 791.

5. Smith, *The Wealth of Nations*, 792–793.

6. Smith, *The Wealth of Nations*, 794.

7. Smith, *The Wealth of Nations*, 797.

8. Nathan Rosenberg, "Some Institutional Aspects of *The Wealth of Nations*," *Journal of Political Economy* (December 1960): 557–570.

9. Gary M. Anderson, "Mr. Smith and the Preachers: The Economics of Religion in *The Wealth of Nations*," *Journal of Political Economy* 96, no. 5 (October 1988): 1066–1088.

10. Smith, *The Wealth of Nations*, 792.

11. Smith, *The Wealth of Nations*, 793.

12. Smith, *The Wealth of Nations*, 808.

13. Smith, *The Wealth of Nations*, 809.

14. Earlier Smith applied the same kind of reasoning to regulated and joint-stock companies. He denounced the monopolizing spirit of the East India Company, the South Sea Company, and the Royal African Company, attributing the inefficiency of each enterprise to its large size and overcapitalization. But he offered qualified praise for the Hudson's Bay Company, which had a more limited market, smaller number of stockholders, and moderate capitalization, which kept its profits in line with "the ordinary profits of trade." Clearly, the central issue for Smith, whether in business or religion, was not the issue of monopoly versus competition per se, but to what extent the internal organization of one or the other produced, or approached, competitive results. Smith, *The Wealth of Nations*, 743–744. See Gary M. Anderson and Robert D. Tollison, "Adam Smith's Analysis of Joint-Stock Companies," *Journal of Political Economy* 90 (December 1982): 1237–1256, for further elaboration on this point.

15. Smith, *The Wealth of Nations*, 809. Charles G. Leathers and J. Patrick Raines assert that Smith advocated religious patronage, an assertion we categorically deny. While Smith's literary criticism on specific topics can be distracting and confusing at times, a careful reading of Book V of *The Wealth of Nations* reveals that Smith regarded religious patronage as the enemy of good ecclesiastical management. Charles G. Leathers and J. Patrick Raines, "Adam Smith on Competitive Religious Markets," in *History of Political Economy* 24, no. 2 (Summer 1992): 513.

16. Smith, *The Wealth of Nations*, 810.

17. Smith, *The Wealth of Nations*, 813.

18. According to "Presbyterian 101: A General Guide to the Facts about the PCUSA" (see http://www.pcusa.org/101/101-unique.htm), the two distinctive aspects of the Presbyterian Church are its adherence to Reformed theology and a form of government that stresses the active, representational leadership of

both ministers and church members. Hence, the democratization of its membership remains a trait of modern Presbyterianism. Note that there is more than one division of Presbyterianism in the United States, although selection processes described herein are quite similar to all.

19. According to Eustace Percy, "The Scottish burghs made their way to wealth and power, not by winning local charters and developing self-government on individual lines as in England, but by lobbying for general legislation. King and Parliament had made them a separate estate of the realm with special privileges. That process robbed Scotland of village industries and village markets ... But such monopolies had not yet made the burghs strong. They were tiny in size; Edinburgh had only some 9,000 inhabitants, Glasgow only half that number, and Aberdeen less than 3,000. Living conditions were bad. ... These little communities were torn by dissensions between the merchant and craft guilds, and between craft guilds and 'unfree' craftsmen. They lived largely on an export trade in which they were mere middlemen; nearly 80 percent of the country's exports consisted of agricultural produce. They were not even independent; the local gentry interfered in the 'abusion and confusions' of their politics." Eustace Percy, *John Knox* (Richmond, Va.: John Knox Press, 1965), 182–183.

20. According to Kevin Reed, *Selected Writings of John Knox: Public Epistles, Treatises, and Expositions to the Year 1559* (Dallas: Presbyterian Heritage Publications, 1995), Knox's religious writings stressed equality among individuals, regardless of wealth or social station. Knox's biographer, Eustace Percy, said, "Though he held firmly that the reformation and purgation of religion appertains chiefly and most principally to the civil power, he had a horror of State-enforced uniformity ... in Knox's view, the less Church and State had to do with each other, the better." Percy, *John Knox*, 223.

21. In a flush of Anglo-Saxon pride, Alfred Marshall argued that "the natural gravity and intrepidity of the stern races that had settled on the shores of England inclined them to embrace the doctrines of the Reformation; and these reacted on their habits of life, and gave a tone to their industry." However, the rest of Marshall's musings on the effects of the Reformation were on its social effects. Alfred Marshall, *Principles of Economics* (London: Macmillan, 1890), 742.

22. Gary M. Anderson is the first to relate Smith's ideas on "pure and rational religion" (a consequence of competition in the religious marketplace) to the peaceful and productive operation of the division of labor. Smith's clear condemnation of the lack of free thought and liberty, and stability and security of civil government under the medieval Roman Catholic Church, together with freedoms afforded under Protestantism, led him to make a connection between Protestantism and economic growth before Weber. Anderson, "Mr. Smith and the Preachers," 1074–1075.

23. Max Weber, *The Protestant Ethic and the Spirit of Capitalism*, trans. Talcott Parsons, with foreword by R. H. Tawney (London: George Allen & Unwin, 1930).

24. R. H. Tawney recognized this and other common misinterpretations of Weber in his *Religion and the Rise of Capitalism* (London: John Murray, 1926), xiv.

25. Anthony Giddens, introduction to Max Weber, *Protestantism and the Spirit of Capitalism* (London: Routledge Classics, 2002).

26. See Barro and McCleary, "Religion and Political Economy in an International Panel"; Robert J. Barro and Rachel M. McCleary, "Religion and Economic Growth," NBER Working Paper no. 9682, May 2003.

27. Weber, *The Protestant Ethic and the Spirit of Capitalism*, 55.

28. Weber, *The Protestant Ethic and the Spirit of Capitalism*, 19.

29. Weber, *The Protestant Ethic and the Spirit of Capitalism*, 71.

30. Weber, *The Protestant Ethic and the Spirit of Capitalism*, 61.

31. When Becker was named recipient of the Nobel Prize in Economics in 1992, the press release of the Alfred Nobel Institute carried the following excerpt: "Gary Becker's research program is founded on the idea that the behavior of an individual adheres to the same fundamental principles in a number of different areas. The same explanatory model should thus, according to Becker, be applicable in analyzing highly diverse aspects of human behavior. The explanatory model which Becker has chosen to work with is based on what he calls an economic approach, which he has applied to one area after another. This approach is characterized by the fact that individual agents—regardless of whether they are households, firms or other organizations—are assumed to behave rationally, i.e., purposefully, and that their behavior can be described as if they maximized a specific objective function, such as utility or wealth. Gary Becker has applied the principle of rational, optimizing behavior to areas where researchers formerly assumed that behavior is habitual and often downright irrational." Not surprisingly, Becker's research has been met in some quarters by skepticism and mistrust. Yet the Nobel Committee noted that "Becker has also had an indirect impact on scientific approaches in social sciences other than economics; more frequently than in the past, sociologists and political scientists work with models based on theories of 'rational choice'."

32. Azzi and Ehrenberg, "Household Allocation of Time and Church Attendance."

33. Iannaccone, "Sacrifice and Stigma."

34. The maximand or goal pursued, called "afterlife consumption," is beset by definitional problems. It is consistently reported that about 30–35 percent of Jews but 85–90 percent of Christians believe in an afterlife, indicating that the construct may differ by religion. Later models of religious participation that built on Azzi and Ehrenberg's framework gradually added other elements to "participation," such as social services, provision of a marriage market, and so forth.

35. D. H. Sullivan, "Simultaneous Determination of Church Contributions and Church Attendance," *Economic Inquiry* 23 (1985): 309–320.

36. Iannaccone, "Introduction to the Economics of Religion."

37. Iannaccone, "Sacrifice and Stigma."

38. Gary M. Becker, "A Theory of Marriage: Parts I and II," *Journal of Political Economy* 81, no. 4 (1973): 813–846; 82, no. 2 (1974): S11–S26.

39. James M. Buchanan, "An Economic Theory of Clubs," *Economica* 32 (1965): 1–14.

40. Smith, *The Wealth of Nations*, 795–796.

41. Buchanan, "An Economic Theory of Clubs."

42. Iannaccone, "Sacrifice and Stigma."

43. Pedro Pita Barros and Nuno Garoupa offer an alternative view of church strictness in which they introduce spatial location models to shore up the analysis. The underlying nature of demand remains ambiguous in their work, however. Pedro Pita Barros and Nuno Garoupa, "An Economic Theory of Church Strictness," *Economic Journal* 112 (2002): 559–576.

44. Eli Berman, "Hamas, Taliban and the Jewish Underground: An Economist's View of Radical Religious Militias," NBER Working Paper no. 10004, September 2003.

45. Sociologists of religion apply the term "sect" to a specific type of religious movement. In the typology of religious movements that has developed from the pioneering work of Ernst Troeltsch, the sect is a formally organized religious body that arises in protest against, and in competition with, the pervasive religion of a society. In Troeltsch's classification, pervasive religions (e.g., Catholicism, Protestantism, Judaism, etc.) are identified by church or denomination. Pervasive religions are highly organized and deeply integrated into a society's social and economic structure; but whereas they make few demands on members for active participation or personal commitment, the sect demands a high degree of participation and a suitable display of individual and spiritual loyalty. Organized churches often compromise and accommodate their doctrines and practices to accommodate secular society, but the sect rejects all such arrangements and promotes a purer doctrine and practice resistant to the blandishments of church and secular society. Most sects are organized and governed more democratically than a church or denomination, but the leadership is frequently less experienced and nonprofessional. The life span of a sect is usually short. Many, but not all, sects gradually lose their sectarian character and acquire the status of a church after a generation or two. The so-called established sect—one that does not shed its sectarian character—manages to avoid accommodation and compromise and keeps its spirit of religious protest and opposition to secular society viable indefinitely. Thus modern Protestant denominations began as sects. Yet not all sects mature into churches. Ernst Troeltsch, *The Social Teachings of the Christian Churches*, 2 vols., trans. O. Wyon (New York: Macmillan, 1931).

46. Robert B. Ekelund Jr., Franklin G. Mixon Jr., and Rand W. Ressler, "Advertising and Information: An Empirical Study of Search, Experience and Credence Goods," *Journal of Economic Studies* 22 (1995): 33–43.

47. M. R. Darby and Edi Karni, "Free Competition and the Optimal Amount of Fraud," *Journal of Law and Economics* 16 (1973): 67–88.

48. Sherwin Rosen, "The Economics of Superstars," *American Economic Review* 71, no. 5 (1981): 845–858.

49. Initially we called religion a joint product, but eventually rejected this terminology because the term has a concise meaning in economic theory that does not capture the circumstances under which the religious product is supplied. The most common, but not the only, situation of joint products implies production under fixed proportions, such that, for example, one hide is produced for the leather market for every steer that is slaughtered for the beef market. No such condition holds in religious markets, as each consumer can draw different bundles of utility from an array of goods and/or services that comprise the product. Going beyond the fixed-proportions of joint supply to the variable proportions case does not alter this basic difference.

50. Kent D. Miller, "Competitive Strategies of Religious Organizations," *Strategic Management Journal* 23 (May 2002): 435–456.

51. Citing Laurence R. Iannaccone, "Why Strict Churches Are Strong," *American Journal of Sociology* 99 (1994): 1180–1211, Kent D. Miller argues, "This strategy prescription appears to contradict the contention that strictness results in strong religious organizations . . . Strictness requires placing demands upon religious adherents, rather than accommodating their preferences. However, accommodating distinct preferences can foster high commitment." Further (and we believe importantly) Miller notes, "Although strictness may be the optimal pricing strategy from a static perspective, it may conflict with the dynamic goal of increasing total organizational resources through growth in the number of participants." Miller, "Competitive Strategies of Religious Organizations," 9.

52. We describe in broad terms how this process is motivated by traditional market theory in chapter 3, and we provide explicit examples of this process in the evolution of Protestant groups in chapter 7.

53. Brooks B. Hull and Gerald F. Moran, "A Preliminary Time Series Analysis of Church Activity in Colonial Woodbury, Connecticut," *Journal for the Scientific Study of Religion* 28 (1989): 478–492; Brooks B. Hull and Gerald F. Moran, "The Churching of Colonial Connecticut: A Case Study," *Review of Religious Research* 41 (1999): 165–183.

54. Jody Lipford, Robert E. McCormick, and Robert D. Tollison, "Preaching Matters," *Journal of Economic Behavior and Organization* 21 (1993): 235–250.

55. Ian Smith, "The Economics of Church Decline in Scotland," *International Journal of Social Economics* 20 (1993). 27–35.

56. Ian Smith, John W. Sawkins, and Paul T. Seaman, "The Economics of Religious Participation: A Cross-Country Study," *Kyklos* 51 (1998): 25–43.

57. Ian Smith and John W. Sawkins, "The Economics of Regional Variation in Religious Attendance," *Applied Economics* 35 (2003): 1577–1588.

58. Jonathan Gruber, "Religious Market Structure, Religious Participation, and Outcomes: Is Religion Good for You?," working paper, Harvard University, 2003.

59. Hull and Bold, "Towards an Economic Theory of the Church."

60. Hull, "Religion, Afterlife, and Property Rights in the High Middle Ages."

61. Richard A. Posner, "A Theory of Primitive Society with Special Reference to Law," *Journal of Law and Economics* 23 (1980): 1–53.

62. Hull, "Religion, Afterlife, and Property Rights in the High Middle Ages."

63. Unfortunately, a good deal of confusion has settled around this term. Gordon Tullock and Ann O. Krueger define rent seeking as the use of real economic resources to obtain a rent transfer from one group of (generally poorly organized) market participants to a group (often well organized and smaller in number) with intense interests in obtaining the monopoly prize. This competition for a fixed prize describes a loss to society resulting from monopoly in addition to the so-called deadweight loss, which is commonly understood as a loss due to any price above marginal cost and is generally associated with tolls, tariffs, and excise taxes (any price that is above marginal cost). The wastes of rent seeking (i.e., the dissipation of wealth) contrast sharply to the pursuit of wealth through profit seeking. The profit seeking monopolist, as identified by economist Joseph A. Schumpeter, directs resources to most valued ends and, in the process, makes profits, thus creating wealth. A competitive process creates value by ensuring that new and competing products or product qualities reduce price-cost margins (monopoly profits) through time. Through profit seeking, the welfare of society is maximized by the productive use of resources. In the rent-seeking case, society's resources are dissipated in unproductive uses rather than in the increased production of utility-creating goods and services. The pursuit of "artificial rents" create losses that may include spending on lawyers, or lobbying, or any other expenditure necessary to obtain a fixed prize. Gordon Tullock, "The Welfare Costs of Tariffs, Monopolies and Theft," *Western Economic Journal* 5 (1967): 224–232; Anne O. Krueger, "The Political Economy of the Rent-Seeking Society," *American Economic Review* 64 (1974): 291–303; J. A. Schumpeter, *The Theory of Economic Development* (New Brunswick, N.J.: Transactions Books, 1983).

64. Robert B. Ekelund Jr., Robert F. Hébert, and Robert D. Tollison, "An Economic Analysis of the Protestant Reformation," *Journal of Political Economy* 110, no. 3 (2002): 646–671; Robert B. Ekelund Jr., Robert F. Hébert, and Robert D. Tollison, "The Economics of the Counter-Reformation: Incumbent Reaction to Market Entry," *Economic Inquiry* 42 (October 2004): 690–705.

65. For the most part, historians have agreed with this basic premise, but some are reluctant to push the argument too far. In her review of *Sacred Trust*, Katherine Fischer Drew said, "No medieval historian would quarrel with this picture of the Church operating as both an economic and a spiritual entity. Nor would they quarrel with the observation that economic good sometimes (perhaps even most

of the time) outweighed spiritual good." Katherine Fischer Drew, "Review of *Sacred Trust: The Medieval Church as an Economic Firm,*" *Journal of Interdisciplinary History* 28 (Spring 1998): 651. Acknowledging that our argument is based on facts gathered from diverse sources, the view from France is that we might have placed too much of a burden on the economic motive of self-interest, thus provoking undue controversy. Jean-Dominique Lafay, for example, notes: "Despite controversy, it is necessary to acknowledge the brilliant pioneer work of the authors of *Sacred Trust.* They were able to go beyond the limits of Jean Touchard's conclusion about Marsile de Padoue: 'These ideas... are too bold to apply immediately. They require that others take them up anew, recast and refine them... apply the penetrating power of the innovator.'" Jean-Dominique Lafay, "L'Eglise médiévale sous le regard de l'analyse économique," *Sociétal* 26 (September 1999): 111.

66. Robert E. McCormick and Robert D. Tollison, *Politicians, Legislation, and the Economy: An Inquiry into the Interest-Group Theory of Government* (Boston: Martinus Nijhoff, 1981); Robert D. Tollison, "Rent Seeking," in *Perspectives on Public Choice: A Handbook,* ed. Dennis C. Mueller (Cambridge: Cambridge University Press, 1997), 506–525; Fred S. McChesney, "Rent Extraction and Rent Creation in the Economic Theory of Regulation," *Journal of Legal Studies* 16 (1987): 101–118.

67. George J. Stigler, "The Theory of Economic Regulation," *Bell Journal of Economics and Management Science* 2 (1971): 3–21.

68. Sam Peltzman, "Toward a More General Theory of Regulation," *Journal of Law and Economics* 19 (1976): 211–240.

69. Douglas Allen, "Order in the Church: A Property Rights Approach," *Journal of Economic Behavior* 27 (1995): 97–117.

70. Dieter Schmidtchen and Achim Mayer, "Established Clergy, Friars and the Pope: Some Institutional Economics of the Medieval Church," *Journal of Institutional and Theoretical Economics* 153 (1997): 122–165.

71. This interesting model received a number of criticisms. Avner Ben-Ner rejects the profit motive as it applies to religious institutions, asserting that "religious products have three important attributes: nonrivalry, nonexcludability, and asymmetric information. The for-profit provision of goods possessing these three attributes will be ineffective and insufficient from the point of view of their users, unless certain market and governmental institutions can compensate." We defer further comment on the nature of the religious good to chapter 3. Avner Ben-Ner, "Comment," *Journal of Institutional and Theoretical Economics* 153 (1997): 157.

72. Audrey Davidson, "The Medieval Monastery as Franchise Monopolist," *Journal of Economic Behavior and Organization* 27 (1995): 119–128.

73. The establishment of the mendicant orders, such as those of Francis and Dominic, were—at least to outward appearances—a response to the Gnostic

and Waldensian criticisms that the church was chiefly concerned with wealth and far removed from the teachings of Christ.

74. Benito Arruñada, "Catholic Confession of Sins as Third-Party Moral Enforcement," working paper, Universitat Pompeu Fabra, Barcelona, Spain, 2004, http://www.econ.upf.es/~arrunada.

75. See the medieval church's indulgence schedules in William E. Lunt, *Papal Revenues in the Middle Ages*, vol. 2 (New York: Columbia University Press, 1934); reprint (New York: Octagon Books, 1965), 481–482. Arruñada ignores the prospect that "optimal enforcement and deterrence" was not the goal of the Church. If this had been the goal of the church we would expect to see lower full prices extracted for minor sins than for serious transgressions (e.g., adultery), which was not the case. The indulgence schedules were based on income and wealth, not sinfulness.

76. Arruñada fails to provide a reason why the elaborate system of "third party enforcement" by priests came about in the high Middle Ages. This system replaced a far looser system of "general confession" that existed in the pre-thirteenth-century church and that is reappearing today due, according to Arruñada, to greater self-enforcement (associated with higher levels of education) and, presumably, higher transactions costs. This medieval system clearly opened up possibilities for rent extractions by the papacy. However, a rent-seeking interpretation is not incompatible with some moral enforcement mechanism. Consider the fact that God alone is the direct enforcer in Protestant theology—eliminating entirely the basis for this sort of religious rent seeking.

77. The function of penance as enforcer of a moral code and as a (public good) promoter of social peace is not entirely persuasive from a logical standpoint. The Catholic system of "sin, confession, penance . . . sin, confession, penance" does not guarantee less crime, for example. The availability of this option may in fact produce more "sin." It is questionable whether civil enforcement mechanisms are (or were) better or worse than religious ones as private or public good promoters of "social peace." Benito Arruñada, "Catholic Confession of Sins as Third-Party Moral Enforcement," working paper, Universitat Pompeu Fabra, Barcelona, Spain, 2004, http://www.econ.upf.es/~arrunada, 23.

78. Emile Durkheim, *The Elementary Forms of the Religious Life* (London: Allen and Unwin, 1915).

79. Werner Sombart, *The Quintessence of Capitalism: A Study of the History and Psychology of the Modern Business Man*, ed. and trans. M. Epstein (New York: Datton, 1915); Tawney, *Religion and the Rise of Capitalism*.

80. Henri Pirenne, *Economic and Social History of Medieval Europe* (New York: Harcourt, Brace, 1937); Ernst Troeltsch, *The Social Teachings of the Christian Churches*, 2 vols., trans. O. Wyon (New York: Macmillan, 1931); Lunt, *Papal Revenues in the Middle Ages*, 2 vols.; William E. Lunt, *Financial Relations of the Papacy with England to 1327* (Cambridge, Mass.: Mediaeval Academy of America, 1939); Robert H. Snape, *English Monastic Finances in the Later Middle Ages* (Cambridge: Cambridge University Press, 1926).

81. Raymond DeRoover, *Money, Banking and Credit in Medieval Bruges* (Cambridge, Mass.: Mediaeval Academy of America, 1948); John T. Noonan, *The Scholastic Analysis of Usury* (Cambridge, Mass.: Harvard University Press, 1927).

82. Andrew M. Greeley, *Unsecular Man: The Persistence of Religion* (New York: Schocken, 1972); Andrew M. Greeley, *Religion: A Secular Theory* (New York: The Free Press, 1982); Rodney Stark and William Sims Bainbridge, *The Future of Religion: Secularization, Revival, and Cult Formation* (Berkeley: University of California Press, 1985); Rodney Stark and William Sims Bainbridge, *A Theory of Religion* (New York: Peter Lang, 1987).

83. Stark and Bainbridge, A *Theory of Religion*, 317.

84. Odd I. Langholm, *Economics in the Medieval Schools: Wealth, Exchange, Value, Money and Usury According to Paris Theological Tradition, 1200–1350* (New York: Brill, 1992); Odd I. Langholm, *The Legacy of Scholasticism in Economic Thought: Antecedents of Choice and Power* (Cambridge: Cambridge University Press, 1998).

85. Richard Newhauser, *The Early History of Greed: The Sin of Avarice in Early Medieval Thought and Literature* (Cambridge: Cambridge University Press, 2000).

86. Barro and McCleary, "Religion and Economic Growth," 1.

87. Some of the factors that the economics of religion cannot easily accommodate as endogenous are typically treated in the same manner as economics treats technology. This does not mean that ideas, ideology, power and power relationships, or other factors outside the standard model are irrelevant in our analysis of historical change; it merely means that on methodological grounds we treat changes in these factors as akin to a change in technology. Ideas and ideology are vitally important in our approach if they create changes in the form of costs and benefits facing economic actors, thereby inducing changes in markets or market structures.

88. See, for example, Douglass North, *Structure and Change in Economic History* (New York: W. W. Norton, 1981). In the context of religion, see also Philippe Simonnot, *Les papes, l'Église et l'argent* (Paris: Bayard, 2005).

89. This view is becoming increasingly common across the social sciences. Hence, William F. Shughart II, an economist, and Anthony Gill, a political scientist, in addition to sociologists Rodney Stark and Williams Sims Bainbridge, defend the use of a standard, neoclassical economic model to analyze religious behavior. Scholars in this area recognize that religious behavior may be motivated by ideological or psychological phenomena; and that economic motivation may itself be observationally equivalent to some religious or ethical behavior. Nevertheless only a scientific theory that formulates propositions in a manner that permits them to be refuted by evidence allows predictions to be made. Commenting on our earlier work in *Sacred Trust*, Gill proclaimed: "Evidence in support of the microeconomic reinterpretation is largely anecdotal... This is *not* a weakness as the authors' reading of history is based on a set of a priori predictions of behavior

and more consistently explains a wide array of behavior than ideational theories that frequently rely on post hoc and ad hoc interpretations of events." Anthony Gill, "Review of *Sacred Trust: The Medieval Church as an Economic Firm*," *Journal of Economic Literature* 36 (September 1998): 1525–1526; W. F. Shughart II, "Review of *Sacred Trust: The Medieval Church as an Economic Firm*," *Public Choice* 94 (1997): 211–216; Anthony Gill, *Rendering unto Caesar: The Catholic Church and the State in Latin America* (Chicago: Chicago University Press, 1998); Stark and Bainbridge, *A Theory of Religion*. See also Katherine Fischer, "Review of *Sacred Trust: The Medieval Church as an Economic Firm*," *Journal of Interdisciplinary History* 28 (1998): 650–651.

3   Religious Markets

1. Ekelund et al., *Sacred Trust*.

2. Brooks B. Hull and Frederick Bold, "Hell, Religion, and Cultural Change," *Journal of Institutional and Theoretical Economics* 150 (1994): 447–464; Brooks B. Hull and Frederick Bold, "Product Variety in Religious Markets," *Review of Social Economy* 56 (Spring 1998): 1–19.

3. Rodney Stark and Roger Finke, *Acts of Faith: Explaining the Human Side of Religion* (Berkeley: University of California Press, 2000), 83–90 and 208–217.

4. Space constraints prohibit detailed treatment of the anthropologic literature on this subject. The interested reader might consult Stark and Finke, *Acts of Faith*; Clifford Geertz, "Religion as a Cultural System," in *Anthropological Approaches to the Study of Religion*, ed. Michael Banton (London: Tavistock Publications, 1966), 1–46; and Guy E. Swanson, *The Birth of the Gods: The Origin of Primitive Beliefs* (Ann Arbor: University of Michigan Press, 1960). Swanson, in particular, offers a brilliant empirical (anecdotal) account of the origin of gods in ancient societies.

5. Joseph Campbell, *The Masks of God: Primitive Mythology* (New York: Penguin, 1959), 22.

6. Some writers regard animism as an unseen operator that exerts influence on human behavior. In economics literature, for example, Thorstein Veblen branded Adam Smith's use of natural law to explain competition as "animistic." Thorstein Veblen, "The Preconceptions of Economic Science," *Quarterly Journal of Economics* 12 (July 1898): 373–397.

7. Tattersall, *The Last Neanderthal*, 94–95.

8. Religion may have had economic purposes also, as noted in "The Primitive Hunter Culture, Pleistocene Extinction, and the Rise of Agriculture" by V. Smith, who argues that "customs," religious practices, anthropomorphism, and magic helped internalize certain externalities connected with overhunting, killing mothers with young, honoring the mating season, and so on.

9. Jared Diamond, *Guns, Germs, and Steel: The Fates of Human Societies* (New York: W. W. Norton, 1999).

10. North, *Structure and Change in Economic History*.

11. Stark and Finke, *Acts of Faith*, 105.

12. Newberg, D'Aquili, and Rause, *Why God Won't Go Away*, 137.

13. Reinhold Niebuhr, *The Children of Light and the Children of Darkness* (New York: Charles Scribner's Sons, 1960).

14. Fenella Saunders, "Tuning in to Sacred Sounds," *Discover* (March 2003), 13.

15. Theodore R. Fehrenbach. *Fire and Blood: A History of Mexico* (New York: Da Capo Press, 1995).

16. For example, see George Will, "Disconnected Youth," *The Washington Post* (September 21, 2003), B07.

17. Newberg, D'Aquili, and Rause, *Why God Won't Go Away*, 9.

18. Pascal Boyer, *Religion Explained: The Evolutionary Origins of Religious Thought* (New York: Basic Books, 2001), 330.

19. See also Alper, *The "God" Part of the Brain*, for an alternative physiological analysis of human spirituality.

20. Boyer, *Religion Explained*, 206.

21. Campbell, *The Masks of God*.

22. In Frank Knight, *The Economic Organization* (New York: Harper & Row, Harper Torchbooks, 1965), 120.

23. Kenneth Scheve and David Stasavage, "Religion and Preferences for Social Insurance," University of Michigan and LSE Working Paper, 2005.

24. Ronald Inglehart and Pippa Norris, *Sacred and Secular: Religion and Politics Worldwide* (New York: Cambridge University Press, 2004).

25. An alternative view is that priestly celibacy permitted the medieval church to more easily concentrate and control its wealth, since it dispensed with the consequences of inheritance among high-ranking prelates.

26. There are also more direct economic benefits that flowed from cathedrals and cathedral building, but we defer discussion of these matters to a later chapter.

27. Other factors lend credence to religions. Network effects wherein the level of credence may be enhanced by the number of adherents is yet another factor affecting an individual's belief.

28. This fact often gives rise to the free-rider problem, which we discussed briefly in chapter 2.

29. Iannaccone, "Sacrifice and Stigma."

30. Gary Becker, "A Theory of the Allocation of Time," *Economic Journal 65*, no. 299 (September 1965): 493–508.

31. Azzi and Ehrenberg, "Household Allocation of Time and Church Attendance." Eli Berman, in "Sect, Subsidy and Sacrifice: An Economist's View of Ultra-Orthodox Jews," *Quarterly Journal of Economics* 115 (2000): 4–29, offers another insight on religious participation among Ultra-Orthodox Jews. Berman maintains that built-in social welfare in the form of mutual aid in the Israeli kibbutz permits men (in this case) to dedicate themselves to full-time religious activities.

32. See Azzi and Ehrenberg, "Household Allocation of Time and Church Attendance," for example.

33. Henry Kraus, *Gold Was the Mortar: The Economics of Cathedral Building* (London: Routledge and Kegan Paul, 1979), 129.

34. Robert A. Scott, *The Gothic Enterprise: A Guide to Understanding the Medieval Cathedral* (Berkeley: University of California Press, 2003), 216–218. A similar argument may be advanced to support the rapid adoption of Christianity in the early days of the Roman Empire. The lack of security provided by Roman governments after the disintegration of dictatorships helped encourage groups of Christians to coalesce around a monotheistic doctrine promising ultimate redemption, temporal communal support and afterlife consumption. Doctrinally, Christians created open access to membership early in the religion's development in order to compete with a multitude of "pagan" sects. Later, in the fourth and fifth centuries, doctrinal strictness was adopted by the church in order to quell internal dissention over official church dogma. See Mario Ferrero, "The Triumph of Christianity in the Roman Empire: An Economic Interpretation," unpublished manuscript, Conference on Religion, Economics and Society, Kansas City, Mo., October 22–24, 2004, http://gunston.gmu.edu/liannacc/ERel/S2-Archives/REC04/Ferrero%20-%20Chistianity%20in%20Roman%20Empire.pdf. Also see Simonnot, *Les papes, l'Église et l'argent*, chapters 3 and 4. We argue, additionally, that other factors were in play that led to the adoption of Christianity, including high taxation and the inability of taxed peasants to combine politically and put pressure on the Emperor Constantine in the fourth century. On the matter of taxation and rent seeking, see Charles D. DeLorme Jr., Stacey Isom, and David R. Kamerschen, "Rent Seeking and Taxation in the Ancient Roman Empire," *Applied Economics* 37 (2005): 705–711.

35. In a related argument, in their article "Hell, Religion, and Cultural Change," Hull and Bold suggest that the religious doctrine of hell produces social benefits in situations where the church is a relatively more stable institution than the family, community or government.

36. Shoshana A. Grossbard-Shechtman and Shoshana Neuman, "Economic Behavior, Marriage and Religiosity," *Journal of Behavioral Science* 15 (Spring/Summer 1986): 71–85.

37. Rodney Stark, *The Rise of Christianity: A Sociologist Reconsiders History* (Princeton, N.J.: Princeton University Press, 1996), 7.

38. Philip Jenkins, *The Next Christendom: The Coming of Global Christianity* (Oxford: Oxford University Press, 2002); Philip Jenkins, "The Next Christianity," *Atlantic Monthly* 290 (October 2002): 53–68.

39. On persistent persecutions of the Mormons, see Jon Krakauer, *Under the Banner of Heaven: A Story of Violent Faith* (New York: Anchor Books, 2003).

40. Campbell, *The Masks of God*, 231.

41. E. Lueas Bridges, *Uttermost Part of the Earth* (London: Hodder & Stoughton, 1948), 232.

42. Quoted in Campbell, *The Masks of God*, 250.

43. Priests were guardians of the calendar from ancient times. The seasons—regarded as a manifestation of the gods—were the province of priestly interpretation. Turning points in the seasonal cycle were thought to have great theological significance as godly communications. (Naturally they also had much to do with agriculture and survival.) This ancient role of priests has evolved to be included in contemporary religions, including Christianity (e.g., the liturgical calendar of the Roman Catholic Church).

44. See Iannaccone, "Sacrifice and Stigma"; and Christian Eilinghoff, "Religious Information and Credibility," in *German Working Papers in Law and Economics*, working paper, University of Hamburg, 2003, http://www.bepress.com/gwp/default/vol2003/iss1/art8.

45. Rosen, "The Economics of Superstars."

46. Iannaccone, "Sacrifice and Stigma."

4   Religious Form Change: Case Studies

1. In appendix 4A to this chapter we also offer two preliminary empirical tests of the determinants of religious forms adopted: the first in an international sample of poor countries where religions defined as "animistic" are tested against "all others" as functions of income and other variables; the second in a U.S. state context that measures the impact of income and other variables on the number of psychics, spiritual advisors, and mediums in forty-six states.

2. Finke and Stark, *The Churching of America, 1776–1990*; Stark and Finke, *Acts of Faith*.

3. Finke and Stark, *The Churching of America, 1776–1990*, 43.

4. Reinhold H. Niebuhr, *The Sources of Denominationalism* (New York: Henry Holt, 1929).

5. Iannaccone, "Sacrifice and Stigma," 238.

6. David A. Rausch and Carl Hermann Voss, *Protestantism—Its Modern Meaning* (Philadelphia: Fortress Press, 1987), 66.

7. Tom W. Smith and Seokho Kim, "The Vanishing Protestant Majority," NORC/University of Chicago, GSS Social Change Report no. 49, July 2004.

8. Hull and Bold, "Product Variety in Religious Markets," 6.

9. See J. Gordon Melton, *Encyclopedia of American Religions*, 7th ed. (Detroit: Gale, 2002); Richard N. Ostling, "Religions by the Thousands," *San Antonio Express News* (March 8, 2003), 7B, 11B.

10. Stark and Finke, *Acts of Faith*, 208–217.

11. Stark and Finke, *Acts of Faith*, 208.

12. The largely derivative accounts of North in *Structure and Change in Economic History* describe a range of authoritarian to democratic societies— Mesopotamia, Persia, Egypt, Greece, and so forth. But it was only in agrarian societies that we first experience wide disparities in income distribution because nomads did not store goods.

13. It is useful to contrast an economic account (such as our own) of the emergence of monotheism in societies with that of anthropologists (see, in particular, Swanson, *The Birth of the Gods*, 55–58) who rely on categories such as hierarchies of sovereign groups in society.

14. We ignore the many controversies surrounding Akhenaton's reign and do not claim to be anthropologically accurate in every detail here; we develop a stylized presentation from numerous works. For details on these many issues see Dominic Montserrat, *Akhenaten: History, Fantasy and Ancient Egypt* (London: Routledge, 2000); Cyril Aldred, *Akhenaten, King of Egypt* (London: Thames and Hudson, 1986); and numerous other works on Akhenaton.

15. A superb study of the forms of magic and its relation to and substance in Egyptian deities is Geraldine Pinch, *Magic in Ancient Egypt* (Austin: University of Texas Press, 1995; originally published by the British Museum Press). Pinch authoritatively describes the extraordinary lengths that Egyptians took in order to quell existential dread.

16. Robert Silverberg, *Akhnaten: The Rebel Pharaoh* (Philadelphia: Chilton Books, 1964), 16.

17. Silverberg, *Akhnaten*, 17–18.

18. In the so-called Great Hymn to Aton, the god's abstract qualities and the anointment of Akhenaton as the god's sole agent or priest is emphasized: "How manifold are thy works! They are hidden from the sight of men, O Sole God, like unto whom there is no other! . . . thou appointest every man to his place and satisfiest his needs." And, emphasizing Akhenaton's uniqueness, the hymn continues, "Thou art in my heart, but there is none other who knows thee save thy son Akhenaton. Thou has made him wise in thy plans and thy power" (qtd. in Aldred, *Akhenaten*, 242–243).

19. James Henry Breasted, *The Dawn of Conscience* (New York: Scribners, 1933), 304.

20. Montserrat, *Akhenaten*, 17.

21. Breasted, *The Dawn of Conscience*, 304.

22. Silverberg, *Akhnaten*, 141.

23. Breasted, *The Dawn of Conscience*, 307.

24. Galileo Galilei, *Dialogue Concerning the Two Chief World Systems— Ptolemaic and Copernican*, trans. Stillman Drake, foreword by Albert Einstein (Berkeley: University of California Press, [1632] 1953).

25. See Elizabeth L. Eisenstein, *The Printing Revolution in Early Modern Europe* (Cambridge: Cambridge University Press, 1983), 225–252.

26. See, for example, Eisenstein, *The Printing Revolution in Early Modern Europe*, 225; Gerald P. Tyson and Sylvia S. Wagonheim, eds., *Print and Culture in the Renaissance: Essays on the Advent of Printing in Europe* (Newark: University of Delaware Press, 1986), 126; and, most particularly, Christiane Andersson, "Popular Imagery in German Reformation Broadsheets," in Gerald P. Tyson and Sylvia S. Wagonheim, eds., *Print and Culture in the Renaissance: Essays on the Advent of Printing in Europe* (Newark: University of Delaware Press, 1986).

27. Eisenstein, *The Printing Revolution in Early Modern Europe*, 145.

28. The first complete edition of Luther's translation of the Bible into German became the most widely read book in Germany and, according to Colin Clair, "influenced decisively the development of the German language." Colin Clair, *A Chronology of Printing* (New York: Frederick A. Praeger, 1969), 46.

29. Jean-François Gilmont, *The Reformation and the Book*, English ed. and trans. Karin Maag (Aldershot, U.K.: Ashgate, 1998), 3–4.

30. The role of printing in the establishment of Protestantism in particular areas and countries of Europe is far more complex than depicted here. See the scholarly studies contained in Gilmont, *The Reformation and the Book*.

31. Eisenstein, *The Printing Revolution in Early Modern Europe*, 176.

32. Edward Burman, *The Inquisition: The Hammer of Heresy* (Leicestershire: Thoth Publications, 1984), 195.

33. For details, see A. Gordon Kinder, "Printing and Reformation Ideas in Spain," in Gilmont, *The Reformation and the Book*.

34. Burman, *The Inquisition*, 163.

35. Clair, *A Chronology of Printing*, 41.

36. Burman, *The Inquisition*, 213.

37. While not rising to full condemnation, Benedict XVI, in an early act of his papacy, issued a severe warning of the dangers to the faithful of reading the popular Harry Potter books.

38. Frederick W. Bell, "The Pope and the Price of Fish," *American Economic Review* 58 (1968): 1346–1350.

39. Gary MacEoin, *The Inner Elite: Dossiers of Papal Candidates* (Kansas City, Mo.: Sheed Andrews and McMeel, 1978), xiv.

40. This dispensation was brought to the New World by Spanish settlers, so Catholics in New Mexico, Arizona, and part of Texas were exempted until 1951. *New York Times* (November 27, 1966), 36.

41. Do not confuse joint production—as in chickens and chicken parts, beef and hides—with the joint production of religious goods. In the former (technical) sense, the production of one good—beef—necessitates in some defined proportion the production of some other goods—hides. In the case of religious goods production, the joint products may include, in addition to a spiritual product, a more efficient marriage market, social insurance and a host of other goods we described in chapter 3.

42. Mark Thornton, "The Pope and the Price of Leather," *Journal of Institutional and Theoretical Economics* 148 (1992): 452–459.

43. Thornton, "The Pope and the Price of Leather," 454.

44. Quoted in Xavier Rynne, *Vatican Council II* (New York: Farrar, Straus and Giroux, 1968), 356.

45. Ault, Ekelund, and Tollison, "The Pope and the Price of Meat," 411.

46. Pope Paul VI, *Poenitemini: Apostolic Constitution on Fast and Abstinence* (Washington, DC: National Catholic Welfare Conference, 1966), 10.

47. Pope Paul VI, *Poenitemini*, 10.

48. This view has been embraced in a number of papers and articles created by European economists. See Lafay, "L'Église médiévale sous le regard de l'analyse économique"; and Gerhard Schmitz, *Monumenta Germaniae Historica* (Zeitschrift: Deutsches Archiv fur Erforschung des Mittelalters (DA) Rezension in Band 53.2, S. 742, 2002), www.mgh.de. Economic historians offering an economic analysis of church history have also included discussions of the Roman Catholic Church as an M-form corporation. An important history, dealing principally with the financial aspects of the papacy and the Church, is by Simonnot, *Les papes, l'Église et l'argent*. Simonnot traces Church organization and finances from the very beginnings to the nineteenth-century losses in temporal power and the Church's dealings with Mussolini. Academic courses, moreover, have been developed around the arguments of Ekelund et al.'s *Sacred Trust*: see Lindsay Porter, "New Three-Semester Class Looks at Church and Economic Monopoly," *The Pendulum Online*, Elon University, April 11, http://www.elon.edu/pendulum/Issues/2002/041102/News/Sacred.html.

49. A study of data sources on the measurement of religions by Marta Reynal-Querol outlines the problems with using alternative data sets, including the *World Christian Encyclopedia*. The author argues (p. 5), however, that the *WCE* underestimates the followers of animist cults in Africa. Marta Reynal-Querol, "A Contribution to the Measurement of Religious Diversity: Data and Indicators" (working paper, Harvard University Weatherhead Center, December 2001), http://www.wcfia.harvard.edu/rsrchpapsum.asp?ID=508.

50. Statistics are obtainable at www.worldbank.org/aboutdata/working-meth.html.

51. In earlier formulations of our test, we found that rural population had no discernable or logical effect on the degree of animism in a country.

52. Melton, *Encyclopedia of American Religions*.

53. In a sample of seventeen Christian countries in their Harvard University working paper, "Religion and Political Economy in an International Panel," Barro and McCleary distinguish between superstition and religion claiming that they are inversely related. What are interesting in their study are high levels of belief in fortune-tellers, horoscopes, and good luck charms in these countries, ranging from 19 percent of the Irish believing in horoscopes to 80 percent of the Latvians believing in fortune-tellers. One possibility, according to Barro and McCleary, is that superstitions substitute for religion. This may be so in some areas but in heavily Catholic countries such as Mexico, fortune-tellers (*curanderos*) are complements to Roman Catholic beliefs.

54. Psychics are licensed by the American Association of Professional Psychics, but membership is voluntary and, according to the association president, vastly miscounts the actual number of psychics in the fifty states.

55. Alaska, Hawaii, New Jersey, and New York were omitted in the reported test, the latter two states due to overlapping listings in the Yellow Pages. Results were unchanged when these two states were included, however.

5   Economies of the Protestant Revolt

1. In Ekelund et al., *Sacred Trust*.

2. Max Weber, *The Protestant Ethic and the Spirit of Capitalism*, 104–105.

3. Max Weber, *The Protestant Ethic and the Spirit of Capitalism*, 10.

4. Gary M. Becker, "Crime and Punishment: An Economic Approach," *Journal of Political Economy* 76, (1968): 169–217; and George J. Stigler, "The Optimum Enforcement of Laws," *Journal of Political Economy* 78 (1970): 526–536.

5. Bronislaw Geremek, *Poverty: A History*, trans. Agnieszka Kolakowska (Oxford, U.K., and Cambridge, Mass.: Blackwell, 1994).

6. Geremek, *Poverty*, 20.

7. Geremek, *Poverty*, 23.

8. B. S. Pullan, *Rich and Poor in Renaissance Venice: The Social Institutions of a Catholic State* (Cambridge: Cambridge University Press, 1971).

9. Smith, *The Wealth of Nations*, 755.

10. The ferment of the "thirteenth-century renaissance," which was stirred by economic changes and by the encounter with Greek philosophy through the mediation of Islam, led to a much more complex religious society than that characterized here. Hence, the assumption of a vertically integrated, dominant firm is an analytical device that is not intended to capture the full texture of European history.

11. E. LeRoy Ladurie, *Montaillou: The Promised Land of Error* (New York: Braziller, 1978).

12. See B. N. Nelson, "The Usurer and the Merchant Prince: Italian Businessmen and the Ecclesiastical Law of Restitution, 1100–1550," *Journal of Economic History* 7 (Summer 1947): 104–122.

13. William E. Lunt, *Financial Relations of the Papacy with England, 1327–1534* (Cambridge, Mass.: Medieval Academy of America, 1962), 422.

14. Lunt, *Financial Relations of the Papacy with England, 1327–1534*, 494.

15. Lunt, *Financial Relations of the Papacy with England, 1327–1534*, 586.

16. Lunt, *Financial Relations of the Papacy with England, 1327–1534*, 602–604.

17. If the goal of the Church had been optimal enforcement and deterrence, we would expect to see lower full prices extracted for minor sins than for serious transgressions (e.g., adultery), which was not the case.

18. Peltzman, "Toward a More General Theory of Regulation," 236.

19. For example, see Lunt, *Financial Relations of the Papacy with England, 1327–1534*, 423; Lunt, *Papal Revenues in the Middle Ages*, vol. 2, 483.

20. Lunt, *Papal Revenues in the Middle Ages*, vol. 2, 483.

21. Lunt, *Papal Revenues in the Middle Ages*, vol. 2, 528.

22. Lunt, *Financial Relations of the Papacy with England, 1327–1534*, 529.

23. R. H. Helmholz, *Marriage Litigation in Medieval England* (Cambridge: Cambridge University Press, 1974), 161; M. Ingram, *Church Courts, Sex and Marriage in England, 1570–1640* (Cambridge: Cambridge University Press, 1987), 57.

24. Lunt, *Papal Revenues in the Middle Ages*, vol. 2, 525.

25. Georges Duby, *Medieval Marriage*, trans. Elbord Forster (Baltimore, Md.: Johns Hopkins University Press, 1978), 30–57.

26. Audrey B. Davidson and Robert B. Ekelund Jr., "The Medieval Church and Rents from Marriage Market Regulations," *The Journal of Economic Behavior and Organization* 32 (February 1997): 215–245.

27. Max Weber, *The Protestant Ethic and the Spirit of Capitalism*, 115.

28. Max Weber, *The Protestant Ethic and the Spirit of Capitalism*, 117.

29. Andrei Shleifer and Robert W. Vishny, *The Grabbing Hand: Government Pathologies and Their Cures* (Cambridge, Mass.: Harvard University Press, 1998), 19–52.

30. Jack Goody, *The Development of the Family and Marriage in Europe.* (Cambridge: Cambridge University Press, 1983), 118; see also Davidson and Ekelund, "The Medieval Church and Rents from Marriage Market Regulations," 228–230.

31. P. Sutter Fichtner, *Protestantism and Primogeniture in Early Modern Germany* (New Haven: Yale University Press, 1989), 52–53.

32. Guy E. Swanson, *Religion and Regime: A Sociological Account of the Reformation* (Ann Arbor: University of Michigan Press, 1967).

33. Lunt, *Financial Relations of the Papacy with England, 1327–1534*, 598.

34. Raymond DeRoover, *The Medici Bank* (New York: New York University Press, 1948), 47.

35. John M. Roberts, "Lombardy," in *European Nobility in the Eighteenth Century*, ed. A. Goodwin (London: Adam and Charles Black, 1953), 71.

36. John McManners, "France," in *European Nobility in the Eighteenth Century*, ed. A. Goodwin (London: Adam and Charles Black, 1953), 31.

37. H. G. Schenk, "Austria," in *European Nobility in the Eighteenth Century*, ed. A. Goodwin (London: Adam and Charles Black, 1953), 105.

38. Winfried Eberhard, "Bohemia, Moravia and Austria," in *The Early Reformation in Europe*, ed. Andrew Pettegree (London: Cambridge University Press, 1992), 32.

39. Robert Scribner, "Germany," in *The Reformation in National Context*, ed. R. Scribner, R. Porter, and M. Teich (London: Cambridge University Press, 1994).

40. Michael Roberts, "Sweden," in *European Nobility in the Eighteenth Century*, ed. A. Goodwin (London: Adam and Charles Black, 1953), 38–40.

41. Gary M. Becker, *A Treatise on the Family* (Cambridge, Mass.: Harvard University Press, 1981), 128, citing G. O. Sayles, *The Medieval Foundations of England*, 2nd ed. (London: Methuen, 1952).

42. G. O. Sayles, *The Medieval Foundations of England* (London: Methuen, 1950), 224–227, only describes the attempt by William the Conqueror to institute military organization through land contracts and through such institutional devices as primogeniture; he does not describe the actual operation and evolution of the system in England.

43. Ralph V. Turner, preface to *Law in Medieval Life and Thought*, ed. E. G. King and S. J. Ridyard (Sewanee, Tenn.: Medieval Society, 1990), 122–123.

44. C. S. K. Kenny, *The Law of Primogeniture in England* (Cambridge: Cambridge University Press, 1978), 57.

45. G. A. Holmes, *The Estates of the Higher Nobility in Fourteenth Century England* (Cambridge: Cambridge University Press, 1957); Alan Simpson, *The Wealth of the Gentry 1540–1660* (Cambridge: Cambridge University Press, 1961).

46. Smith, *The Wealth of Nations*, 363.

47. J. M. W. Bean, *The Decline of English Feudalism, 1250–1540* (New York: Barnes & Noble, 1968).

48. Becker, *A Treatise on the Family*, 128n.8.

49. Smith, *The Wealth of Nations*, 362.

50. Eyre Lloyd, *The Succession Laws of Christian Countries* (London: Stevens and Haynes, 1877), 2.

51. Eileen Spring, *Law, Land and Family: Aristocratic Inheritance in England, 1300–1800* (Chapel Hill: University of North Carolina Press, 1993), 32. Adam Smith expressed similar sentiments about primogeniture in his *Lectures on Jurisprudence*, ed. R. L. Meek, D. D. Raphael, and P. G. Stein (Oxford: Oxford University Press, 1978), 69. See also Lloyd, *The Succession Laws of Christian Countries.*

52. Diarmaid MacCulloch, "England," in *The Early Reformation in Europe*, ed. Andrew Pettegree (London: Cambridge University Press, 1992), 166.

53. Simpson, *The Wealth of the Gentry 1540–1660*, 36.

54. Julian Goodare, "Scotland," in *The Reformation in National Context*, eds. B. Scribner, R. Porter, and M. Teich (London: Cambridge University Press, 1994), 97.

55. T. A. Brady Jr., *Turning Swiss: Cities and Empire, 1450–1550* (Cambridge: Cambridge University Press, 1985).

56. Brady, *Turning Swiss: Cities and Empire, 1450–1550*, 45–46.

57. Scribner, "Germany," 219–220.

58. Paul Bairoch, Jean Bateau, and Pierre Chèvre, *La Population des villes européenes, 800–1850: Banque de données et analyse sommaire des résultats* (Geneva: Librairie Droz, 1988).

59. Shleifer and Vishny, *The Grabbing Hand*, 27–30.

60. Scribner, "Germany," 219–220.

61. George C. Broderick, "The Law and Custom of Primogeniture," in *Systems of Land Tenure in Various Countries*, ed. J. W. Probyn (London: Stevens and Haynes, 1881), 99.

62. Turner, Preface to *Law in Medieval Life and Thought*, 133.

63. Holmes, *The Estates of the Higher Nobility in Fourteenth Century England*, 7; see also Simpson, *The Wealth of the Gentry 1540–1660*, 28–29.

64. A. G. Dickens, *Reformation and Society in Sixteenth-Century Europe* (New York: Harcourt, Brace & World, 1966), 12–14.

65. Roberts, "Lombardy," 67.

66. Raymond Carr, "Spain," in *European Nobility in the Eighteenth Century*, ed. A. Goodwin (London: Adam and Charles Black, 1953), 48.

67. A. B. Boswell, "Poland," in *European Nobility in the Eighteenth Century*, ed. A. Goodwin (London: Adam and Charles Black, 1953), 156.

6   The Counter-Reformation: Incumbent-Firm Reaction to Market Entry

1. In implying that "Reformation" and "Counter-Reformation" were sequential episodes we rely on a stylized version of history. Some modern historians, such as

Wolfgang Reinhard, hold that the Reformation and the Counter-Reformation were not mutually exclusive in either their temporal or their material aspects. Wolfgang Reinhard, "Reformation, Counter-Reformation, and the Early Modern State: A Reassessment," *The Catholic Historical Review* 75 (1989): 384.

2. Harro Hopfl, ed. and trans., *Luther and Calvin on Secular Authority* (Cambridge: Cambridge University Press, 1991), xviii–xix.

3. By analogy to contemporary deregulatory practice (e.g., the breakup of AT&T into regional firms; or competitive/technological incursions into the postal monopoly by private couriers such as Federal Express, or by new technology such as e-mail), when Protestant sects enter as competitors, the price of religious services should fall to industry marginal costs. This would apply to a competitive supply of religion. In this context, however, we are here considering what amounts to spatial monopoly in the supply of religious services.

4. There is no welfare loss due to Protestant entry at the "tithe-price" P_p in figure 6.2. Since the Catholic Church continued to perfectly price discriminate below P_p, a competitive amount of religious services was provided.

5. Yet a fifth implication of our theory is that the "savings" in consumer surplus from entry (triangle ABP_p in figure 6.2) meant that rent-seeking investment in churches fell by the recouped triangle and was freed up for productive investment in the private sector, spurring economic growth. This circumstance is relevant to a reconsideration of Max Weber's celebrated thesis, which we take up in chapter 8.

6. On the regulation of benefices see H. J. Schroeder, trans., *The Canons and Decrees of The Council of Trent* (Rockford, Ill.: TAN Books and Publishers, 1978), 56–58, 113, 204–206, 237, 239. On residency requirements for bishops and clergy, see pp. 46–49, 164–166. On supervision of priests and monks, see pp. 49, 141, 198–199. On minimum competency qualifications of clergy, see pp. 55, 60, 83, 111, 153–154, 167–169, 171–174, 200–202. On restoring and renewing piety among priests, monks, and nuns, see pp. 152–153, 156–157, 217–218, 224. On establishing procedural norms for the election of bishops and cardinals, see pp. 190–192. On penalties for concubinage and other public offenses, see pp. 188, 226, 246–248.

7. On attempts to prohibit bishops from selling rights and offices, see Schroeder, *The Canons and Decrees of The Council of Trent*, 113, 136, 241. On elimination of charges for selling certain church services (e.g., dispensations), see pp. 250–251. On the prohibition of certain leases of church property, see p. 245. On enjoining cardinals and prelates from using church property to enrich their families, see pp. 232–233. On requiring that clerics be compelled to pay what they owe, see pp. 60–61. On restricting abuse of wills and bequests by opportunistic clergy, see p. 156. On restrictions put on the conversions of benefices, see p. 249. On quality control over the doctrine of purgatory and the veneration of sacred relics, and efforts to abolish "all evil traffic" in indulgences, see p. 253.

8. On various attempts to "advertise" and disseminate knowledge of its product, see Schroeder, *The Canons and Decrees of The Council of Trent*, pp. 24–28,

175–179, 195–198. On attempts to improve financial assistance to poor parishes, see p. 205. On efforts to soften some of its punishments, such as the use of excommunication, see pp. 235–236. On removal of certain impediments to marriage, see pp. 186–187.

9. Andrew Pettegree, *Europe in the Sixteenth Century* (Oxford: Blackwell Publishing, 2002), 2.

10. Jerome Blum, Rondo Cameron, and Thomas G. Barnes, *The European World: A History* (Boston: Little, Brown and Co., 1966), 208.

11. Robert Bireley, *The Refashioning of Catholicism, 1450–1700* (Washington, D.C.: Catholic University of America Press, 1999), 18–19.

12. Burman, *The Inquisition*, 176.

13. Cited in Burman, *The Inquisition*, 168.

14. Burman, *The Inquisition*, 201.

15. Michel Foucault, *Discipline and Punish: The Birth of the Prison*, trans. A. Sheridan (New York: Pantheon Books, 1977), 40.

16. *The Canons and Decrees of the Council of Trent*, 24.

17. *The Canons and Decrees of the Council of Trent*, 26.

18. *The Canons and Decrees of the Council of Trent*, 195–198.

19. Michael Foss, *The Founding of the Jesuits, 1540* (New York: Weybright and Talley, 1969), 157.

20. B. D. Hill, ed., *Church and State in the Middle Ages* (New York: John Wiley & Sons, 1970), 148.

21. On these matters, including documents that accompanied the dispute, see Brian Tierney, *The Crisis of Church and State 1050–1300* (Englewood Cliffs, N.J.: Prentice-Hall, 1964), 172–190.

22. Denys Hay, *The Church in Italy in the Fifteenth Century* (London: Cambridge University Press, 1977), 27.

23. Hay, *The Church in Italy in the Fifteenth Century*, 26.

24. Hay, *The Church in Italy in the Fifteenth Century*, 32.

25. The decree *Frequens*, promulgated in 1417 at the Council of Constance (1414–1418) is replicated in C. M. D. Crowder, *Unity, Heresy and Reform, 1378–1460* (New York: St. Martin's Press, 1977), 128–129.

26. Brian Tierney, *The Crisis of Church and State 1050–1300*, 1.

27. Robert Bireley, *The Refashioning of Catholicism, 1450–1700*, 15.

28. Crowder, *Unity, Heresy and Reform, 1378–1460*, 20.

29. Denys Hay reports on the resentment of French monarchs to paying church tribute: "Charles VII or Louis XI of France might huff and puff, but French bishops and abbots [nominated by the monarchs themselves] paid their dues, however belatedly, and so did English prelates until the break with Rome." Hay, *The Church in Italy in the Fifteenth Century*, 33.

30. Crowder, *Unity, Heresy and Reform, 1378–1460*, 23.

31. J. J. Scarisbrick, "Clerical Taxation in England, 1485 to 1547," *Journal of Ecclesiastical History* 11 (1960): 50.

32. Foss, *The Founding of the Jesuits, 1540*, 156.

33. Hay, *The Church in Italy in the Fifteenth Century*, 42–43.

34. B. M. Hallman, *Italian Cardinals, Reform, and the Church as Property* (Berkeley: University of California Press, 1985).

35. *The Canons and Decrees of the Council of Trent*, 232.

36. Hallman, *Italian Cardinals, Reform, and the Church as Property*.

37. The *scudo* was first struck as a gold coin by several Italian states in the early sixteenth century. At 3.35 grams, it was slightly smaller than the standard gold trade coin of the period, the Venetian ducat (3.50 grams). If the market price of gold was US$500 per ounce, each gram would be worth approximately US$18, establishing the value of a *scudo* at approximiately US$60. *Scudo* comes from the same root as the French *ecu*, named for the shield that appeared on most of the coin types, and was first issued in Lucca and Naples when they were under French occupation.

38. Hallman, *Italian Cardinals, Reform, and the Church as Property*, 157.

39. Bireley, *The Refashioning of Catholicism, 1450–1700*, 157.

40. Hallman, *Italian Cardinals, Reform, and the Church as Property*, 131.

41. Hallman, *Italian Cardinals, Reform, and the Church as Property*, 139.

42. Hallman, *Italian Cardinals, Reform, and the Church as Property*, 1.

43. Hallman, *Italian Cardinals, Reform, and the Church as Property*, 79.

44. Hallman, *Italian Cardinals, Reform, and the Church as Property*, 94.

45. These "expectancies" were papal grants of benefices that were already occupied. They were granted in anticipation of the death of the holder, effectively establishing a futures market in benefices. Hallman, *Italian Cardinals, Reform, and the Church as Property*, 43.

46. Geremek, *Poverty*; John H. Pullen, *The English Catholics in the Reign of Queen Elizabeth* (New York: Burt Franklin Reprint, [1920] 1971).

7   The Establishment and Evolution of Protestantism

1. This view is derivative of the pioneer work of E. H. Chamberlin. It is most often associated with K. J. Lancaster, but Ekelund and Hébert have shown that the crux of the idea already existed in the writings of the French engineer, Jules Dupuit (1804–1866). E. H. Chamberlin, *The Theory of Monopolistic Competition* (Cambridge, Mass.: Harvard University Press, 1933); K. J. Lancaster, "A New Approach to Consumer Theory," *Journal of Political Economy* 74 (1966): 132–157; Robert B. Ekelund, Jr., and Robert F. Hébert, "Dupuit's

Characteristics-Based Theory of Consumer Behavior and Entrepreneurship," *Kyklos* 44, no. 1 (1991): 19–34; Jules Dupuit, "De l'influence des péages sur l'utilité des voies de communication," *Annales des Ponts et Chaussées: Mémoires et Documents*, 2d ser., 17, no. 1 (1849): 170–248; reprinted in *De utilité et de sa mesure: Écrits choisis et republies par Mario de Bernardi* (Torino: La Riforma Sociale, 1933), 99–162.

2. Bodo Nischan, "Ritual and Protestant Identity in Late Reformation Germany," in *Protestant History and Identity in Sixteenth Century Europe, Vol. 2: The Later Reformation*, ed. Bruce Gordon (Aldershot, U.K.: Scholar Press, 1996), 145 (emphasis added).

3. Steven Ozment, *Protestants: The Birth of a Revolution* (New York: Doubleday, 1992), x.

4. Andrew Pettegree, *The Early Reformation in Europe* (Cambridge: Cambridge University Press, 1992).

5. Diarmaid MacCulloch, *The Reformation* (New York: Viking, 2004), 47.

6. MacCulloch, *The Reformation*, 50.

7. Emile G. Leonard, *A History of Protestantism, Vol. I: The Reformation*, trans. Joyce M. H. Reid (Indianapolis: Bobbs-Merrill, 1968), 97–115.

8. MacCulloch, *The Reformation*, 156.

9. Bruce Gordon, "The Changing Face of Protestant History and Identity in the Sixteenth Century," in *Protestant History and Identity in Sixteenth Century Europe, Vol. 2: The Later Reformation*, ed. Gordon, 18.

10. MacCulloch, *The Reformation*, 171.

11. MacCulloch, *The Reformation*, 174.

12. MacCulloch, *The Reformation*, 233.

13. Nischan, "Ritual and Protestant Identity in Late Reformation Germany," 149.

14. MacCulloch, *The Reformation*, 381.

15. MacCulloch, *The Reformation*, 369.

16. An important part of the Reformation in Scandinavia was the transition from Latin to the domestic language for use in church services and in translation of the Bible. Because of this the reformers, Olaus Petri and Mikael Agricola, also played an instrumental role in the development of Swedish and Finnish as written languages.

17. Although, strictly speaking, nationalism and nationalization are not the same thing, Albert Breton's economic analysis of nationalism is instructive on this point. Breton concludes that societies that invest in nationality or ethnicity receive a lower return on investment than if resources were economically invested in alternative uses; the motivation for such investment is income redistribution rather than the creation of wealth. Albert Breton, "The Economics of Nationalism," *Journal of Political Economy* 72, no. 4 (1964): 376–386.

18. David Hempton, "A Tale of Preachers and Beggars: Methodism and Money in the Great Age of Transatlantic Expansion, 1780–1830," in *God and Mammon*, ed. Mark A. Noll (Oxford: Oxford University Press, 2002), 139–140.

19. Robin Klay and John Lunn, "Protestants and the American Economy in the Postcolonial Period: An Overview," in *God and Mammon*, ed. Mark A. Noll (Oxford: Oxford University Press, 2002), 30–53.

20. Klay and Lunn, "Protestants and the American Economy in the Postcolonial Period," 48.

21. See www.sda.co.uk/twickurc/pewrent.htm.

22. www.sda.co.uk/twickurc/pewrent.htm.

8 Catholicism, Protestantism, and Economic Performance

1. Research on the link between religion and economic growth remains vigorous, as demonstrated in recent studies by Ulrich Blum and Leonard Dudley, "Religion and Economic Growth: Was Weber Right?," *Journal of Evolutionary Economics* 11 (2001): 207–230, and Robert J. Barro and Rachel M. McCleary, "Religion and Economic Growth"; whereas since Kurt Samuelsson, *Religion and Economic Action: A Critique of Max Weber*, trans. E. G. French, ed. D. C. Coleman (New York: Basic Books, 1961), the consensus scholarly opinion is that Weber's study was seriously flawed.

2. Schmuel N. Eisenstadt, *The Protestant Ethic and Modernization: A Comparative View* (New York: Basic Books, 1968).

3. Franz-Xaver Kaufmann, "Religion and Modernization in Europe," *Journal of Institutional and Theoretical Economics* 153, no. 1 (1997).

4. Weber, *The Protestant Ethic and the Spirit of Capitalism*, 53.

5. Weber, *The Protestant Ethic and the Spirit of Capitalism*, 52.

6. Weber, *The Protestant Ethic and the Spirit of Capitalism*, 53–54.

7. Weber, *The Protestant Ethic and the Spirit of Capitalism*, 52.

8. Michael H. Lessnoff, *The Spirit of Capitalism and the Protestant Ethic: An Enquiry into the Weber Thesis* (Aldershot, U.K.: Edward Elgar, 1994).

9. Weber, *The Protestant Ethic and the Spirit of Capitalism*.

10. Lessnoff, *The Spirit of Capitalism and the Protestant Ethic*.

11. Weber, *The Protestant Ethic and the Spirit of Capitalism*, 55.

12. George J. Stigler and Gary S. Becker, *"De Gustibus Non Est Disputandum,"* *American Economic Review* (March 1977): 76–90.

13. By analogy to contemporary deregulatory practice (e.g., the breakup of AT&T into regional firms; or competitive/technological incursions into the postal monopoly by private couriers such as Federal Express, or by new technology such as e-mail), when Protestant sects enter as competitors, the price of religious

services should fall to industry marginal costs (i.e., the sum of marginal costs for all religions).

14. There is no welfare loss due to Protestant entry at the "tithe-price" P_p in figure 8.2. Since the Catholic Church continued to perfectly price discriminate below P_p, a competitive amount of religious services was provided, both before and after entry.

15. Hopfl, *Luther and Calvin on Secular Authority*, xviii–xix.

16. Georges Duby, *The Europe of the Cathedrals, 1140–1280*, trans. Stuart Gilbert (Geneva: Editions d'Art Albert Skira, 1966), 8.

17. Duby, *The Europe of the Cathedrals, 1140–1280*, 8.

18. Duby, *The Europe of the Cathedrals, 1140–1280*, 35.

19. Duby, *The Europe of the Cathedrals, 1140–1280*, 36.

20. Duby, *The Europe of the Cathedrals, 1140–1280*, 37.

21. Patrick J. Geary, *Furta Sacra: Thefts of Relics in the Central Middle Ages* (Princeton: Princeton University Press, 1990); Ernst Tyerman, *The Social Teachings of the Christian Churches*, 2 vols, trans. O. Wyon (New York: Macmillan, 1931).

22. Charles M. Tiebout, "A Pure Theory of Local Expenditures," *Journal of Political Economy* (October 1956): 416–424.

23. Ann Mitchell, *Cathedrals of Europe* (Feltham, U.K.: Hamlyn Publishing Group, 1968), 9.

24. Robert A. Scott, *The Gothic Enterprise: A Guide to Understanding the Medieval Cathedral* (Berkeley: University of California Press, 2003), 40.

25. H. Thomas Johnson, "Cathedral Building and the Medieval Economy," *Explorations in Entrepreneurial History 5*, no. 1 (1967): 110; Scott, *The Gothic Enterprise*; Richard Morris, *Cathedrals and Abbeys of England and Wales: The Building Church, 600–1540* (New York: W. W. Norton, 1979).

26. Virginia Lee Owen, "The Economic Legacy of Gothic Cathedral Building: France and England Compared," *Journal of Cultural Economics* (June 1989): 92.

27. Scott, *The Gothic Enterprise*, 11, citing Jean Gimpel, *The Cathedral Builders* (New York: Grove Press, 1961).

28. Scott, *The Gothic Enterprise*, 36.

29. Owen, "The Economic Legacy of Gothic Cathedral Building," 92.

30. Hamilton R. Armstrong, "Art and Liturgy: The Splendor of Faith," *Crisis* (October 1998), http://www.crisismagazine.com/pastissues.htm.

31. Mitchell, *Cathedrals of Europe*, 183.

32. See "An inventory of goods and vestments at Holy Trinity church, 1552, taken by John Britts and Thomas Pellman, churchwardens," http://www.dartfordarchive.org.uk/early_modern/religion.shtml.

33. Eamon Duffy, *The Stripping of the Altars* (New Haven: Yale University Press, 1992).

34. Gregory Dix, *The Shape of the Liturgy* (New York: Seabury Press, 1982).

35. While this is a valid generalization in making comparisons between Protestantism and Catholicism, it should not be allowed to obscure the fact that within Protestantism liturgy and ritual became tools of product differentiation (as discussed in chapter 7). Lutherans and Calvinists, for example, held different views on sacramentality. Achatius, a member of the (Lutheran) Brandenburg Consistory, defended old rituals as useful devices to instruct believers in how to keep the true faith. And Zacharias Rivander of Saxony, where Calvinist ideas were held at bay, described how a "simple layman" could easily spot a Calvinist minister: "If he distributes Holy Communion without reverence... [and] runs to the altar like a hog to its trough... he surely is a secret sacramentarian." Nischan, "Ritual and Protestant Identity in Late Reformation Germany," 145–146.

36. Diana Webb, "Saints and Cities in Medieval Italy," *History Today* 43 (July 1993): 15–22.

37. Hutton Webster, *Rest Days: The Christian Sunday, the Jewish Sabbath, and Their Historical and Anthropological Prototypes* (New York: Macmillan, 1916), 305–306.

38. Earl J. Hamilton, "American Treasure and the Rise of Capitalism (1500–1700)," *Economica* 27 (1929): 342.

39. Duffy, *The Stripping of the Altars*, 42.

40. H. J. Voth, "Height, Nutrition, and Labor: Recasting the 'Austrian Model,'" *Journal of Interdisciplinary History* 25, no. 4 (1995): 627–636; John Komlos and Albrecht Ritschl, "Holy Days, Work Days, and the Standard of Living in the Hapsburg Monarchy," *Journal of Interdisciplinary History* 26, no. 1 (1995): 57–66.

41. Jean Gimpel, *The Cathedral Builders*, trans. Carl F. Barnes Jr. (New York: Grove Press, 1961), xxx; Scott, *The Gothic Enterprise*, 29.

42. Dorothy Gladys Spicer, *Festivals of Western Europe* (New York: H. W. Wilson, 1958), 269–275.

43. Nolan and Nolan, *Christian Pilgrimage in Modern Western Europe*, 99–100.

44. Quoted in Richard Bauman, "The Place of Festival in the Worldview of the Seventeenth-Century Quakers," in *Time Out of Time: Essays on the Festival*, ed. Alessandro Falassi (Albuquerque: University of New Mexico Press, [1682] 1987), 95.

45. Richard Cantillon, *Essai sur la nature du commerce en general*, ed. and trans. Henry Higgs (London: Macmillan, for the Royal Economic Society, [1755] 1931), 95.

46. Jacques Delacroix, "Religion and Economic Action: The Protestant Ethic, the Rise of Capitalism, and the Abuses of Scholarship," *Journal for the Scientific*

Study of Religion, 34 (1995): 126–127. Others have cast doubt on the specific mechanism whereby the Protestant ethic is transformed into the profit ethic embodied in capitalism. For example, see Eisenstadt, *The Protestant Ethic and Modernization* and Lessnoff, *The Spirit of Capitalism and the Protestant Ethic.* The latter indicts Weber for failing to give any theological explanation at all for the profit ethic.

47. Nolan and Nolan, *Christian Pilgrimage in Modern Western Europe*, 87, table 4-2.

48. Robin Grier, "The Effect of Religion on Economic Development: A Cross National Study of 63 Former Colonies," *Kyklos* 57, no. 1 (1997): 47.

49. Barro and McCleary, "Religion and Economic Growth."

50. J. Bradford Delong and Andrei Shleifer, "Princes and Merchants: European City Growth Before the Industrial Revolution," *Journal of Law and Economics* 36 (1993): 671–702.

51. Daron Acemoglu, Simon H. Johnson, and James A. Robinson, "The Rise of Europe: Atlantic Trade, Institutional Change and Economic Growth," MIT Department of Economics Working Paper no. 02-43; MIT Sloan Working Paper no. 4269-02, 2002, http://ssrn.com/abstract=355880.

52. P. Bairoch, J. Bateau, and P. Chèvre, *La Population des villes europeenes, 800–1850.*

53. Delong and Shleifer, "Princes and Merchants."

54. Acemoglu, Johnson, and Robinson, "The Rise of Europe: Atlantic Trade, Institutional Change and Economic Growth," 3.

55. Acemoglu, Johnson, and Robinson, "The Rise of Europe: Atlantic Trade, Institutional Change and Economic Growth," 7.

56. Acemoglu, Johnson, and Robinson, "The Rise of Europe: Atlantic Trade, Institutional Change and Economic Growth," 3.

57. Blum and Dudley, "Religion and Economic Growth," 210.

58. Weber, *The Protestant Ethic and the Spirit of Capitalism*, 125.

59. Blum and Dudley, "Religion and Economic Growth," 221.

60. Douglass North, *Structure and Change in Economic History* (New York: W. W. Norton, 1981); Douglass North and Robert P. Thomas, *The Rise of the Western World* (Cambridge: Cambridge University Press, 1973).

61. For example, Deepak Lal, *Unintended Consequences: The Impact of Factor Endowments, Culture, and Politics on Long-Run Economic Performance* (Cambridge, Mass.: MIT Press, 1998).

62. Martin Paldam, "Corruption and Religion: Adding to the Economic Model," *Kyklos* 54, nos. 2/3 (2001): 384.

63. Paul Johnson, *British Cathedrals* (New York: William Morrow, 1980), 21.

64. Mitchell, *Cathedrals of Europe*, 9.

65. Bairoch, Bateau, and Chèvre, *La Population des villes europeenes, 800–1850.*

66. Julius Baum, *German Cathedrals* (New York: Vanguard, 1956), 47.

67. Martin Erbstösser, *Heretics in the Middle Ages*, trans. Janet Fraser (Leipzig: Edition Leipzig, 1984).

68. Dennis Carlton and J. M. Perloff, *Modern Industrial Organization* (Boston: Addison Wesley, 2005), 360.

69. Benjamin Klein and Keith Leffler, "The Role of Market Forces in Assuring Contractual Performance," *Journal of Political Economy* 89, no. 4 (1981): 615–641.

70. R. Kieckhefer, *European Witch Trials: Their Foundations in Popular and Learned Culture, 1300–1500* (London: Routledge & Kegan Paul, 1976), 108–147.

71. Swanson, *Religion and Regime.*

72. Johnson, *British Cathedrals.*

73. Johnson, *British Cathedrals*, 22.

9 The Competitive Revolution in Christianity

1. Robert J. Barro, *Determinants of Economic Growth: A Cross-Country Empirical Study* (Cambridge, Mass.: MIT Press, 1997).

2. Barro and McCleary, "Religion and Political Economy in an International Panel"; Barro and McCleary, "Religion and Economic Growth"; Robert J. Barro and Rachel M. McCleary, "Which Countries Have State Religions?," working paper, Harvard University, March 2004.

3. Barro and McCleary, "Religion and Political Economy in an International Panel."

4. Will Carrington Heath, Melissa S. Waters and John Keith Watson, "Religion and Economic Welfare: An Empirical Analysis of State Per Capita Income," *Journal of Economic Behavior and Organization* 27 (1995): 129–142. This finding does not of course conflict with research that shows that religious attendance is associated with higher household incomes and lower welfare participation and divorce within communities of predominately one religion. See Jonathan Gruber, "Religious Market Structure, Religious Participation and Outcomes: Is Religion Good for You?," NBER Working Paper no. 11377, 2005, or the summary of this report by Linda Gorman, "Is Religion Good for You?" *The NBER Digest* (October 2005): 2.

5. Heath, Waters and Watson, "Religion and Economic Welfare," 120.

6. See Richard Florida, *Rise of the Creative Class* (New York: Basic Books, 2002).

7. See Finke and Stark, *The Churching of America, 1776–1990.*

8. MacCulloch, *The Reformation*, 675.

9. Rausch and Voss, *Protestantism—Its Modern Meaning*, 45.

10. Rausch and Voss, *Protestantism—Its Modern Meaning*, 48.

11. John Cornwell, *Hitler's Pope: The Secret History of Pius XII* (New York: Viking, 1999).

12. MacCulloch, *The Reformation*, 678.

13. Frank S. Mead and Samuel S. Hill, *Handbook of Denominations in the United States*, 11th ed. (Nashville: Abingdon Press, 2001).

14. Mead and Hill, *Handbook of Denominations in the United States*, 66.

15. J. Gordon Melton, *The Encyclopedia of American Religions*, 7th ed. (Detroit: Gale Research, 2002).

16. Melton, *The Encyclopedia of American Religions*, 24–33.

17. Melton, *The Encyclopedia of American Religions*, xvii, xlvi.

18. MacCulloch, *The Reformation*.

19. Melton, *The Encyclopedia of American Religions*, xlvi.

20. Finke and Stark, *The Churching of America, 1776–1990*.

21. Finke and Stark, *The Churching of America, 1776–1990*; Iannacone, "Introduction to the Economics of Religion."

22. Jenkins, "The Next Christianity."

23. Gill, *Rendering unto Caesar*.

24. Rosa Castro Aguilar, "Religion and Family: Catholic Experiences in Peru," in Anna Peterson, Manuel Vasquez and Philip Williams (eds.), *Christianity, Social Change, and Globalization in the Americas* (New Brunswick, N.J.: Rutgers University Press, 2001), 47–48.

25. Illeana Gomez, "Rebuilding Community in the Wake of War: Churches and Civil Society in Monazan," in *Christianity, Social Change, and Globalization in the Americas*, ed. Peterson, Vasquez, and Williams, 135.

26. In 2003 a university theologian and students walked out of the commencement exercise at Georgetown University during which speaker Cardinal Francis Arinze of Nigeria said that the family is "mocked by homosexuality," a clear clash of Northern and Southern versions of belief among young American Catholics. *USA Today* (May 13, 2004), 4D.

27. Stark and Finke, *Acts of Faith*, chapter 3.

28. See Jan Klos, "Liberty, Progress Individualism: On the Relationship between Christianity and Liberalism in the Nineteenth Century," *Journal des Economistes et des Etudes Humaines* 13 (Juin/Septembre 2003) 197–212.

29. Christoph Schönborn, "Finding Design in Nature," *New York Times* (July 7, 2005), www.nytimes.com/2005/07/07/opinion/07schonborn.html.

30. Despite pleas from some members of his own party, President George W. Bush failed to provide support for stem cell research. In contrast, Britain opened

a national stem cell bank in 2004. As such it was the first nation to authorize funding aimed at cloning human embryos for research.

31. William Breit and Barry T. Hirsch, *Lives of the Laureates: Eighteen Nobel Economists*, 4th ed. (Cambridge, Mass.: MIT Press, 2004).

32. Charles M. North and Carl R. Gwin, "Religious Freedom and the Unintended Consequences of State Religion," *Southern Economic Journal* 71 (July 2004): 103–117.

33. Marla Prather and Charles F. Stuckey, eds., *Gauguin: A Retrospective* (New York: Park Lane, 1987): 132–133.

34. Smith and Kim, "The Vanishing Protestant Majority."

35. Cathy Lynn Grossman, "Can Politics be a Litmus Test for Communion?" *USA Today* (June 15, 2004), 10D.

36. This is, of course, not to criticize or condemn research based upon available empirics. One must start somewhere.

37. See J. Gordon Melton, Jerome Clark, and Aidan A. Kelly, *New Age Almanac* (New York: Visible Ink Press, 1991).

38. MacCulloch, *The Reformation*, 681.

39. See Cathy Lynn Grossman, "God Have Mercy on His Church," *USA Today* (August 5, 2003), 7D.

40. Kevin Eckstrom, "Catholic College See Views Shift Left," *San Antonio Express-News* (March 8, 2003), 7B. Inroads of academic freedom—some labeled "liberalism" and "secularism"—are being made at many Catholic colleges and universities. Some Catholic universities—Notre Dame being one—do not allow an officially sanctioned group of gay and lesbian students. Many others do. According to the Reverend Charles L. Currie, president of the Association of Jesuit Universities and Colleges, twenty-four of the twenty-eight members permit gay and lesbian associations at their schools. See Neela Banerjee, "At Religious Universities, Disputes Over Faith and Academic Freedom," *The New York Times* (February 18, 2006), http:www.nytimes.com/2006/02/18/national/18notredame .html.

41. See Cathy Lynn Grossman and In-Sung Yoo, "Civil Marriage on Rise Across USA," *USA Today* (October 7, 2003), 1A; Cathy Lynn Grossman, "Public Opinion Is Divided on Gay Marriages," *USA Today* (October 7, 2003b), 21A.

42. Richard N. Ostling, "Southern Baptists Quit Worldwide Baptist Group" (Associated Press) *Opelika-Auburn News* (June 16, 2004), 8A.

43. Ostling, "Southern Baptists Quit Worldwide Baptist Group," 3A.

44. Cathy Lynn Grossman, "God Have Mercy on His Church," *USA Today* (August 5, 2003a), 6D.

45. Richard N. Ostling, "Questions Persist: Can 77 Million Anglicans Avoid an Eventual Crackup?" (Associated Press) *Opelika-Auburn News* (November 13, 2004), 2C. See also Martha T. Moore, "Episcopal Church Torn by Gay Issue as More Parishes Leave U.S. Branch," *USA Today* (March 3–5, 2006), 1A.

46. Mead and Hill, *Handbook of Denominations in the United States*, 336.

47. Reported in Cathy Lynn Grossman and Anthony DeBarros, *USA Today* (November 7, 2004), 1D.

48. Elisabeth Rosenthal, "For Fruit Flies, Gene Shift Tilts Sex Orientation," *New York Times* (June 3, 2005), http://www.nytimes.com/2005/06/03/science/03cell.html.

49. It was long after the conquest of Mexico by Cortez in 1519 that the indigenous populations were declared by the papacy to be "fully human."

50. Gill, *Rendering unto Caesar*.

51. André Suares, *Péguy*, cited in *Bartlett's Familiar Quotations*, 15th ed. (Boston: Little Brown, 1980), 726.

52. All statistics are reported in Iannaccone, "Introduction to the Economics of Religion." See also Hull and Bold, "Hell, Religion, and Cultural Change." High attendance statistics are not replicated in western or eastern Europe. Of 25 million Britons who identify their denomination as the Church of England, only 1.2 million attend weekly church services. In Italy where 33 percent of respondents in a Gallup poll described religion as "very important" to them, only 15–33 percent of all Italians go to church each week. Frank Bruni, "The Changing Church: Faith Fades Where It Once Burned Strong," *New York Times* (October 13, 2003). www.nytimes.com/2003/10/13/international/europe/13CHUR.html. Competitive Christianity in the United States has taken on a distinctly American flavor with the development of churches as giant corporations with "pastorpreneurs" (rather than entrepreneurs) modeling themselves on business principles. Evangelical megachurches—dubbed "Six Flags over Jesus" or "Fort Gods" by some critics—are rapidly developing in all areas of the country but particularly in the states of middle America. Pastorpreneurs are shaping their products to the tastes of demanders. Lakewood Church in Houston, Texas, for example, passed a 30,000-a-week attendance record in 2005. See "Jesus, CEO: Churches as Businesses," *The Economist* (February 23, 2006), http://www.economist.com/displaystory.cfm?story_id=5323597. Modern high-tech wide-screen presentations, mortgage lending, entertainment such as movie theaters and bowling alleys, and extravaganzas of all sorts typify some of these behemoths. Most of these pastors and churches are evangelical in nature, with softer come-ons to new and potential members. Other product innovations include complete kits for pastors and franchised churches around the United States and internationally. The success of Rick Warren's *Purpose-Driven Life: What on Earth Am I Here For?* (Grand Rapids, Mich.: Zondervan, 2002) has led him and other contemporary preachers to develop Web sites that contain complete resources for pastors, including canned sermons. Warren's site (http://www.pastors.com) provides pastors with "tools for healthy, growing churches" and poses questions such as "Why spend thousands of dollars to have others raise funds for your ministry when we can show you how to do it?" And, a long tradition of ties between religions and the political process have also come into play. Most of these churches are evangelical and conservative in nature, taking positions in favor of the Re-

publican Party that sometimes overstep the rules of the Internal Revenue Service. See Stephanie Strom, "I.R.S. Finds Sharp Increase in Illegal Political Activity," *The New York Times* (February 25, 2006), http://www.nytimes.com/2006/02/25/national/25charity.html?th&emc=th. We would only note that the nature of modern religious "products" offered by Christian churches, while modern in nature, are not different than those described for the medieval church in chapters 5, 6, and 7. In medieval times cathedrals were offered as meeting places, places of business, and houses of curiosities and relics. The Roman Catholic Church offered many products and social services to those outside the Church in addition to afterlife consumption. Competition, then and now, takes place on many margins.

53. We are not, of course, "Veblenians" except in the sense that we adhere to his view that some institutions are temporally static (religion, law, government) and others (technology, science, incomes) are dynamic. When there is a rift between the two, the static institutions change. Further, Veblen's argument is only superficially similar to Marx's view of history. Marx used pre-Darwinian (deterministic) elements to arrive at the stasis of socialism. Veblen's evolutionary view is dynamic and he did not, as did writers such as Henri de Saint-Simon and Auguste Comte, suggest that science would finally triumph over religion. We make no such suggestion.

54. Arnold Toynbee, *An Historian's Approach to Religion* (London: Oxford University Press, 1956), 286.

A Brief Chronology of Christianity

Editorial note: This brief, selective chronology is intended to help the reader to trace some of the highlights in the development of Christianity and to place this book's discussions in a broader historical context. **Some times are approximate.**

A.D.

1	First year in Christian calendar
1–36?	Life of Jesus Christ
36	Paul of Tarsus has Stephen martyred and the Jerusalem Church destroyed
36–66	Oral tradition of Christianity established; the first Gospel (Mark) written; original Christians disperse; Peter leads the new Christian Church, moves seat of the Church to Rome
37	Paul of Tarsus converts to Christianity
48–49	Council of Jerusalem, First Christian Council, adopts doctrine regarding circumcision and dietary law
60	Paul imprisoned in Rome (martyred for treason in Rome, two years later)
66–70	Roman-Jewish War; final destruction of Herod's Temple
67	Peter martyred, crucified in Rome
67–78	Pope Linus, second pope, succeeds Peter
70	Collapse of Jewish self-government in Judea; destruction of the Temple in Jerusalem
75–90	Gospel according to Luke and Acts of the Apostles written

90–100	Gospel according to John written
200?	Latin Bible translations begun, most likely in Carthage
230–250	Christian Council of Rome called to dispel renunciations of Virgin Birth
240–250	Christian Council of Carthage
250	Rome intensifies persecution of Christians; martyrs revered as saints
254–257	Major schism over rebaptizing heretics and apostates
303–311	End of Christian persecutions in Rome
306–337	Reign of Roman Emperor Constantine, who converts to Christianity
313	Edict of Milan; Constantine establishes toleration of Christianity
314	Council of Arles called by Constantine against Donatist schism
318	Roman law passed denying the competence of a civil court if appeal is made to the court of a Christian bishop
321	Constantine declares Sunday as official Roman-Christian day of rest
325	Council of Nicaea, called by Constantine against Arianism (denial of Jesus' divinity)
350?	Codex Sinaiticus; Codex Vaticanus; first Christian Bibles
350–400	Interval between first Christian Bible and first Western Christian Bible, during which the books that comprise the Bible varied
360	Books (codex) begin to replace scrolls
380	Christianity declared official state religion by Emperor Theodosius
381	Council of Theodosius at Constantinople declares Jesus had a human soul
384	St. Jerome presents Pope Damasus I with new Latin gospels; originals lost
400?	Vulgate (Latin) Bible by St. Jerome (?) becomes standard Western Christian Bible

401–417	Pope Innocent I, fortieth pope, decrees Roman custom the norm for Christianity
410	Visigoths sack Rome under King Alaric
430	Death of St. Augustine (b. 354), author of *The City of God* and *Confessions*
431	Council of Ephesus, third ecumenical, decrees Mary the Mother of God; Syrian Christianity splits into East and West
432	St. Patrick begins mission in Ireland
451	Council of Chalcedon declares Jesus is two natures, both human and divine in one, a compromise solution of Jesus god/man schisms
480–547	Life of St. Benedict, founder of Benedictine monastic order
484–519	Acacian schism (controversy over divine paternity of Jesus) divides Eastern (Greek) and Western (Roman) churches
491	Armenian Church secedes from Eastern (Byzantium) and Western (Rome) Churches
498–506	Lawrencian schism; Anti-Pope Lawrence
500	First plans made for Vatican
570?	Birth of Mohammad
587	Visigoths of Spain converted to Christianity
589	Lombards of Italy converted to Christianity
611	Mohammed's reported vision of Allah on Mount Hira
625	Mohammed begins dictation of Que'ran (Koran) to his scribe
628	Mohammed captures Mecca, explains Islam to world rulers
632	First Islamic Caliphate established at Medina by Abu Bekr; death of Mohammed
636	Southern Irish Church submits to Roman Catholicism
637	Capture of Jerusalem by Islam

690?	Earliest Bible translations into English vernacular; continued work by Bede, author of "The Ecclesiastical History of the English People"
1054	Split between Eastern and Western churches formalized; Eastern Orthodox Church founded
1095–1291	Ten crusades, first called by Pope Urban II to restore Asia Minor to Byzantium and conquer the Holy Land from the Turks
1215	Fourth Lateran Council establishes aural confession as "a matter of faith"; Dominican Order established
1223	Franciscan Order established
1225–1274	Life of Thomas Aquinas, Italian theologian and philosopher in the scholastic (Aristotelian) tradition and author of *Summa Theologica*
1309–1378	Babylonian captivity; papacy moves to France (Avignon)
1321?	Publication of *The Divine Comedy* by Dante Alighieri
1347–1351	Black Death ravages Europe
1378–1417	Great Schism: divisions within Christendom produce two (Rome vs. Avignon) and then three popes (popes and antipopes)
1380–1382	John Wycliffe, eminent Oxford scholar, completes English translations of Old and New Testaments; preaches against abuses, the use of relics, and clerical celibacy; expresses unorthodox views of the sacraments, especially Penance and the Eucharist
1390?	Wycliffe's teachings condemned repeatedly in England
1408	In reaction to Wycliffe Bible, Council of Oxford forbids translations of Scripture into the vernacular unless and until approved by Church authority
1415	Council of Florence condemns all of Wycliffe's works, but his bibles continue to be used (and tacitly accepted by Catholics)

1450?	Johann Gutenberg (c. 1398–1468) develops a method of printing with movable metal type; his first book is the Holy Bible
1453	Ottoman Empire replaces Byzantium
1473–1481	Sistine Chapel built in Vatican under supervision of Giovanni de Dolci
1478	Inquisition begins in Spain for suppression of heresy, as determined by the Spanish monarchy and the Catholic Church
1490	Spanish Inquisition burns six thousand books at Salamanca and Hebrew Bibles at Seville
1492	Columbus discovers North America; Spanish colonization of the New World begins; Spain drives Jews and Moslems from country unless "conversions" are made to Christianity
1498	Savonarola, Italian reformer and Dominican friar, executed for criticizing Church policy and Pope Alexander VI
1509	Desiderius Erasmus writes *The Praise of Folly*, aimed at the bellicose and corrupt Roman papacy of Julius II
1516	Erasmus (c. 1466–1536) publishes a critical edition of the Greek New Testament
1517	Martin Luther (1483–1546) posts his Ninety-five Theses in Germany (protesting authority of the pope, sale of indulgences, and priestly celibacy), preaches faith alone requisite to salvation; Reformation begins
1520	Luther excommunicated by Pope Leo X
1522	Luther translates New Testament into German
1523	Martin Bucer (1491–1551) excommunicated; goes on to become a Protestant reformer, mediator, and liturgical scholar best known for his attempts to make peace between conflicting reform groups
1524	Peasants' Revolt in South Germany, massive rural uprisings against Catholic Church; begins one hundred years of religious wars in Europe

1529	Reformer Huldrych Zwingli (1484–1531) wages war against Catholic communities of Switzerland; ultimately, each parish or village is given the right to choose which religion to adopt
1529	The Church in Sweden becomes a state institution by action of the Swedish Diet
1530	Augsburg Confession, summation of Lutheran faith, presented to Emperor Charles V; Luther founds the Lutheran Church
1534	Henry VIII breaks with Catholic Church, confiscates monasteries in Britain; Episcopal Church established; Jesuit Order founded by Ignatius Loyola (1491–1566)
1539	Publication of the first English Bible authorized for public use in English churches, translated by Myles Coverdale and directed by Thomas Cromwell
1541	John Calvin (1509–1564) establishes theocracy in Geneva; preaches predetermination and advocates good conduct and success as signs of election
1542	Holy Office instituted, through which the pope governs the Roman Catholic Church
1545–1563	Council of Trent marks beginning of the Catholic Reformation, or Counter-Reformation: condemned Protestant beliefs; defined an official theology; sought to reform practice of simony (the buying or selling of a church office or preferment) but fails to reform practices of the upper levels of the Church
1549	Publication of the Book of Common Prayer (Episcopal Church)
1553	Founding of Pontifical Gregorian University within the Vatican
1555	Peace of Augsburg ends religious wars in Germany and recognizes Lutherans
1559	List of prohibited books by the Roman Catholic Church appears in connection with the Spanish Inquisition

1560	John Knox (c. 1514–1572), establishes Scottish Presbyterian Church over disagreement with Luther regarding sacraments and church government; Scottish Parliament declares Presbyterianism the state religion
1563	Thirty-nine Articles (Episcopal Church) established
1588	Spanish Armada sets sail with intent of restoring Catholic ruler to the British throne
1590	Completion of Michelangelo's dome in St. Peter's Basilica
1609	Baptist Church formed by John Smyth due to objections to infant baptism and demands for separation of church and state
1611	King James (Authorized) Version of Bible printed
1618	Thirty Years' War begins
1620	English Puritans aboard the *Mayflower* arrive in Massachusetts, establish Plymouth Colony
1633	Galileo Galilei (1564–1642) is condemned to life imprisonment by the Roman Inquisition for promoting Copernicus's theory that the earth revolves around the sun
1648	Peace of Westphalia ends Thirty Years' War; England, Scotland, Netherlands, Scandinavia and large parts of South Germany declared "Protestant" lands, while rest of Europe remained Roman Catholic
1738	Methodist Church founded by Reverend John Wesley
1776	Publication of *An Inquiry into the Nature and Causes of the Wealth of Nations*, written by Scottish social philosopher and political economist Adam Smith (c. 1723–1790), establishes the basis for modern economics and provides the first analysis of the economics of religion; British colonies in America declare independence from England
1805	Spanish Index of Forbidden Books issued under the aegis of the Catholic Church banned hundreds of titles, including Adam Smith's *The Wealth of Nations* and Burke's *Reflections on the Revolution in France*
1827	Mormon Church founded by Joseph Smith

1832   Reformist Presbyterians establish the Church of Christ (disciples)

1858   Reported apparition of Mary at Lourdes, France, considered "worthy of belief" by the Catholic Church

1869–1870   First Vatican Council affirms doctrine of papal infallibility

1879   Charles Taze Russell founded Jehovah's Witness Movement

1901   Pentecostal Church founded in Topeka, Kansas, in reaction to loss of evangelical fervor by Methodists and others

1904–1905   Publication of Max Weber's (1864–1920) *The Protestant Ethic and the Spirit of Capitalism*, which asserts that Calvinism breeds a work ethic and an avoidance of trivial pleasures, resulting in the rapid accumulation of capital in Protestant states

1908   Pope Pius X drops the formal "Inquisition," but reasserts its spirit by assigning watchdog duties to the Congregation of the Holy Office

1910   Five Point Statement by the Presbyterian General Assembly, also adopted by the Fundamentalists

1917–1945   The Index of Forbidden Books of the Church comes to include more than four thousand titles, is reinvigorated by Cardinal Merry del Val, ardent conservative and opponent of "secularization" and "relativism"; del Val and Eugenio Pacelli (later Pope Pius XII) also restructure canon law to favor centralized authority in Rome over bishops of the world

1919   World's Christian Fundamentals Association founded

1925   Scopes "monkey" trial stirs public controversy and division among Fundamentalists over teaching of theory of evolution

1957   United Church of Christ founded by ecumenical union of Congregationalists and Evangelicals and Reformed, representing Calvinists and Lutherans

1959   Statement of Faith (United Church of Christ)

1962–1965   Second Vatican Council called by Pope John XXIII and concluded by Pope Paul VI; its avowed purpose is to "to increase the fervor and energy of Catholics, to serve the needs of Christian people"

1966   Pope Paul VI reasserts Church's opposition to birth control and establishes the Sacred Congregation for the Doctrine of the Faith, successor to the Inquisition; continues to condemn secularism and "relativism"

1970   The Universal Fellowship of Metropolitan Community Church founded, ministering chiefly to gays and lesbians but to heterosexuals as well

1978–2005   Papacy of John Paul II, who reaffirms conservative moral traditions and the prohibition of women in the priesthood; he elevates numerous individuals to sainthood

1994   Declaration of cooperation between Catholics and Evangelicals on matters of common interest such as condemnation of abortion and homosexuality

2000–2006   The teaching of "intelligent design" and "creationism" to replace Darwinism as taught in school science becomes a central issue for many evangelical denominations in the United States and elsewhere

2003   Churches who ordain either openly gay or women clergy and/or bless same-sex unions in the United States include Evangelical Lutheran Church, the African Methodist Episcopal Church, Assemblies of God, the Presbyterian Church USA, the Episcopal Church, the American Baptist Church and the United Church of Christ

2004   Southern Baptist Convention (SBC) votes to secede from the World Baptist Alliance, a global federation of Baptist denominations, the latter being deemed "too liberal" with respect to the role of women and other policies

2005   Benedict XVI, formerly Cardinal Joseph Ratzinger who headed the Sacred Congregation for the Doctrine of Faith (successor to the Roman Inquisition), elected pope;

Benedict moves quickly to reassert Pope John Paul II's conservative ideology and moral traditions

2006   Number of Roman Catholics worldwide claiming to attend weekly services falls from 44 percent in 1998 to 33 percent

2006   More than 2,500 distinct types of religion exist in the United States with large and growing numbers of Christian sects

Note: Most data drawn from http://www.cwo.com/~pentrack/catholic/chron.html.

Glossary

afterlife consumption   A product that is consumed in the afterlife such as heaven, eternal peace, a beatific vision, communion with God, Valhalla, and so on. Acquisition of this product is premised upon certain types of behavior prescribed by religions in this life.

animism   The attribution of a living soul to inanimate objects and natural phenomena. (OED)

Apostle's Creed   A statement of faith used in the Roman Catholic, Anglican, and many Protestant churches. (EBO)

arbitrage   Buying a good or asset in one market where price is low, and simultaneously selling in another market where price is higher. (DE)

asymmetric information   A situation where economic agents do not all have the same information. (DE)

Augsburg Confession   The twenty-eight articles that constitute the basic confession of the Lutheran churches, presented June 25, 1530, at the Diet of Augsburg to the emperor Charles V by seven Lutheran princes and two imperial free cities. (EBO)

average cost pricing   A price that represents the average cost of producing some good or service. In a competitive market, competition causes price to gravitate to average cost of producing the good or service.

average price   A simple average of a set of prices. If n is the number of prices, the total sum of all prices considered is divided by n.

barriers to entry   Any restriction or cost that an entrant must pay in order the enter a market for a good or service.

Becker, Gary   (born 1930) American economist, awarded the Nobel Prize for Economics in 1992. He applied the methods of economics to aspects of human behavior previously considered more or less the exclusive domain of sociology, criminology, anthropology, and demography. (EBO)

benefice   A term originally used for a grant of land for life as a reward for services, in canon law it came to imply an ecclesiastical office that prescribed certain duties or conditions for the due discharge of which it provided certain revenues. (COD)

bishop   In some Christian churches, the chief pastor and overseer of a diocese, an area containing several congregations. (EBO)

British Nonconformist   An English Protestant who does not conform to the doctrines or practices of the established Church of England. (EBO)

canon law   The body of ecclesiastical rules or laws imposed by authority in matters of faith, morals, and discipline. (COD)

capital   Man-made means of production. (DE)

capital goods   Goods intended for use in production, rather than by consumers. (DE)

cardinal   The title, at first applied to any priest permanently attached to a church, came to be restricted to the clergy of Rome. These gradually formed a college and became the pope's immediate counselors. (COD)

cartel   An alliance of firms that act collusively to reduce output and increase price in an industry in order to increase profits. (ET)

Chamberlinian product group   A group of products that are different from one another in some unspecified way, yet equally likely to appeal to any given buyer. (MB)

chancery   The papal chancery is the name attached in the late twelfth century to the pope's secretariat. In the fourteenth century the chancery exercised quasi-legislative powers, but from the fifteenth century on its influence diminished. (COD)

club good   An intermediate case between purely public goods and private goods. With the club good exclusion is feasible, but the optimal size of the club is in general larger than one individual. (MITD)

Coase, Ronald   (born 1910) British-born economist, awarded the Nobel Prize for Economics in 1991 for his seminal work in the theory of the firm and in the economics of externalities. (MITD)

comparative advantage   An economic entity's (an individual's or a nation's) ability to produce a good at a lower marginal opportunity cost than some other entity. (ET)

competition   A market that functions under two conditions—no collusion among sellers or buyers (which occurs with a large number or buyers and sellers) and freedom to enter and exit the market. Competition results in prices equal to the costs of production plus a normal profit for sellers. (ET)

competitive entry   Entry by businesses or entrepreneurs into a market when price exceeds average costs of producing a good or service, meaning that there is a profit opportunity.

competitive margin   The margin or basis upon which competition takes place. Competition may take place on many margins such as price, quality differences, appearance, or location.

conciliarists   People who believed that the authority in the Roman church rested in a general council composed of clergy, theologians, and laypeople, rather than in the pope alone. (HWS)

Congregationalism   The form of Church polity which rests on the independence and autonomy of each local Church. Modern Congregationalism dates from the Reformation. (COD)

constraint-driven   This is a situation in which behavior is determined by what one is able to do rather than what one wants to do.

consumer sovereignty   The proposition that it is the tastes of consumers rather than the preferences of producers that determine what goods are provided. (DE)

consumers' surplus   The difference between what consumers are willing to pay for a given quantity of a good or service (the total consumer valuation) and what they have to pay (their total expenditure). (ET)

contiguous markets   Markets that abut one another in location. Intercommunication between buyers and sellers in contiguous markets is expected, leading to a tendency to a common market in prices, interest rates, and so on.

correlation   A term indicating a relation between one variable or quantity and another. Correlation is not to be confused with causation.

cost-benefit analysis   The attempt to compare the total social costs and benefits of an activity, usually expressed in money terms. (DE)

cost inflation   Inflation due to increases in particular prices or wage rates being passed round the economy. (DE)

Council of Trent   The nineteenth ecumenical council of the Roman Catholic Church (1545–1563), highly important for its sweeping decrees on self-reform and for its dogmatic definitions that clarified virtually every doctrine contested by the Protestants. (EBO)

Counter-Reformation or Catholic Reformation   The revival of the Roman Catholic Church in Europe, usually considered as extending from the middle of the sixteenth century to the period of the Thirty Years' War (1618–1648). (COD)

covenant   A bond entered into voluntarily by two parties in which each pledges to do something for the other. The notion was used in a range of secular contexts before being employed as a model for the relationship between God and Israel. (COD)

credence good   A good whose utility impact is difficult or impossible for the consumer to ascertain; unlike experience goods, the utility gain or loss is difficult to measure after consumption as well. (W)

curia   The papal court and its functionaries, especially those through whom the government of the Roman Catholic Church is administered. (COD)

demand   The quantity of a good or service that people want to buy. (DE)

demand curve   A graphic representation of the quantities of a product that people are willing and able to purchase at all possible prices. (ET)

demand shifter   Any factor other than full price, such as income, risk tolerance, tastes, or the price of some similar or substitute good, that shifts the demand curve rightward or leftward. That shift ordinarily changes the price and quantity consumed of the good.

demand-side   Economic forces that affect the economy arising from changes in factors affecting demand such as price, preferences, tastes, risk tolerance, income, and so on.

differential pricing   Charging different prices to different consumers. If not based on cost differences, such pricing is called price discrimination.

direct costs   Costs that vary with the level of output—for example, labor costs. Also known as variable costs. (MITD)

dominant firm   A firm with a position of strong leadership in its markets. (DE)

dynamic efficiency   A condition summarized in the idea that monopolies may, over time, be more innovative and efficient than competitive firms at developing new products and new production techniques. (ET)

ecumenism   The doctrine, or quality, of universality (especially of the Christian church). (OED)

efficiency   Getting any given results with the smallest possible inputs, or getting the maximum possible output from given resources. (DE)

elastic demand   A situation in which buyers are relatively responsive to price changes; the percent change in quantity demanded is greater than the percent change in price. (ET)

elasticity of demand   The ratio between proportional change in quantity demanded and proportional change in price. This is on the assumption that income and other prices remain unchanged. (DE)

endogamy   The custom of marrying only within the limits of a clan or tribe. (OED)

endogenous   Arising from the working of a system. This is contrasted with exogenous, which means imposed on a system from outside. (DE)

entry control   Any artificial barrier placed on entry by a government entity.

entry costs   Costs associated with the development and production of a substitute product or service.

entry-deterring devices   *See* barriers to entry.

episcopal (consistory) form   Of a church: Constituted on the principle of episcopacy, or government of the church by bishops; the system of church government that comprises three distinct orders, bishops, presbyters or priests, and deacons. (OED)

equilibrium price   The price at which quantity demanded is equal to quantity supplied; other things being equal, there is no tendency for this price to change. (ET)

equilibrium full price   The money and time price that reflects all of the cost of consumption or production.

Establishment Clause   The clause in the First Amendment of the U.S. Constitution that prohibits the establishment of religion by Congress. (NOAD)

Eucharist   A Christian sacrament commemorating the action of Jesus at the Last Supper with His disciples. Also called Holy Communion, or the Lord's Supper. (EBO)

Evangelical   From the eighteenth century applied to that school of Protestants that maintains that the essence of the Gospel consists in the doctrine of salvation by faith in the atoning death of Christ, and denies that either good works or the sacraments have any saving efficacy. (OED)

exchange costs   The opportunity costs of the resources used in making trades; includes transaction costs, transportation costs, and artificial barriers to trade. (ET)

exclusion   The legal right and practical ability to prevent others from using a good. (DE)

excommunication   An ecclesiastical censure that excludes those subject to it from the communion of the faithful and imposes certain other deprivations and disabilities. (COD)

exegesis   The act of explaining a text—in theology, usually a sacred text. (COD)

exogenous variable   A variable whose value is not determined within an economic model, but that plays a role in the determination of the values of endogenous variables. Also known as a predetermined variable. (MITD)

explicit markets   An explicit market is one in which prices are observable, such as the stock market or the market for bananas.

externality   Benefits or costs of an individual's activity that the individual does not receive or bear. (ET)

feast days   Ecclesiastical feasts come under three main headings: (1) Sundays, the weekly commemoration of the Resurrection; (2) movable feasts, the most important of which is Easter; and (3) immovable feasts, notably Christmas and the Epiphany. (COD)

franchise monopoly   A monopoly that finds it efficient to use franchise contracts rather than vertical integration of subsidiaries.

free rider   An individual who receives the benefit of consuming a public good or service without paying for it. (ET)

full price   The total opportunity cost to an individual of obtaining a good; includes money price and all other costs, such as transportation costs or waiting costs. (ET)

function   A relation between two or more variables. If y is a function of x, written $y = f(x)$, when the value of the argument x is known, the function tells us how to find the value of y. If y is a single-valued function of x, for each value of x there is only one value of y. (DE)

Fundamentalism A movement in various Protestant bodies reacting against evolutionary theories, liberal theology, and biblical criticism. It began in the late nineteenth century and developed after the First World War (1914–1918), especially in the United States. In a wider sense, the term is applied to other religious and political groups. (COD)

game theory A theory involving decision making in an atmosphere of mutual interdependence and imperfect information. (ET)

gross domestic product (GDP) A measure of the final goods and services produced by a country with resources located within that country. (ET)

gross national product (GNP) The value measured at market prices of all final goods and services produced in an economy in one year regardless of where the resources are located.

Gnosticism A complex religious movement that in its Christian form came into prominence in the second century. A central importance was attached to gnosis, the supposedly revealed knowledge of God and of the origin and destiny of mankind, by means of which the spiritual element in man could receive redemption. (COD)

Great Schism This term refers to two different periods. The first, in 1054, refers to the separation of the Roman Catholic Church and the Greek Orthodox Church; the second, to the period from 1378 to 1417, when the church had two separate popes, one in Rome and one in Avignon, France. (MOW)

Holy Office Official Roman Catholic agency founded in 1542 to combat international doctrinal heresy and to promote sound doctrine on faith and morals. (HWS)

Holy See The term commonly denotes the papacy. (COD)

homogeneous product A good or service for which the consumer is indifferent as to which firm produces it; each firm's product is a perfect substitute for other firms' products in the eyes of the consumer. (ET)

humanism A literary and intellectual movement that arose in the early fifteenth century to valorize the writings of Greco-Roman antiquity; it was so named because its practitioners studied and supported the liberal arts, or humanities. (MOW)

implicit contract A situation when people or firms expect to have continuing dealings with one another, and so need to agree on the terms on which these will take place, but a formal or explicit contract between them is impossible or impracticable. (DE)

implicit markets Markets with imputed rather than posted prices on goods and services.

income distribution The division of total income between different recipients. Functional income distribution is the division of income between the owners of the different factors of production. Personal income distribution is the distribution of incomes classified by size. (DE)

income effect The change in the quantity demanded of a good that results from a change in real income. (ET)

incumbent firm A firm that is already in position in a market. (DE)

indicator A variable used in deciding on the use of policy instruments. (DE)

indulgence In Roman Catholic doctrine, a remission of sin earned by performing certain religious tasks to avoid purgatory after death; indulgences were in use by the thirteenth century. (MOW)

industrial organization Traditionally, the field of applied price theory. It is concerned with the working of the market economy and generally organizes its approach in terms of market structure, conduct, and performance. (MITD)

inefficiency Not getting the best possible results from the use of resources. (DE)

inelastic demand A situation in which buyers are relatively unresponsive to price changes; the percent change in quantity demanded is less than the percent change in price. (ET)

inferior good A good that a consumer chooses to purchase in smaller quantities as income rises or in larger amounts as income falls. (ET)

information cost The cost to a consumer of obtaining information concerning the price, quality, or other aspects of a good or service.

information networks Any group of individuals that has some common economic or social basis to share information such as an interest group.

input monopoly A situation that occurs when the supplier of an input into the production of a good or service has complete control over the supply of the input.

interdict An ecclesiastical penalty in the Roman Catholic Church excluding the faithful from participation in spiritual things, but without loss of Communion of the Church. (COD)

joint products Commodities that have the property that in production a change in the rate of output of one brings about a similar change in the other(s). (MITD)

joint supply The supply conditions when outputs are produced jointly. (DE)

Keynesian A term used to describe macroeconomic theories of the level of economic activity using the techniques developed by John Maynard Keynes (1883–1946). The methodology of Keynesian economics may be distinguished by its concern with aggregate behavior, especially the income-generating effect of total expenditure and the emphasis placed on the investment component in determining the level of activity. (MITD)

Kirk The Scottish equivalent of "church." (COD)

labor All human resources available to society for use in the process of production. (MITD)

law of demand   The price of a product or service and the amount purchased are inversely related. If price rises, then quantity demanded falls; if price falls, quantity demanded increases, all other things held constant. (ET)

law of entail   Laws limiting the laws of inheritance of property to a specified succession of heirs.

law of supply   The price of a product or service and the amount that producers are willing and able to offer for sale are positively related. If price rises, then quantity supplied rises; if price decreases, then quantity supplied decreases. (ET)

Laws of Toro   Spanish law specifying conditions for adult sons to inherit their father's property.

limit pricing   A pricing policy consisting of temporarily setting a price lower than the short-run profit-maximizing price in order to deter entry and maximize profits in the long run. (ET)

liturgy   The word is used in two senses: (1) all of the prescribed services of the church, as contrasted with private devotion; and (2) especially in the Eastern Church, as a title for the Eucharist. (COD)

locational competition   Competition that takes place between firms when positioning themselves within a physical market area. On which street corner do I locate?

macroeconomics   Analysis of the behavior of an economy as a whole. (ET)

Malthus, Thomas   (1766–1834) English economist and demographer who is best known for his theory that population growth will always tend to outrun the food supply and that betterment of humankind is impossible without stern limits on reproduction. (EBO)

marginal cost   The additional cost of producing one more unit of output; the change in total cost divided by the change in output. (ET)

marginal product   The additional output produced by employing one additional unit of a variable input. (ET)

marginal revenue   The change in total revenue resulting from the sale of one additional unit of output; the change in total revenue divided by the change in output. (ET)

market entry   Access to a market by a new supplier. An entrant may be a new firm, or a firm that has previously been active in other markets. (DE)

market structure   The pattern of market shares in an industry. This is concerned with how many firms there are, and how they vary in size. (DE)

Marx, Karl   (1818–1883) Revolutionary, sociologist, historian, and economist. His writings and others by Marx and Friedrich Engels form the basis of the body of thought and belief known as Marxism. (EBO)

mendicant friars   Members of those orders that were forbidden to own property in common; they work or beg for their living and are not bound to one church. (COD)

meta-credence good   Any good or service, such as eternal salvation or any after-life consumption, whose qualities cannot be known given any amount of human time or money.

M-form corporation   A common type of internal organization adopted by large corporations in response to managerial slack. Responsibility for production activities is decentralized by the formation of operating divisions, each of which possesses its own managerial structures. (MITD)

microeconomics   Analysis of the behavior of individual decision-making units, including individuals, households, and business firms. (ET)

monopoly   A market situation with only one seller. (DE)

moral hazard   The danger that if a contract promises people payments on certain conditions, they will change their conduct so as to make these conditions more likely to occur. (DE)

neoclassical economics   The approach in economics of analyzing how individuals and firms should behave to maximize their own objective functions, assuming that activities are coordinated by the price mechanism, and that markets clear so that the economy is in equilibrium at all times. (DE)

net utility   The total of all utility gained from comsuming a product, including meta-credence services, less the cost attached to consuming that good or service.

network effects   The process by which a network becomes more valuable as more people sign up to use it. Microsoft Word would be a network.

network externality   An external economy derived from being connected to other people, for example, through the Internet. (DE)

Niebuhr, Reinhold   (1892–1971) American theologian who sought to return to the categories of the biblical revelation and was critical of both liberal theology and metaphysics; he reinstated the doctrine of original sin. (COD)

non-competing (complementary) consumption   The consumption of goods that are joined in final usage. Gin and tonic. A case where an addition in consumption of one unit of a good does not detract from the consumption of other buyers. Examples include production processes where joint goods (beef and hides) are produced and the production of public goods such as national defense.

nonexcludability   A situation where, when once produced, the consumption benefits of a good cannot be excluded from all consumers.

normal good   A good that a consumer chooses to purchase in smaller (larger) amounts as income falls (rises). (ET)

one-tailed test   A statistical procedure for determining the confidence with which one can view a particular statistical result. It is based on a specific cause and effect relationship between two variables.

opportunistic behavior   Taking strategic advantage of a situation, such as shirking in a team production process or group process; to free-ride on others.

opportunity cost   The highest-valued alternative forgone in making any choice. (ET)

optimal deterrence   The calibration of marginal punishments so as to coincide with the marginal severity of some crime or infraction.

optimum   The "best" situation or state of affairs. (MITD)

ordinary least squares (OLS)   A basic statistical practice for testing the validity of some theory about the behavior of a particular variable.

papal bull   A written mandate of the pope of a more serious and weighty kind than a "brief." (COD)

Papal camera   One of the departments of the papal curia assuming the duties of a treasury. (OED)

papal investiture   The (often debated) right of the papacy to appoint local or regional prelates. That right was sometimes exercised or claimed by secular authorities.

predestination   John Calvin's doctrine that God preordained salvation or damnation for each person before creation. (MOW)

prelate   The term was originally of wide connotation, but it came to be restricted to church officials of high rank. (COD)

price discrimination   The practice of charging one buyer or group of buyers a different price than that charged to others. The price difference is not due to differences in the cost of supplying the two groups. (ET)

primogeniture   The right of succession or inheritance belonging to the first-born. (OED)

private good   Any good or service that if used by one individual or firm is not available to others. (DE)

probit   The unit that forms the scale into which percentages may be transformed so that data evenly distributed between 0 and 100 percent become normally distributed with a standard deviation of one probit. (OED)

product differentiation   The marketing of generally similar products with minor variations that make them imperfect substitutes for consumers. (DE)

profit-maximizing price   The price associated with the quantity sold at which the difference between total revenue and total cost is greatest; the price associated with the quantity sold at which marginal revenue equals marginal cost. (ET)

public choice   The economic analysis of political decision making, politics, and the democratic process. (ET)

public good   A good such that, once produced, one individual's consumption of the good does not reduce or exclude the ability of other individuals to consume the good. (ET)

public-interest theory   A view that government or church tries to create the greatest good for the greatest number in its promulgation of its policies.

real income The buying power of a consumer's budget, determined by the consumer's money income and the prices of goods and services; the quantity of goods and services that money income can buy. (ET)

Reformation The term is sometimes used to describe a series of changes in Western Christendom between the fourteenth and seventeenth centuries, but is usually restricted to the early sixteenth-century movement prompted by Martin Luther. Luther attacked transubstantiation, clerical celibacy, and the religious orders, and demanded the abolition of papal power in Germany. (COD)

regression A statistical method of measuring the extent to which variations in one variable are associated with variations in others. (DE)

rent A payment to a factor of production in excess of the factor's opportunity cost. (ET)

rent distribution The allocation of the spoils of some rent-seeking regulation or control.

rent extraction The case where a government or ruling authority threatens costly regulations to extort money or resources from producers.

rent-seeking Spending time and money not on the production of real goods and services, but rather on trying to get the government to change the rules so as to make one's business more profitable. (DE)

residual demand curve A demand curve facing a supplier after the price and quantities sold by all other competitors are subtracted from the total market demand curve.

risk premium The extra return required to induce a risk-averse individual to undertake a project with uncertain returns. (DE)

rota Also known as the Rota Romana. The normal Roman Catholic appeal tribunal for judging cases brought before the Holy See. (COD)

sacrament Religious sign or symbol, especially associated with Christian churches, in which a sacred or spiritual power is believed to be transmitted through material elements viewed as channels of divine grace. (EBO)

schism Formal and willful separation from the unity of the church. It is distinguished from heresy in that the separation involved is not doctrinal in basis. (COD)

separable markets Markets that are separated by some natural factor (such as location, sex or eye color) or that are separated artificially by such factors as product differentiation.

signaling Actions taken not for the sake of their direct results, but to inform prospective customers or employers. (DE)

simony The purchase or sale of spiritual things. (COD)

sinecure Any office or position that has no work or duties attached to it, especially one that yields some stipend or gain. (OED)

single-price monopolists   A monopolist charging a single price in contrast to one engaging in price discrimination and charging multiple prices.

spatial competition   Competition between firms for customers within some physically defined market area; locational competition.

spatial equilibrium   A locational equilibrium wherein established firms are optimally located given respective market sales areas.

specialization   Concentrating activity in those lines of production in which the individual or firm has some natural or acquired advantage. (MITD)

stock   An accumulation by accretion of goods, talents, or things of value.

substitution effect   The change in the quantity demanded of a good that results only from a change in the relative price of the good. (ET)

superstar effect   An extreme consumption externality where increases in the number of customers or adherents increases the utility of each consumer. As with network effects and externalities, concentration is expected in such markets.

supply   The amount of a good or service offered for sale. (DE)

supply curve   A graphic representation of the quantities of a product or service that producers are willing and able to sell at all possible prices. (ET)

supply-side economics   The view that real growth in the economy depends to a considerable extent even in the short run, and almost completely in the long run, on factors affecting supply rather than on effective demand. (DE)

synod   In the Christian church, a local or provincial assembly of bishops and other church officials meeting to resolve questions of discipline or administration. (EBO)

Teutonic Order   This religious order of knights, priests, and lay brothers played a major role in eastern Europe in the late Middle Ages and underwent various changes in organization and residence from its founding in 1189–1190 to the present. (COD, EBO)

Tiebout model   An analysis of the provision of public goods that argues that if certain public services are provided at the level of local governments, individuals can indicate their preferences concerning these services and obtain a combination of public services and taxes that corresponds with their preferences by moving between local government areas. (MITD)

trade-off   The process of deciding whether to give up some of one good or one objective to obtain more of another. (DE)

transaction costs   Those costs other than price that are incurred in trading goods and services. (MITD)

transubstantiation   In Christianity, the change by which the substance (though not the appearance) of the bread and wine in the Eucharist becomes Christ's real presence—that is, His body and blood. (EBO)

Tridentine   Having reference to the Council of Trent. (COD)

Tridentine Index   Officially known as *Index Librorum Prohibitorum* (Lat., "List of prohibited books"), in short, "the Index." The official list of books issued by the Roman Catholic Church that its members were normally forbidden to read or possess. The first Index was issued in 1557. In 1966 the Index ceased to have the force of ecclesiastical law but is said to retain its moral force. (COD)

two-tailed test   A procedure to evaluate a statistical regression that does not make a specific prediction about whether the cause and effect relation is positive or negative.

usury   The fact or practice of lending money at interest; especially in later use, the practice of charging, taking, or contracting to receive excessive or illegal rates of interest for money on loan. (OED)

utility   A measure of the satisfaction that the consumption of goods or services yields an individual. (ET)

vector   A compact notation used to refer to a list of variables, which may themselves be numbers or algebraic expressions. Vectors provide a convenient notation for referring to lists of the quantities or prices of goods. (DE)

vertical integration   The combination in one firm of two or more stages of production normally operated by separate firms. (DE)

Waldensians   Since the twelfth century the name "Waldenses" has been applied to several groups of heretics. In the sixteenth century one group adopted Calvinism and formed a Waldensian Protestant Church, the Chiesa Evangelica Valdese. With the advent of Protestantism, the Waldenses lost their separate identity except in the parts of the Alpine valleys. From 1561 they were usually tolerated but sometimes persecuted. (COD)

wholesale   The sale of goods to distributors rather than to the general public. Wholesale traders usually deal in larger quantities than retailers; they break bulk and sell in smaller quantities than their purchases from manufacturers. (DE)

Z-good   A concept of the consumption of ultimate services of products that emphasizes that individuals do not buy commodities or services as such but for the various services that one obtains from commodities; people do not buy apartments but housing services.

COD = *The Concise Oxford Dictionary of the Christian Church* (online)

DE = Black, *Dictionary of Economics, 2nd. ed.*, OUP (online)

EBO = Encyclopedia Britannica Online

ET = Ekelund, Tollison, *Economics: Private Markets and Public Choice, 6th ed.*

HWS = McKay, Hill, Buckler, *History of Western Society, 7th ed.*, online glossary

MB = Robert H. Frank, *Microeconomics and Behavior, 4th ed.*, McGraw-Hill

MITD = *MIT Dictionary of Modern Economics, 4th ed.*

MOW = Hunt, Martin, et al., *The Making of the West, 2nd ed.*

NOAD = *New Oxford American Dictionary, 2nd. ed.*, 2005, OUP (online)

OED = *Oxford English Dictionary* (online)

W = Wikipedia.org

Index

World Christian Encyclopedia, 98
World Values Survey, 265
Wycliffe, John, 81

Z-goods, 163
  Counter-Reformation and, 135–138
  market analysis and, 55–56, 63
  Protestant Reformation and, 105,
    110–111
Zola, Emile, 84
Zwingli, Huldrych, 72
  competition and, 239, 248
  Protestant evolution and, 163, 170–
    175